MARVEL BOY. Contains material originally published in magazine form as MARVEL BOY #1-6. Second edition. First printing 2014. ISBN# 978-0-7851-9107-0. Published by MARVEL WORLDWIDE, INC., a subsidiary of MARVEL ENTERTAINMENT, LLC. OFFICE OF PUBLICATION: 135 West 50th Street, New York, NY 10020. Copyright © 2000, 2001 and 2014 Marvel Characters, Inc. All rights reserved. All characters featured in this issue and the distinctive names and likenesses thereof, and all related indicia are trademarks of Marvel Characters, Inc. No similarity between any of the names, characters, persons, and/or institutions in this magazine with those of any living or dead person or institution is intended, and any such similarity which may exist is purely coincidental. **Printed in the U.S.A.** ALAN FINE, EVP - Office of the President, Marvel Worldwide, Inc. and EVP & CMO Marvel Characters B.V.; DAN BUCKLEY, Publisher & President - Print, Animation & Digital Divisions; JOE QUESADA, Chief Creative Officer; TOM BREVOORT, SVP of Publishing; DAVID BOGART, SVP of Operations & Procurement, Publishing; C.B. CEBULSKI, SVP of Creator & Content Development; DAVID GABRIEL, SVP Print, Sales & Marketing; JIM O'KEEFE, VP of Operations & Logistics; DAN CARR, Executive Director of Publishing Technology; SUSAN CRESPI, Editorial Operations Manager; ALEX MORALES, Publishing Operations Manager; STAN LEE, Chairman Emeritus. For information regarding advertising in Marvel Comics or on Marvel.com, please contact Niza Disla, Director of Marvel Partnerships, at ndisla@marvel.com. For Marvel subscription inquiries, please call 800-217-9158. **Manufactured between 4/4/2014 and 5/12/2014 by R.R. DONNELLEY, INC., SALEM, VA, USA.**

10 9 8 7 6 5 4 3 2 1

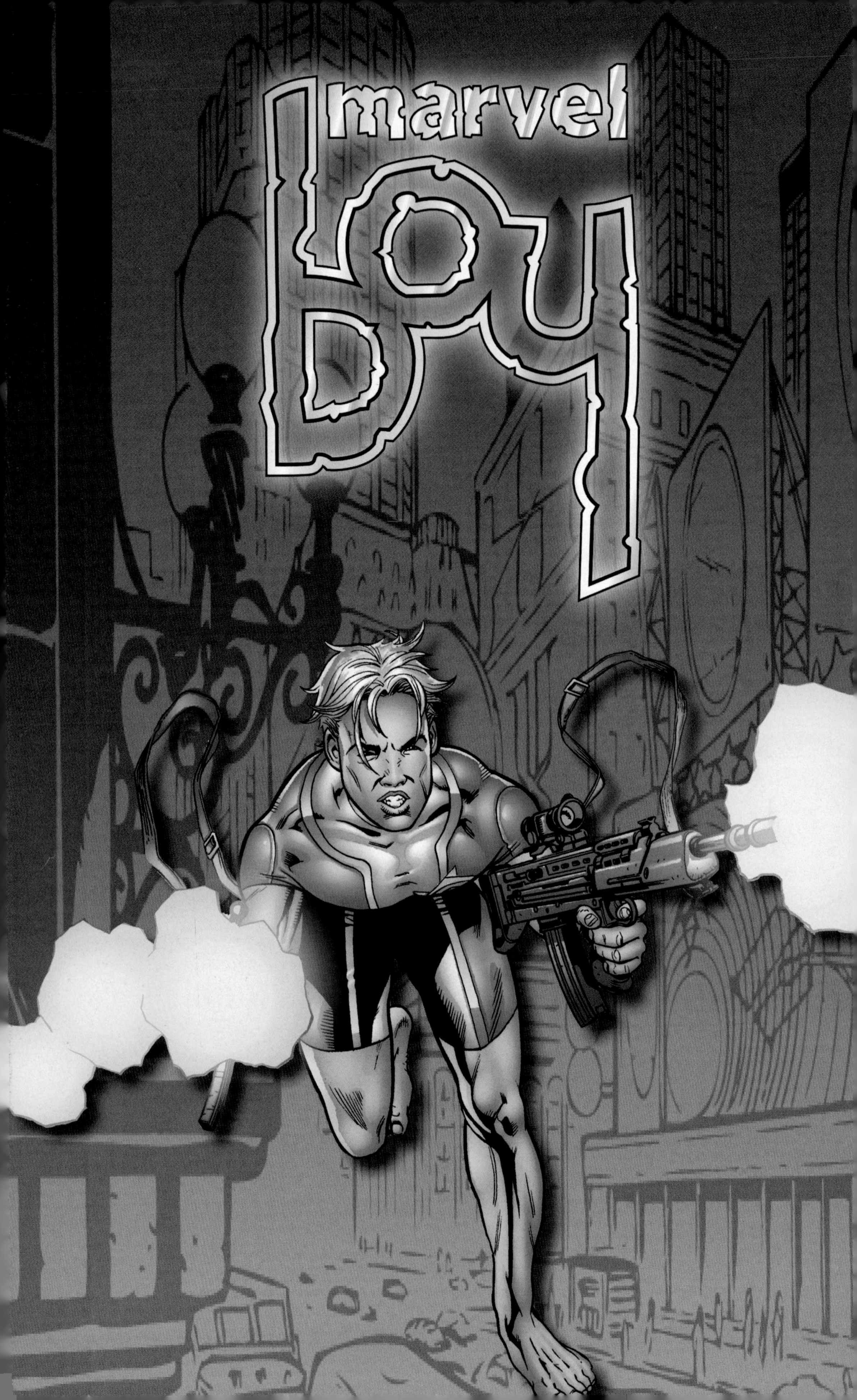
marvel
boy

Writer
Grant Morrison

Pencils
J.G. Jones
with Ryan Kelly (issue #6, p. 20)

Inks
J.G. Jones
with Sean Parsons (issues #5-6)

Letters
Richard Starkings & Comicraft's Wes Abbott

Colors
Avalon Studios & Matt Milla

Editors
Joe Quesada & Jimmy Palmiotti

Managing Editor
Nanci Dakesian

Collection Editor: Mark D. Beazley

Associate Managing Editor: Alex Starbuck

Editor, Special Projects: Jennifer Grünwald

Senior Editor, Special Projects: Jeff Youngquist

SVP Print, Sales & Marketing: David Gabriel

Book Designer: Spring Hoteling

Editor in Chief: Axel Alonso

Chief Creative Officer: Joe Quesada

Publisher: Dan Buckley

Executive Producer: Alan Fine

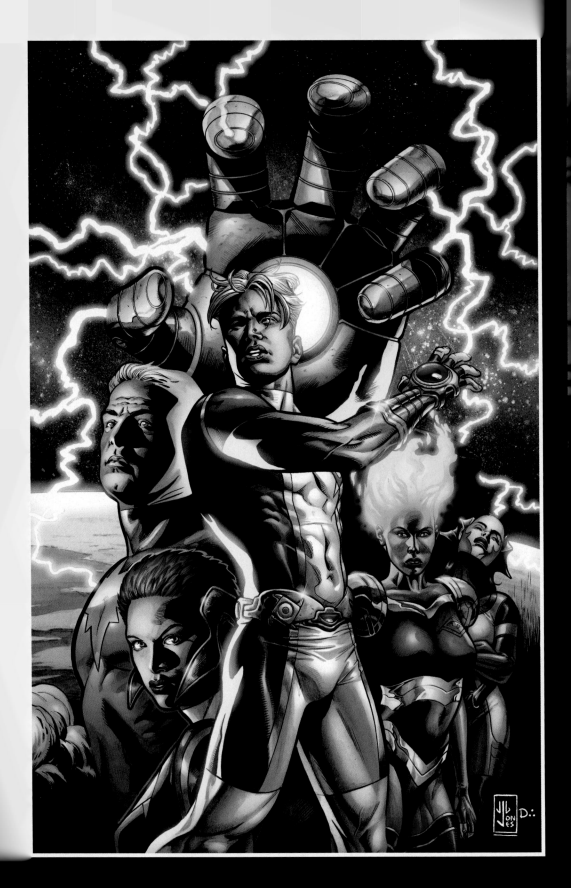

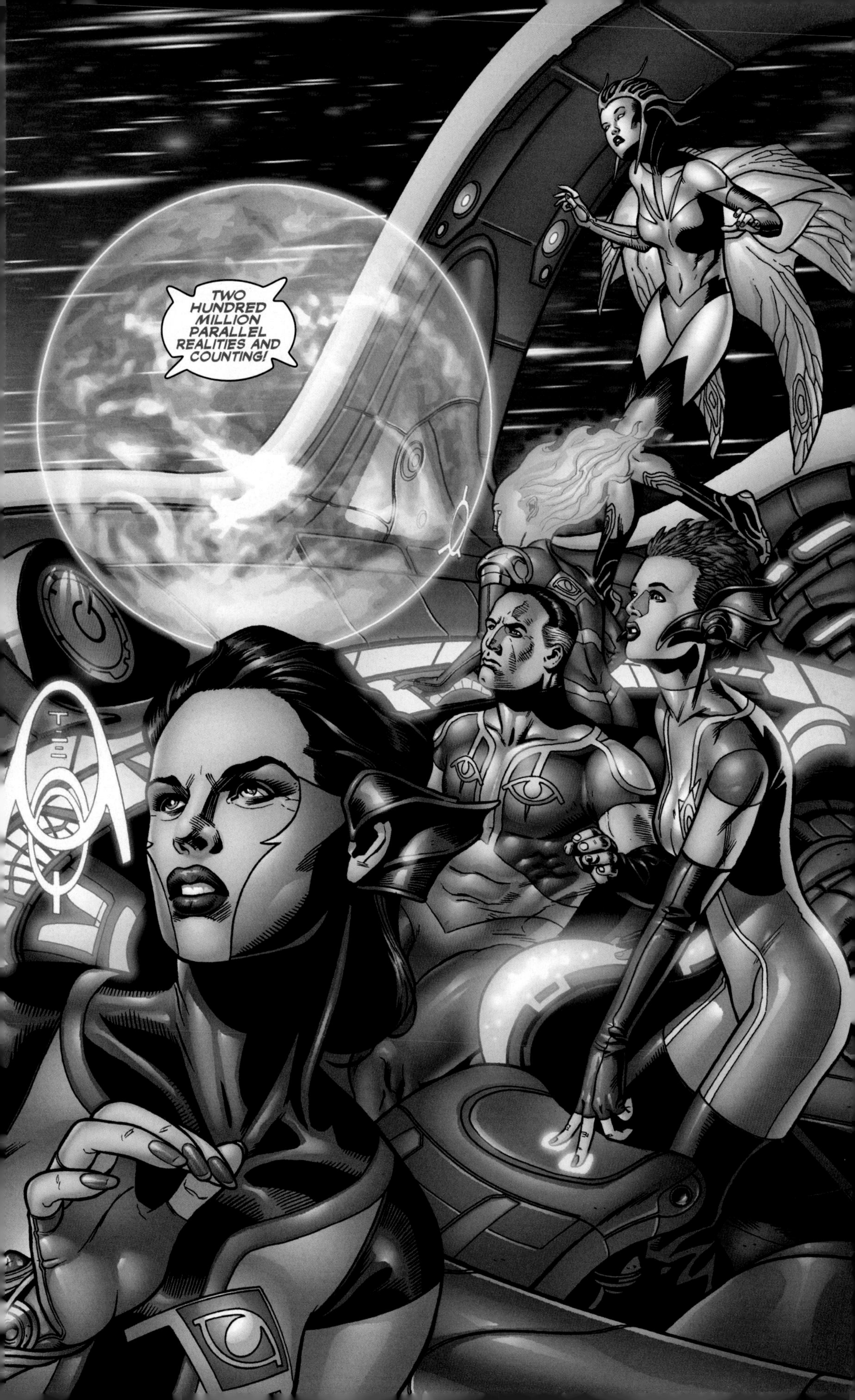
TWO HUNDRED MILLION PARALLEL REALITIES AND COUNTING!

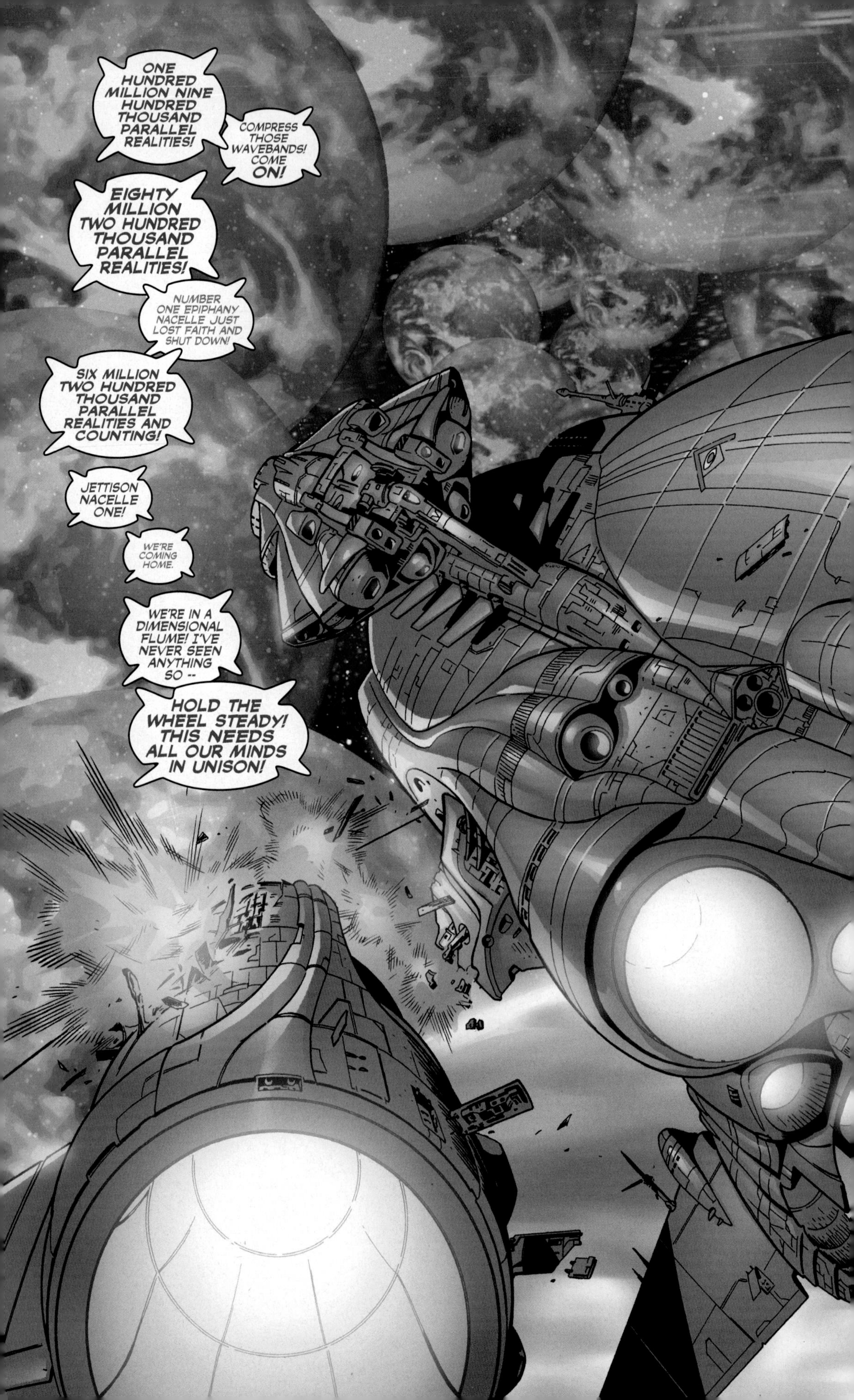

ONE HUNDRED MILLION NINE HUNDRED THOUSAND PARALLEL REALITIES!
COMPRESS THOSE WAVEBANDS! COME ON!
EIGHTY MILLION TWO HUNDRED THOUSAND PARALLEL REALITIES!
NUMBER ONE EPIPHANY NACELLE JUST LOST FAITH AND SHUT DOWN!
SIX MILLION TWO HUNDRED THOUSAND PARALLEL REALITIES AND COUNTING!
JETTISON NACELLE ONE!
WE'RE COMING HOME.
WE'RE IN A DIMENSIONAL FLUME! I'VE NEVER SEEN ANYTHING SO --
HOLD THE WHEEL STEADY! THIS NEEDS ALL OUR MINDS IN UNISON!

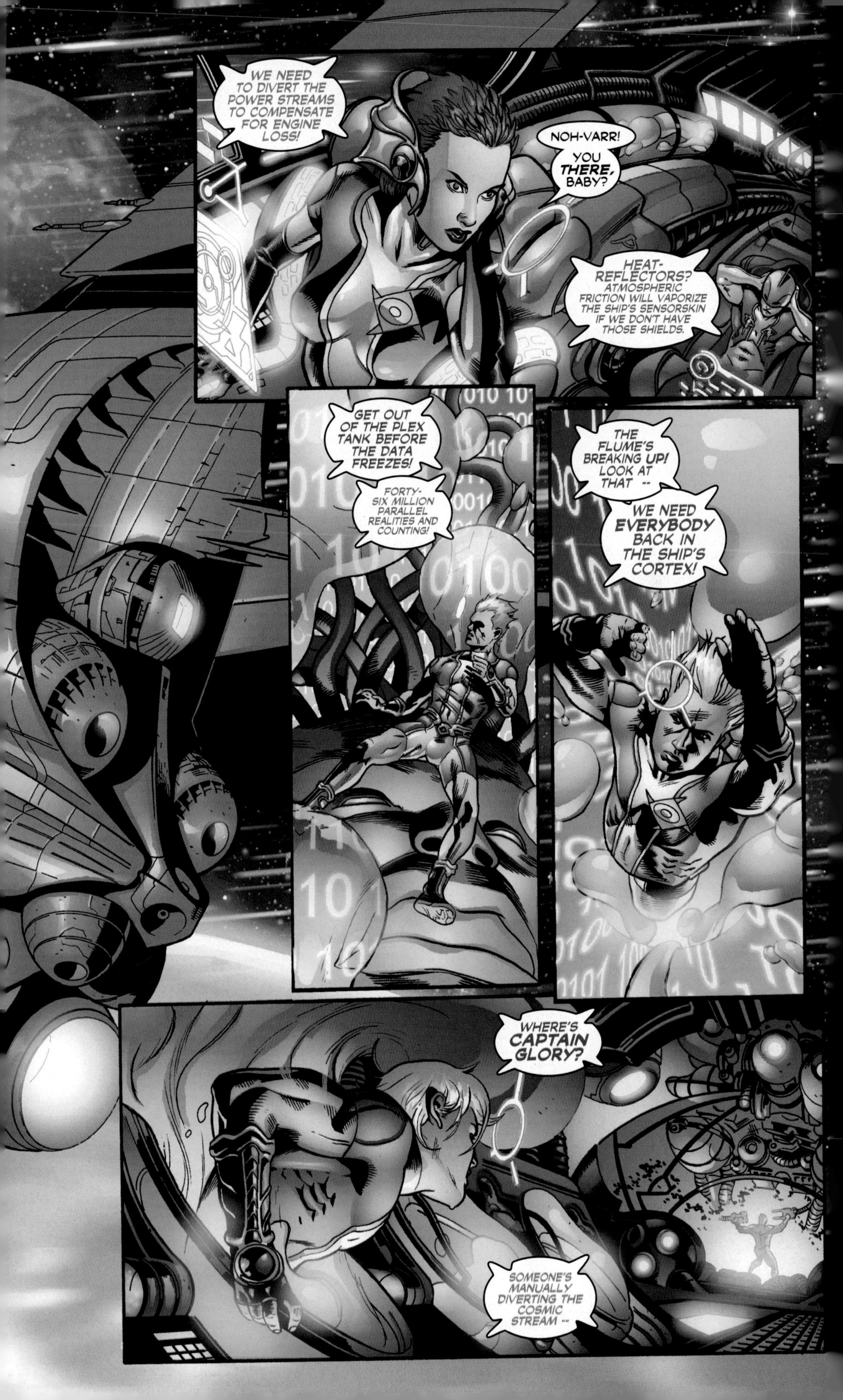

WE NEED TO DIVERT THE POWER STREAMS TO COMPENSATE FOR ENGINE LOSS!
NOH-VARR!
YOU THERE, BABY?
HEAT-REFLECTORS? ATMOSPHERIC FRICTION WILL VAPORIZE THE SHIP'S SENSORSKIN IF WE DON'T HAVE THOSE SHIELDS.
GET OUT OF THE PLEX TANK BEFORE THE DATA FREEZES!
FORTY-SIX MILLION PARALLEL REALITIES AND COUNTING!
THE FLUME'S BREAKING UP! LOOK AT THAT --
WE NEED EVERYBODY BACK IN THE SHIP'S CORTEX!
WHERE'S CAPTAIN GLORY?
SOMEONE'S MANUALLY DIVERTING THE COSMIC STREAM --

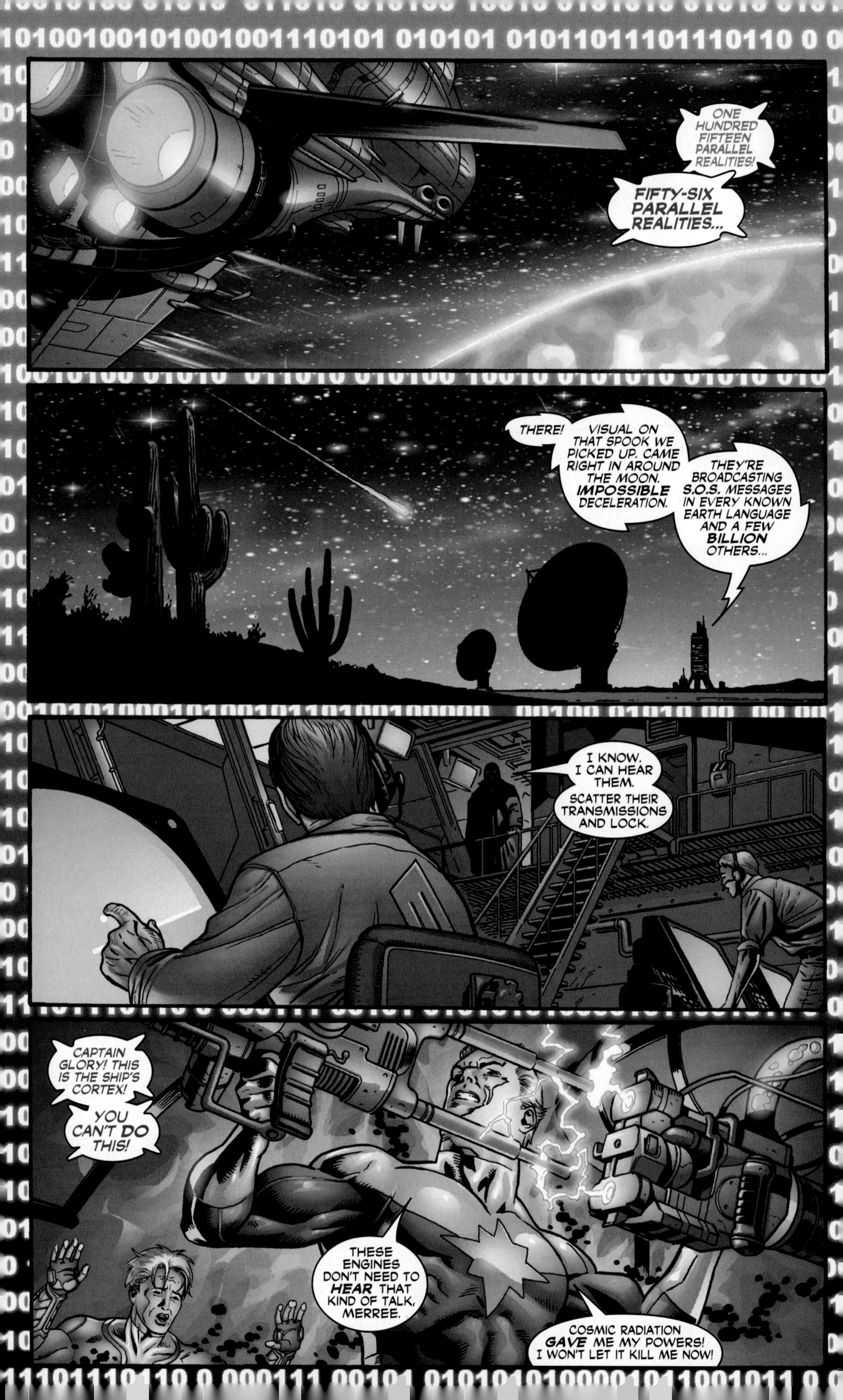
ONE HUNDRED FIFTEEN PARALLEL REALITIES!
FIFTY-SIX PARALLEL REALITIES...
THERE!
VISUAL ON THAT SPOOK WE PICKED UP. CAME RIGHT IN AROUND THE MOON. IMPOSSIBLE DECELERATION.
THEY'RE BROADCASTING S.O.S. MESSAGES IN EVERY KNOWN EARTH LANGUAGE AND A FEW BILLION OTHERS...
I KNOW. I CAN HEAR THEM.
SCATTER THEIR TRANSMISSIONS AND LOCK.
CAPTAIN GLORY! THIS IS THE SHIP'S CORTEX!
YOU CAN'T DO THIS!
THESE ENGINES DON'T NEED TO HEAR THAT KIND OF TALK, MERREE.
COSMIC RADIATION GAVE ME MY POWERS! I WON'T LET IT KILL ME NOW!

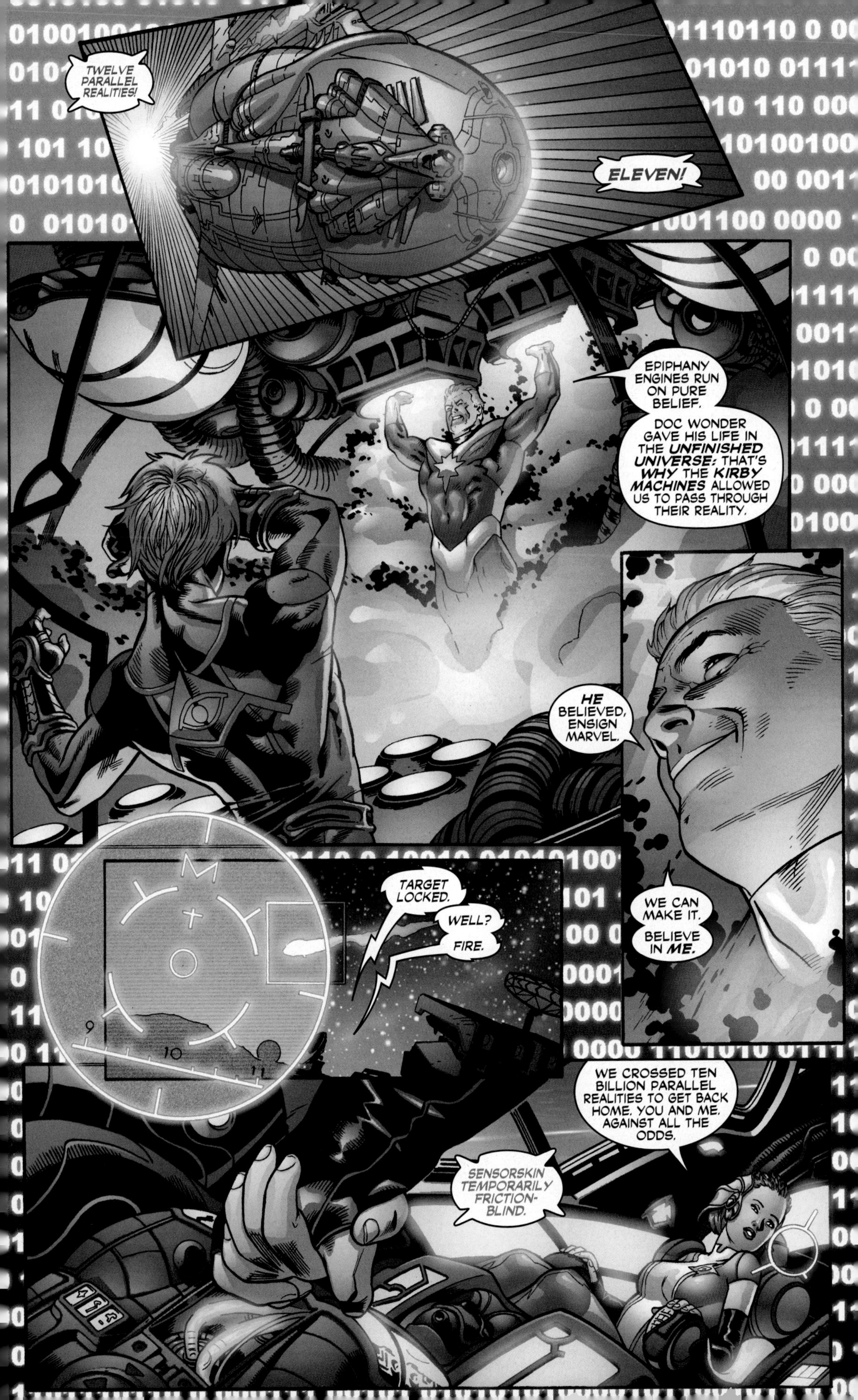
TWELVE PARALLEL REALITIES!
ELEVEN!
EPIPHANY ENGINES RUN ON PURE BELIEF.
DOC WONDER GAVE HIS LIFE IN THE UNFINISHED UNIVERSE: THAT'S WHY THE KIRBY MACHINES ALLOWED US TO PASS THROUGH THEIR REALITY.
HE BELIEVED, ENSIGN MARVEL.
WE CAN MAKE IT.
BELIEVE IN ME.
TARGET LOCKED.
WELL?
FIRE.
WE CROSSED TEN BILLION PARALLEL REALITIES TO GET BACK HOME, YOU AND ME, AGAINST ALL THE ODDS.
SENSORSKIN TEMPORARILY FRICTION-BLIND.

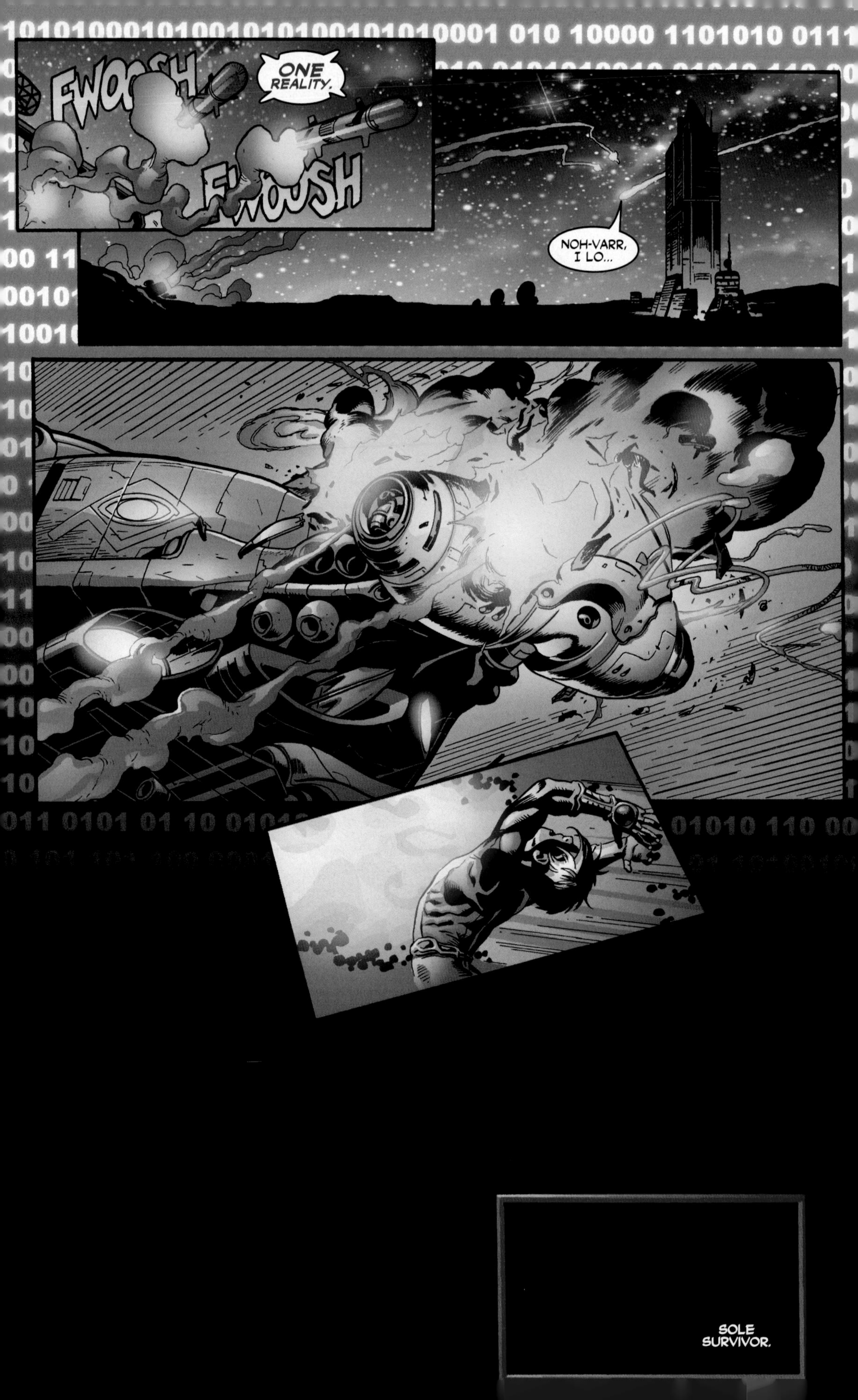
FWOOSH
ONE REALITY.
FWOOSH
NOH-VARR, I LO...
SOLE SURVIVOR.

Script

J.G. JONES Art

marvel boy

HELLO CRUEL WORLD

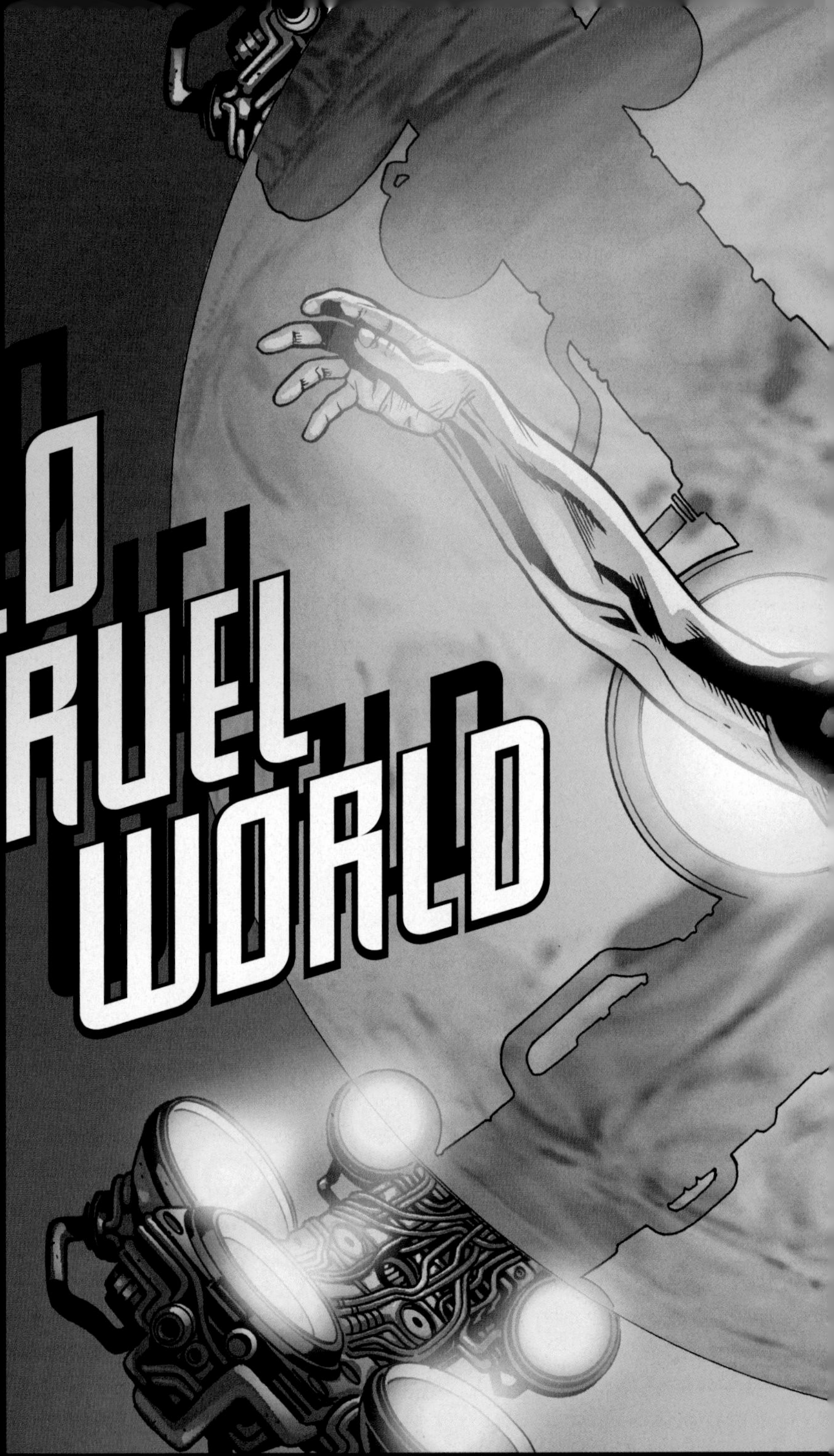

AVALON STUDIOS & MATT MILLA Colors

RICHARD STARKINGS & COMICRAFT'S WES ABBOTT Letters

JOE QUESADA & JIMMY PALMIOTTI Editors

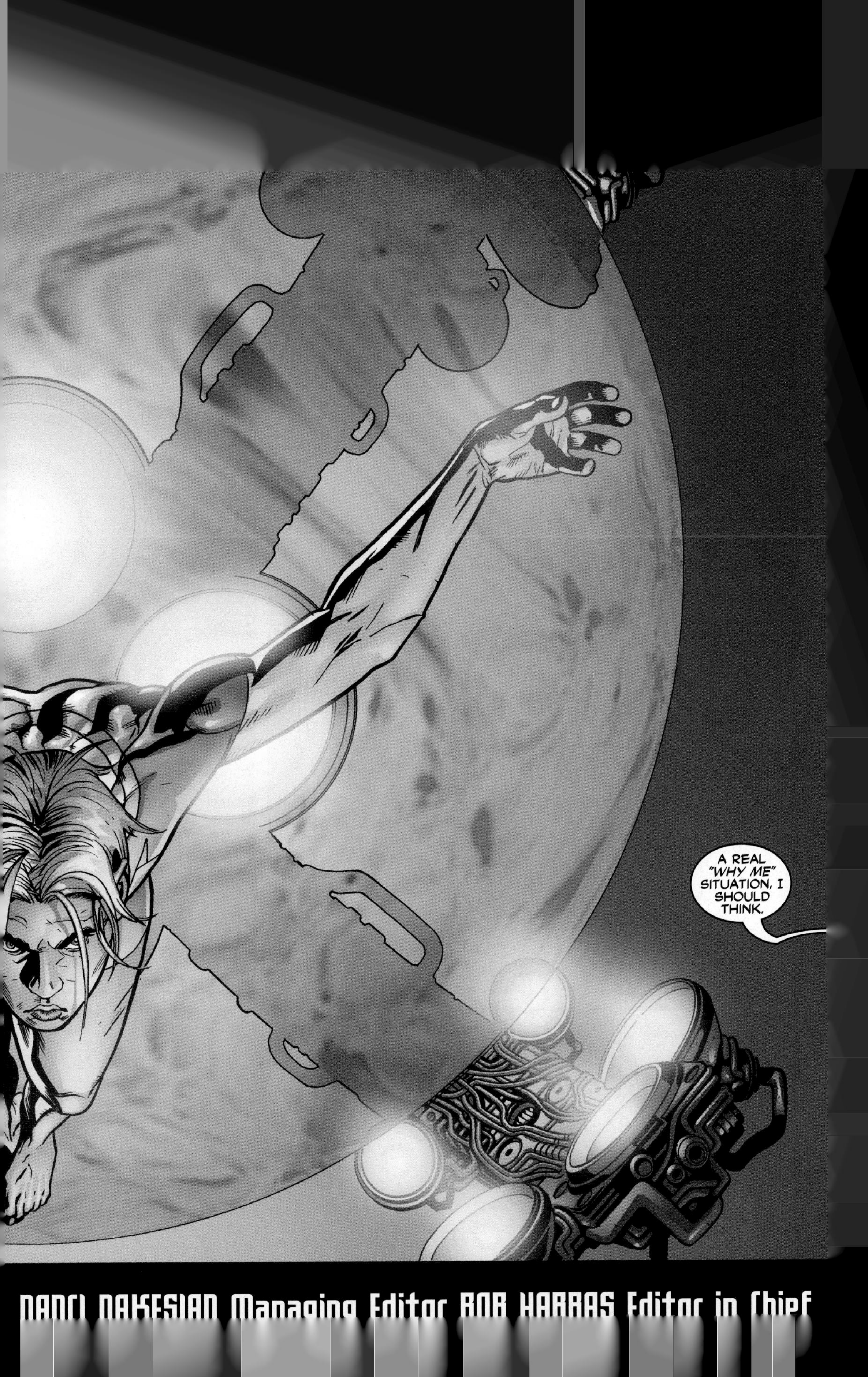
A REAL "WHY ME" SITUATION, I SHOULD THINK.

NANCI DAKESIAN Managing Editor BOB HARRAS Editor in Chief

LOOK AT IT THIS WAY; NONE OF THIS IS REAL. YOUR *PAIN* IS NOT REAL. NOT *OFFICIALLY* REAL.

YOUR FEAR AND CONFUSION ARE NOT OFFICIALLY REAL.

THIS BUILDING DOES NOT EXIST. *OFFICIALLY* --

-- I DO NOT EXIST.

THEREFORE, *YOU* DO NOT EXIST. LOGIC AT WORK.

I CAN DO *ANYTHING* TO YOU. YOU HAVE NO ADVOCATE HERE. NO ONE TO BARGAIN FOR YOUR RELEASE.

THE *CHURCH* HAD THE IRON MAIDEN AND THE *RACK.*

WE HAVE *THE BUBBLE.*

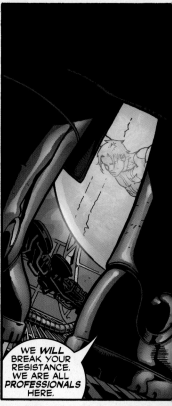

WE *WILL* BREAK YOUR RESISTANCE. WE ARE ALL *PROFESSIONALS* HERE.

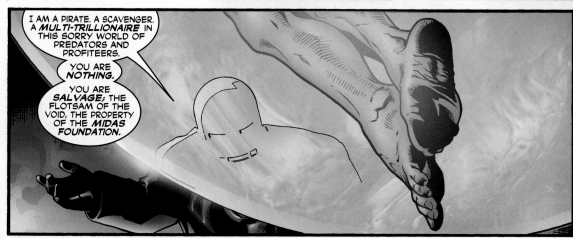

I AM A PIRATE. A SCAVENGER. A *MULTI-TRILLIONAIRE* IN THIS SORRY WORLD OF PREDATORS AND PROFITEERS.

YOU ARE *NOTHING.*

YOU ARE *SALVAGE;* THE FLOTSAM OF THE VOID, THE PROPERTY OF THE *MIDAS FOUNDATION.*

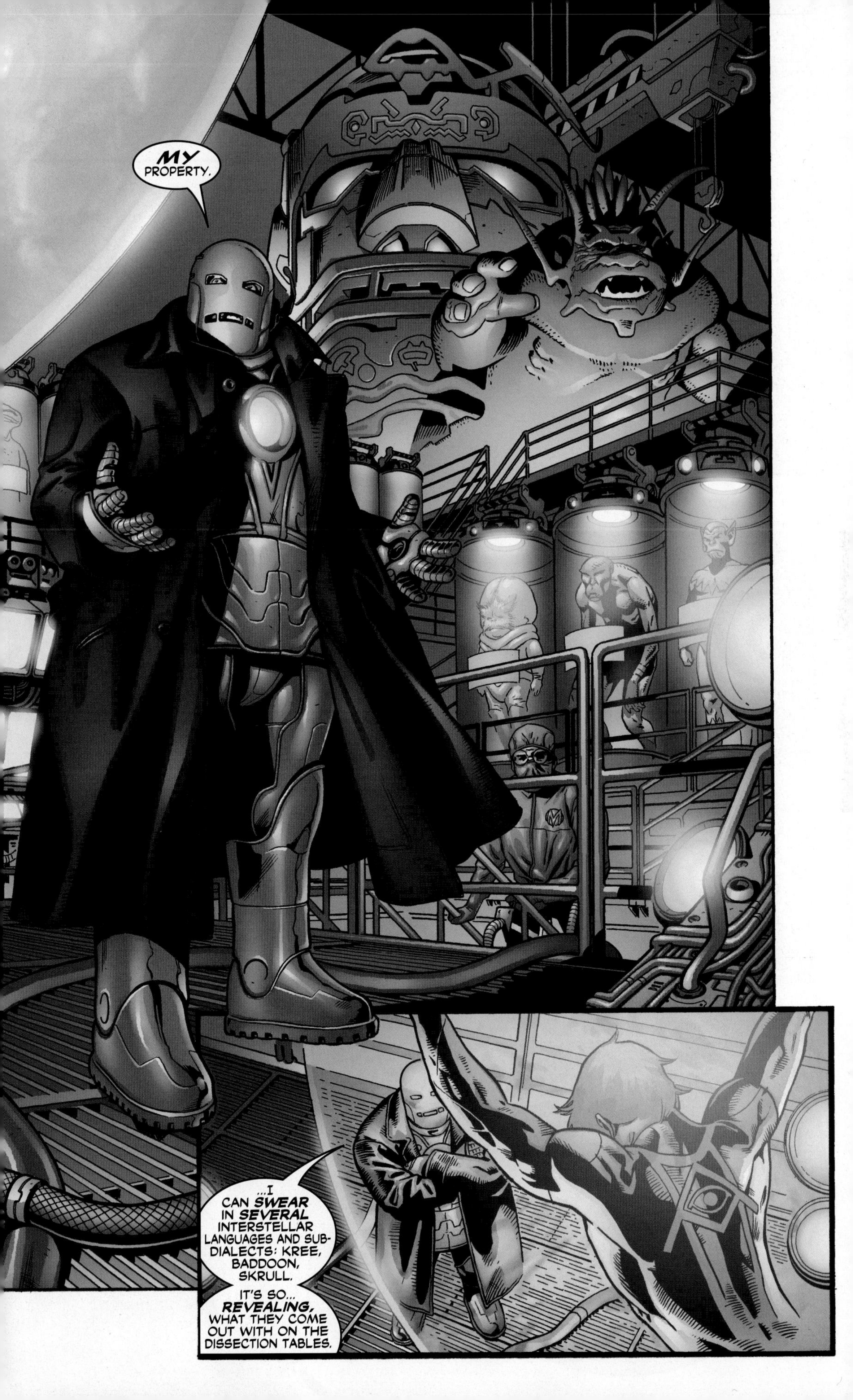
MY PROPERTY.
...I CAN SWEAR IN SEVERAL INTERSTELLAR LANGUAGES AND SUB-DIALECTS: KREE, BADDOON, SKRULL.
IT'S SO... REVEALING, WHAT THEY COME OUT WITH ON THE DISSECTION TABLES.

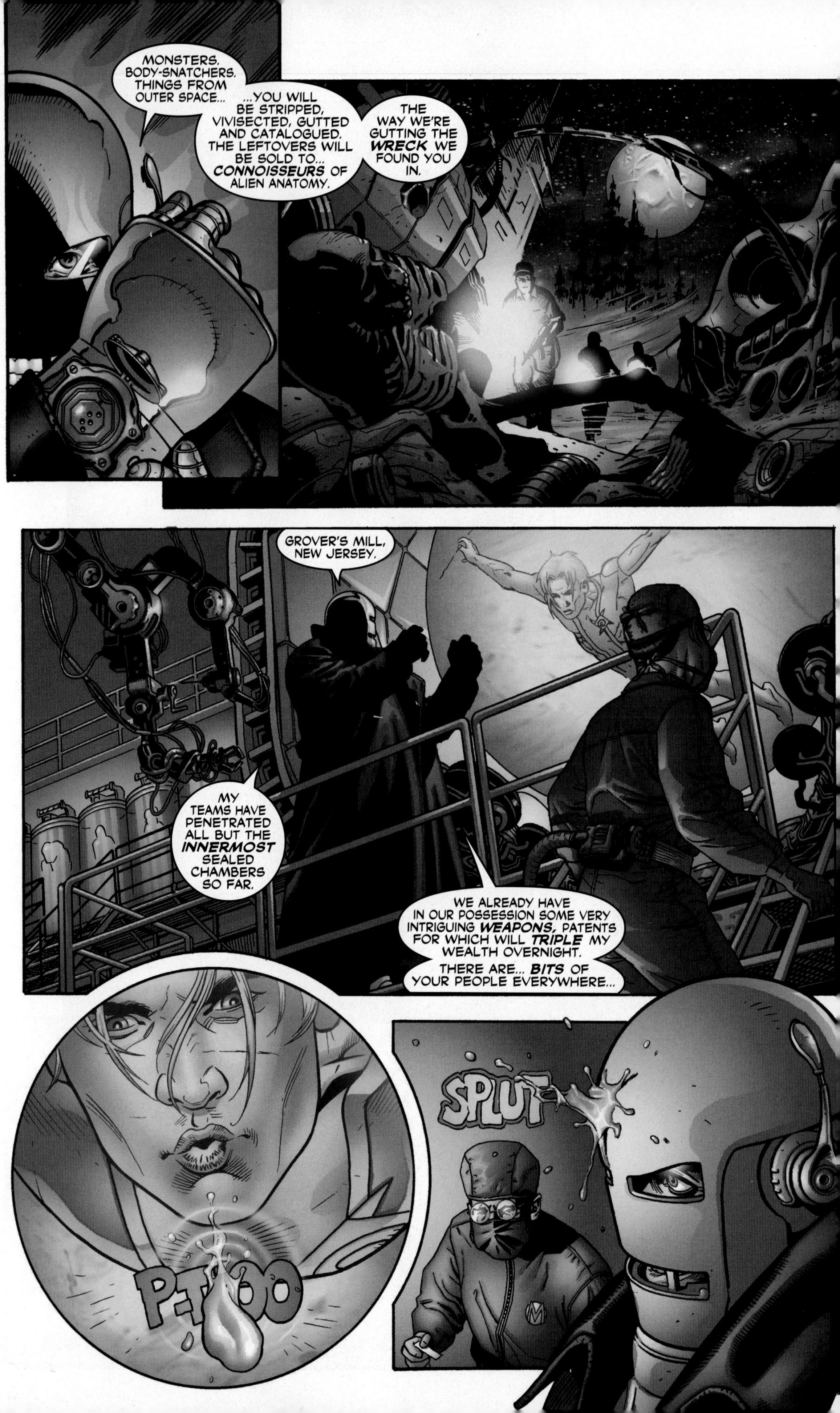
MONSTERS. BODY-SNATCHERS. THINGS FROM OUTER SPACE...
...YOU WILL BE STRIPPED, VIVISECTED, GUTTED AND CATALOGUED. THE LEFTOVERS WILL BE SOLD TO... CONNOISSEURS OF ALIEN ANATOMY.
THE WAY WE'RE GUTTING THE WRECK WE FOUND YOU IN.
GROVER'S MILL, NEW JERSEY.
MY TEAMS HAVE PENETRATED ALL BUT THE INNERMOST SEALED CHAMBERS SO FAR.
WE ALREADY HAVE IN OUR POSSESSION SOME VERY INTRIGUING WEAPONS, PATENTS FOR WHICH WILL TRIPLE MY WEALTH OVERNIGHT.
THERE ARE... BITS OF YOUR PEOPLE EVERYWHERE...
PTOO
SPLUT

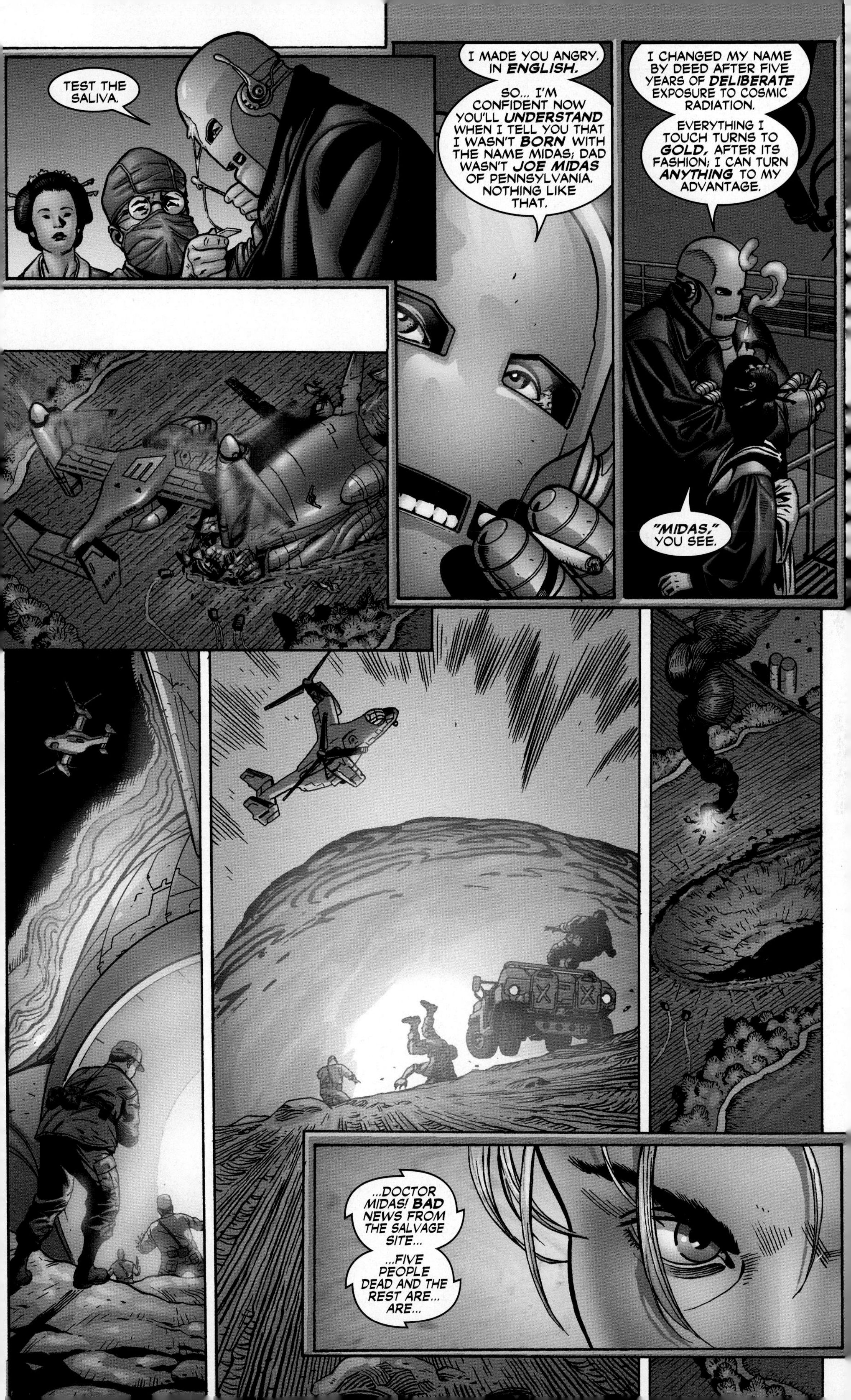
TEST THE SALIVA.
I MADE YOU ANGRY. IN ENGLISH.
SO... I'M CONFIDENT NOW YOU'LL UNDERSTAND WHEN I TELL YOU THAT I WASN'T BORN WITH THE NAME MIDAS; DAD WASN'T JOE MIDAS OF PENNSYLVANIA, NOTHING LIKE THAT.
I CHANGED MY NAME BY DEED AFTER FIVE YEARS OF DELIBERATE EXPOSURE TO COSMIC RADIATION.
EVERYTHING I TOUCH TURNS TO GOLD, AFTER ITS FASHION; I CAN TURN ANYTHING TO MY ADVANTAGE.
"MIDAS," YOU SEE.
...DOCTOR MIDAS! BAD NEWS FROM THE SALVAGE SITE...
...FIVE PEOPLE DEAD AND THE REST ARE... ARE...

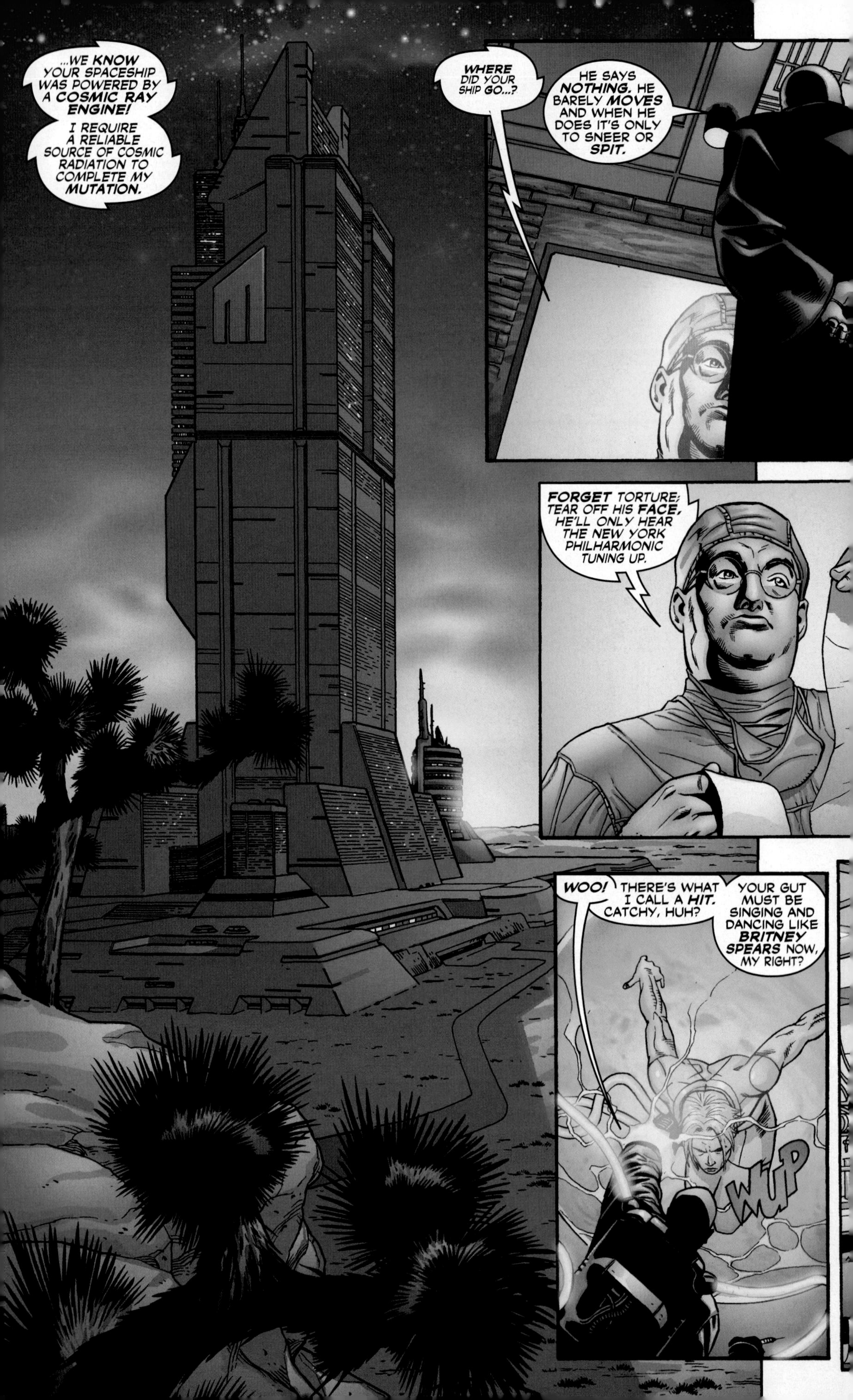
...WE KNOW YOUR SPACESHIP WAS POWERED BY A COSMIC RAY ENGINE!
I REQUIRE A RELIABLE SOURCE OF COSMIC RADIATION TO COMPLETE MY MUTATION.
WHERE DID YOUR SHIP GO...?
HE SAYS NOTHING. HE BARELY MOVES AND WHEN HE DOES IT'S ONLY TO SNEER OR SPIT.
FORGET TORTURE; TEAR OFF HIS FACE, HE'LL ONLY HEAR THE NEW YORK PHILHARMONIC TUNING UP.
WOO!
THERE'S WHAT I CALL A HIT. CATCHY, HUH?
YOUR GUT MUST BE SINGING AND DANCING LIKE BRITNEY SPEARS NOW, MY RIGHT?
WUP

YOUR EYES KEEP **DRIFTING**...

DAD, YOU'RE DISGUSTING. I'M TRYING TO IDENTIFY HIS WEAK POINTS.

THE PLACES HE'D **BREAK.**

...**NOT** IMPOSSIBLE, DOCTOR MIDAS; THE BUBBLE HAS STATE-OF-THE-ART **VIRTUAL SENSORS;** HE CAN'T HAVE A LOUD **THOUGHT** WITHOUT IT SHOWING UP HERE.

THERE'S THE PROOF: HE'S REROUTING **PAIN** SIGNALS INTO HIS **AUDITORY** CORTEX.

...**BLOOD.** I NEED A BLOOD SAMPLE FOR MY BOSS, DRACULA.

SO DON'T **LAUGH.**

YOU'RE THE GUY THAT TURNS PAIN INTO **MUSIC,** RIGHT?

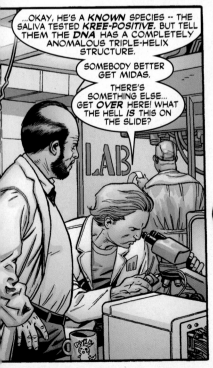

...OKAY, HE'S A **KNOWN** SPECIES -- THE SALIVA TESTED **KREE-POSITIVE.** BUT TELL THEM THE **DNA** HAS A COMPLETELY ANOMALOUS TRIPLE-HELIX STRUCTURE.

SOMEBODY BETTER GET MIDAS.

THERE'S SOMETHING ELSE... GET **OVER** HERE! WHAT THE HELL **IS** THIS ON THE SLIDE?

LAB

ALIEN **SUBSPECIES, ZERO** RIGHTS, END OF STORY. A DAMN **BACTERIA** GROWING ON THE TOILET WALL HERE'S GONNA GET THE VOTE BEFORE YOU DO, SO WELCOME TO **PLANET**...

HE'S SEETHING WITH SUBMICROTECH!

HIS BODY FLUIDS ARE NANOACTIVE!

XENOHAZARD ALERT!

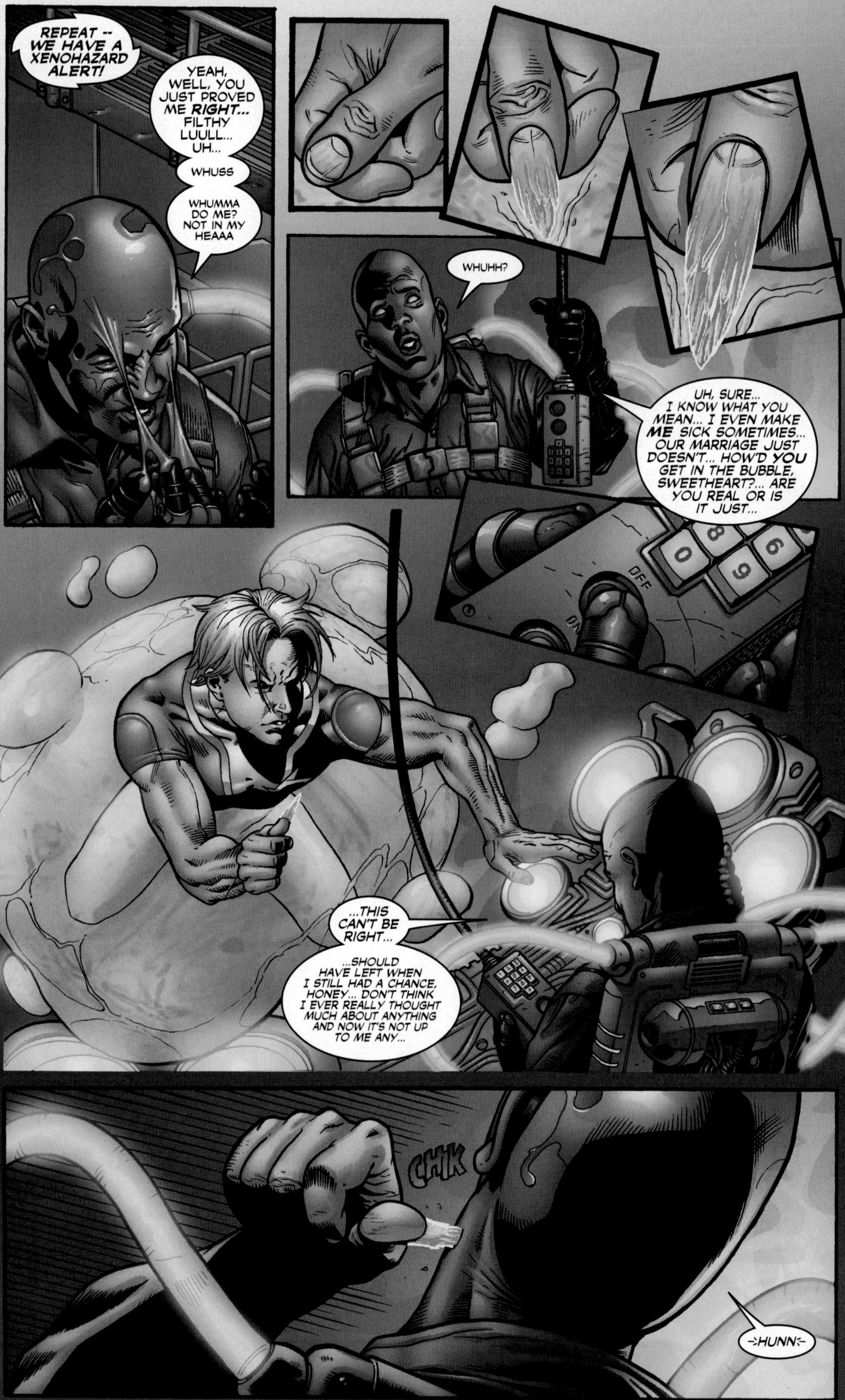
REPEAT -- WE HAVE A XENOHAZARD ALERT!
YEAH, WELL, YOU JUST PROVED ME RIGHT... FILTHY LUULL... UH...
WHUSS
WHUMMA DO ME? NOT IN MY HEAAA
WHUHH?
UH, SURE... I KNOW WHAT YOU MEAN... I EVEN MAKE ME SICK SOMETIMES... OUR MARRIAGE JUST DOESN'T... HOW'D YOU GET IN THE BUBBLE, SWEETHEART?... ARE YOU REAL OR IS IT JUST...
OFF
...THIS CAN'T BE RIGHT...
...SHOULD HAVE LEFT WHEN I STILL HAD A CHANCE, HONEY... DON'T THINK I EVER REALLY THOUGHT MUCH ABOUT ANYTHING AND NOW IT'S NOT UP TO ME ANY...
CHK
HUNN

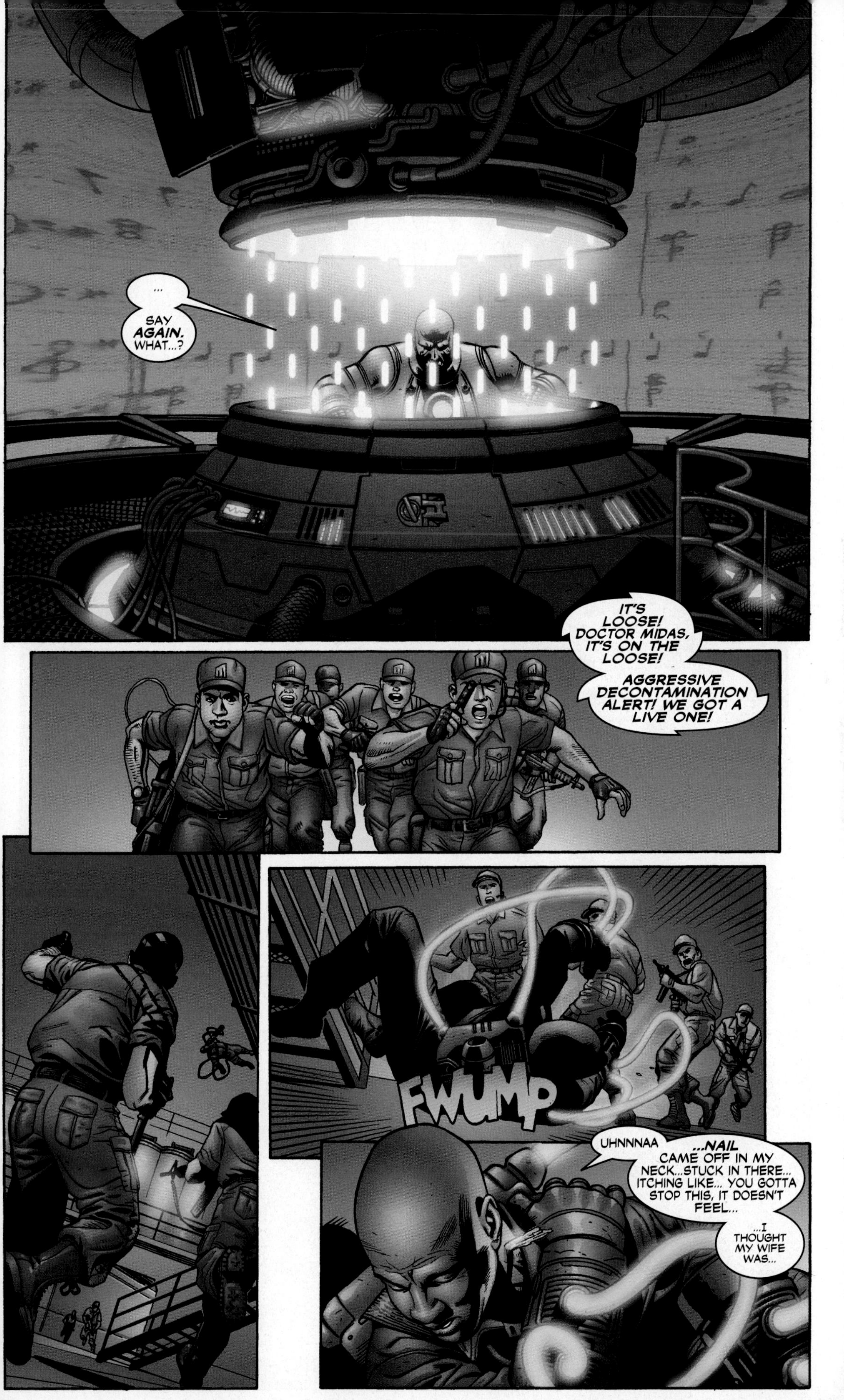
...
SAY AGAIN. WHAT...?
IT'S LOOSE! DOCTOR MIDAS, IT'S ON THE LOOSE!
AGGRESSIVE DECONTAMINATION ALERT! WE GOT A LIVE ONE!
FWUMP
UHNNNAA
...NAIL CAME OFF IN MY NECK...STUCK IN THERE... ITCHING LIKE... YOU GOTTA STOP THIS, IT DOESN'T FEEL...
...I THOUGHT MY WIFE WAS...

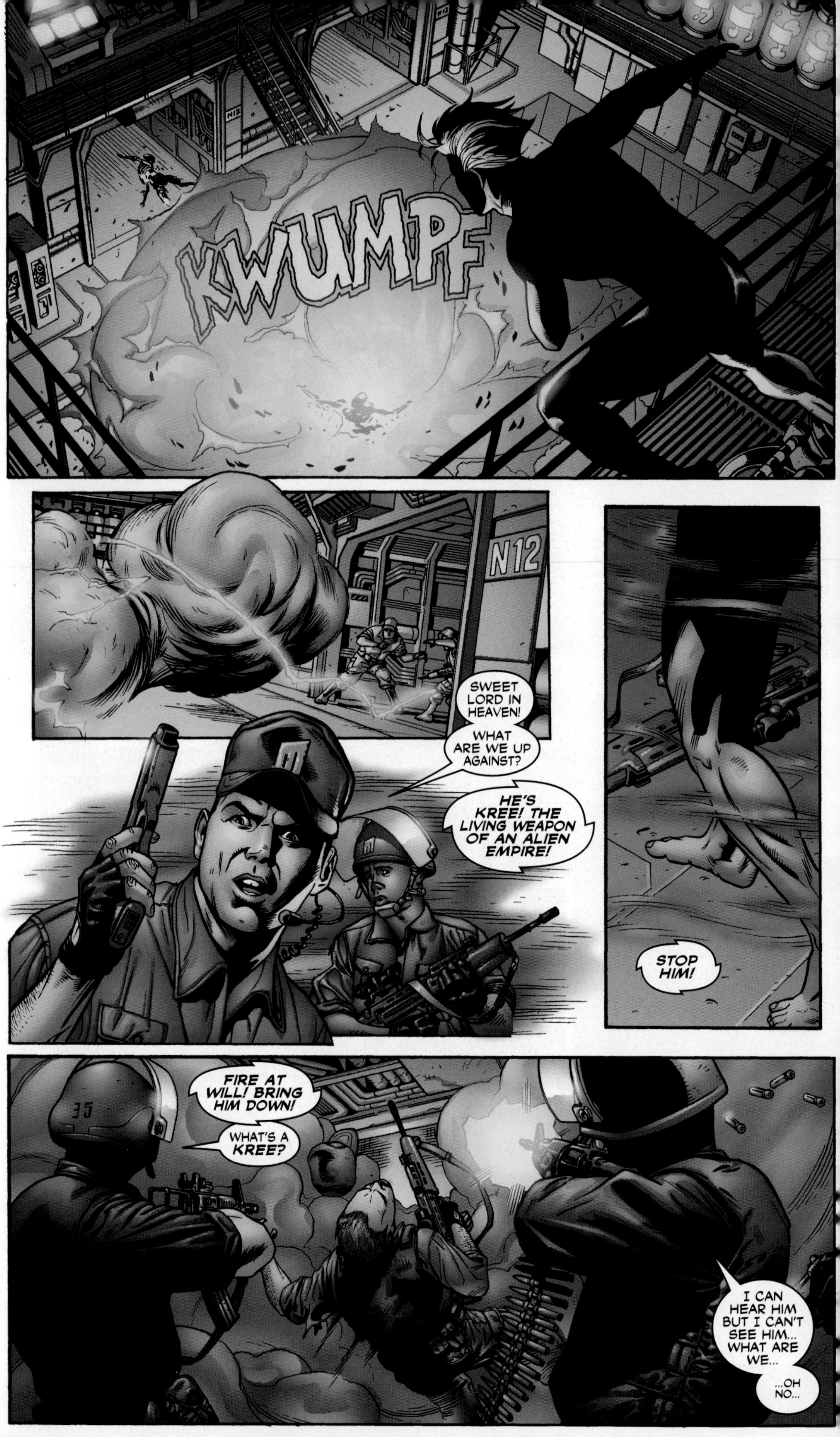
KWUMPF
SWEET LORD IN HEAVEN!
WHAT ARE WE UP AGAINST?
HE'S KREE! THE LIVING WEAPON OF AN ALIEN EMPIRE!
STOP HIM!
FIRE AT WILL! BRING HIM DOWN!
WHAT'S A KREE?
I CAN HEAR HIM BUT I CAN'T SEE HIM... WHAT ARE WE...
...OH NO...

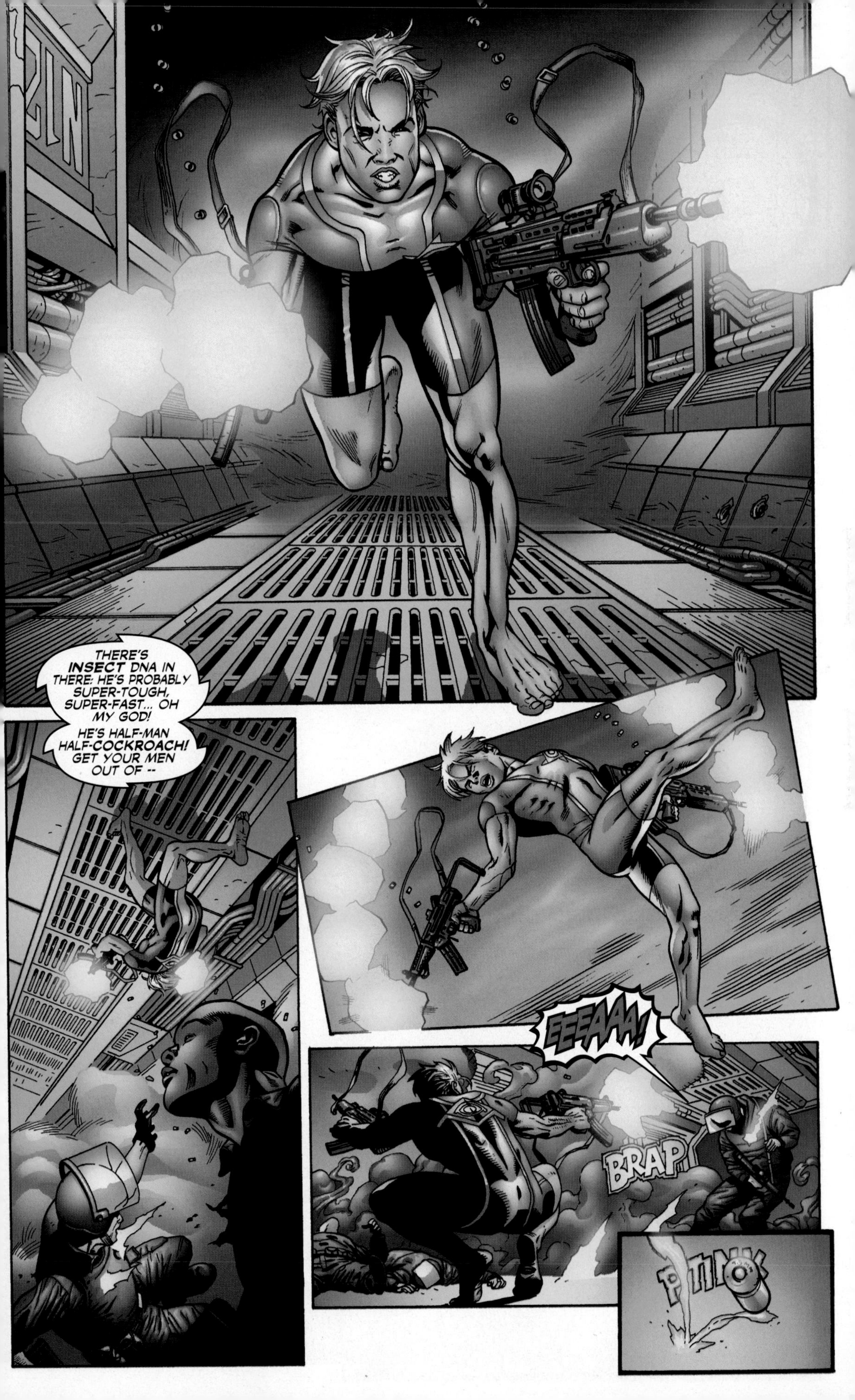
THERE'S INSECT DNA IN THERE: HE'S PROBABLY SUPER-TOUGH, SUPER-FAST... OH MY GOD!
HE'S HALF-MAN HALF-COCKROACH! GET YOUR MEN OUT OF --
EEEAAA!
BRAP

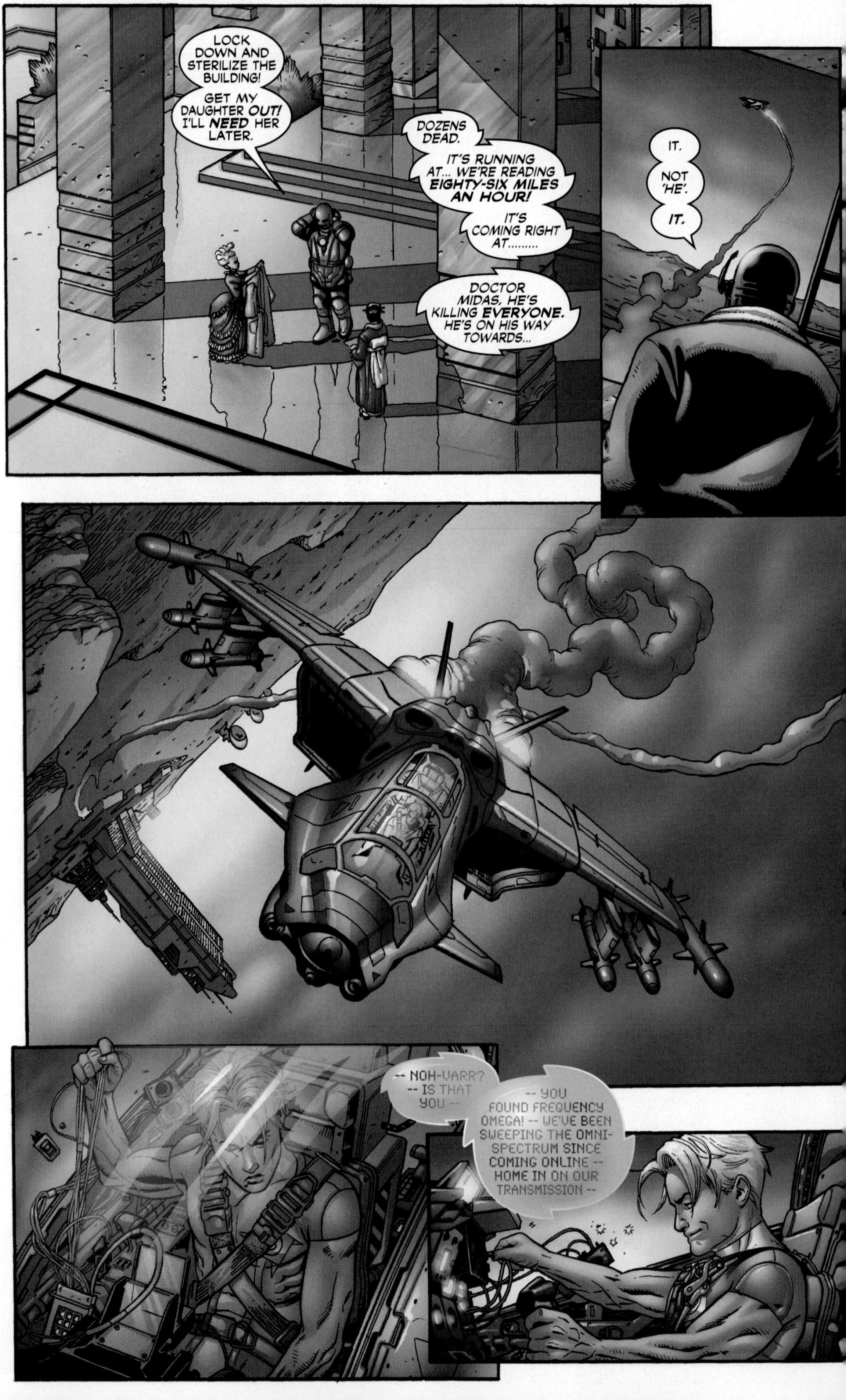
LOCK DOWN AND STERILIZE THE BUILDING!
GET MY DAUGHTER OUT! I'LL NEED HER LATER.
DOZENS DEAD.
IT'S RUNNING AT... WE'RE READING EIGHTY-SIX MILES AN HOUR!
IT'S COMING RIGHT AT.........
DOCTOR MIDAS, HE'S KILLING EVERYONE. HE'S ON HIS WAY TOWARDS...
IT.
NOT 'HE'.
IT.
-- NOH-VARR? -- IS THAT YOU --
-- YOU FOUND FREQUENCY OMEGA! -- WE'VE BEEN SWEEPING THE OMNI-SPECTRUM SINCE COMING ONLINE -- HOME IN ON OUR TRANSMISSION --

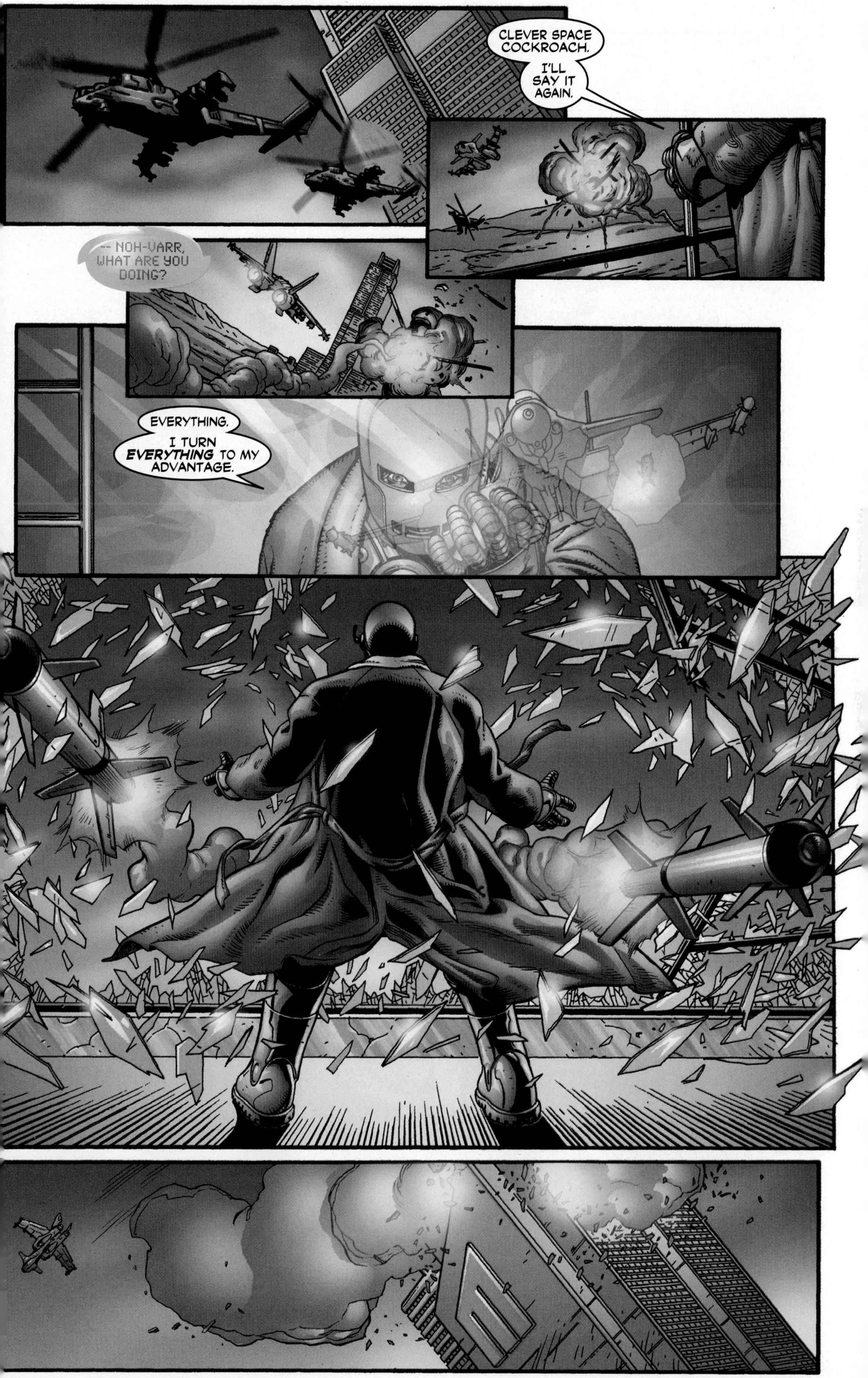
CLEVER SPACE COCKROACH.
I'LL SAY IT AGAIN.
-- NOH-VARR, WHAT ARE YOU DOING?
EVERYTHING.
I TURN EVERYTHING TO MY ADVANTAGE.

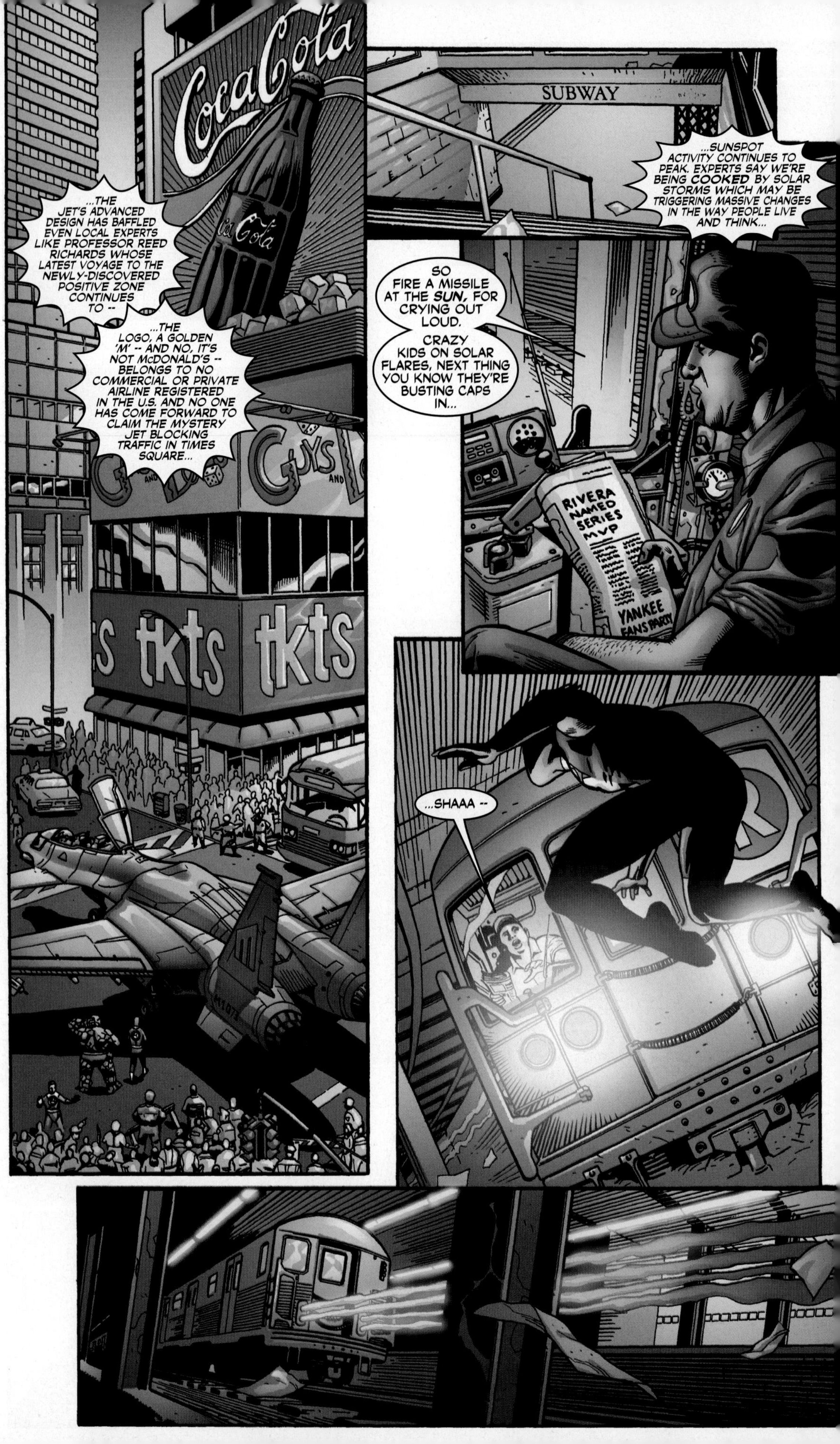
Coca-Cola
Coca-Cola
...THE JET'S ADVANCED DESIGN HAS BAFFLED EVEN LOCAL EXPERTS LIKE PROFESSOR REED RICHARDS WHOSE LATEST VOYAGE TO THE NEWLY-DISCOVERED POSITIVE ZONE CONTINUES TO --
...THE LOGO, A GOLDEN 'M' -- AND NO, IT'S NOT McDONALD'S -- BELONGS TO NO COMMERCIAL OR PRIVATE AIRLINE REGISTERED IN THE U.S. AND NO ONE HAS COME FORWARD TO CLAIM THE MYSTERY JET BLOCKING TRAFFIC IN TIMES SQUARE...
GUYS AND
tkts tkts
SUBWAY
...SUNSPOT ACTIVITY CONTINUES TO PEAK. EXPERTS SAY WE'RE BEING COOKED BY SOLAR STORMS WHICH MAY BE TRIGGERING MASSIVE CHANGES IN THE WAY PEOPLE LIVE AND THINK...
SO FIRE A MISSILE AT THE SUN, FOR CRYING OUT LOUD.
CRAZY KIDS ON SOLAR FLARES, NEXT THING YOU KNOW THEY'RE BUSTING CAPS IN...
RIVERA NAMED SERIES MVP
YANKEE FANS PARTY
...SHAAA --

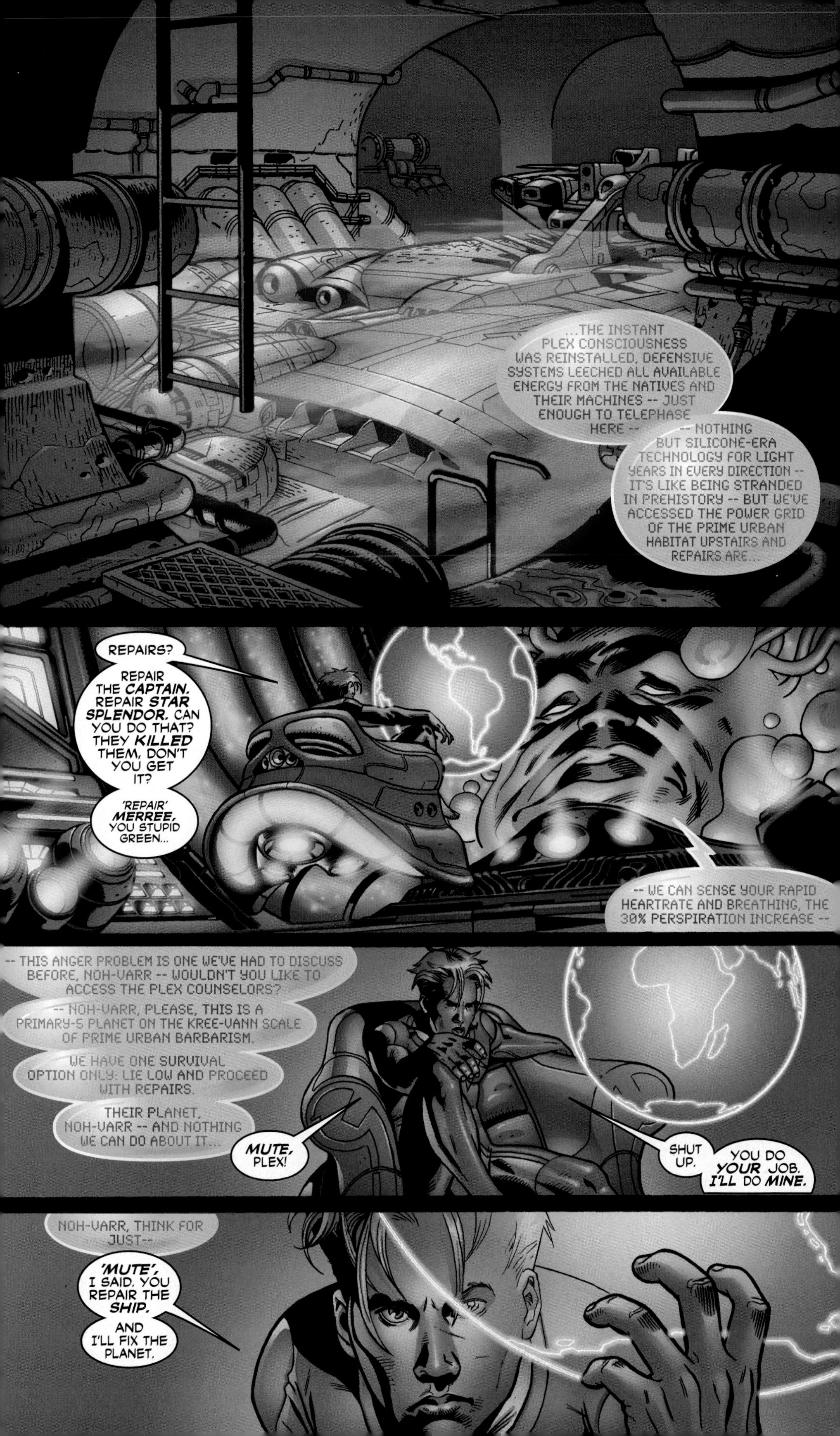
...THE INSTANT PLEX CONSCIOUSNESS WAS REINSTALLED, DEFENSIVE SYSTEMS LEECHED ALL AVAILABLE ENERGY FROM THE NATIVES AND THEIR MACHINES -- JUST ENOUGH TO TELEPHASE HERE --
-- NOTHING BUT SILICONE-ERA TECHNOLOGY FOR LIGHT YEARS IN EVERY DIRECTION -- IT'S LIKE BEING STRANDED IN PREHISTORY -- BUT WE'VE ACCESSED THE POWER GRID OF THE PRIME URBAN HABITAT UPSTAIRS AND REPAIRS ARE...
REPAIRS?
REPAIR THE CAPTAIN. REPAIR STAR SPLENDOR. CAN YOU DO THAT? THEY KILLED THEM, DON'T YOU GET IT?
'REPAIR' MERREE, YOU STUPID GREEN...
-- WE CAN SENSE YOUR RAPID HEARTRATE AND BREATHING, THE 30% PERSPIRATION INCREASE --
-- THIS ANGER PROBLEM IS ONE WE'VE HAD TO DISCUSS BEFORE, NOH-VARR -- WOULDN'T YOU LIKE TO ACCESS THE PLEX COUNSELORS?
-- NOH-VARR, PLEASE, THIS IS A PRIMARY-5 PLANET ON THE KREE-VANN SCALE OF PRIME URBAN BARBARISM.
WE HAVE ONE SURVIVAL OPTION ONLY: LIE LOW AND PROCEED WITH REPAIRS.
THEIR PLANET, NOH-VARR -- AND NOTHING WE CAN DO ABOUT IT...
MUTE, PLEX!
SHUT UP.
YOU DO YOUR JOB. I'LL DO MINE.
NOH-VARR, THINK FOR JUST--
'MUTE', I SAID. YOU REPAIR THE SHIP.
AND I'LL FIX THE PLANET.

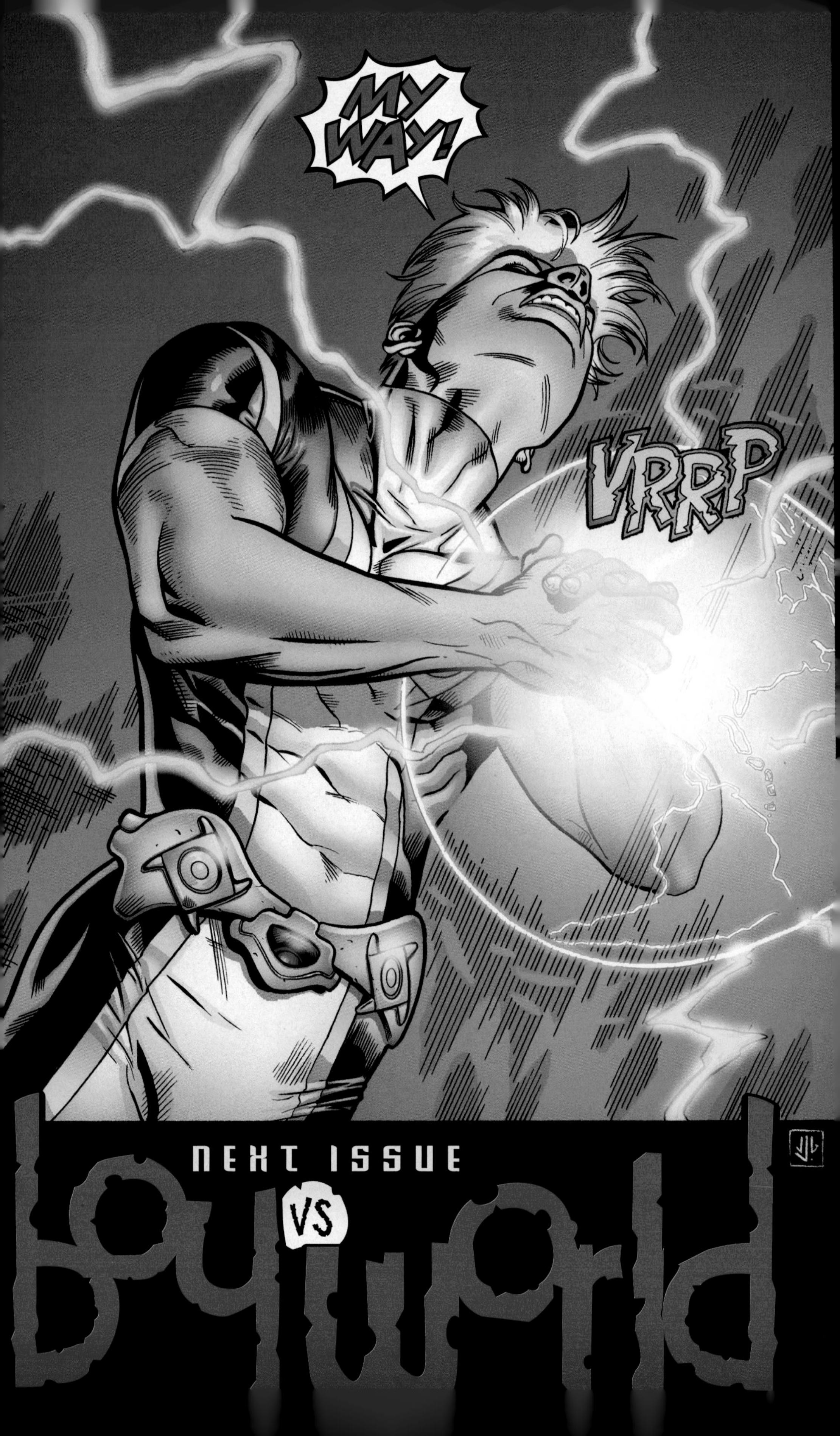
MY WAY!
VRRP
NEXT ISSUE
VS
boyworld

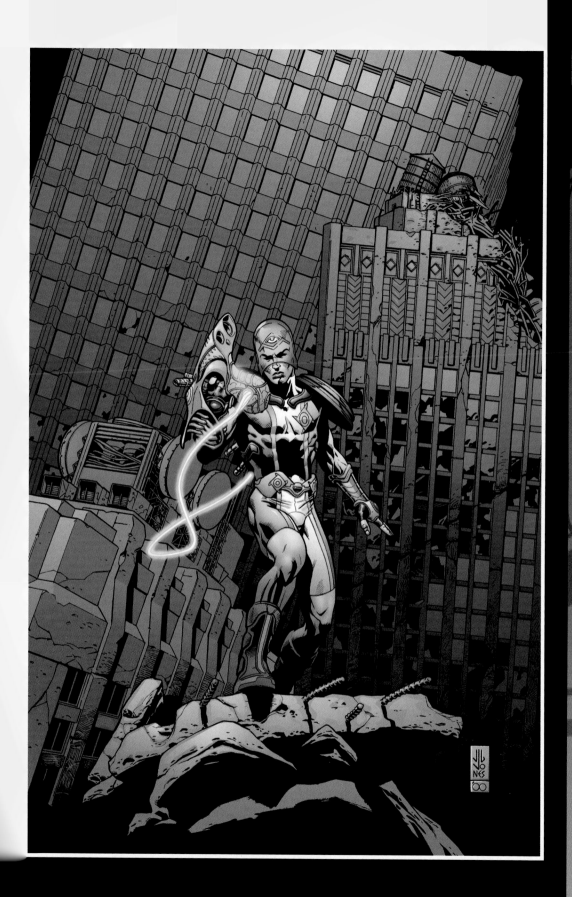

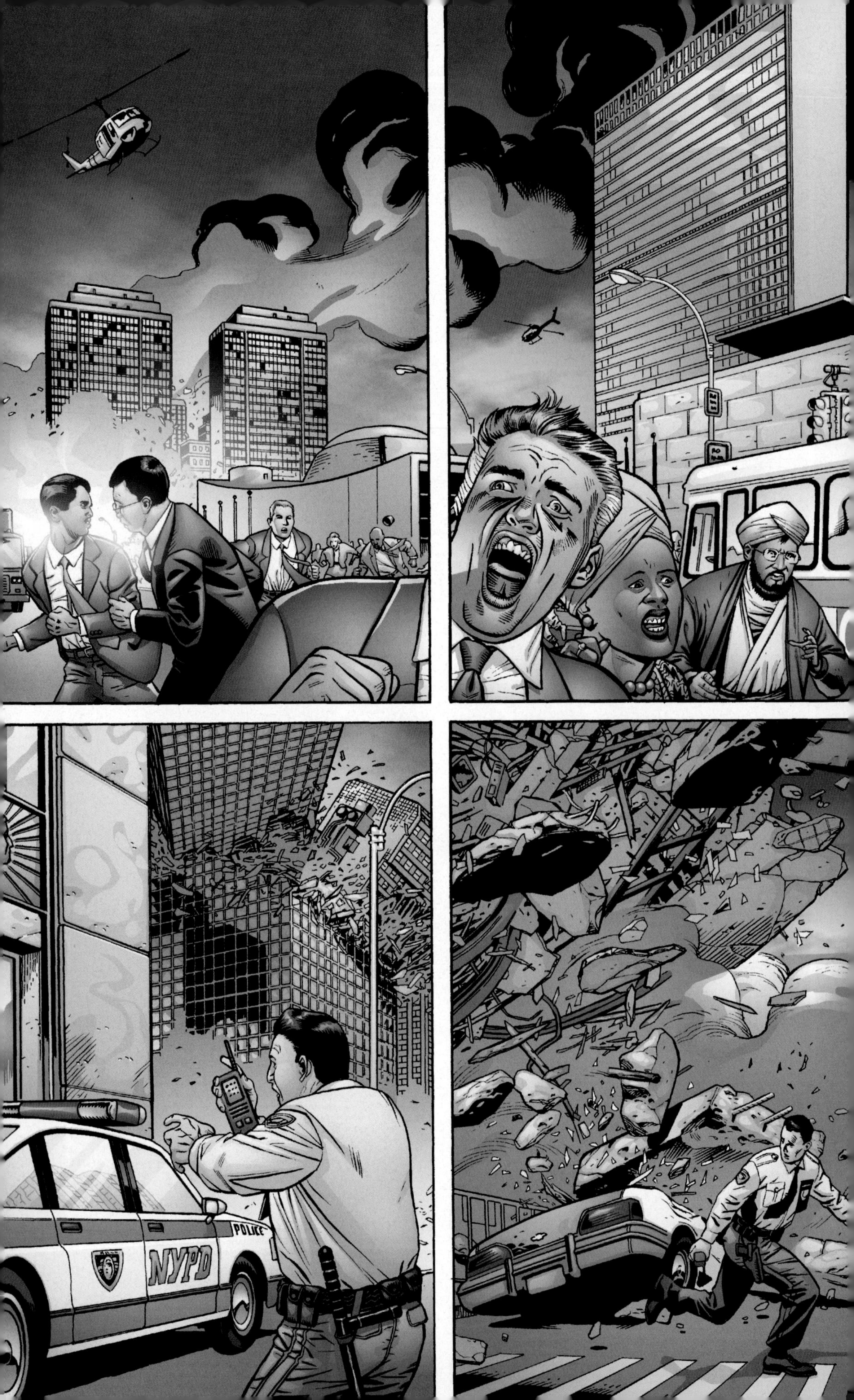
POLICE
NYPD

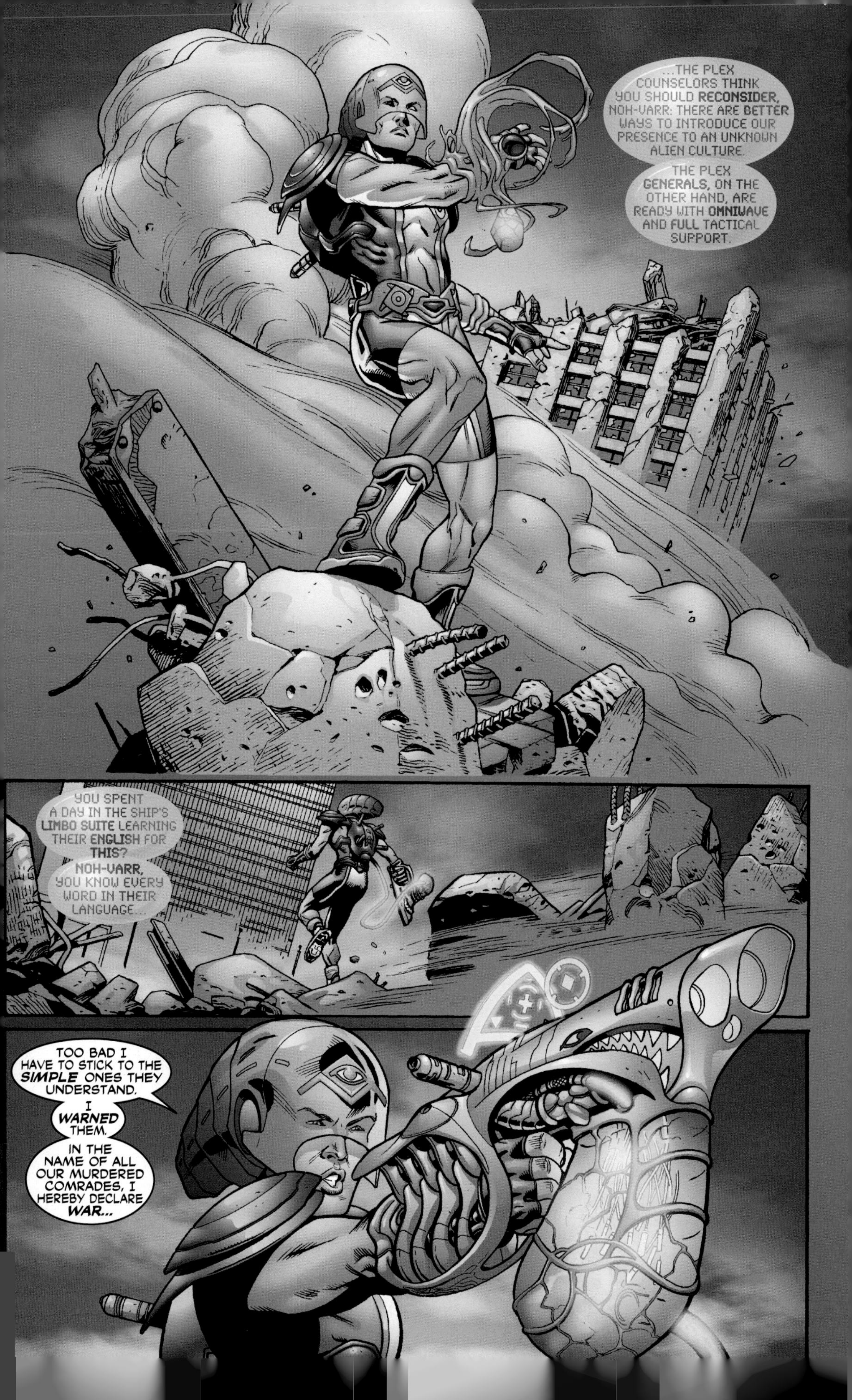
...THE PLEX COUNSELORS THINK YOU SHOULD RECONSIDER, NOH-VARR: THERE ARE BETTER WAYS TO INTRODUCE OUR PRESENCE TO AN UNKNOWN ALIEN CULTURE.
THE PLEX GENERALS, ON THE OTHER HAND, ARE READY WITH OMNIWAVE AND FULL TACTICAL SUPPORT.
YOU SPENT A DAY IN THE SHIP'S LIMBO SUITE LEARNING THEIR ENGLISH FOR THIS?
NOH-VARR, YOU KNOW EVERY WORD IN THEIR LANGUAGE...
TOO BAD I HAVE TO STICK TO THE SIMPLE ONES THEY UNDERSTAND.
I WARNED THEM.
IN THE NAME OF ALL OUR MURDERED COMRADES, I HEREBY DECLARE WAR...

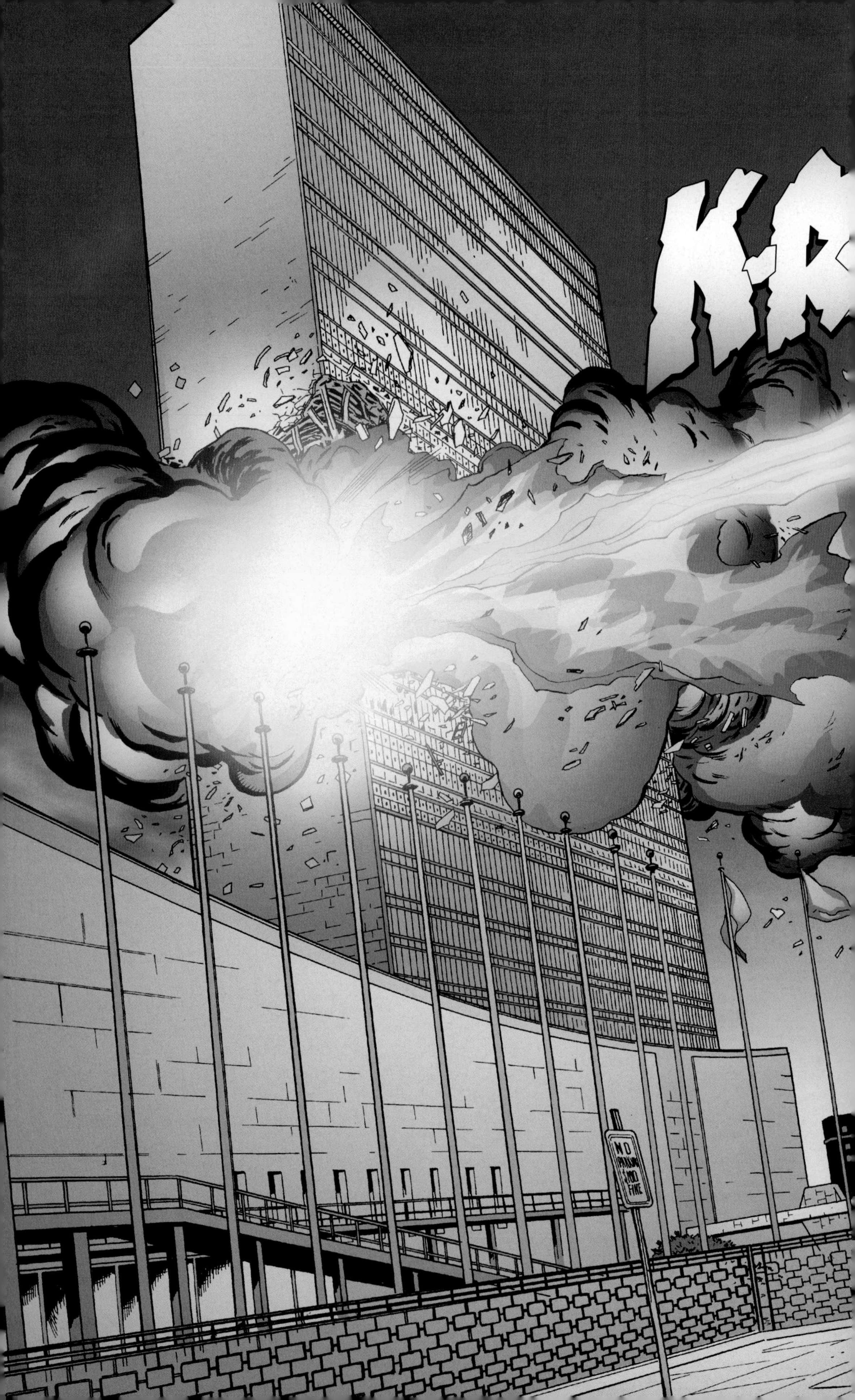
K-R
NO PARKING $100 FINE

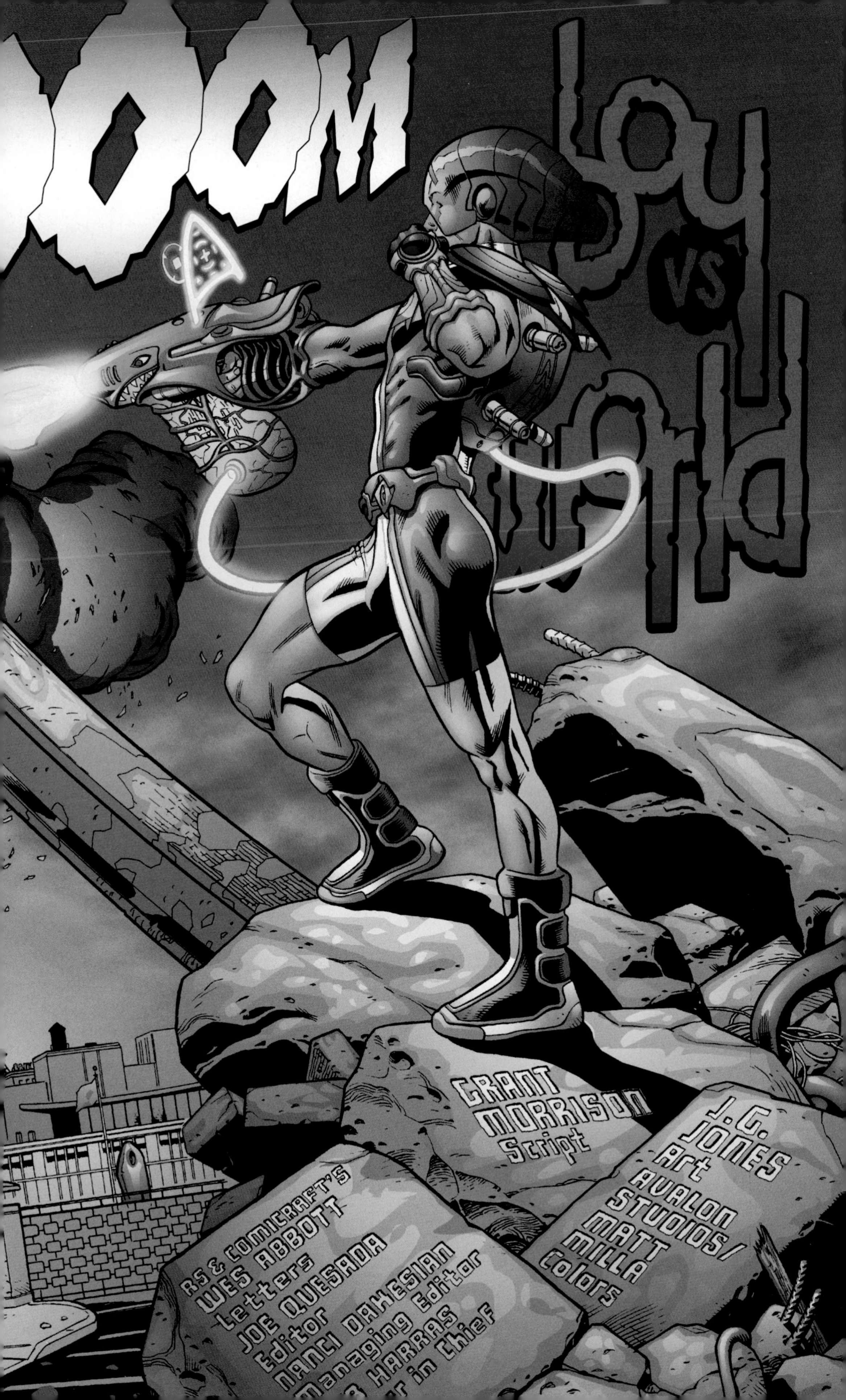
OOM
VS
GRANT MORRISON Script
J.G. JONES Art
AVALON STUDIOS/ MATT MILLA Colors
WES ABBOTT Letters
JOE QUESADA Editor
NANCI DAKESIAN Managing Editor
HARRAS
in Chief

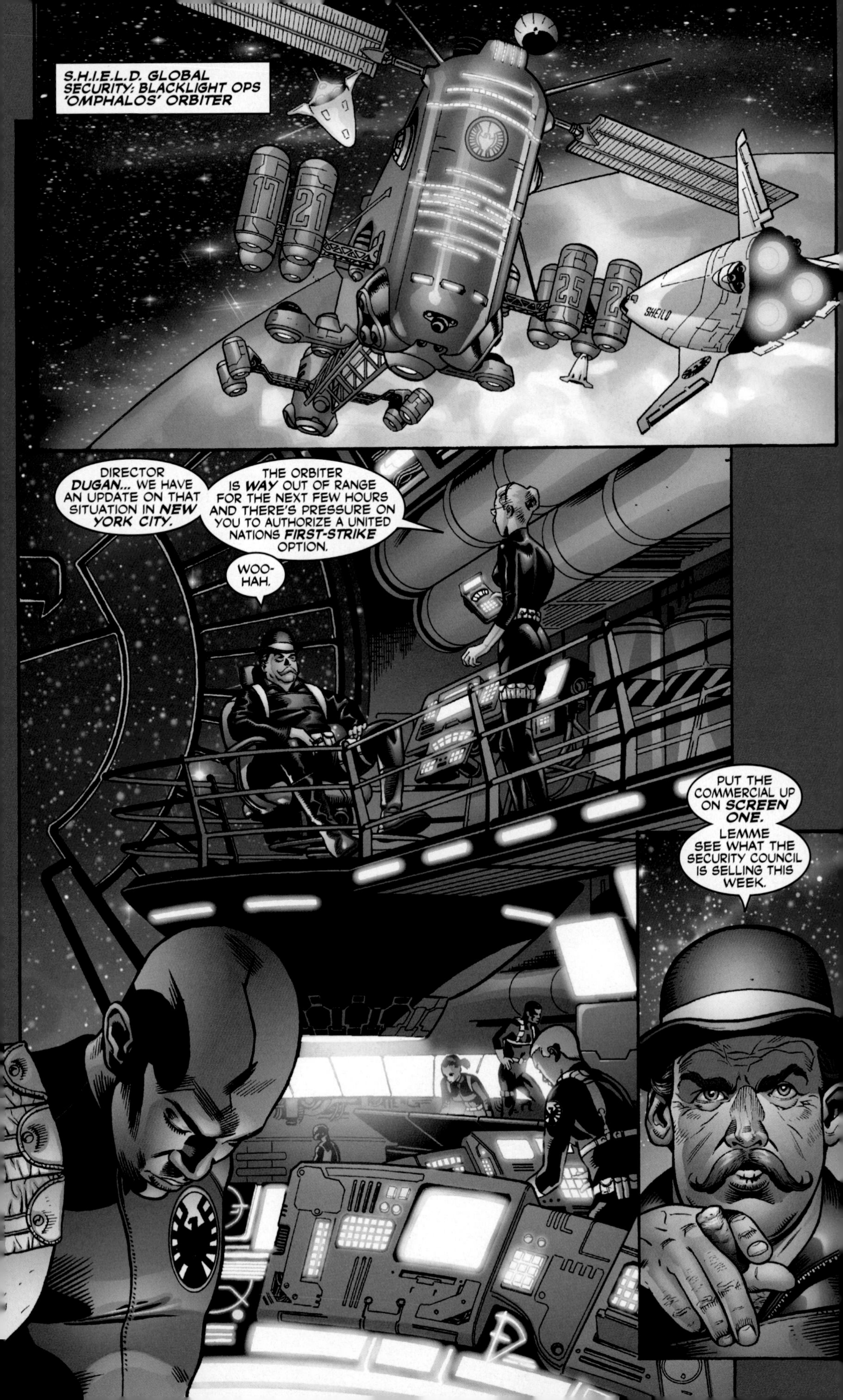
S.H.I.E.L.D. GLOBAL SECURITY: BLACKLIGHT OPS 'OMPHALOS' ORBITER
SHEILO
DIRECTOR DUGAN... WE HAVE AN UPDATE ON THAT SITUATION IN NEW YORK CITY.
THE ORBITER IS WAY OUT OF RANGE FOR THE NEXT FEW HOURS AND THERE'S PRESSURE ON YOU TO AUTHORIZE A UNITED NATIONS FIRST-STRIKE OPTION.
WOO-HAH.
PUT THE COMMERCIAL UP ON SCREEN ONE.
LEMME SEE WHAT THE SECURITY COUNCIL IS SELLING THIS WEEK.

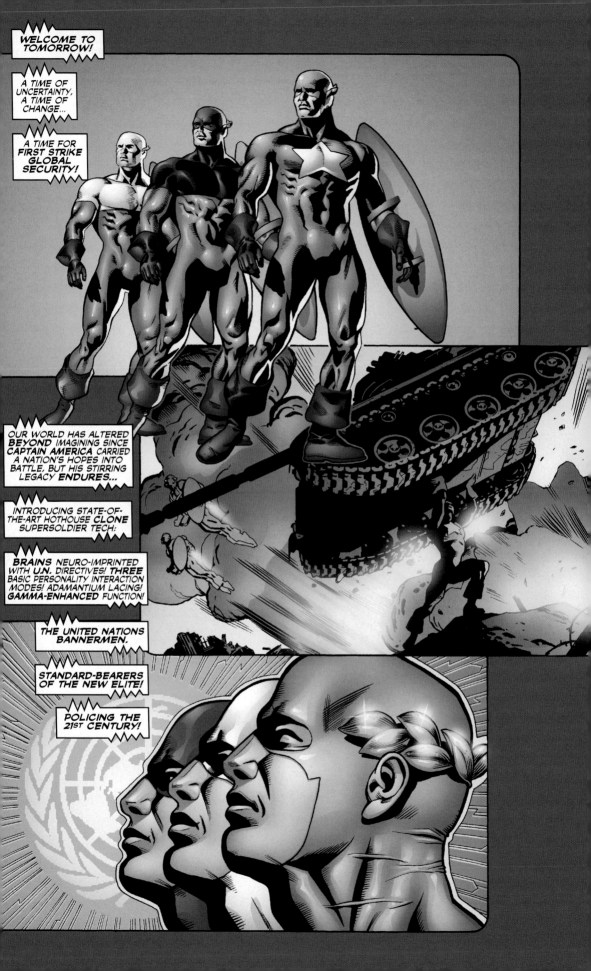

WELCOME TO TOMORROW!

A TIME OF UNCERTAINTY, A TIME OF CHANGE...

A TIME FOR FIRST STRIKE GLOBAL SECURITY!

OUR WORLD HAS ALTERED **BEYOND** IMAGINING SINCE **CAPTAIN AMERICA** CARRIED A NATION'S HOPES INTO BATTLE, BUT HIS STIRRING LEGACY **ENDURES**...

INTRODUCING STATE-OF-THE-ART HOTHOUSE **CLONE** SUPERSOLDIER TECH:

BRAINS NEURO-IMPRINTED WITH **U.N.** DIRECTIVES! **THREE** BASIC PERSONALITY INTERACTION MODES! ADAMANTIUM LACING! **GAMMA-ENHANCED** FUNCTION!

THE UNITED NATIONS BANNERMEN.

STANDARD-BEARERS OF THE NEW ELITE!

POLICING THE 21ST CENTURY!

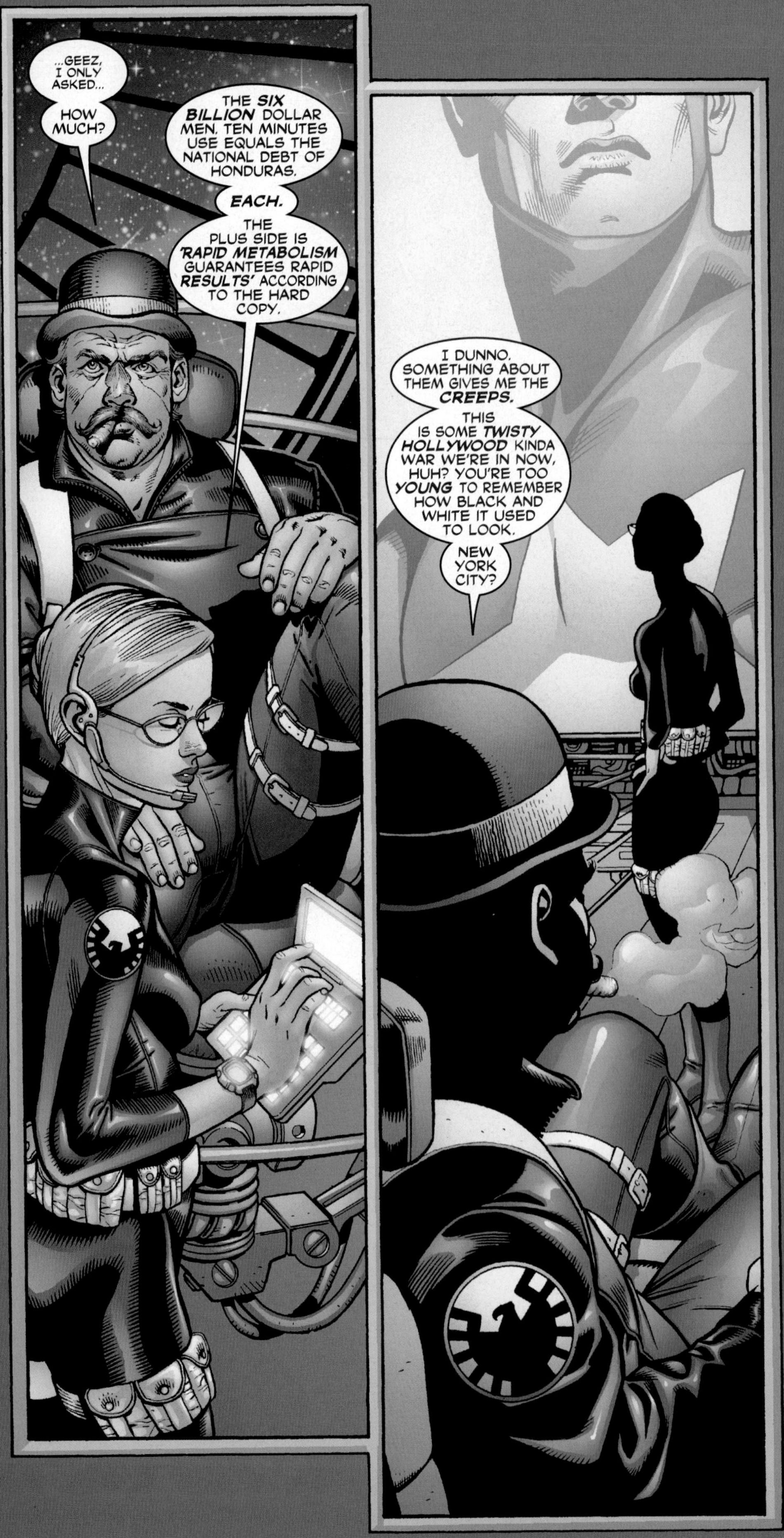
...GEEZ, I ONLY ASKED...
HOW MUCH?
THE SIX BILLION DOLLAR MEN. TEN MINUTES USE EQUALS THE NATIONAL DEBT OF HONDURAS.
EACH.
THE PLUS SIDE IS 'RAPID METABOLISM GUARANTEES RAPID RESULTS' ACCORDING TO THE HARD COPY.
I DUNNO. SOMETHING ABOUT THEM GIVES ME THE CREEPS.
THIS IS SOME TWISTY HOLLYWOOD KINDA WAR WE'RE IN NOW, HUH? YOU'RE TOO YOUNG TO REMEMBER HOW BLACK AND WHITE IT USED TO LOOK.
NEW YORK CITY?

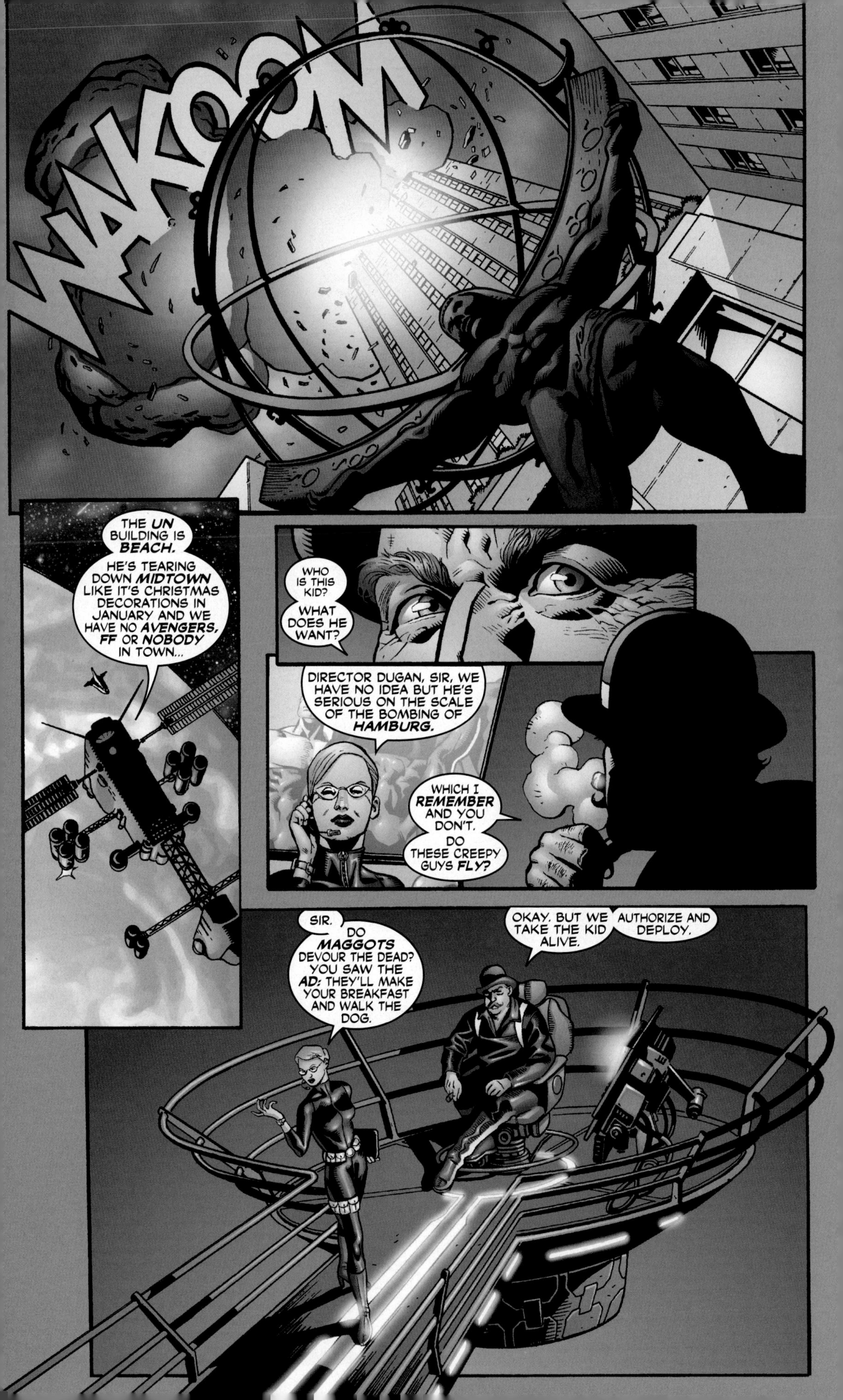
WAKOOM
THE UN BUILDING IS BEACH.
HE'S TEARING DOWN MIDTOWN LIKE IT'S CHRISTMAS DECORATIONS IN JANUARY AND WE HAVE NO AVENGERS, FF OR NOBODY IN TOWN...
WHO IS THIS KID?
WHAT DOES HE WANT?
DIRECTOR DUGAN, SIR, WE HAVE NO IDEA BUT HE'S SERIOUS ON THE SCALE OF THE BOMBING OF HAMBURG.
WHICH I REMEMBER AND YOU DON'T.
DO THESE CREEPY GUYS FLY?
SIR.
DO MAGGOTS DEVOUR THE DEAD? YOU SAW THE AD: THEY'LL MAKE YOUR BREAKFAST AND WALK THE DOG.
OKAY. BUT WE TAKE THE KID ALIVE.
AUTHORIZE AND DEPLOY.

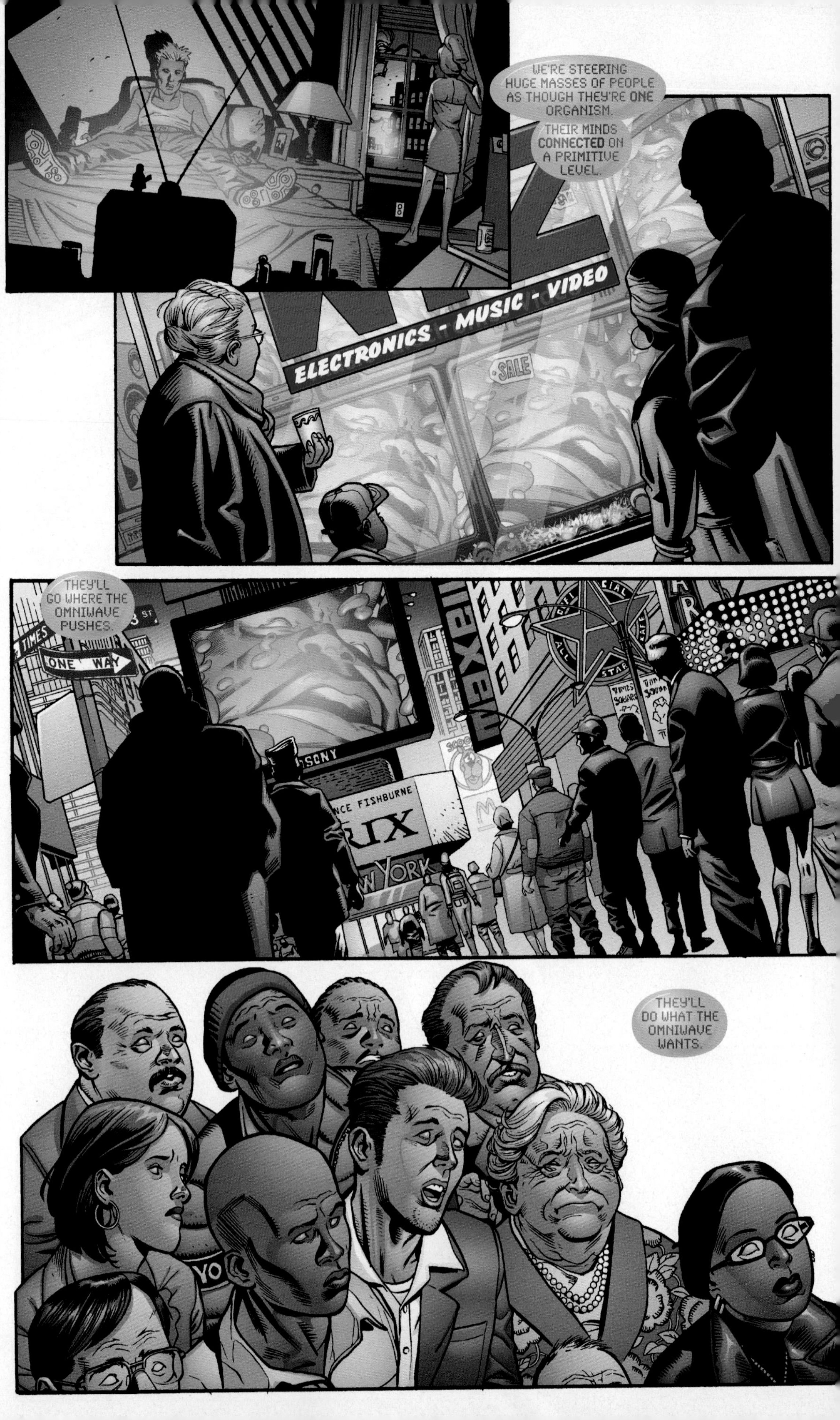

WE'RE STEERING HUGE MASSES OF PEOPLE AS THOUGH THEY'RE ONE ORGANISM.
THEIR MINDS CONNECTED ON A PRIMITIVE LEVEL.
ELECTRONICS - MUSIC - VIDEO
SALE
THEY'LL GO WHERE THE OMNIWAVE PUSHES.
ONE WAY
SONY
THEY'LL DO WHAT THE OMNIWAVE WANTS.

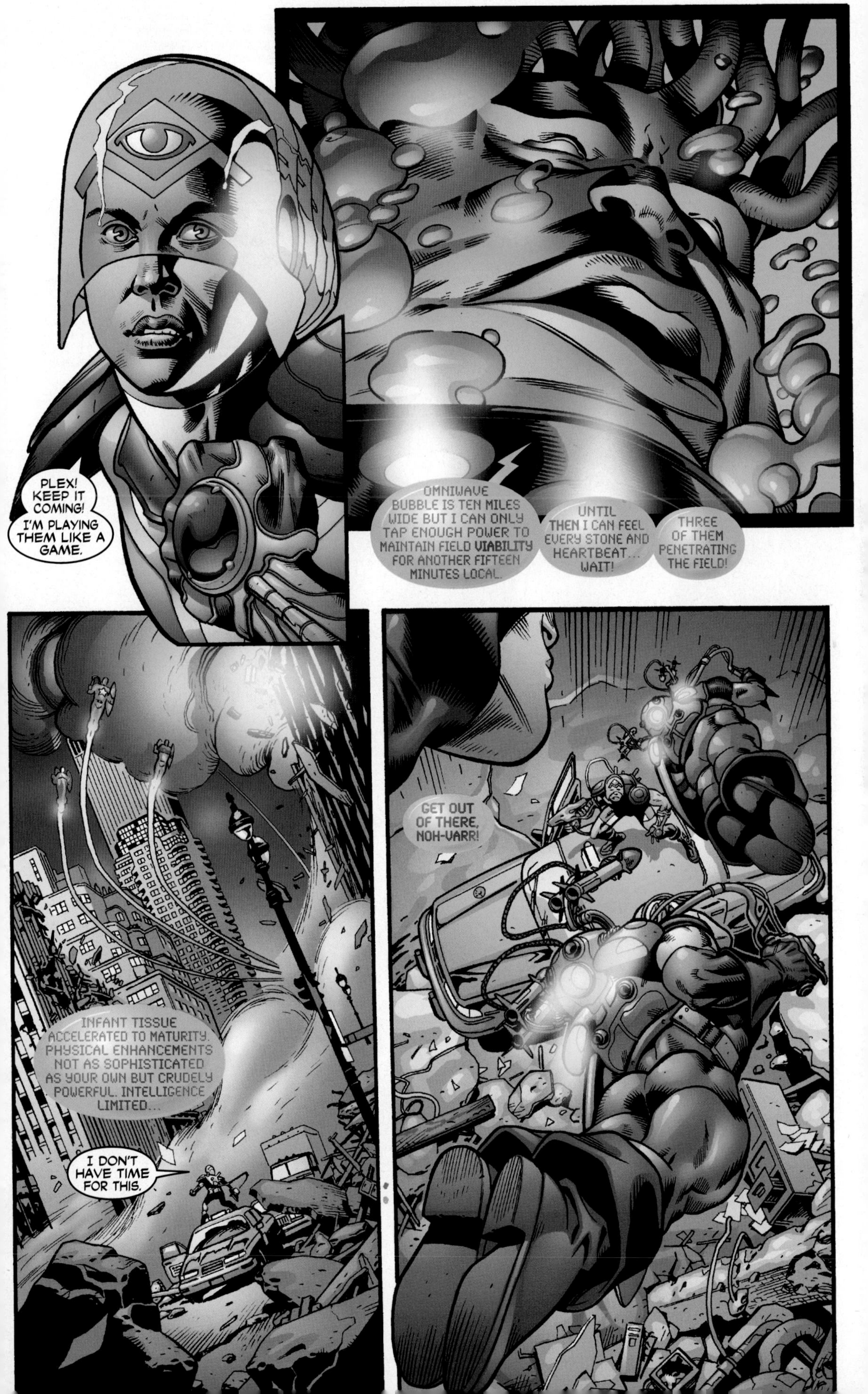
PLEX! KEEP IT COMING! I'M PLAYING THEM LIKE A GAME.
OMNIWAVE BUBBLE IS TEN MILES WIDE BUT I CAN ONLY TAP ENOUGH POWER TO MAINTAIN FIELD VIABILITY FOR ANOTHER FIFTEEN MINUTES LOCAL.
UNTIL THEN I CAN FEEL EVERY STONE AND HEARTBEAT... WAIT!
THREE OF THEM PENETRATING THE FIELD!
INFANT TISSUE ACCELERATED TO MATURITY. PHYSICAL ENHANCEMENTS NOT AS SOPHISTICATED AS YOUR OWN BUT CRUDELY POWERFUL. INTELLIGENCE LIMITED...
I DON'T HAVE TIME FOR THIS.
GET OUT OF THERE, NOH-VARR!

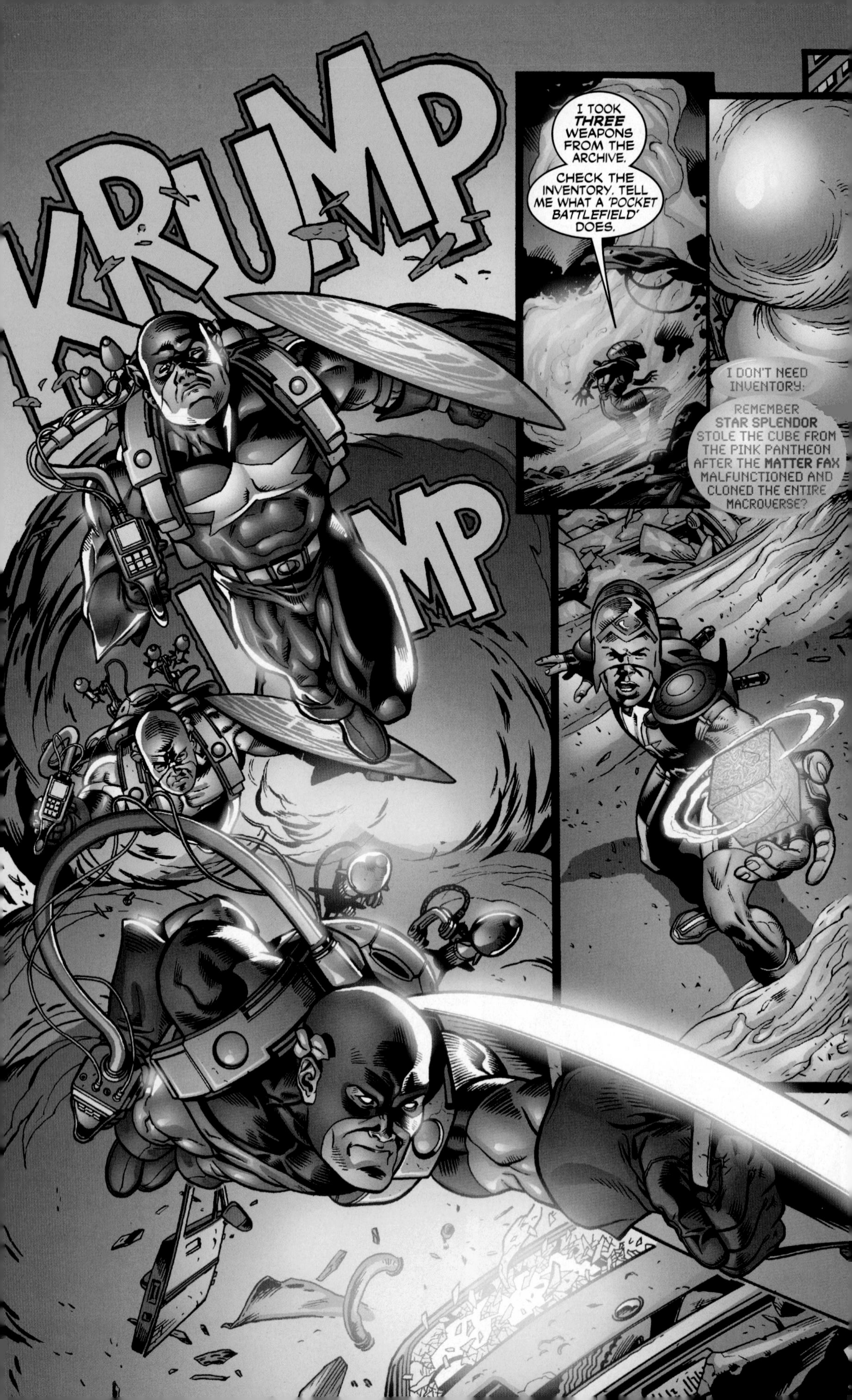
VRUMP
VRUMP
I TOOK THREE WEAPONS FROM THE ARCHIVE.
CHECK THE INVENTORY. TELL ME WHAT A 'POCKET BATTLEFIELD' DOES.
I DON'T NEED INVENTORY:
REMEMBER STAR SPLENDOR STOLE THE CUBE FROM THE PINK PANTHEON AFTER THE MATTER FAX MALFUNCTIONED AND CLONED THE ENTIRE MACROVERSE?

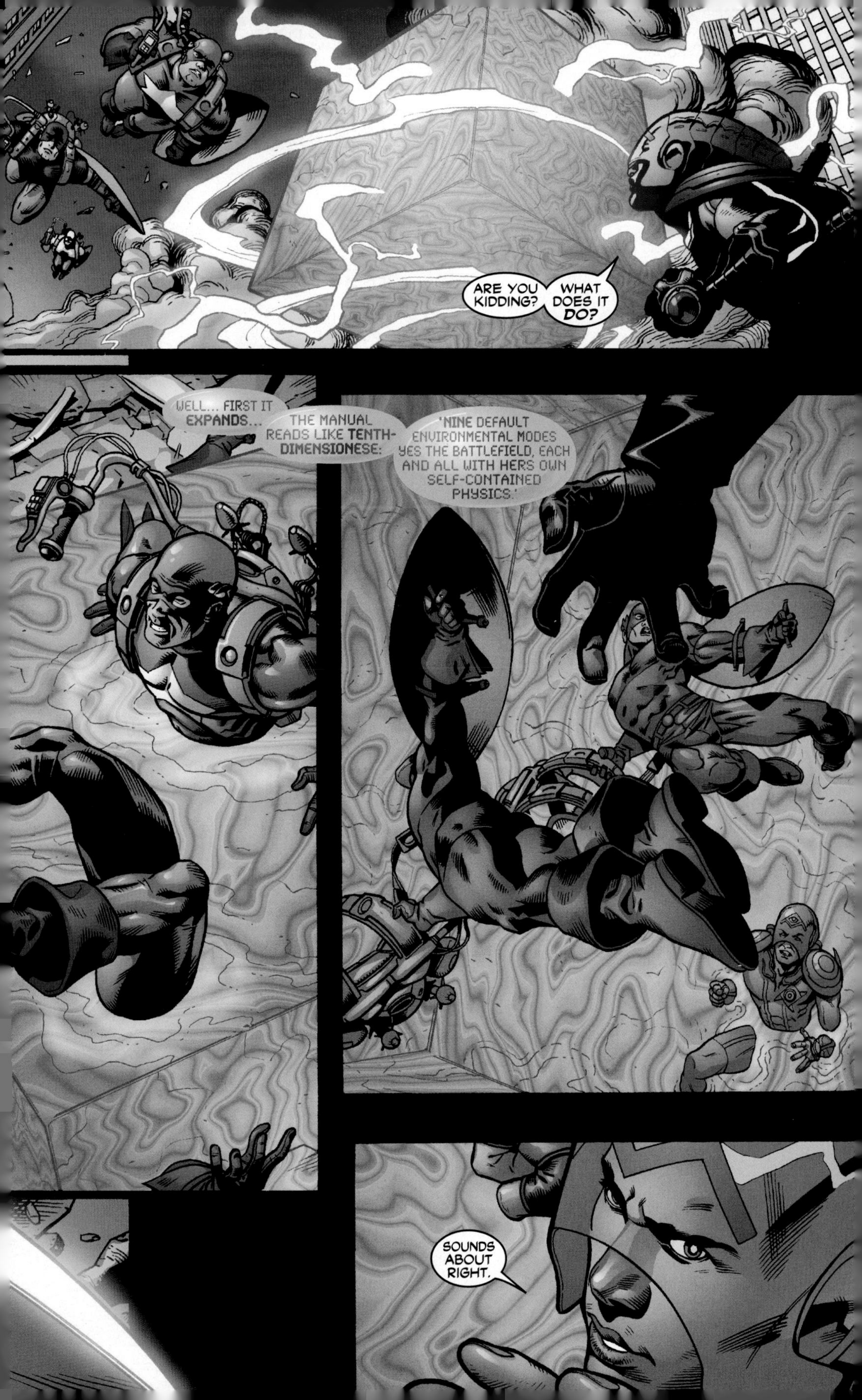
ARE YOU KIDDING?
WHAT DOES IT DO?
WELL... FIRST IT EXPANDS...
THE MANUAL READS LIKE TENTH-DIMENSIONESE:
'NINE DEFAULT ENVIRONMENTAL MODES YES THE BATTLEFIELD, EACH AND ALL WITH HERS OWN SELF-CONTAINED PHYSICS.'
SOUNDS ABOUT RIGHT.

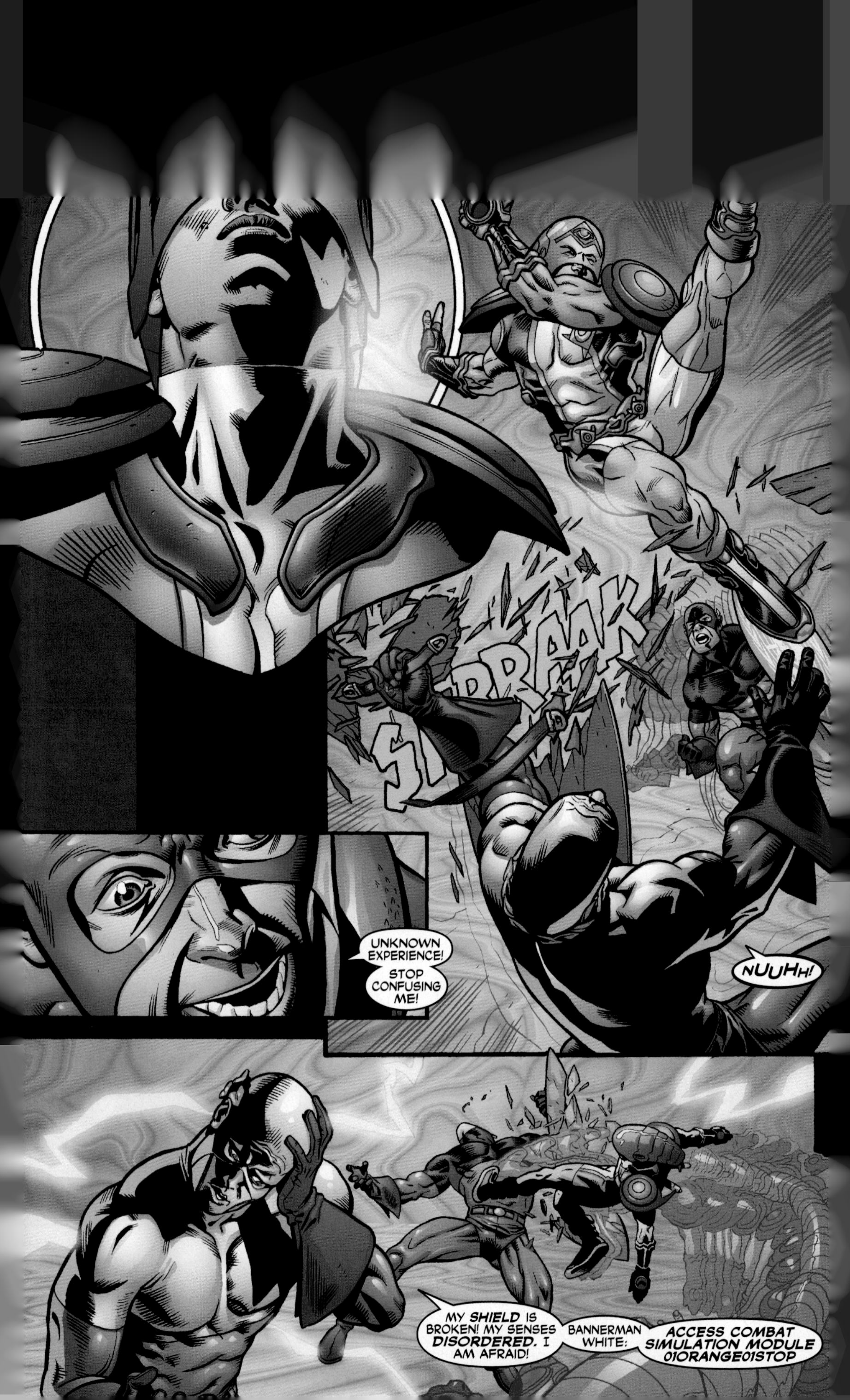
SPRAAK
UNKNOWN EXPERIENCE!
STOP CONFUSING ME!
NUUHH!
MY SHIELD IS BROKEN! MY SENSES DISORDERED. I AM AFRAID!
BANNERMAN WHITE:
ACCESS COMBAT SIMULATION MODULE 01ORANGE01STOP

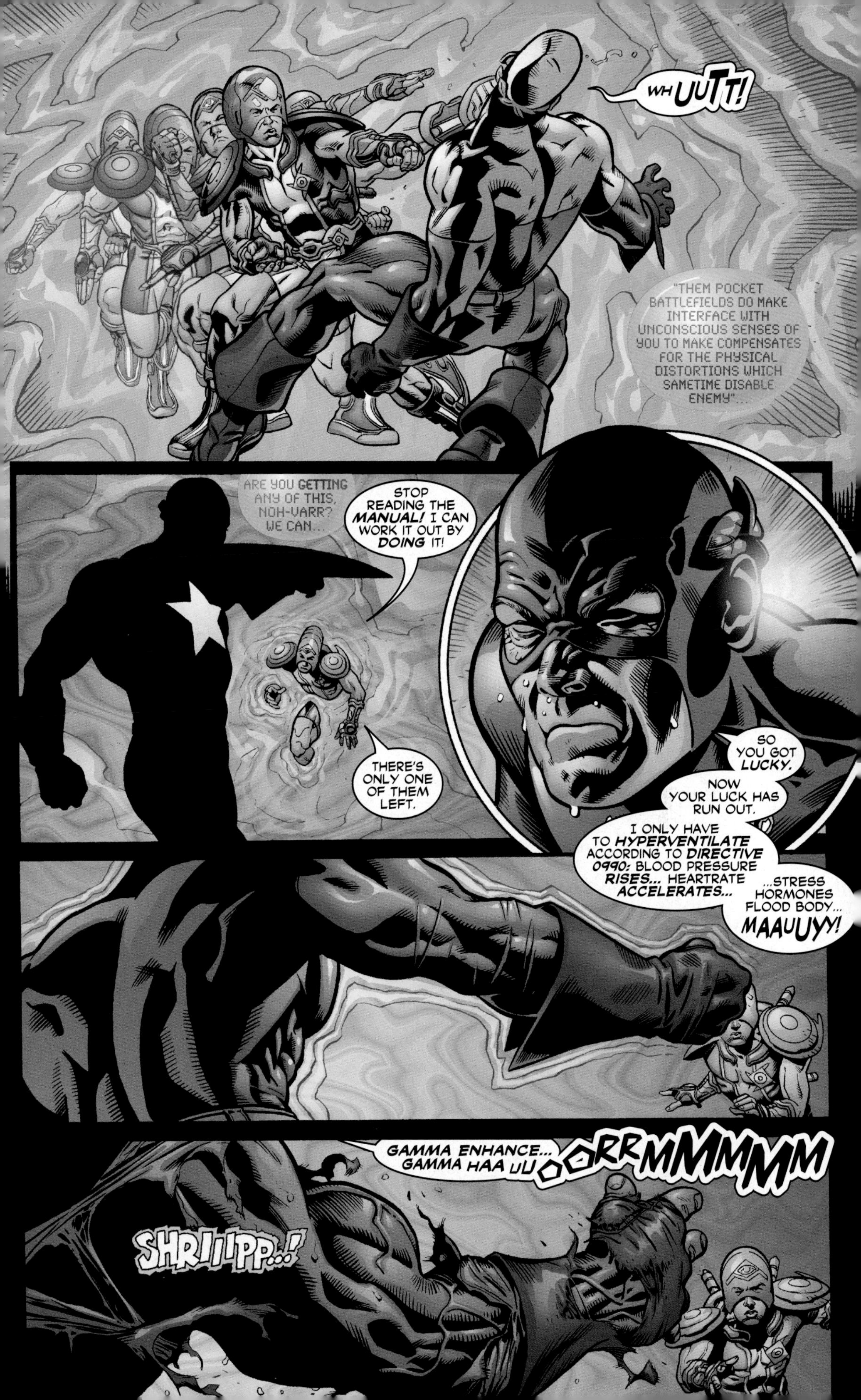
WH UUTT!
"THEM POCKET BATTLEFIELDS DO MAKE INTERFACE WITH UNCONSCIOUS SENSES OF YOU TO MAKE COMPENSATES FOR THE PHYSICAL DISTORTIONS WHICH SAMETIME DISABLE ENEMY"...
ARE YOU GETTING ANY OF THIS, NOH-VARR? WE CAN...
STOP READING THE MANUAL! I CAN WORK IT OUT BY DOING IT!
THERE'S ONLY ONE OF THEM LEFT.
SO YOU GOT LUCKY.
NOW YOUR LUCK HAS RUN OUT.
I ONLY HAVE TO HYPERVENTILATE ACCORDING TO DIRECTIVE 0990: BLOOD PRESSURE RISES... HEARTRATE ACCELERATES...
...STRESS HORMONES FLOOD BODY... MAAUUYY!
GAMMA ENHANCE... GAMMA HAA UU OORRMMMMMM
SHRIIIPP..!

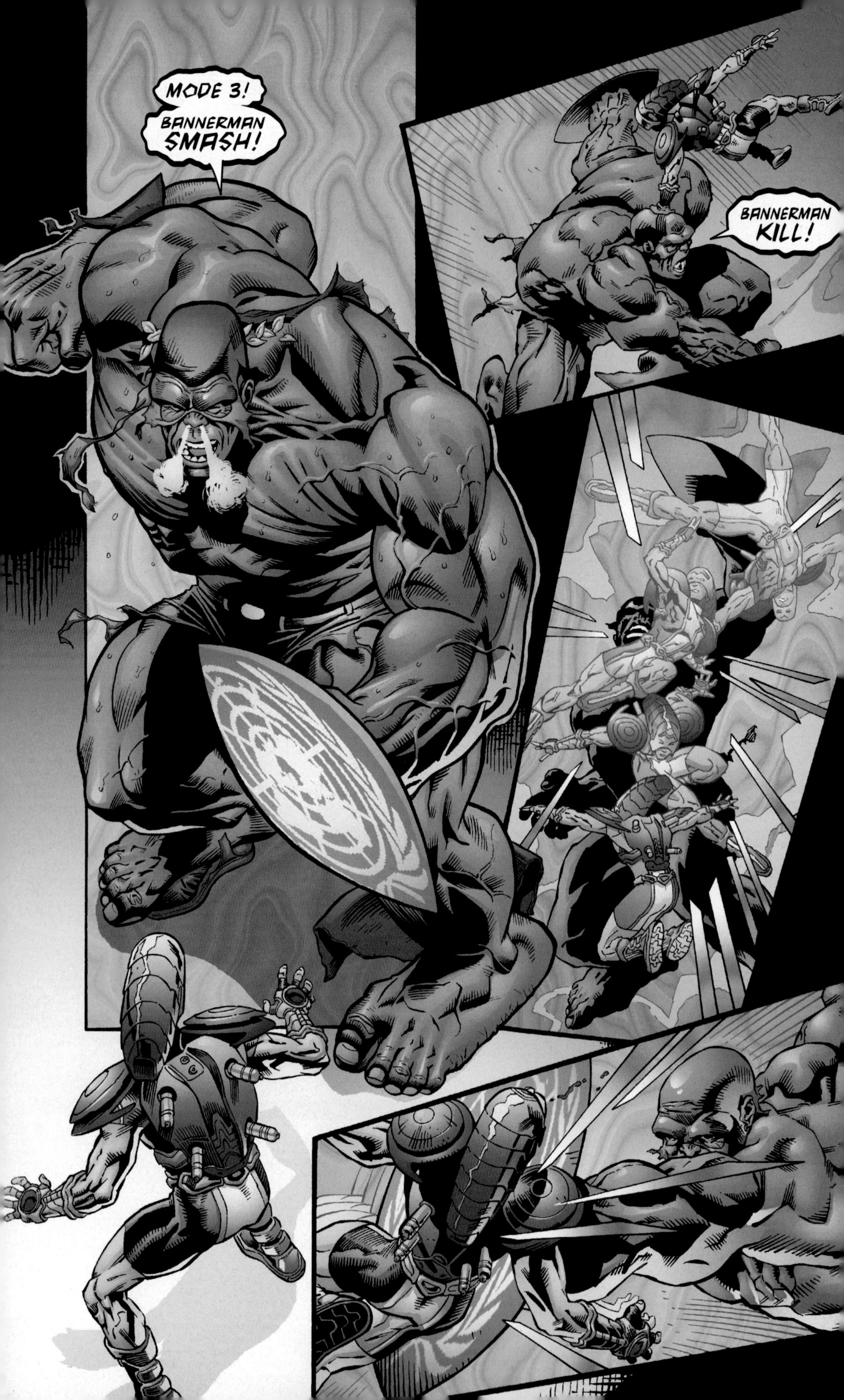
MODE 3!
BANNERMAN SMASH!
BANNERMAN KILL!

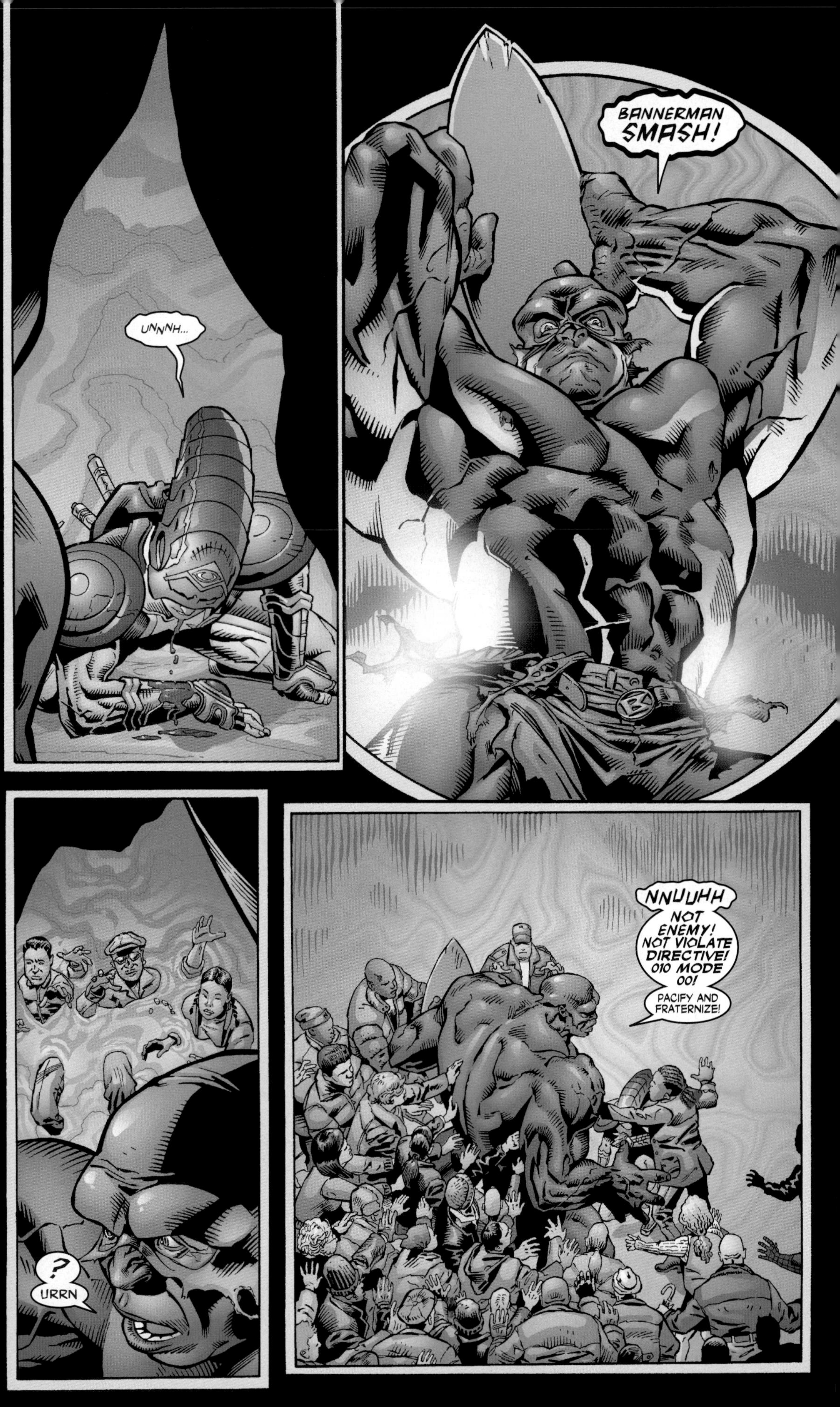
UNNNH...
BANNERMAN SMASH!
?
URRN
NNUUHH
NOT ENEMY! NOT VIOLATE DIRECTIVE! 010 MODE 00!
PACIFY AND FRATERNIZE!

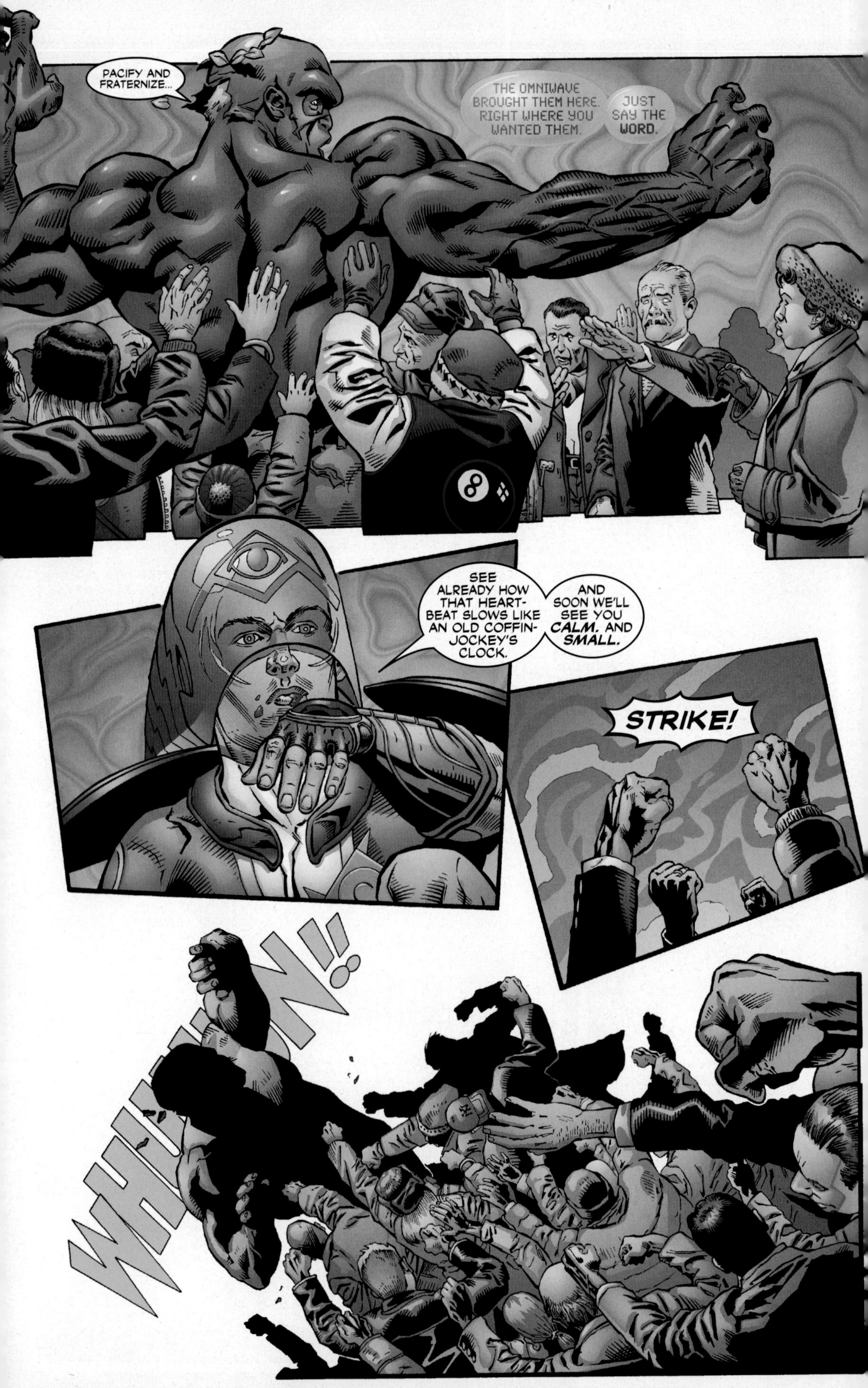

PACIFY AND FRATERNIZE...
THE OMNIWAVE BROUGHT THEM HERE. RIGHT WHERE YOU WANTED THEM.
JUST SAY THE WORD.
SEE ALREADY HOW THAT HEART-BEAT SLOWS LIKE AN OLD COFFIN-JOCKEY'S CLOCK.
AND SOON WE'LL SEE YOU CALM. AND SMALL.
STRIKE!

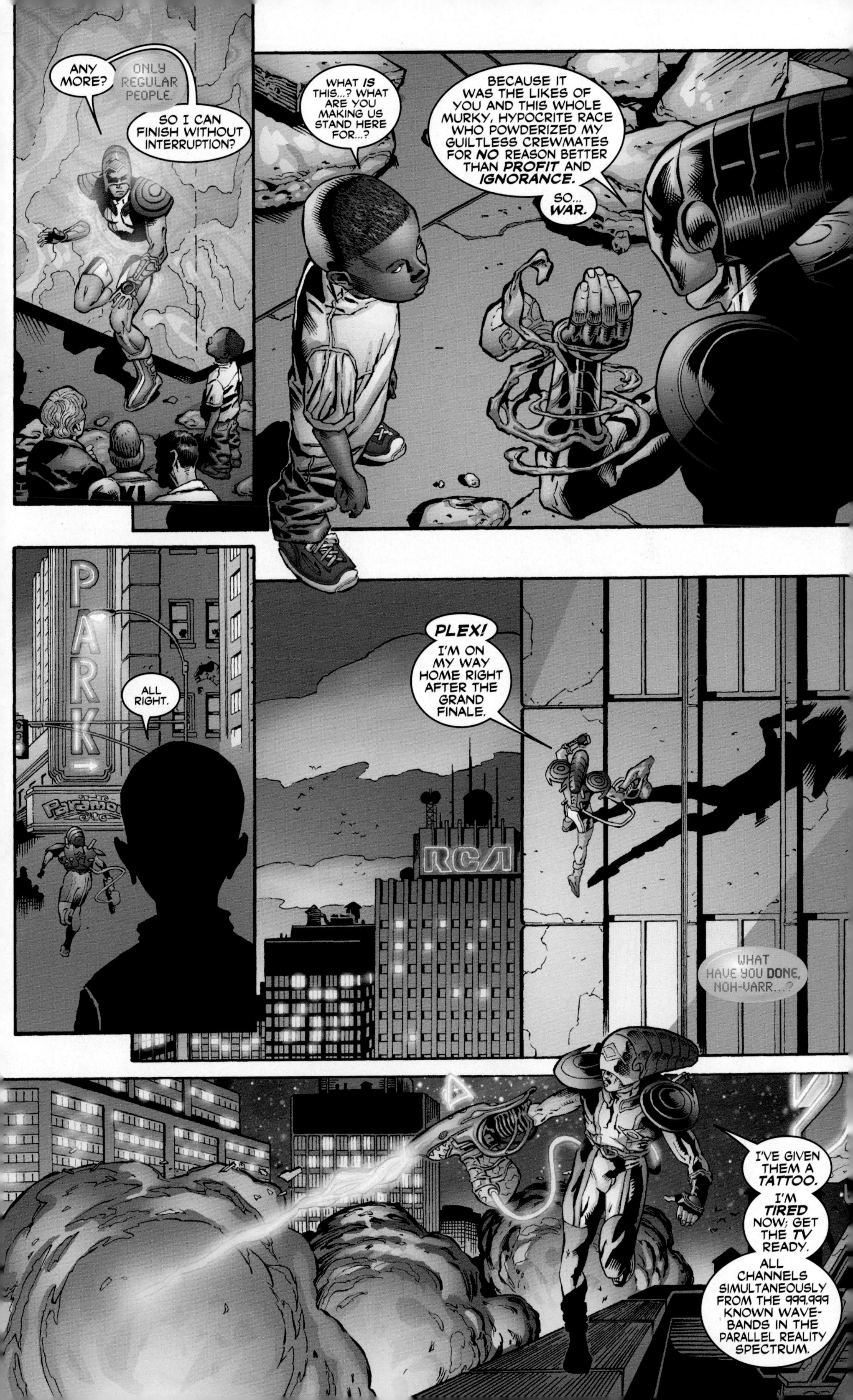
ANY MORE?
ONLY REGULAR PEOPLE.
SO I CAN FINISH WITHOUT INTERRUPTION?
WHAT IS THIS...? WHAT ARE YOU MAKING US STAND HERE FOR...?
BECAUSE IT WAS THE LIKES OF YOU AND THIS WHOLE MURKY, HYPOCRITE RACE WHO POWDERIZED MY GUILTLESS CREWMATES FOR NO REASON BETTER THAN PROFIT AND IGNORANCE.
SO... WAR.
PARK
ALL RIGHT.
PLEX! I'M ON MY WAY HOME RIGHT AFTER THE GRAND FINALE.
RCA
WHAT HAVE YOU DONE, NOH-VARR...?
I'VE GIVEN THEM A TATTOO.
I'M TIRED NOW; GET THE TV READY.
ALL CHANNELS SIMULTANEOUSLY FROM THE 999,999 KNOWN WAVE-BANDS IN THE PARALLEL REALITY SPECTRUM.

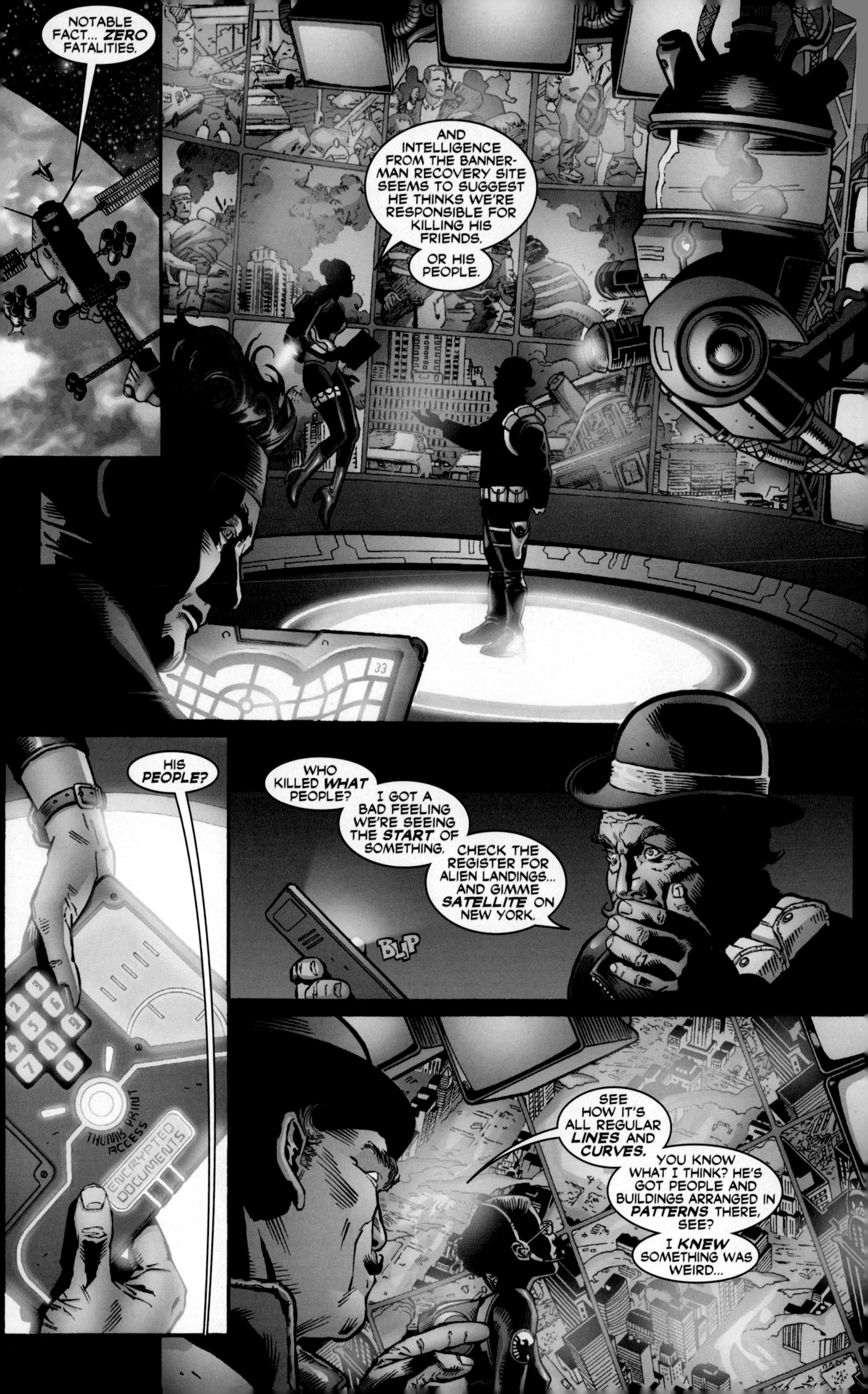
NOTABLE FACT... ZERO FATALITIES.
AND INTELLIGENCE FROM THE BANNERMAN RECOVERY SITE SEEMS TO SUGGEST HE THINKS WE'RE RESPONSIBLE FOR KILLING HIS FRIENDS.
OR HIS PEOPLE.
33
HIS PEOPLE?
WHO KILLED WHAT PEOPLE?
I GOT A BAD FEELING WE'RE SEEING THE START OF SOMETHING.
CHECK THE REGISTER FOR ALIEN LANDINGS... AND GIMME SATELLITE ON NEW YORK.
BLIP
THUMB PRINT ACCESS
ENCRYPTED DOCUMENTS
SEE HOW IT'S ALL REGULAR LINES AND CURVES.
YOU KNOW WHAT I THINK? HE'S GOT PEOPLE AND BUILDINGS ARRANGED IN PATTERNS THERE, SEE?
I KNEW SOMETHING WAS WEIRD...

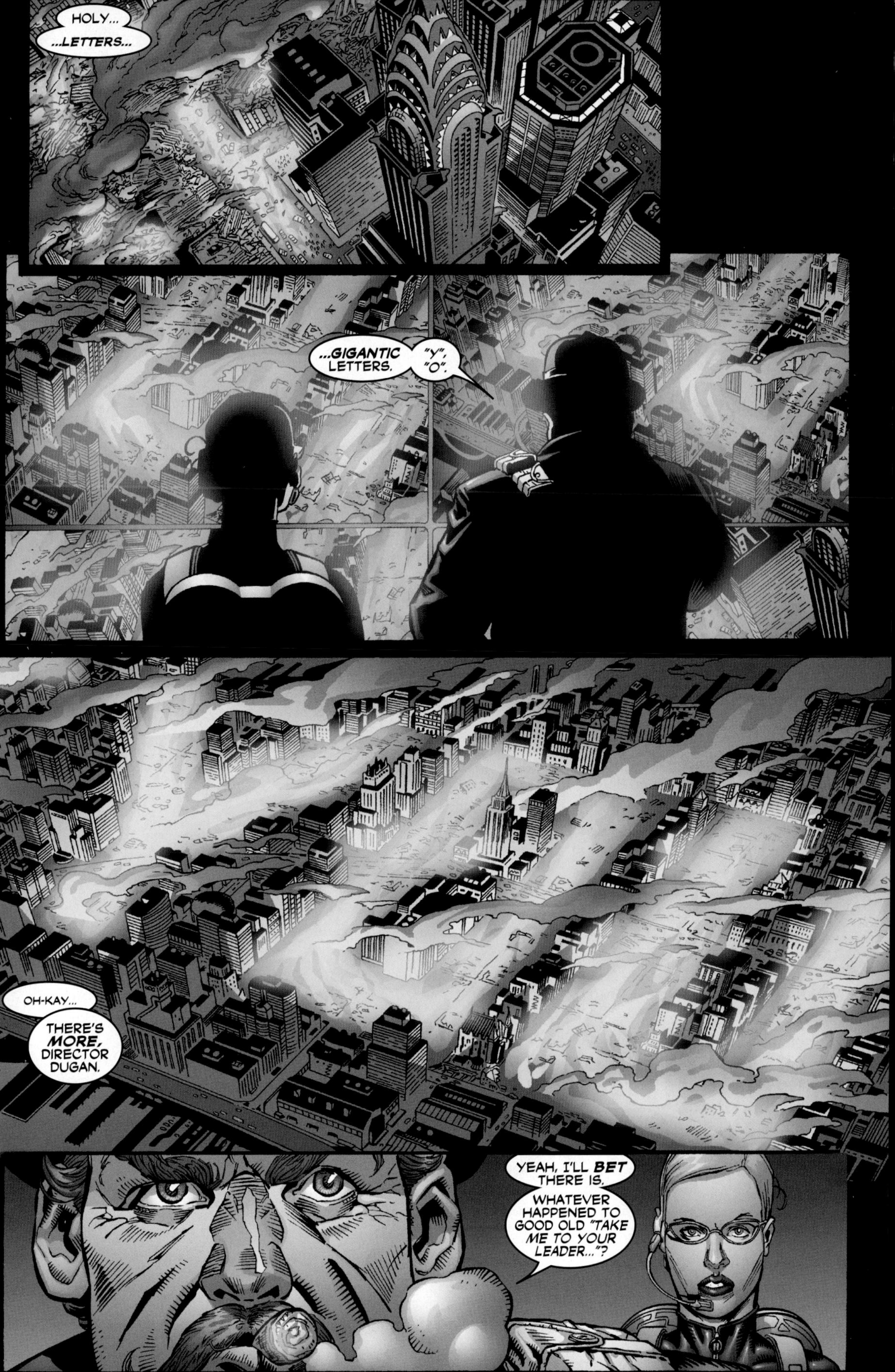
HOLY...
...LETTERS...
...GIGANTIC LETTERS.
"Y", "O".
OH-KAY...
THERE'S MORE, DIRECTOR DUGAN.
YEAH, I'LL BET THERE IS.
WHATEVER HAPPENED TO GOOD OLD "TAKE ME TO YOUR LEADER..."?

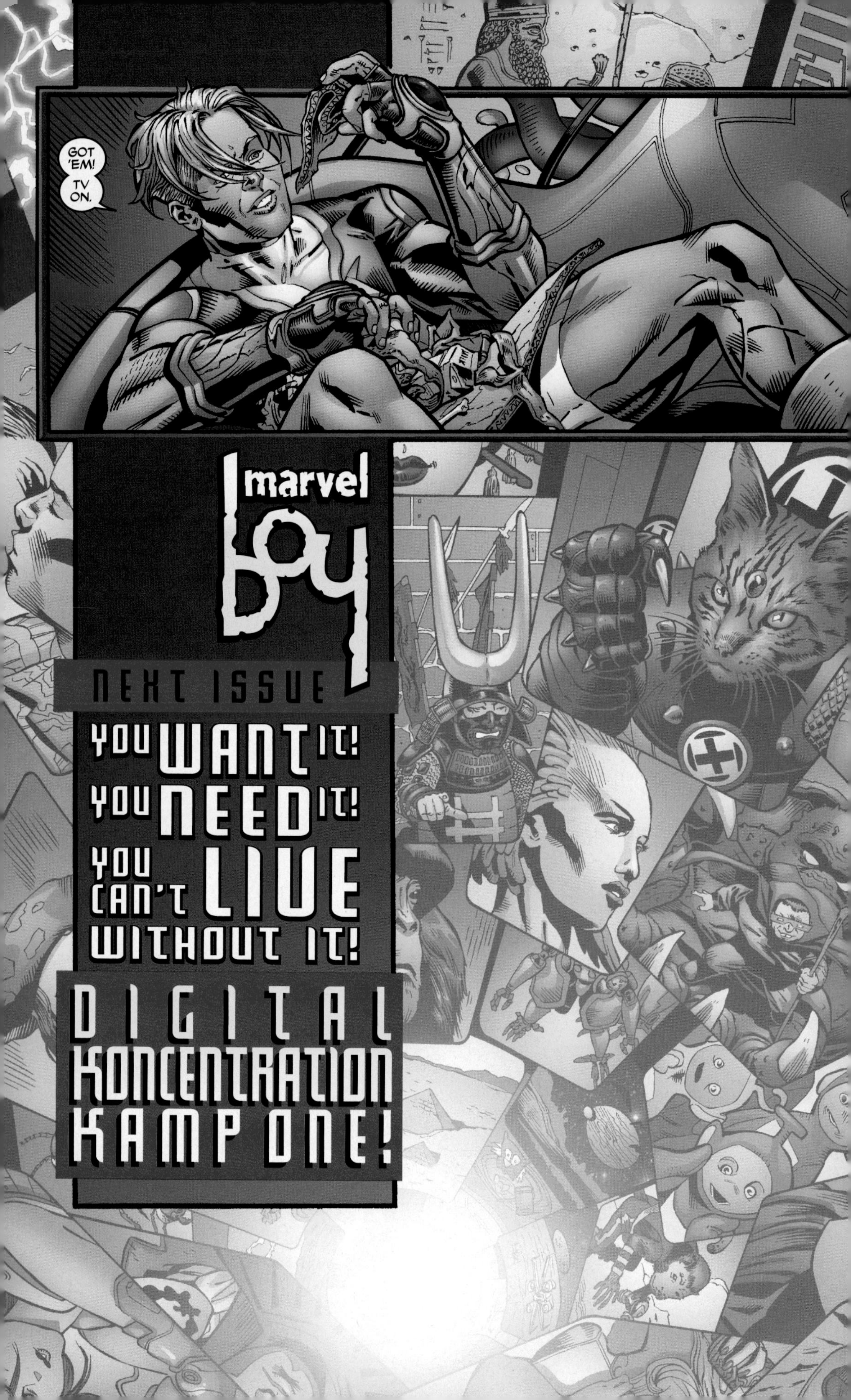
GOT 'EM! TV ON.
marvel boy
NEXT ISSUE
YOU WANT IT!
YOU NEED IT!
YOU CAN'T LIVE WITHOUT IT!
DIGITAL KONCENTRATION KAMP ONE!

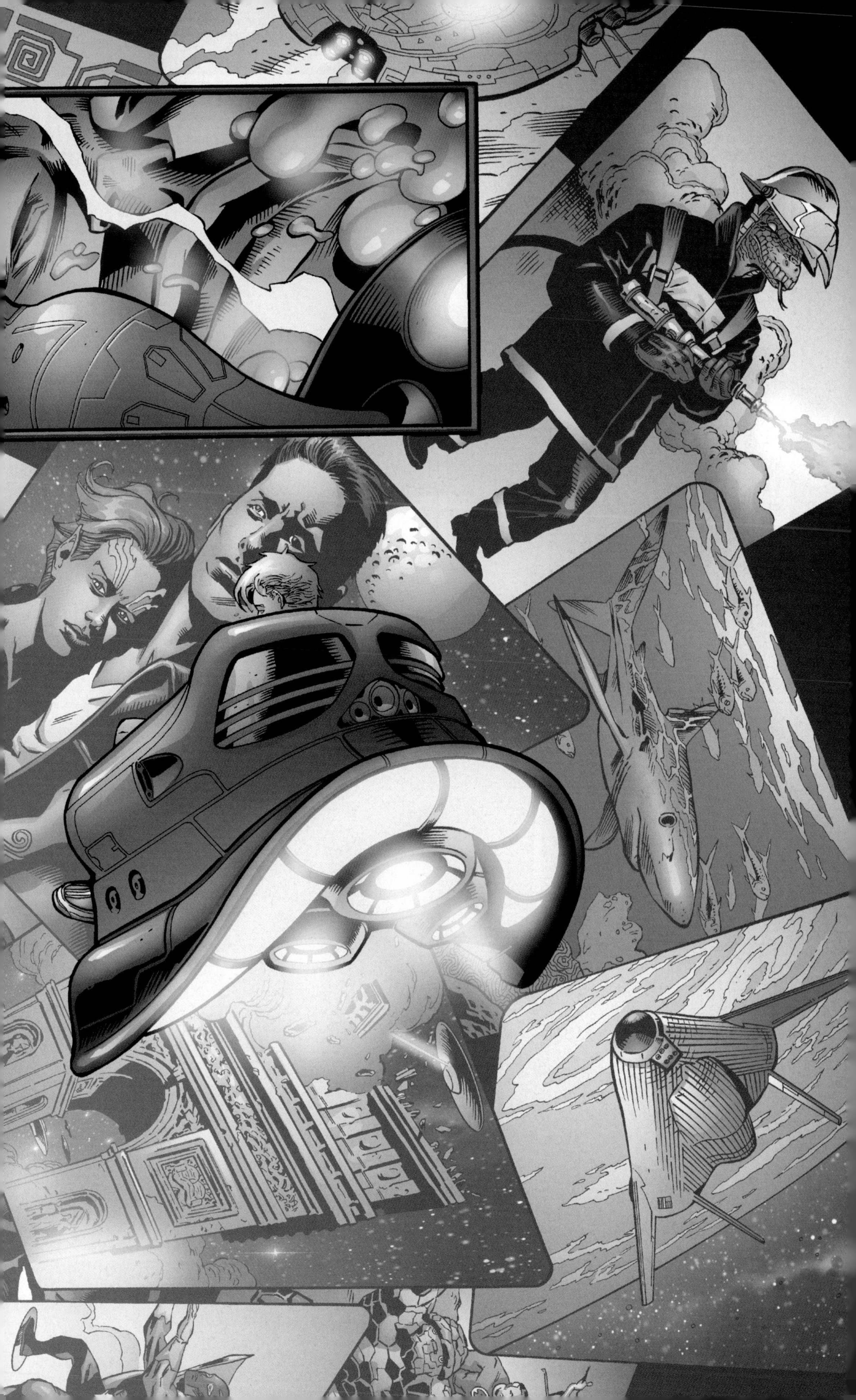

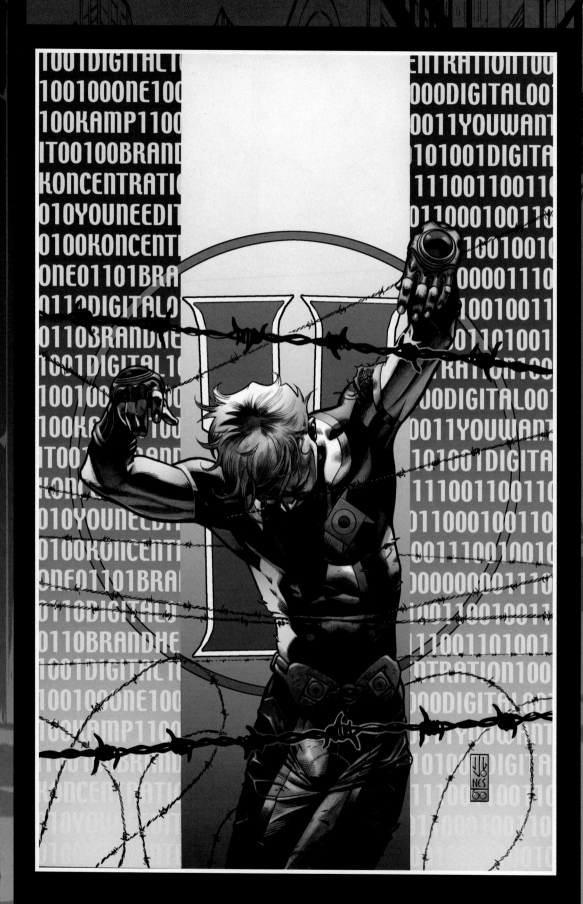

(3)

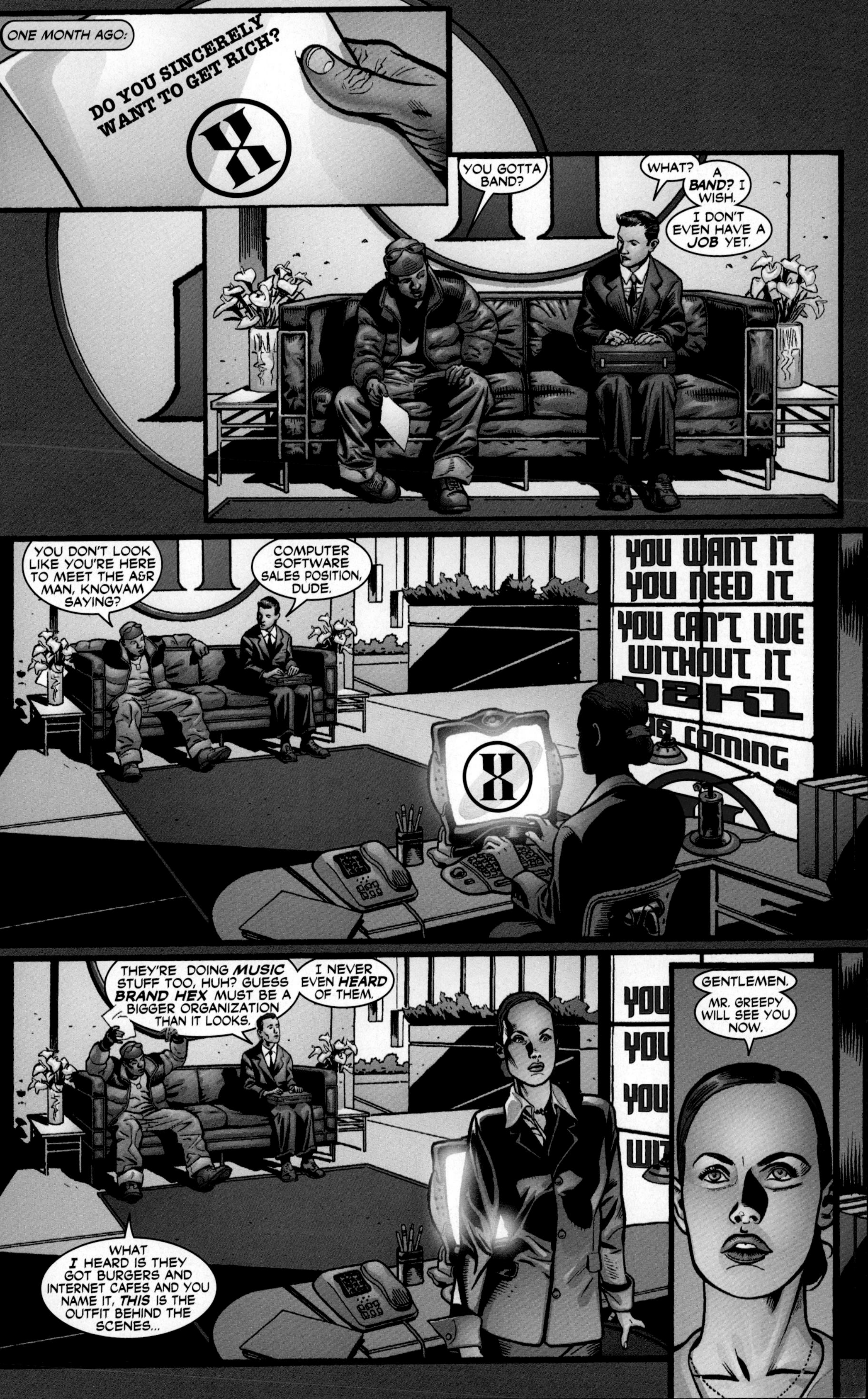
ONE MONTH AGO:
DO YOU SINCERELY WANT TO GET RICH?
YOU GOTTA BAND?
WHAT?
A BAND? I WISH.
I DON'T EVEN HAVE A JOB YET.
YOU DON'T LOOK LIKE YOU'RE HERE TO MEET THE A&R MAN, KNOWAM SAYING?
COMPUTER SOFTWARE SALES POSITION, DUDE.
YOU WANT IT
YOU NEED IT
YOU CAN'T LIVE WITHOUT IT
COMING
THEY'RE DOING MUSIC STUFF TOO, HUH? GUESS BRAND HEX MUST BE A BIGGER ORGANIZATION THAN IT LOOKS.
I NEVER EVEN HEARD OF THEM.
WHAT I HEARD IS THEY GOT BURGERS AND INTERNET CAFES AND YOU NAME IT, THIS IS THE OUTFIT BEHIND THE SCENES...
GENTLEMEN,
MR. GREEPY WILL SEE YOU NOW.

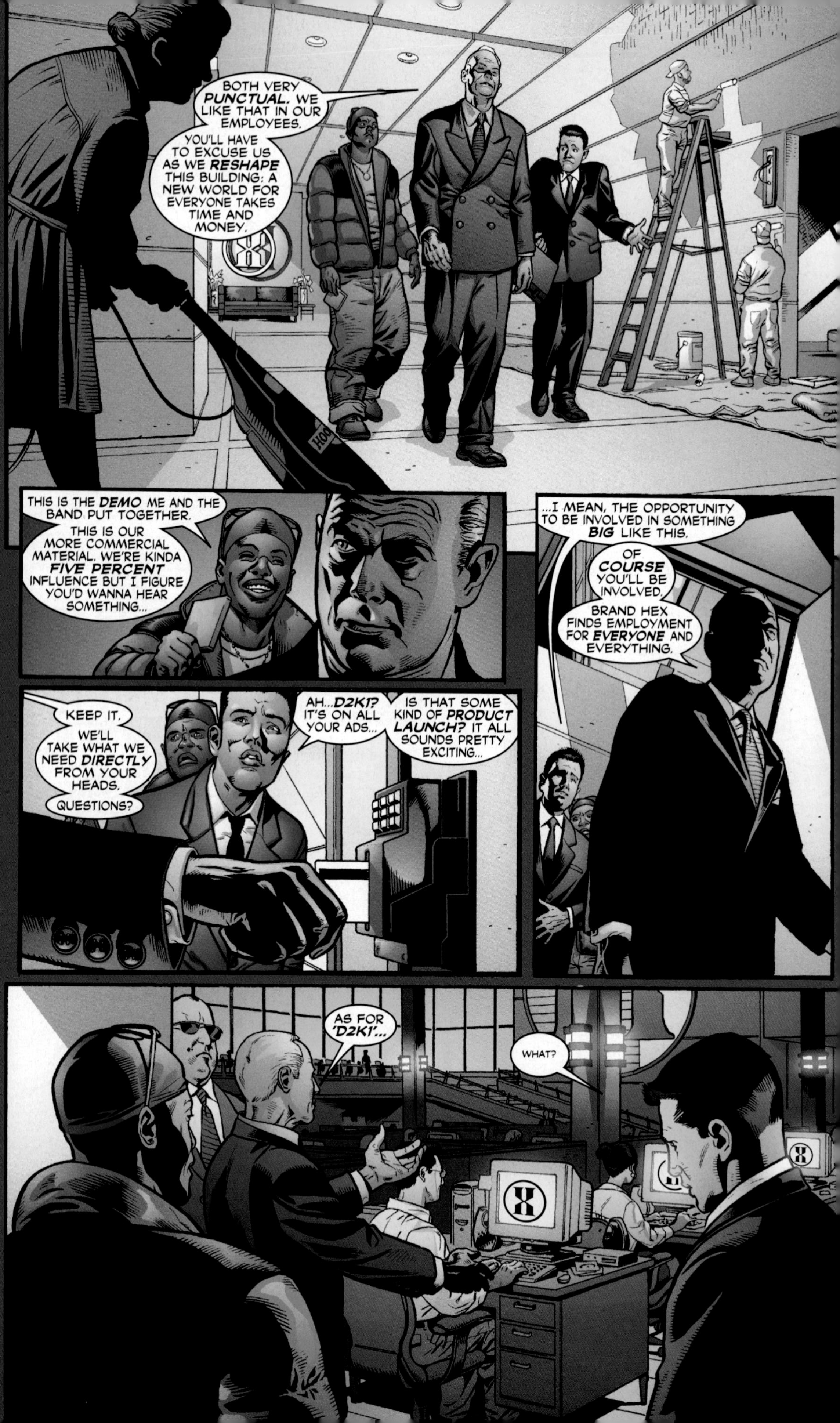

BOTH VERY PUNCTUAL. WE LIKE THAT IN OUR EMPLOYEES.
YOU'LL HAVE TO EXCUSE US AS WE RESHAPE THIS BUILDING: A NEW WORLD FOR EVERYONE TAKES TIME AND MONEY.
THIS IS THE DEMO ME AND THE BAND PUT TOGETHER.
THIS IS OUR MORE COMMERCIAL MATERIAL. WE'RE KINDA FIVE PERCENT INFLUENCE BUT I FIGURE YOU'D WANNA HEAR SOMETHING...
KEEP IT.
WE'LL TAKE WHAT WE NEED DIRECTLY FROM YOUR HEADS.
QUESTIONS?
AH...D2K1? IT'S ON ALL YOUR ADS...
IS THAT SOME KIND OF PRODUCT LAUNCH? IT ALL SOUNDS PRETTY EXCITING...
...I MEAN, THE OPPORTUNITY TO BE INVOLVED IN SOMETHING BIG LIKE THIS.
OF COURSE YOU'LL BE INVOLVED.
BRAND HEX FINDS EMPLOYMENT FOR EVERYONE AND EVERYTHING.
AS FOR 'D2K1'...
WHAT?

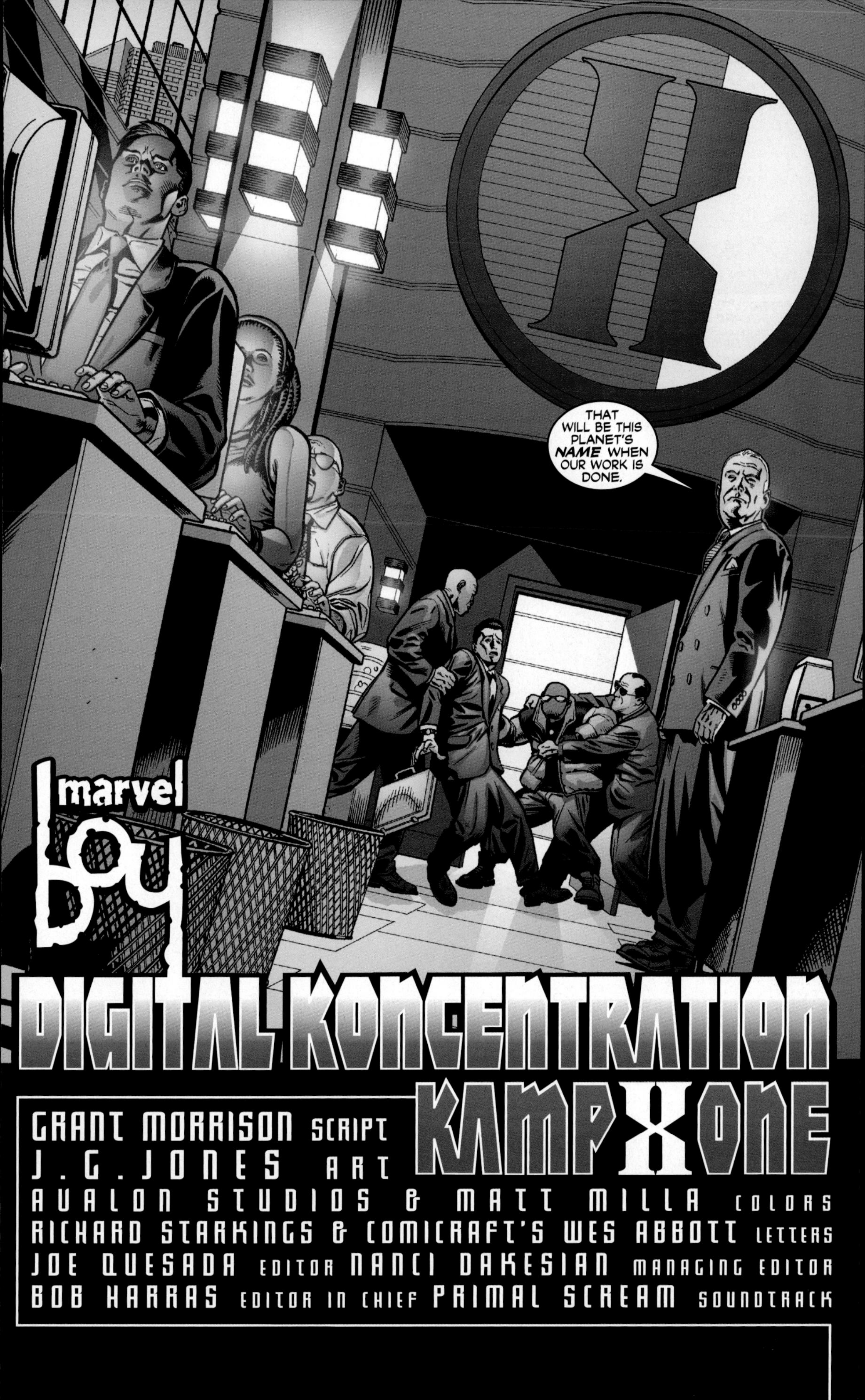

THAT WILL BE THIS PLANET'S NAME WHEN OUR WORK IS DONE.
marvel boy
DIGITAL KONCENTRATION
KAMP X ONE
GRANT MORRISON SCRIPT
J.G.JONES ART
AVALON STUDIOS & MATT MILLA COLORS
RICHARD STARKINGS & COMICRAFT'S WES ABBOTT LETTERS
JOE QUESADA EDITOR NANCI DAKESIAN MANAGING EDITOR
BOB HARRAS EDITOR IN CHIEF PRIMAL SCREAM SOUNDTRACK

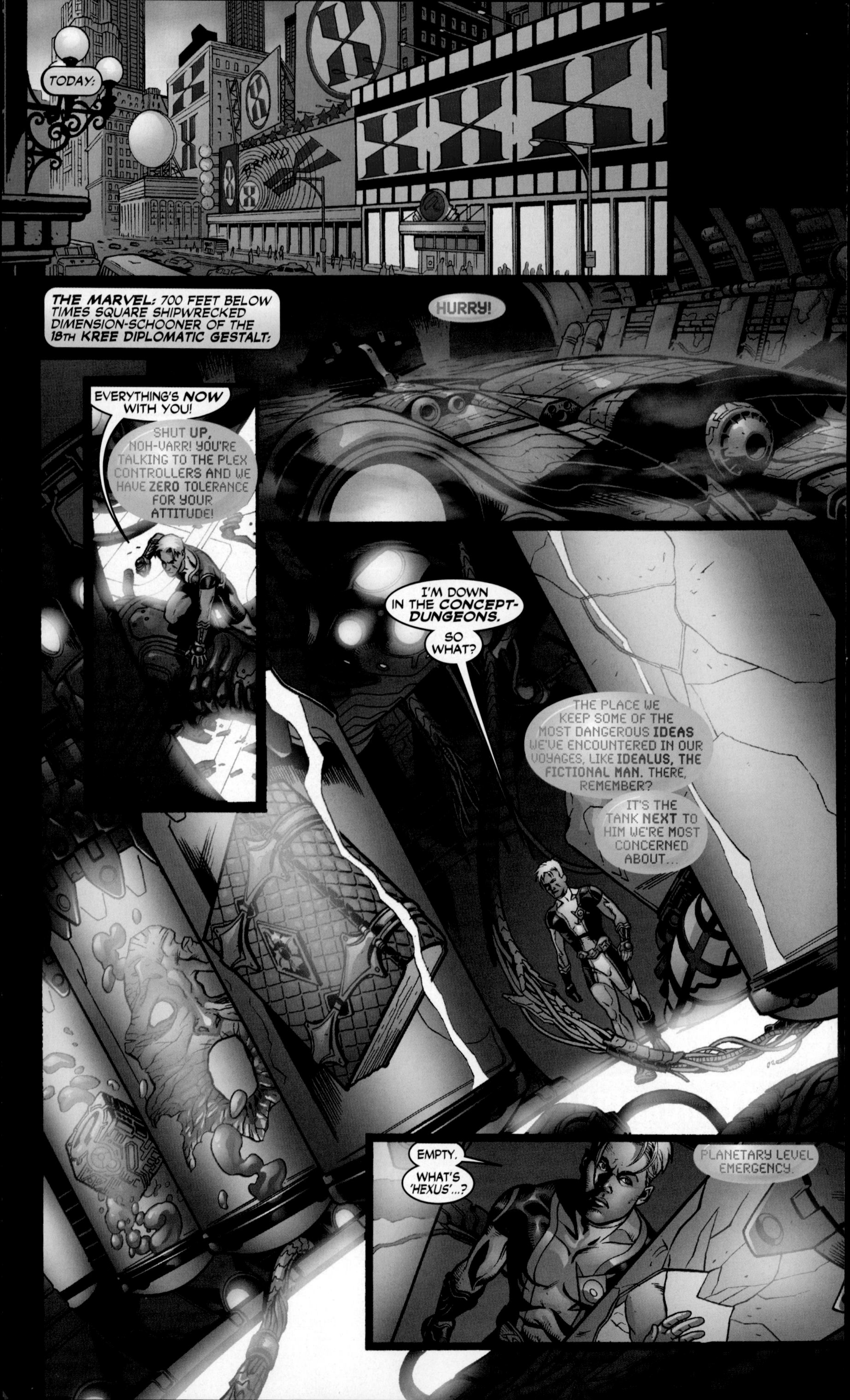
TODAY:
THE MARVEL: 700 FEET BELOW TIMES SQUARE SHIPWRECKED DIMENSION-SCHOONER OF THE 18TH KREE DIPLOMATIC GESTALT:
HURRY!
EVERYTHING'S NOW WITH YOU!
SHUT UP, NOH-VARR! YOU'RE TALKING TO THE PLEX CONTROLLERS AND WE HAVE ZERO TOLERANCE FOR YOUR ATTITUDE!
I'M DOWN IN THE CONCEPT-DUNGEONS.
SO WHAT?
THE PLACE WE KEEP SOME OF THE MOST DANGEROUS IDEAS WE'VE ENCOUNTERED IN OUR VOYAGES, LIKE IDEALUS, THE FICTIONAL MAN. THERE, REMEMBER?
IT'S THE TANK NEXT TO HIM WE'RE MOST CONCERNED ABOUT...
EMPTY.
WHAT'S 'HEXUS'...?
PLANETARY LEVEL EMERGENCY.

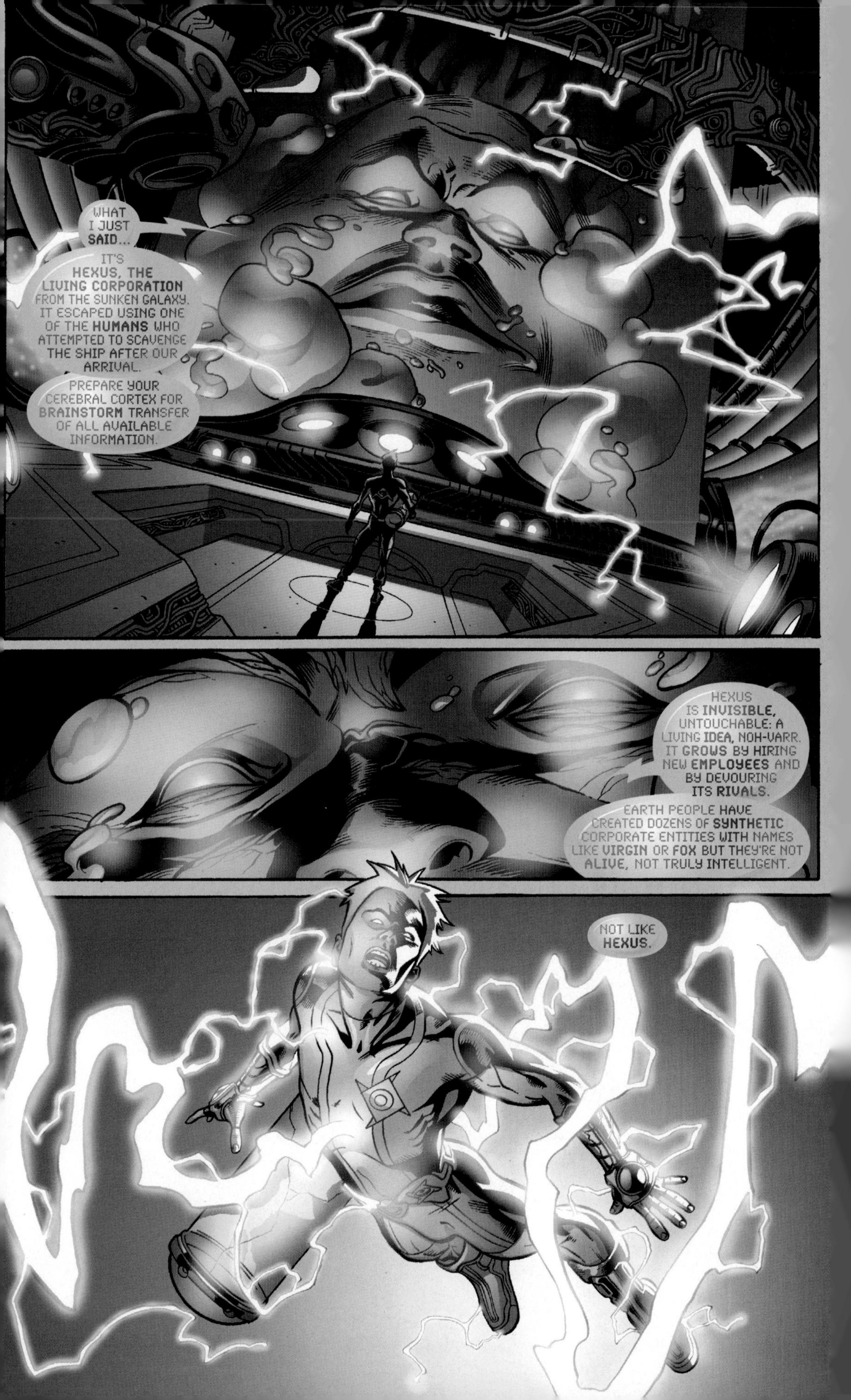
WHAT I JUST SAID...
IT'S HEXUS, THE LIVING CORPORATION FROM THE SUNKEN GALAXY. IT ESCAPED USING ONE OF THE HUMANS WHO ATTEMPTED TO SCAVENGE THE SHIP AFTER OUR ARRIVAL.
PREPARE YOUR CEREBRAL CORTEX FOR BRAINSTORM TRANSFER OF ALL AVAILABLE INFORMATION.
HEXUS IS INVISIBLE, UNTOUCHABLE: A LIVING IDEA, NOH-VARR. IT GROWS BY HIRING NEW EMPLOYEES AND BY DEVOURING ITS RIVALS.
EARTH PEOPLE HAVE CREATED DOZENS OF SYNTHETIC CORPORATE ENTITIES WITH NAMES LIKE VIRGIN OR FOX BUT THEY'RE NOT ALIVE, NOT TRULY INTELLIGENT.
NOT LIKE HEXUS.

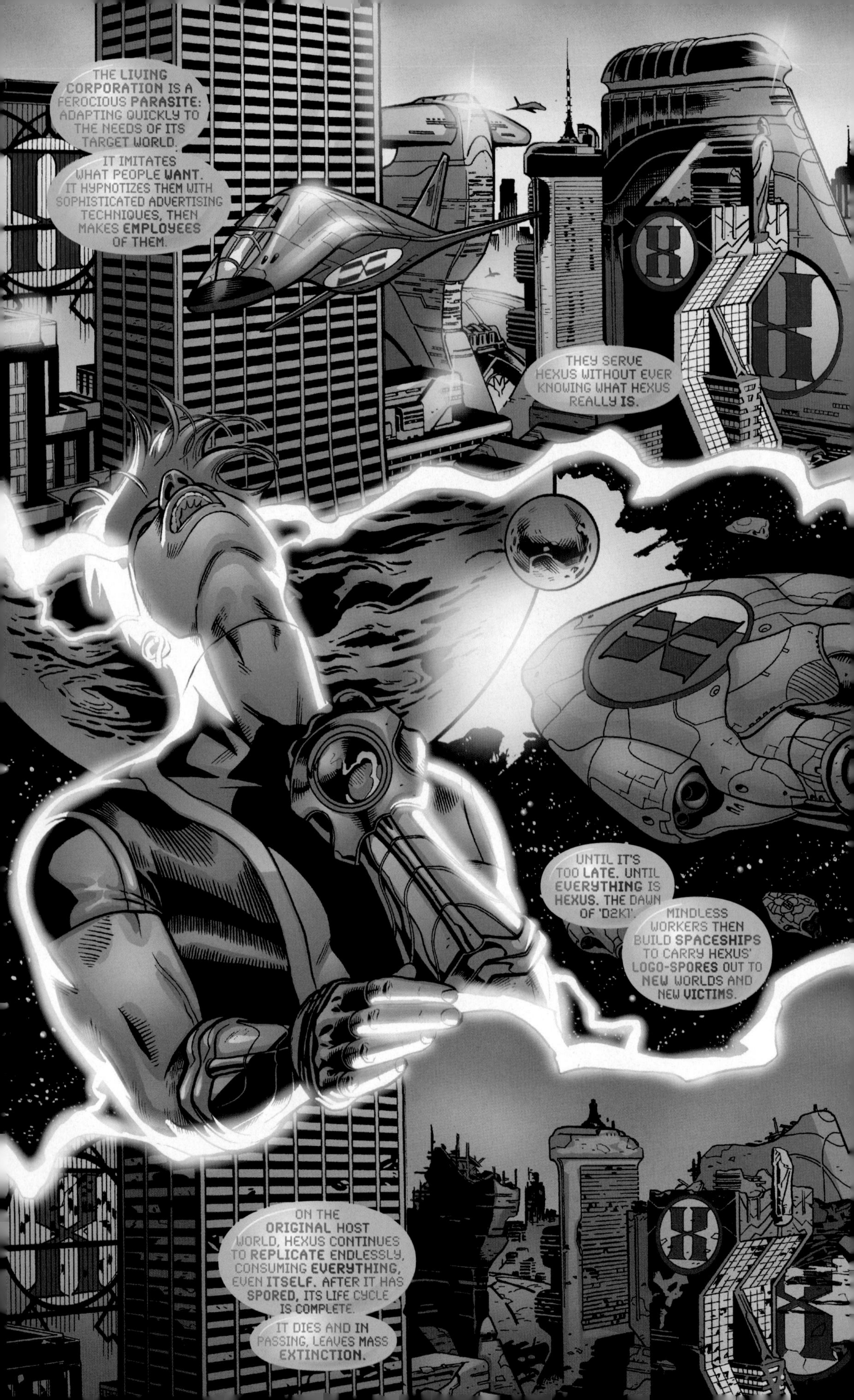
THE LIVING CORPORATION IS A FEROCIOUS PARASITE: ADAPTING QUICKLY TO THE NEEDS OF ITS TARGET WORLD.
IT IMITATES WHAT PEOPLE WANT. IT HYPNOTIZES THEM WITH SOPHISTICATED ADVERTISING TECHNIQUES, THEN MAKES EMPLOYEES OF THEM.
THEY SERVE HEXUS WITHOUT EVER KNOWING WHAT HEXUS REALLY IS.
UNTIL IT'S TOO LATE. UNTIL EVERYTHING IS HEXUS. THE DAWN OF 'D2K1'.
MINDLESS WORKERS THEN BUILD SPACESHIPS TO CARRY HEXUS' LOGO-SPORES OUT TO NEW WORLDS AND NEW VICTIMS.
ON THE ORIGINAL HOST WORLD, HEXUS CONTINUES TO REPLICATE ENDLESSLY, CONSUMING EVERYTHING, EVEN ITSELF. AFTER IT HAS SPORED, ITS LIFE CYCLE IS COMPLETE.
IT DIES AND IN PASSING, LEAVES MASS EXTINCTION.

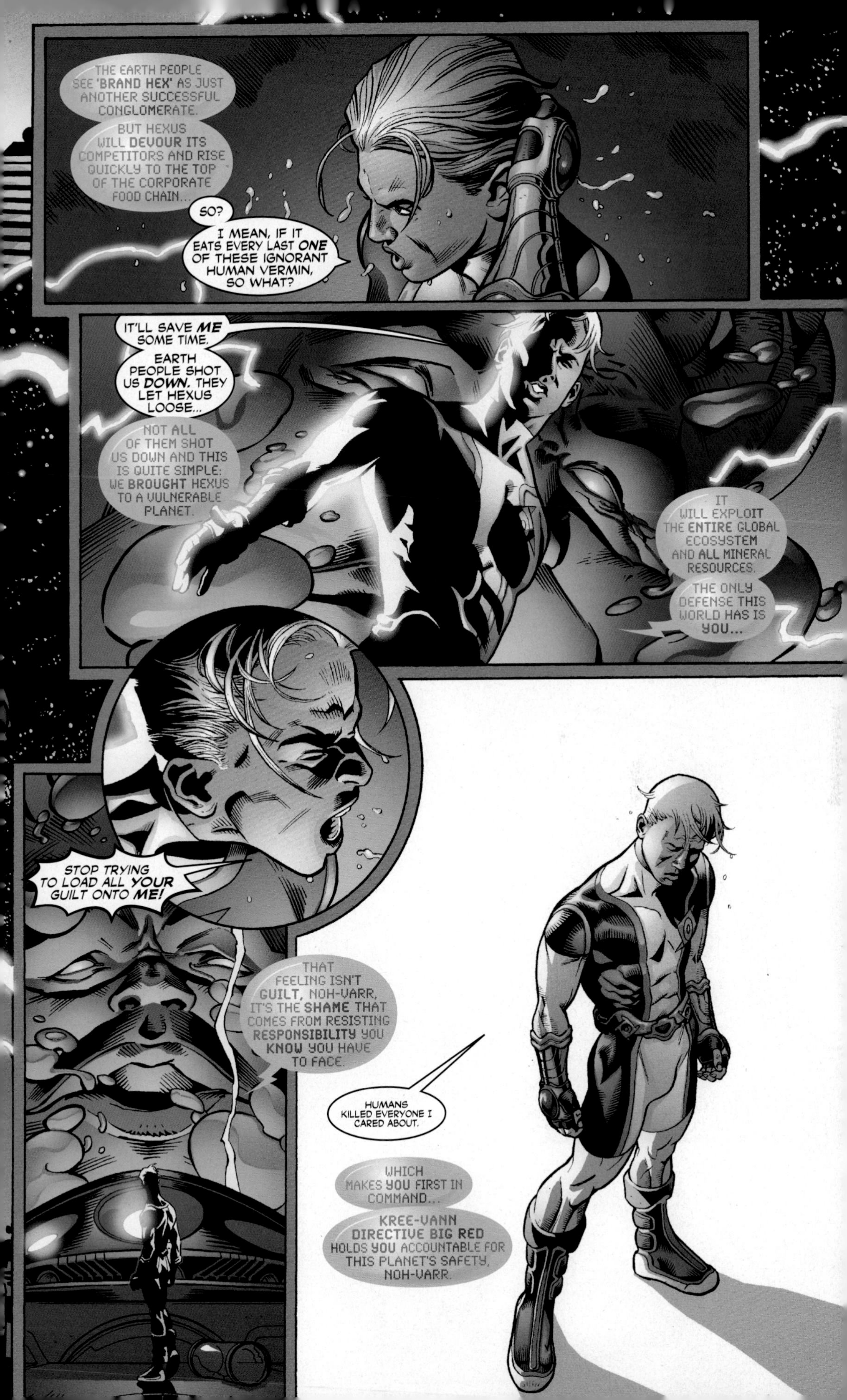
THE EARTH PEOPLE SEE 'BRAND HEX' AS JUST ANOTHER SUCCESSFUL CONGLOMERATE.
BUT HEXUS WILL DEVOUR ITS COMPETITORS AND RISE QUICKLY TO THE TOP OF THE CORPORATE FOOD CHAIN...
SO?
I MEAN, IF IT EATS EVERY LAST ONE OF THESE IGNORANT HUMAN VERMIN, SO WHAT?
IT'LL SAVE ME SOME TIME.
EARTH PEOPLE SHOT US DOWN. THEY LET HEXUS LOOSE...
NOT ALL OF THEM SHOT US DOWN AND THIS IS QUITE SIMPLE: WE BROUGHT HEXUS TO A VULNERABLE PLANET.
IT WILL EXPLOIT THE ENTIRE GLOBAL ECOSYSTEM AND ALL MINERAL RESOURCES.
THE ONLY DEFENSE THIS WORLD HAS IS YOU...
STOP TRYING TO LOAD ALL YOUR GUILT ONTO ME!
THAT FEELING ISN'T GUILT, NOH-VARR, IT'S THE SHAME THAT COMES FROM RESISTING RESPONSIBILITY YOU KNOW YOU HAVE TO FACE.
HUMANS KILLED EVERYONE I CARED ABOUT.
WHICH MAKES YOU FIRST IN COMMAND...
KREE-VANN DIRECTIVE BIG RED HOLDS YOU ACCOUNTABLE FOR THIS PLANET'S SAFETY, NOH-VARR.

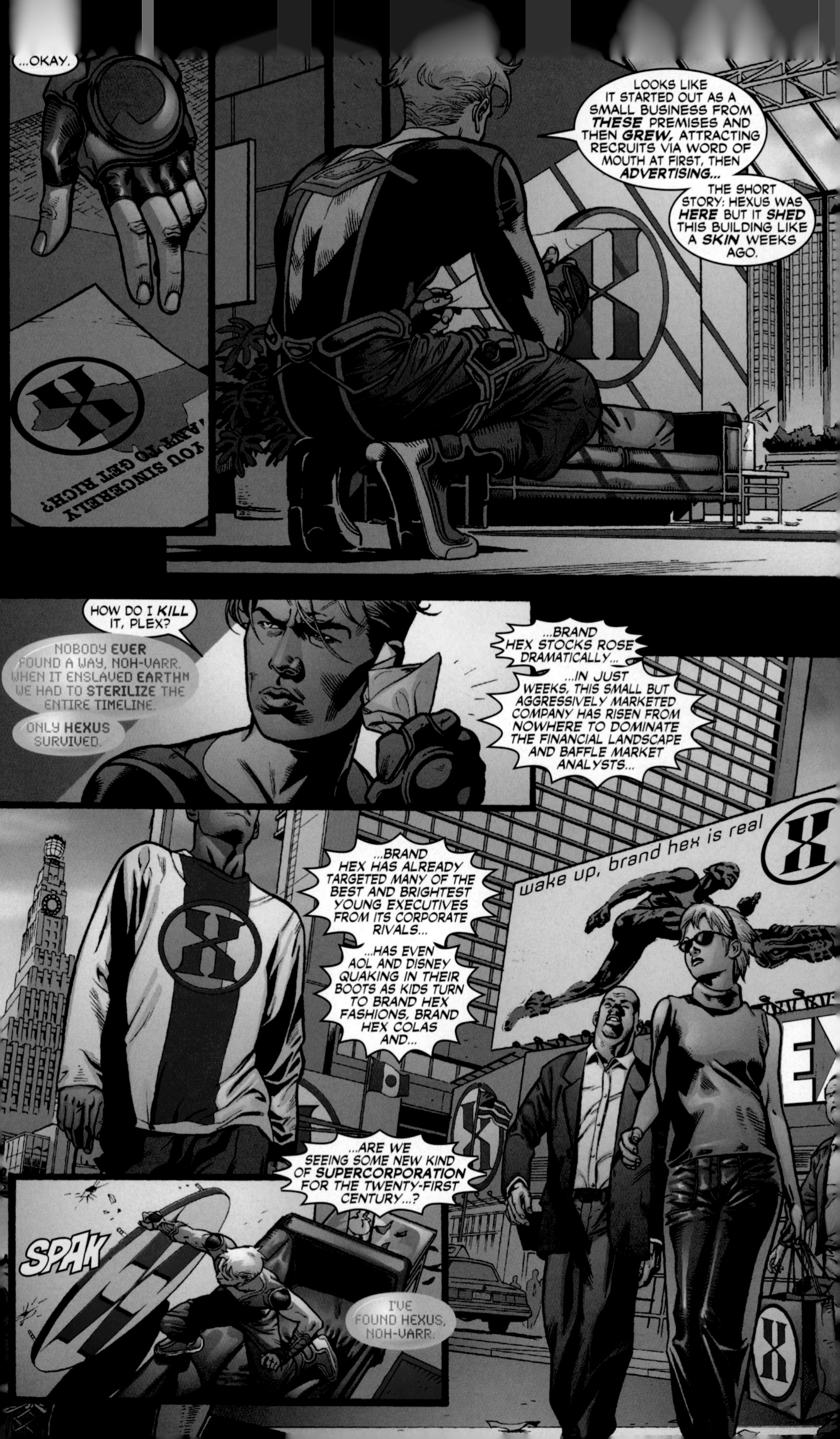

...OKAY.
YOU SINCERELY
ANT TO GET RICH?
LOOKS LIKE IT STARTED OUT AS A SMALL BUSINESS FROM THESE PREMISES AND THEN GREW, ATTRACTING RECRUITS VIA WORD OF MOUTH AT FIRST, THEN ADVERTISING...
THE SHORT STORY: HEXUS WAS HERE BUT IT SHED THIS BUILDING LIKE A SKIN WEEKS AGO.
HOW DO I KILL IT, PLEX?
NOBODY EVER FOUND A WAY, NOH-VARR. WHEN IT ENSLAVED EARTH WE HAD TO STERILIZE THE ENTIRE TIMELINE.
ONLY HEXUS SURVIVED.
...BRAND HEX STOCKS ROSE DRAMATICALLY...
...IN JUST WEEKS, THIS SMALL BUT AGGRESSIVELY MARKETED COMPANY HAS RISEN FROM NOWHERE TO DOMINATE THE FINANCIAL LANDSCAPE AND BAFFLE MARKET ANALYSTS...
wake up, brand hex is real
...BRAND HEX HAS ALREADY TARGETED MANY OF THE BEST AND BRIGHTEST YOUNG EXECUTIVES FROM ITS CORPORATE RIVALS...
...HAS EVEN AOL AND DISNEY QUAKING IN THEIR BOOTS AS KIDS TURN TO BRAND HEX FASHIONS, BRAND HEX COLAS AND...
...ARE WE SEEING SOME NEW KIND OF SUPERCORPORATION FOR THE TWENTY-FIRST CENTURY...?
SPAK
I'VE FOUND HEXUS, NOH-VARR.

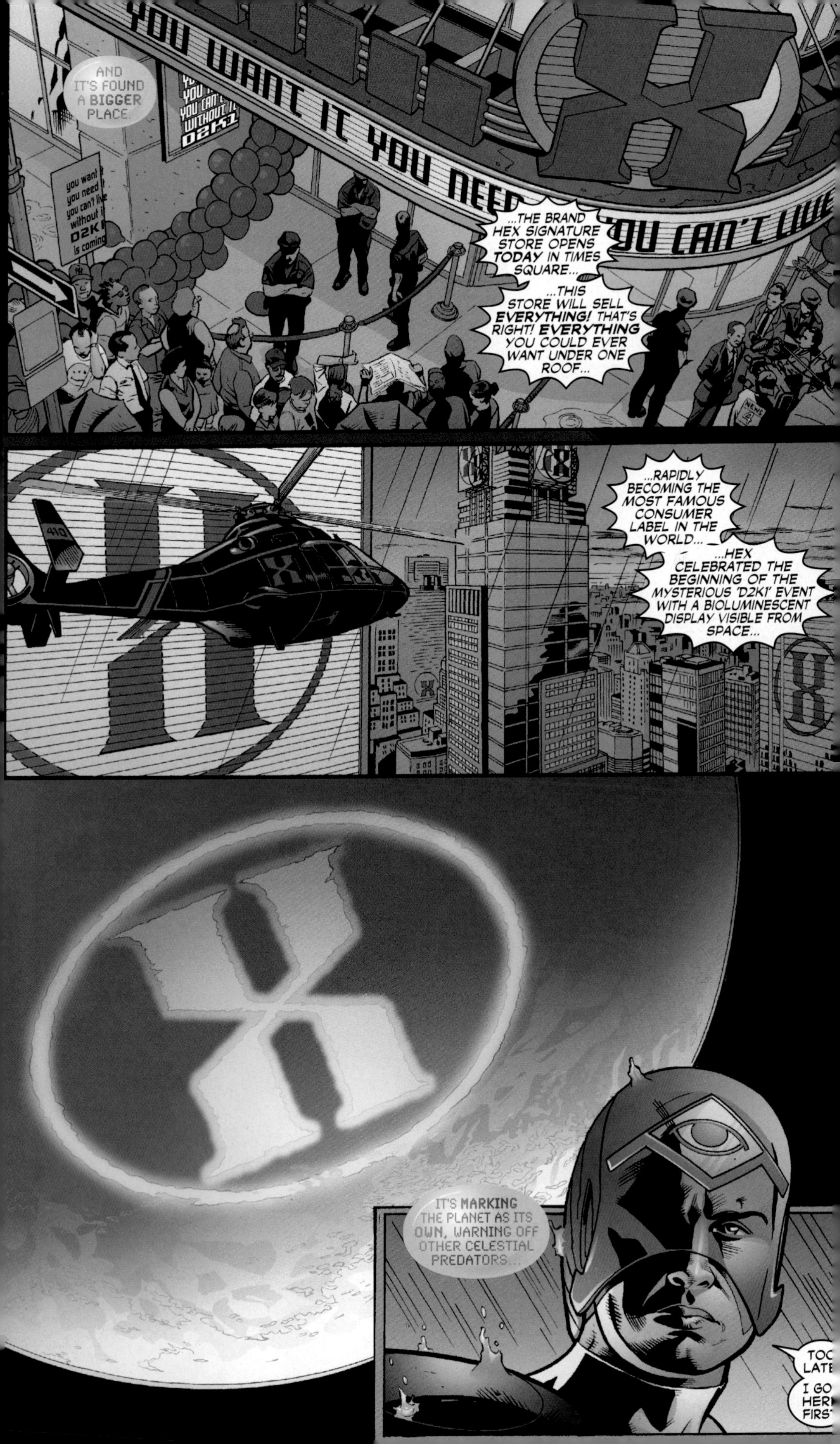
YOU WANT IT YOU NEED
YOU CAN'T LIVE
D2K1
is coming
AND IT'S FOUND A BIGGER PLACE.
...THE BRAND HEX SIGNATURE STORE OPENS TODAY IN TIMES SQUARE...
...THIS STORE WILL SELL EVERYTHING! THAT'S RIGHT! EVERYTHING YOU COULD EVER WANT UNDER ONE ROOF...
...RAPIDLY BECOMING THE MOST FAMOUS CONSUMER LABEL IN THE WORLD...
...HEX CELEBRATED THE BEGINNING OF THE MYSTERIOUS 'D2K1' EVENT WITH A BIOLUMINESCENT DISPLAY VISIBLE FROM SPACE...
IT'S MARKING THE PLANET AS ITS OWN, WARNING OFF OTHER CELESTIAL PREDATORS...

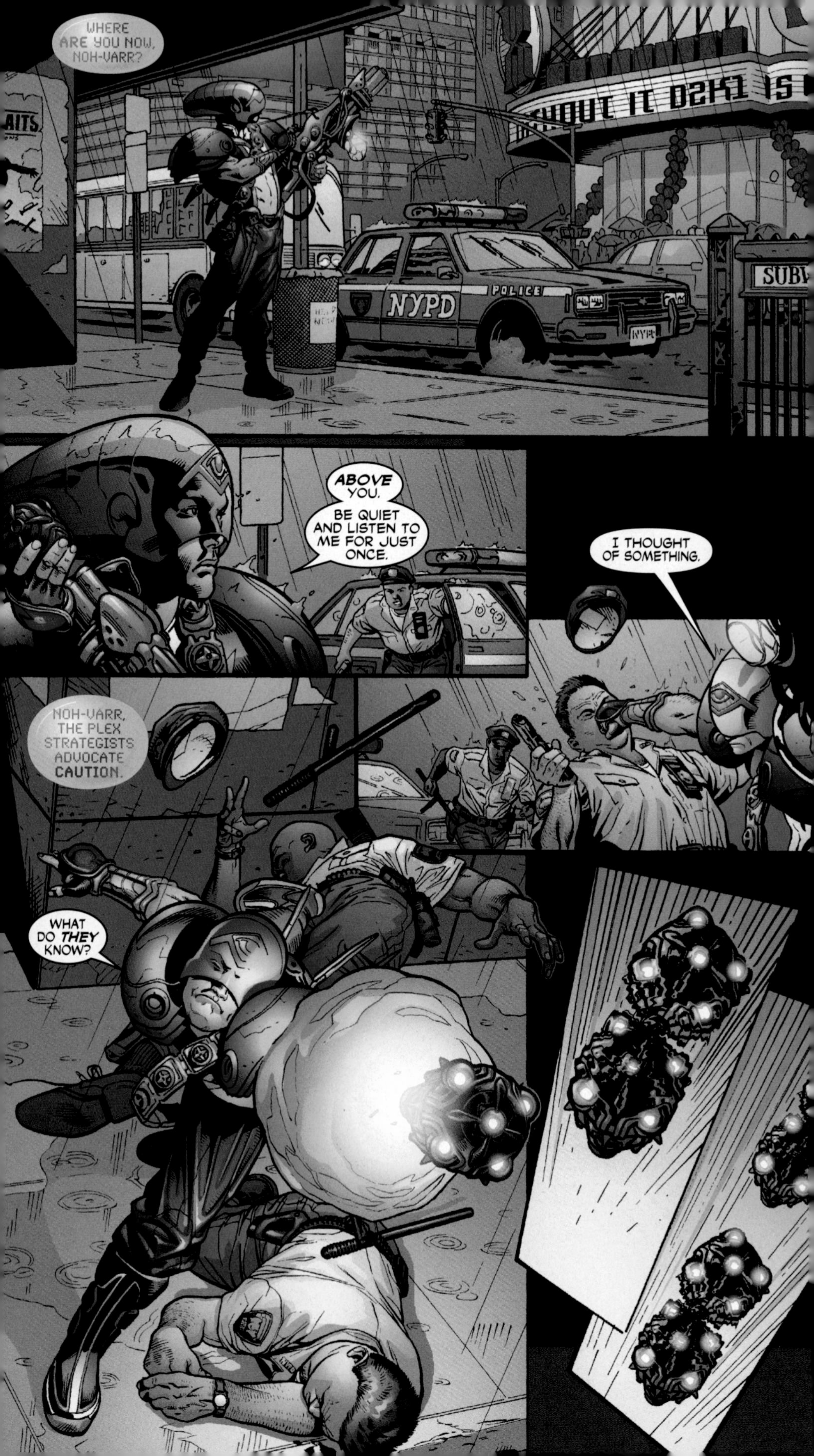
WHERE ARE YOU NOW, NOH-VARR?
NYPD
POLICE
SUBW
ABOVE YOU. BE QUIET AND LISTEN TO ME FOR JUST ONCE.
I THOUGHT OF SOMETHING.
NOH-VARR, THE PLEX STRATEGISTS ADVOCATE CAUTION.
WHAT DO THEY KNOW?

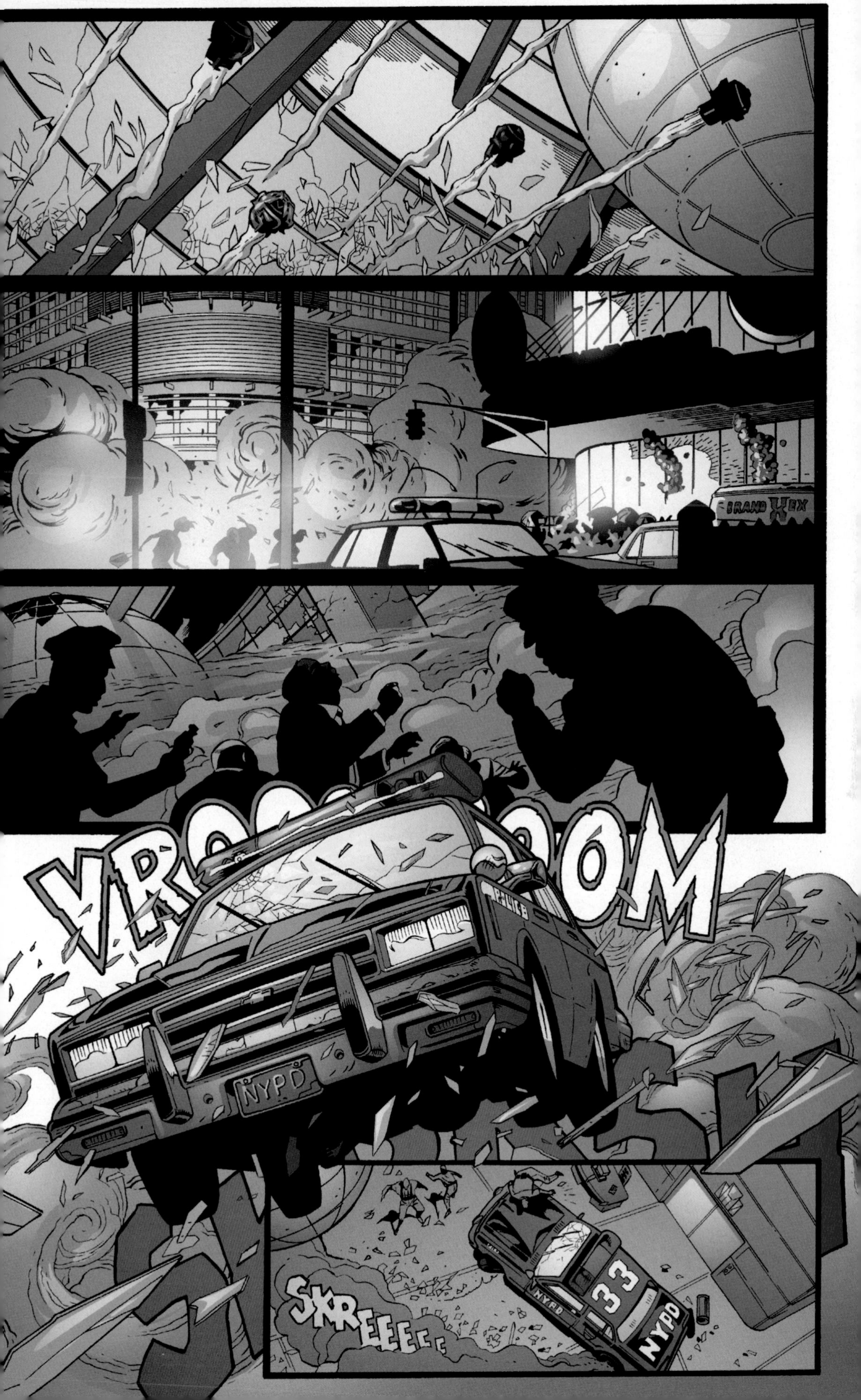
BRAND NEW HEX
VROOOOOOM
POLICE
NYPD
SKREEEEEEE
NYPD
33
NYPD

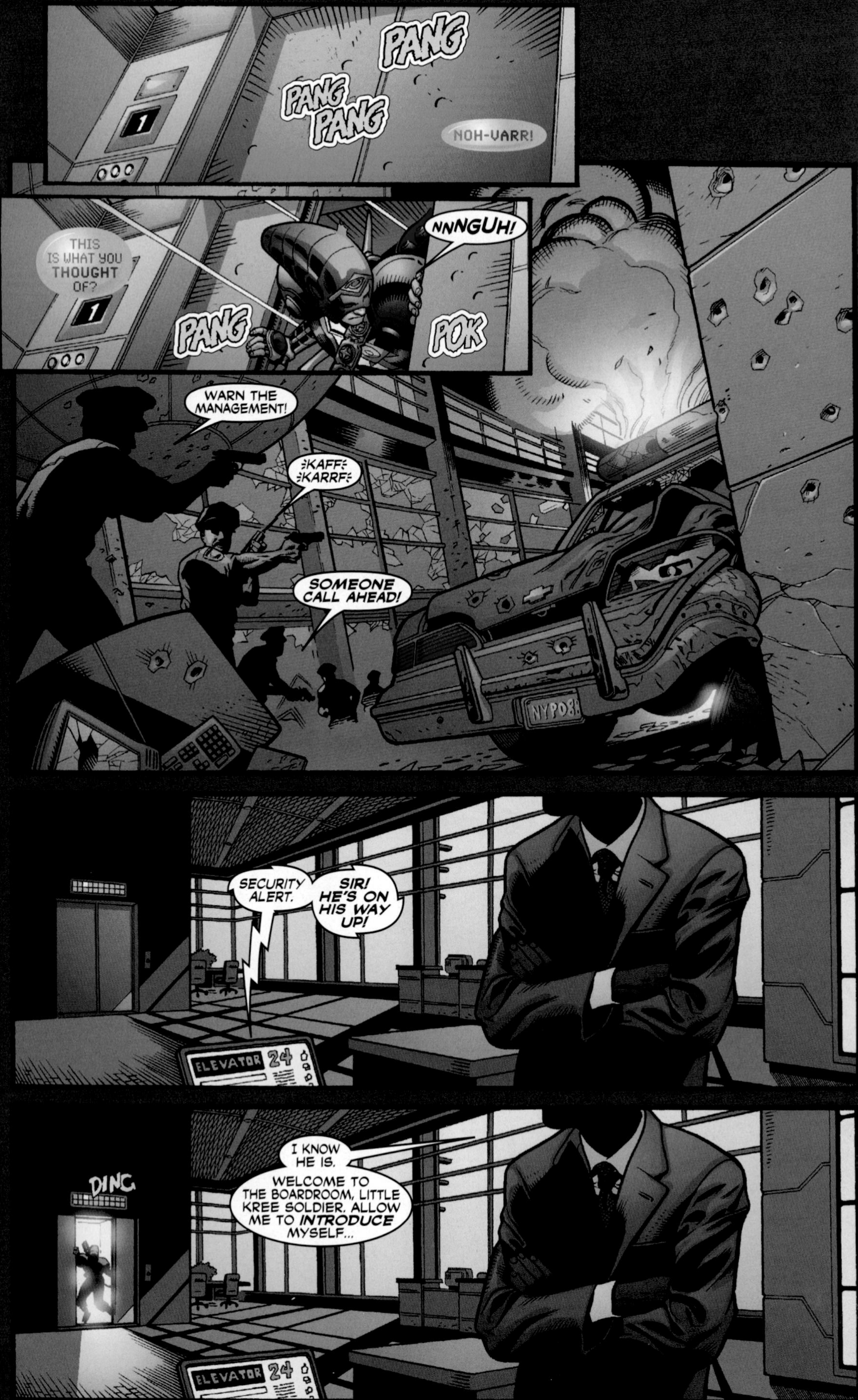
PANG
PANG PANG
NOH-VARR!
THIS IS WHAT YOU THOUGHT OF?
NNNGUH!
PANG
POK
WARN THE MANAGEMENT!
KAFF KARRF
SOMEONE CALL AHEAD!
NYPD88
SECURITY ALERT.
SIR! HE'S ON HIS WAY UP!
ELEVATOR 24
DING
I KNOW HE IS.
WELCOME TO THE BOARDROOM, LITTLE KREE SOLDIER. ALLOW ME TO INTRODUCE MYSELF...
ELEVATOR 24

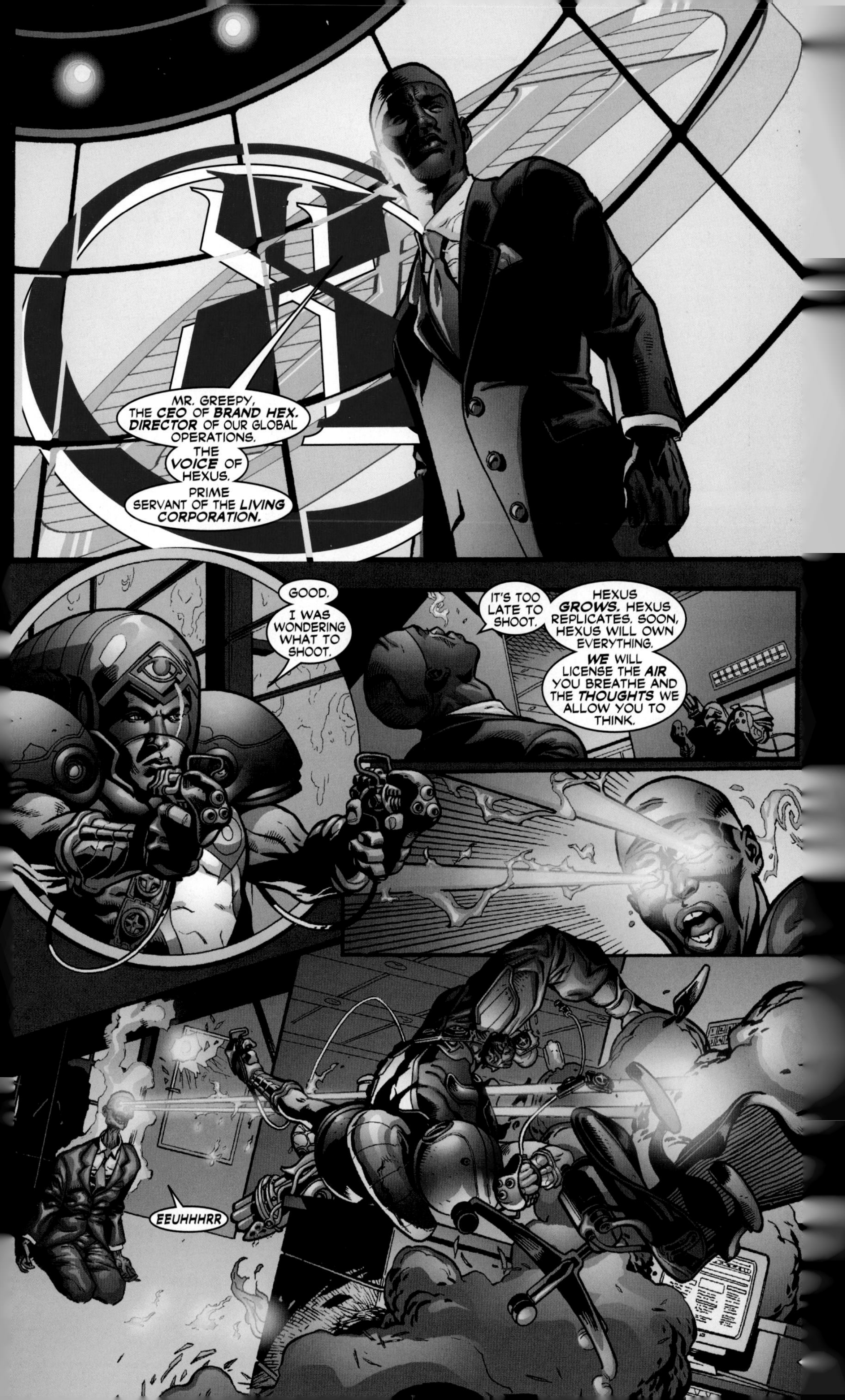
MR. GREEPY, THE CEO OF BRAND HEX. DIRECTOR OF OUR GLOBAL OPERATIONS.
THE VOICE OF HEXUS.
PRIME SERVANT OF THE LIVING CORPORATION.
GOOD.
I WAS WONDERING WHAT TO SHOOT.
IT'S TOO LATE TO SHOOT.
HEXUS GROWS. HEXUS REPLICATES. SOON, HEXUS WILL OWN EVERYTHING.
WE WILL LICENSE THE AIR YOU BREATHE AND THE THOUGHTS WE ALLOW YOU TO THINK.
EEUHHHRR

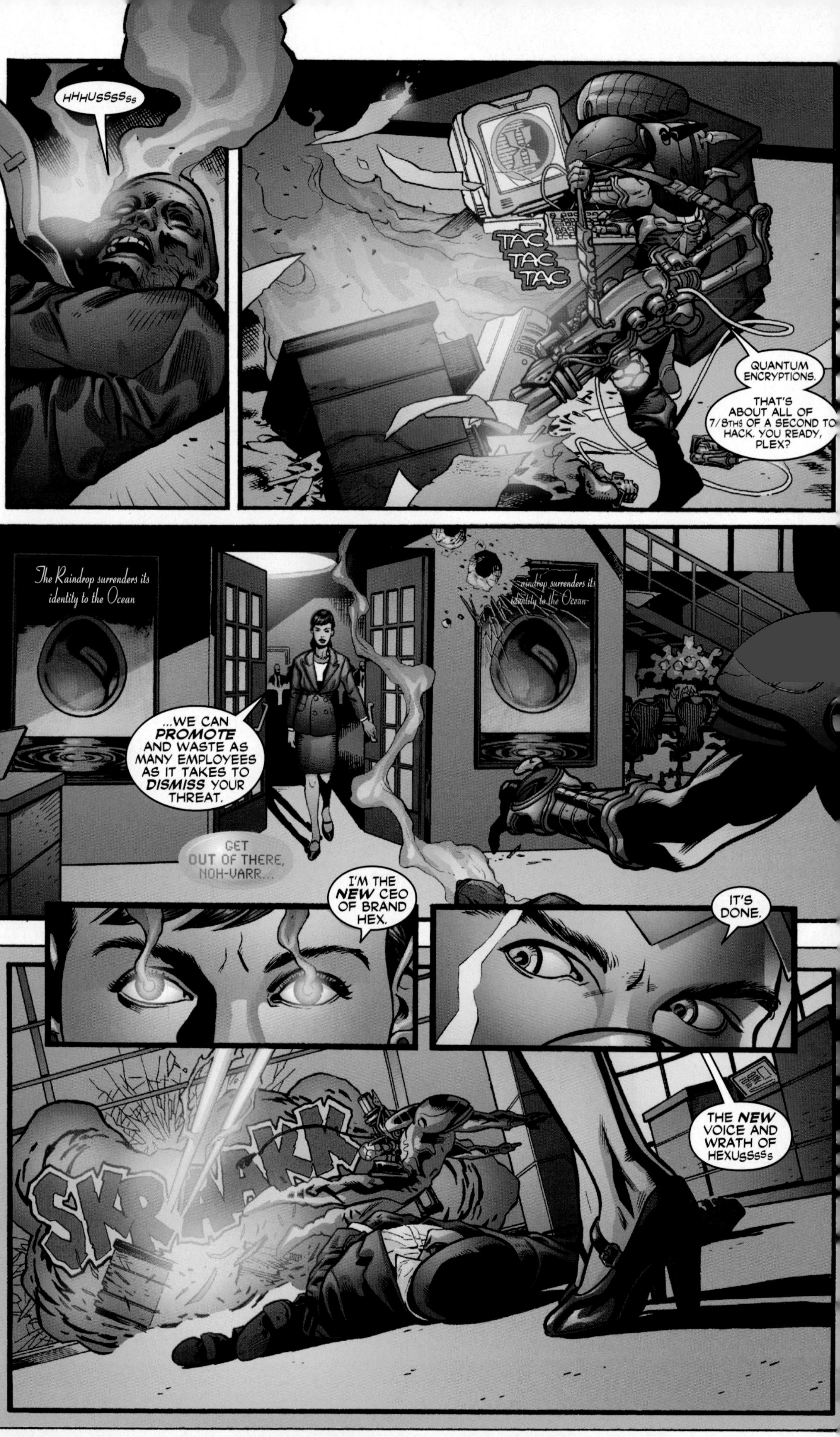
HHHUSSSSSS
TAC TAC TAC
QUANTUM ENCRYPTIONS.
THAT'S ABOUT ALL OF 7/8THS OF A SECOND TO HACK. YOU READY, PLEX?
The Raindrop surrenders its identity to the Ocean
...WE CAN PROMOTE AND WASTE AS MANY EMPLOYEES AS IT TAKES TO DISMISS YOUR THREAT.
GET OUT OF THERE, NOH-VARR...
I'M THE NEW CEO OF BRAND HEX.
IT'S DONE.
THE NEW VOICE AND WRATH OF HEXUSSSSS
SKRAAKK

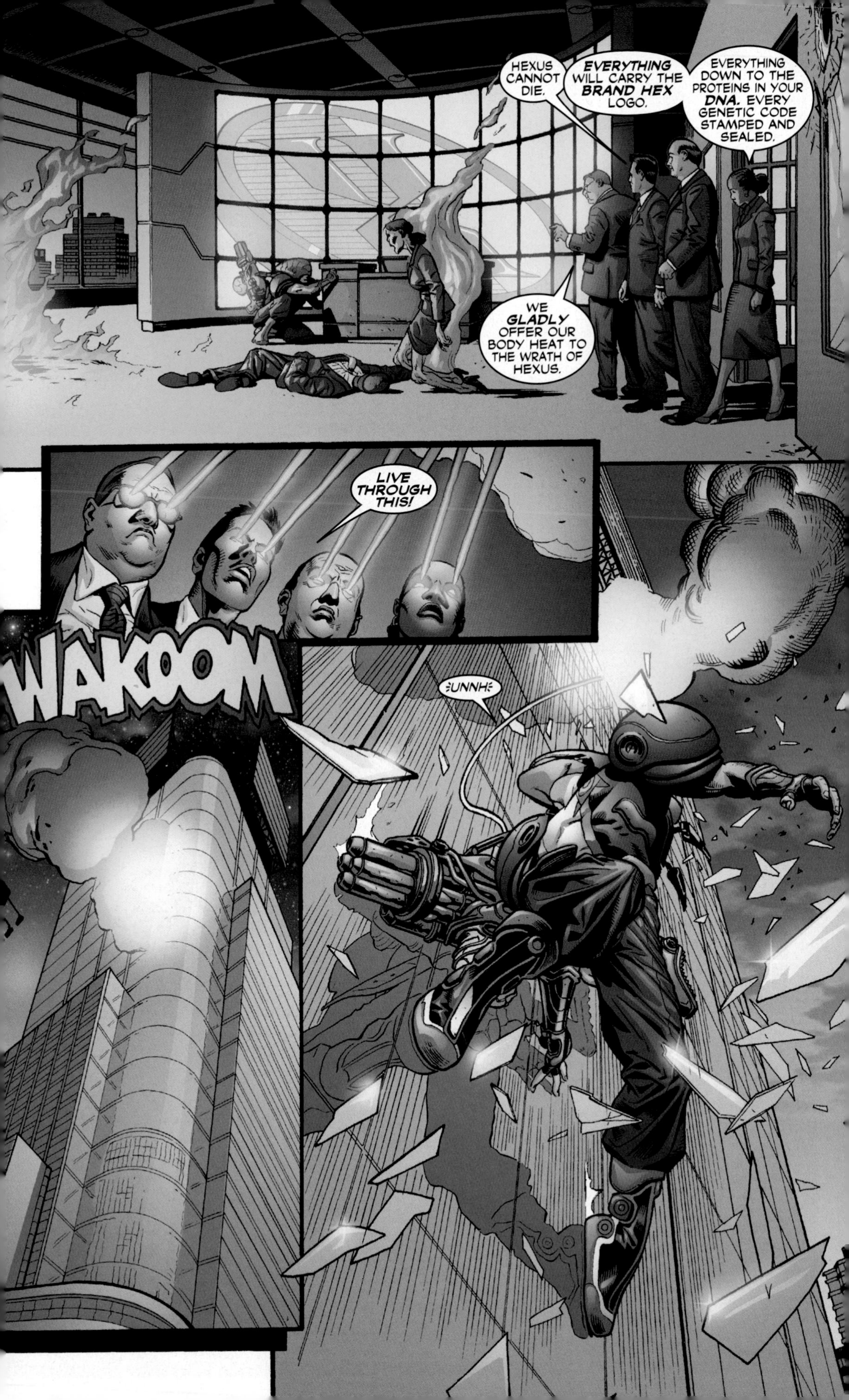
HEXUS CANNOT DIE.
EVERYTHING WILL CARRY THE BRAND HEX LOGO.
EVERYTHING DOWN TO THE PROTEINS IN YOUR DNA. EVERY GENETIC CODE STAMPED AND SEALED.
WE GLADLY OFFER OUR BODY HEAT TO THE WRATH OF HEXUS.
LIVE THROUGH THIS!
WAKOOM
UNNH

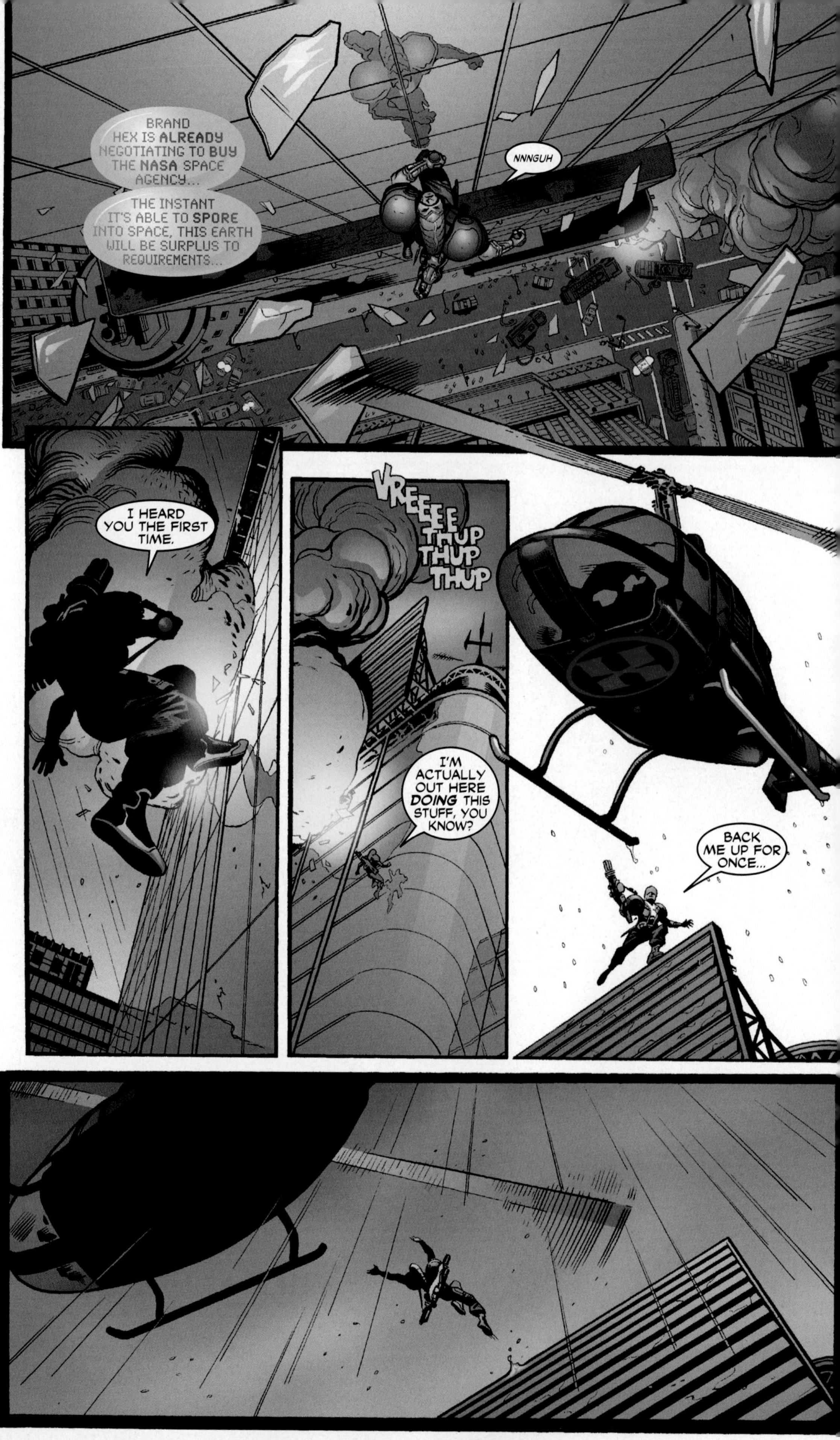
BRAND HEX IS **ALREADY** NEGOTIATING TO **BUY** THE **NASA** SPACE AGENCY...
THE INSTANT IT'S ABLE TO **SPORE** INTO SPACE, THIS EARTH WILL BE SURPLUS TO REQUIREMENTS...
NNNGUH
I HEARD YOU THE FIRST TIME.
VREEEEE
THUP THUP THUP
I'M ACTUALLY OUT HERE ***DOING*** THIS STUFF, YOU KNOW?
BACK ME UP FOR ONCE...

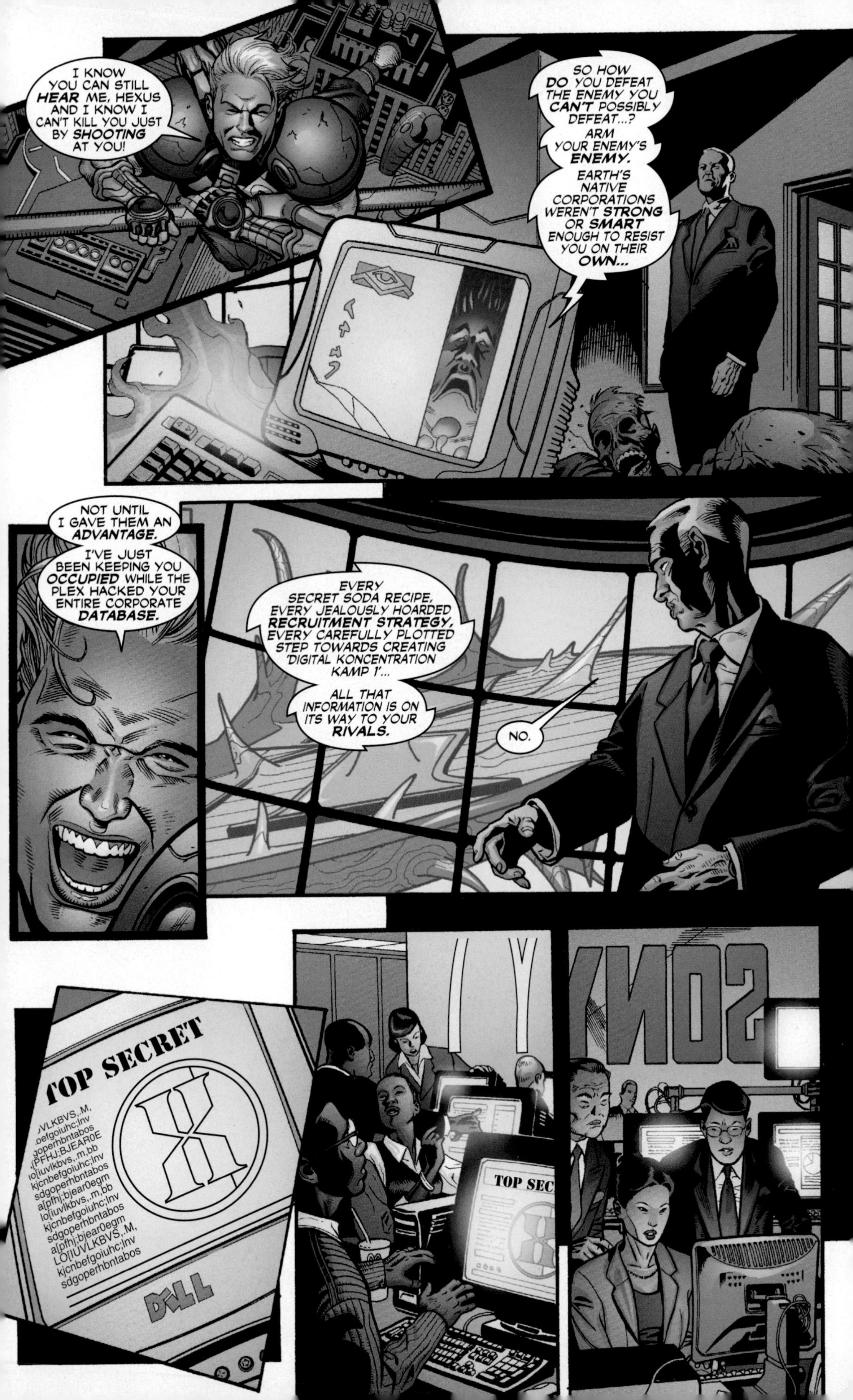
I KNOW YOU CAN STILL HEAR ME, HEXUS AND I KNOW I CAN'T KILL YOU JUST BY SHOOTING AT YOU!
SO HOW DO YOU DEFEAT THE ENEMY YOU CAN'T POSSIBLY DEFEAT...?
ARM YOUR ENEMY'S ENEMY.
EARTH'S NATIVE CORPORATIONS WEREN'T STRONG OR SMART ENOUGH TO RESIST YOU ON THEIR OWN...
NOT UNTIL I GAVE THEM AN ADVANTAGE.
I'VE JUST BEEN KEEPING YOU OCCUPIED WHILE THE PLEX HACKED YOUR ENTIRE CORPORATE DATABASE.
EVERY SECRET SODA RECIPE, EVERY JEALOUSLY HOARDED RECRUITMENT STRATEGY, EVERY CAREFULLY PLOTTED STEP TOWARDS CREATING 'DIGITAL KONCENTRATION KAMP 1'...
ALL THAT INFORMATION IS ON ITS WAY TO YOUR RIVALS.
NO.
TOP SECRET
DELL
TOP SEC

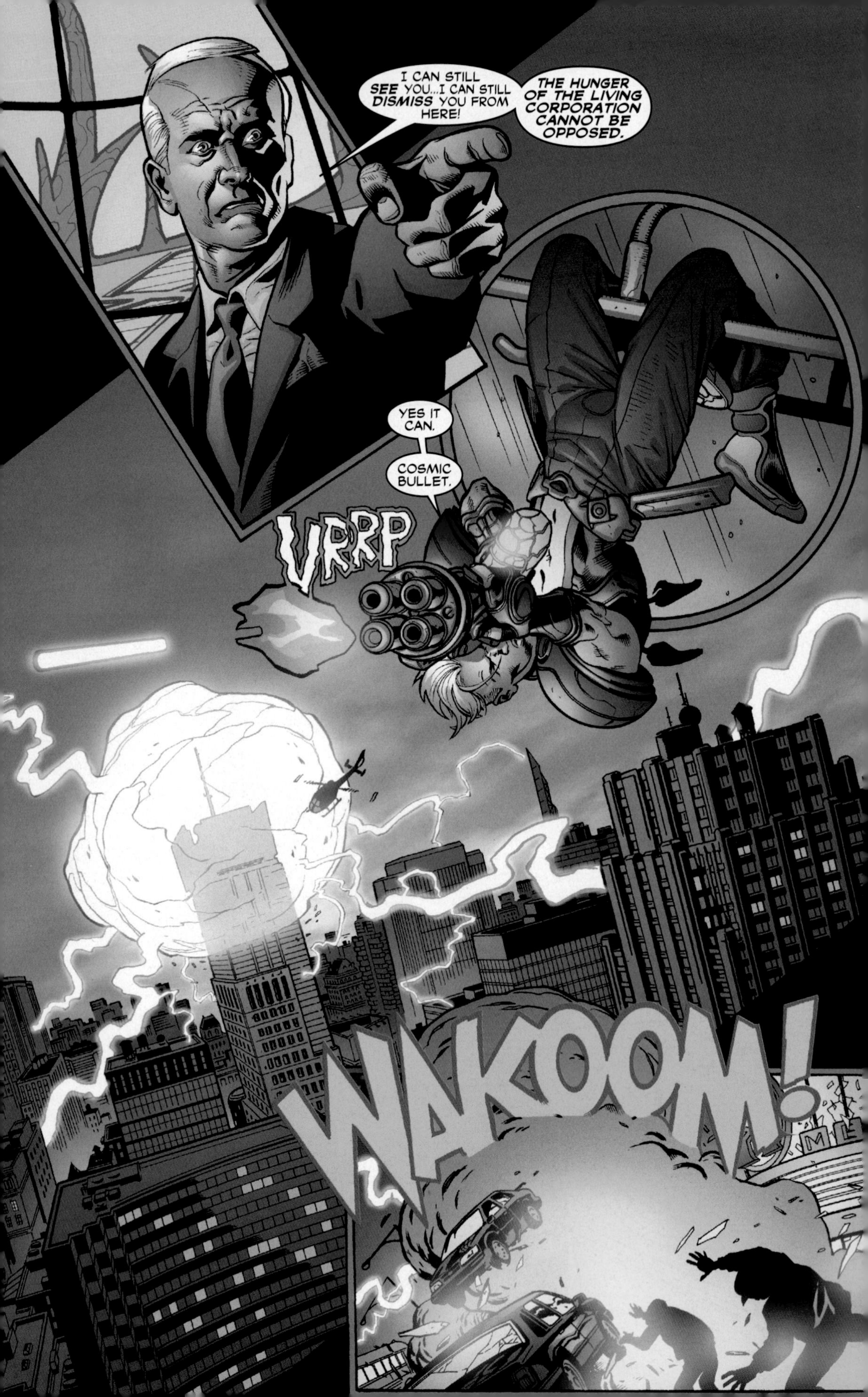
I CAN STILL SEE YOU...I CAN STILL DISMISS YOU FROM HERE!
THE HUNGER OF THE LIVING CORPORATION CANNOT BE OPPOSED.
YES IT CAN.
COSMIC BULLET.
VRRP
WAKOOM!

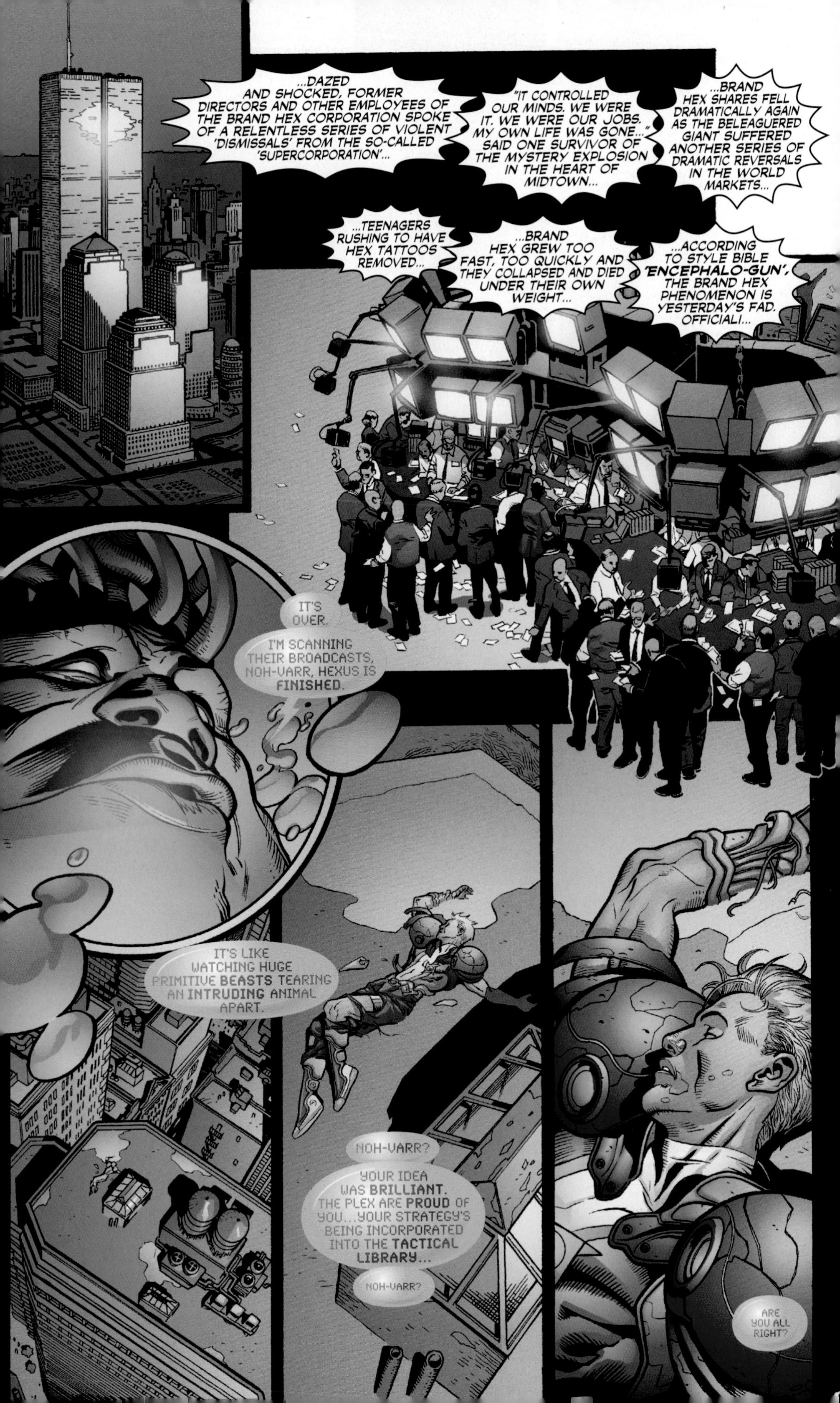
...DAZED AND SHOCKED, FORMER DIRECTORS AND OTHER EMPLOYEES OF THE BRAND HEX CORPORATION SPOKE OF A RELENTLESS SERIES OF VIOLENT 'DISMISSALS' FROM THE SO-CALLED 'SUPERCORPORATION'...
"IT CONTROLLED OUR MINDS. WE WERE IT. WE WERE OUR JOBS. MY OWN LIFE WAS GONE..." SAID ONE SURVIVOR OF THE MYSTERY EXPLOSION IN THE HEART OF MIDTOWN...
...BRAND HEX SHARES FELL DRAMATICALLY AGAIN AS THE BELEAGUERED GIANT SUFFERED ANOTHER SERIES OF DRAMATIC REVERSALS IN THE WORLD MARKETS...
...TEENAGERS RUSHING TO HAVE HEX TATTOOS REMOVED...
...BRAND HEX GREW TOO FAST, TOO QUICKLY AND THEY COLLAPSED AND DIED UNDER THEIR OWN WEIGHT...
...ACCORDING TO STYLE BIBLE 'ENCEPHALO-GUN', THE BRAND HEX PHENOMENON IS YESTERDAY'S FAD. OFFICIAL!...
IT'S OVER.
I'M SCANNING THEIR BROADCASTS, NOH-VARR, HEXUS IS FINISHED.
IT'S LIKE WATCHING HUGE PRIMITIVE BEASTS TEARING AN INTRUDING ANIMAL APART.
NOH-VARR?
YOUR IDEA WAS BRILLIANT. THE PLEX ARE PROUD OF YOU...YOUR STRATEGY'S BEING INCORPORATED INTO THE TACTICAL LIBRARY...
NOH-VARR?
ARE YOU ALL RIGHT?

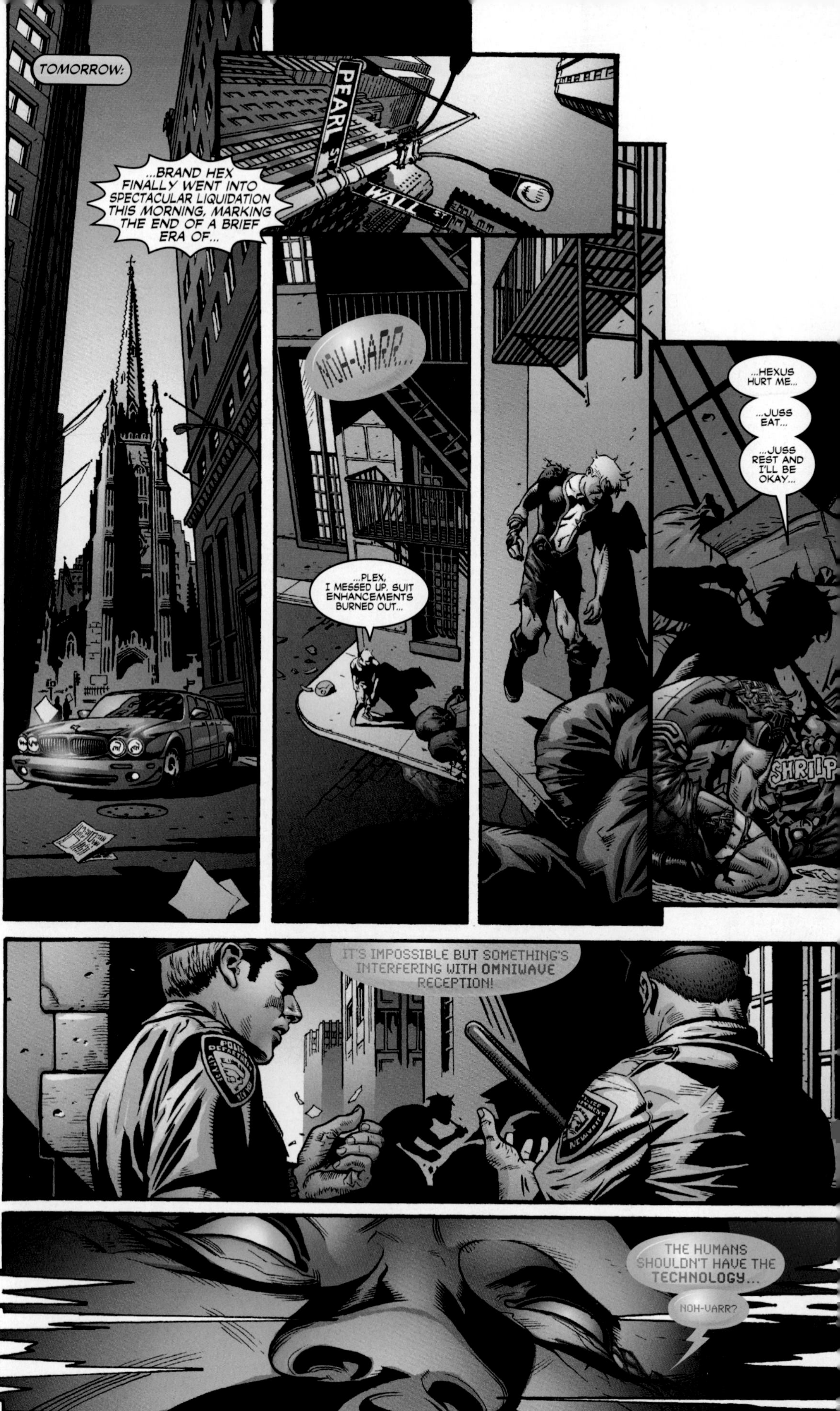

TOMORROW:
...BRAND HEX FINALLY WENT INTO SPECTACULAR LIQUIDATION THIS MORNING, MARKING THE END OF A BRIEF ERA OF...
PEARL ST
WALL ST
NOH-VARR...
...PLEX, I MESSED UP. SUIT ENHANCEMENTS BURNED OUT...
...HEXUS HURT ME...
...JUSS EAT...
...JUSS REST AND I'LL BE OKAY...
SHRIIP
IT'S IMPOSSIBLE BUT SOMETHING'S INTERFERING WITH OMNIWAVE RECEPTION!
THE HUMANS SHOULDN'T HAVE THE TECHNOLOGY...
NOH-VARR?

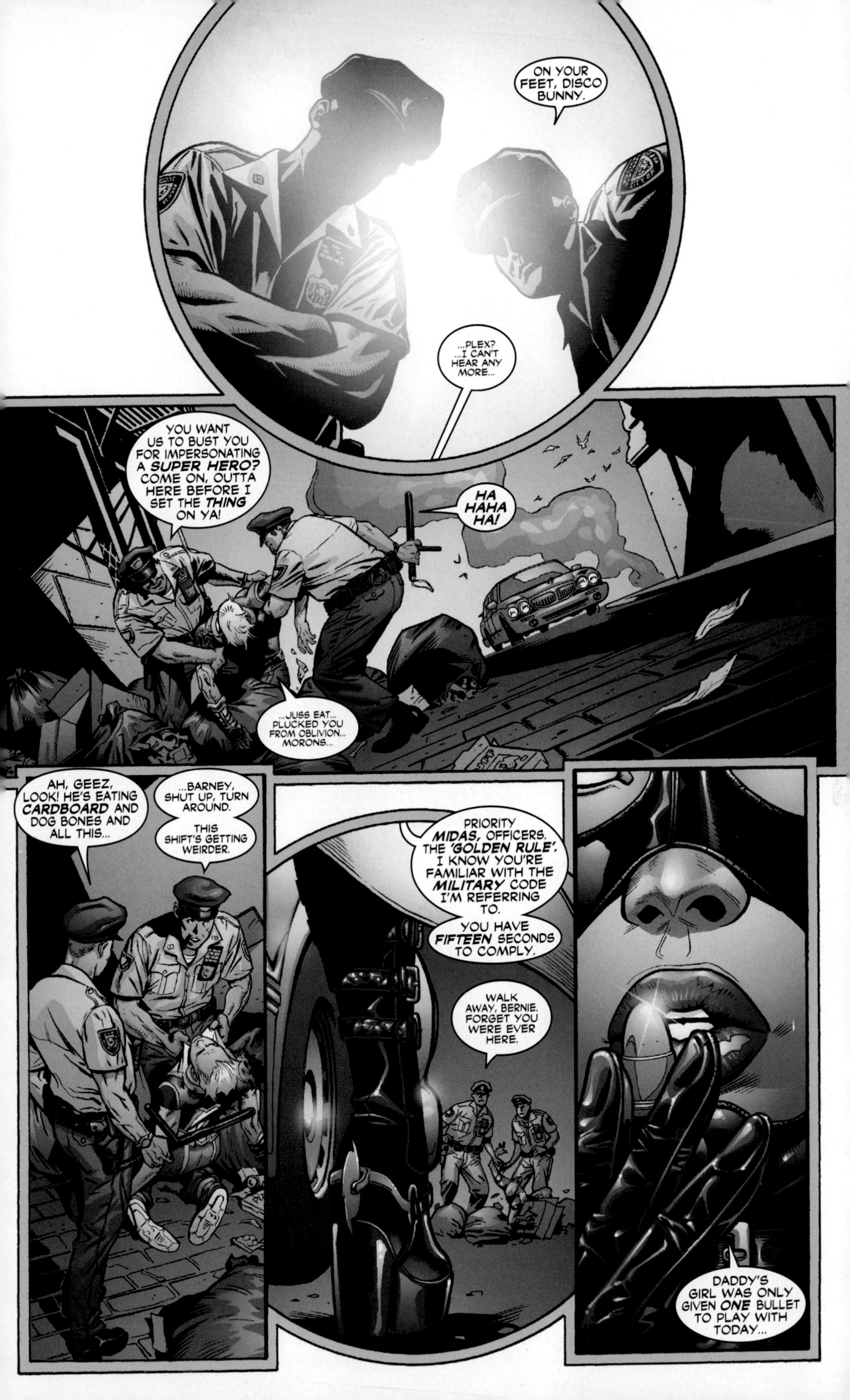

ON YOUR FEET, DISCO BUNNY.
...PLEX? ...I CAN'T HEAR ANY MORE...
YOU WANT US TO BUST YOU FOR IMPERSONATING A SUPER HERO? COME ON, OUTTA HERE BEFORE I SET THE THING ON YA!
HA HAHA HA!
...JUSS EAT... PLUCKED YOU FROM OBLIVION... MORONS...
AH, GEEZ, LOOK! HE'S EATING CARDBOARD AND DOG BONES AND ALL THIS...
...BARNEY, SHUT UP, TURN AROUND.
THIS SHIFT'S GETTING WEIRDER.
PRIORITY MIDAS, OFFICERS. THE 'GOLDEN RULE'. I KNOW YOU'RE FAMILIAR WITH THE MILITARY CODE I'M REFERRING TO.
YOU HAVE FIFTEEN SECONDS TO COMPLY.
WALK AWAY, BERNIE. FORGET YOU WERE EVER HERE.
DADDY'S GIRL WAS ONLY GIVEN ONE BULLET TO PLAY WITH TODAY...

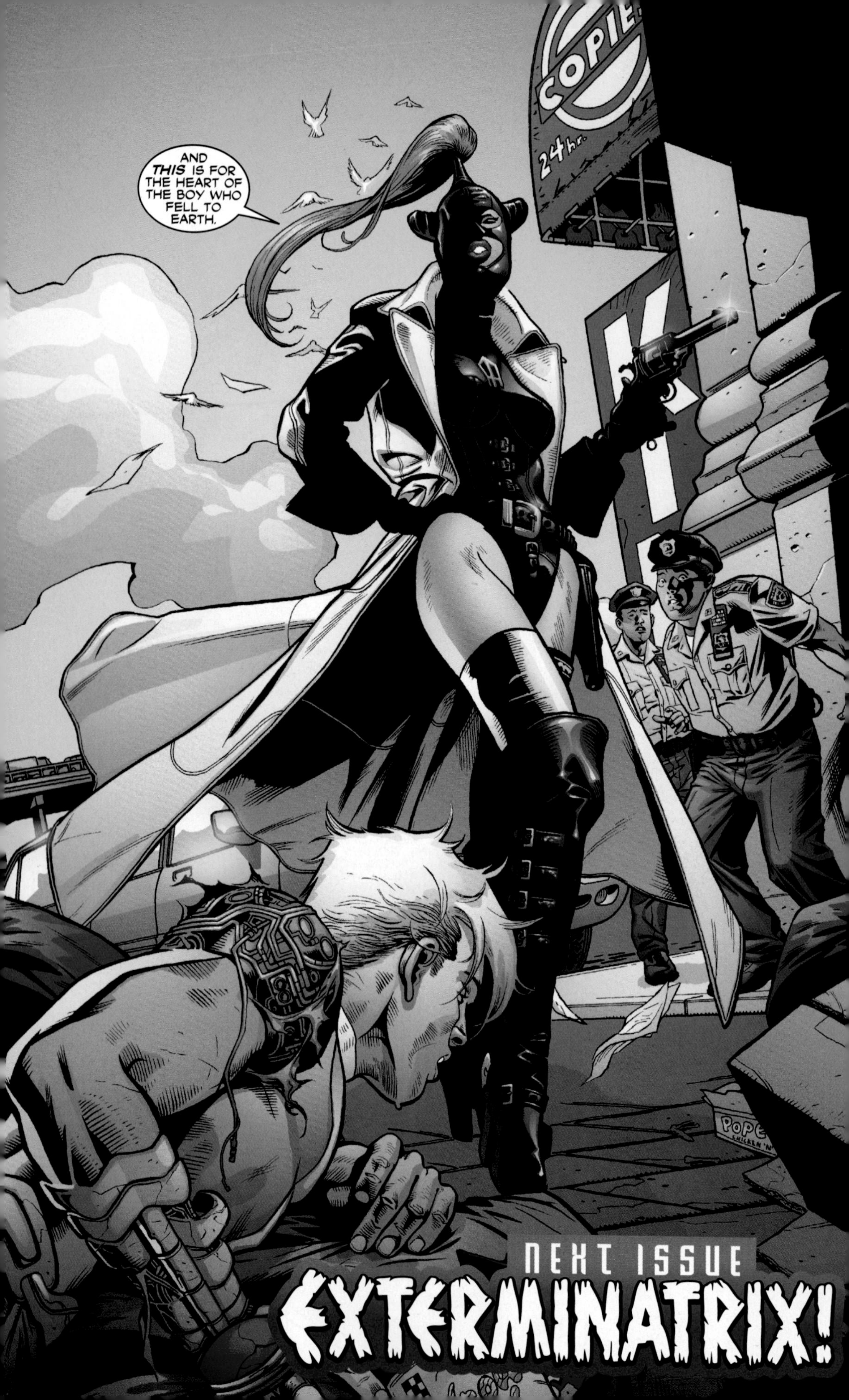
AND *THIS* IS FOR THE HEART OF THE BOY WHO FELL TO EARTH.
NEXT ISSUE
EXTERMINATRIX!

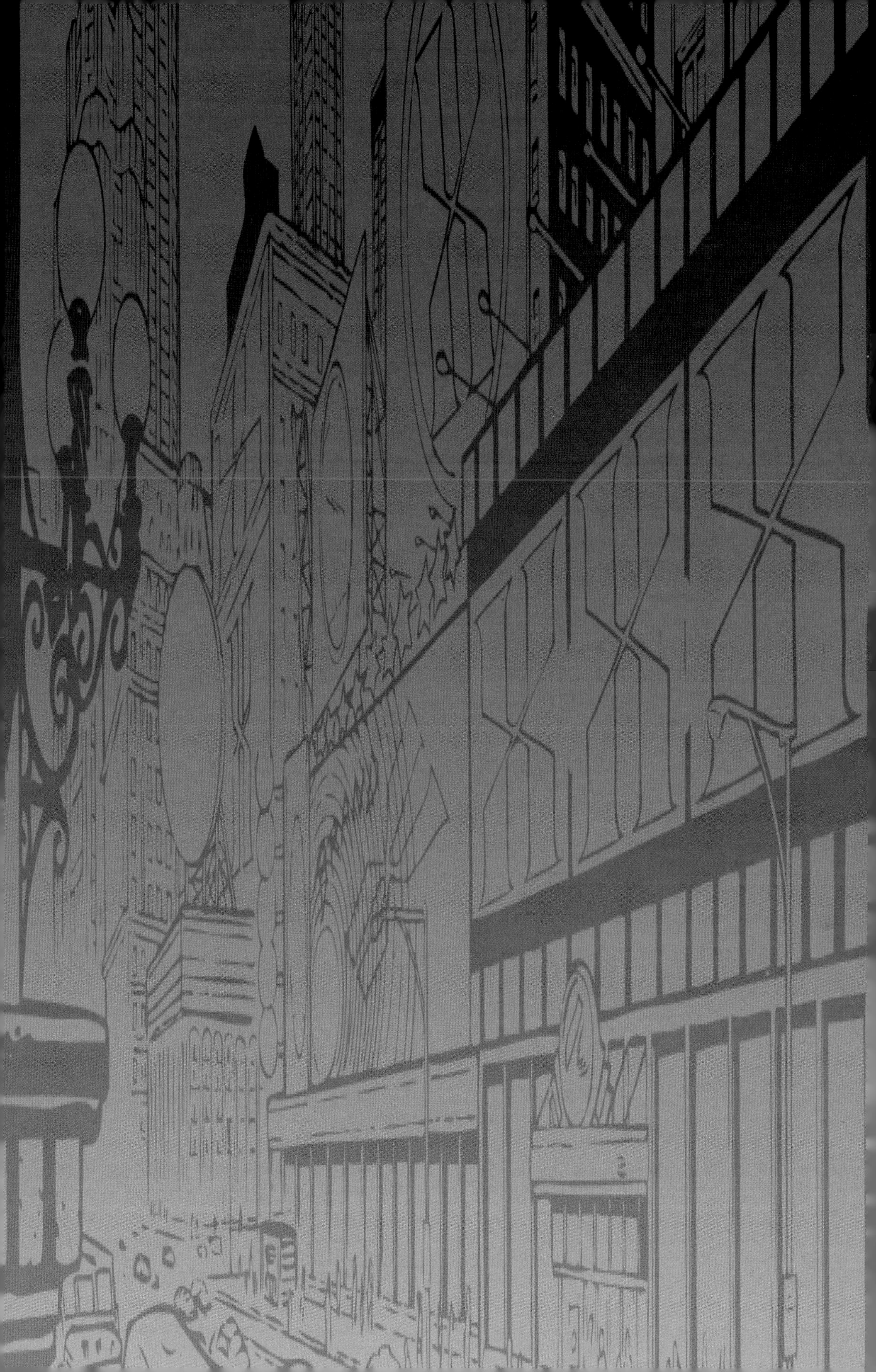

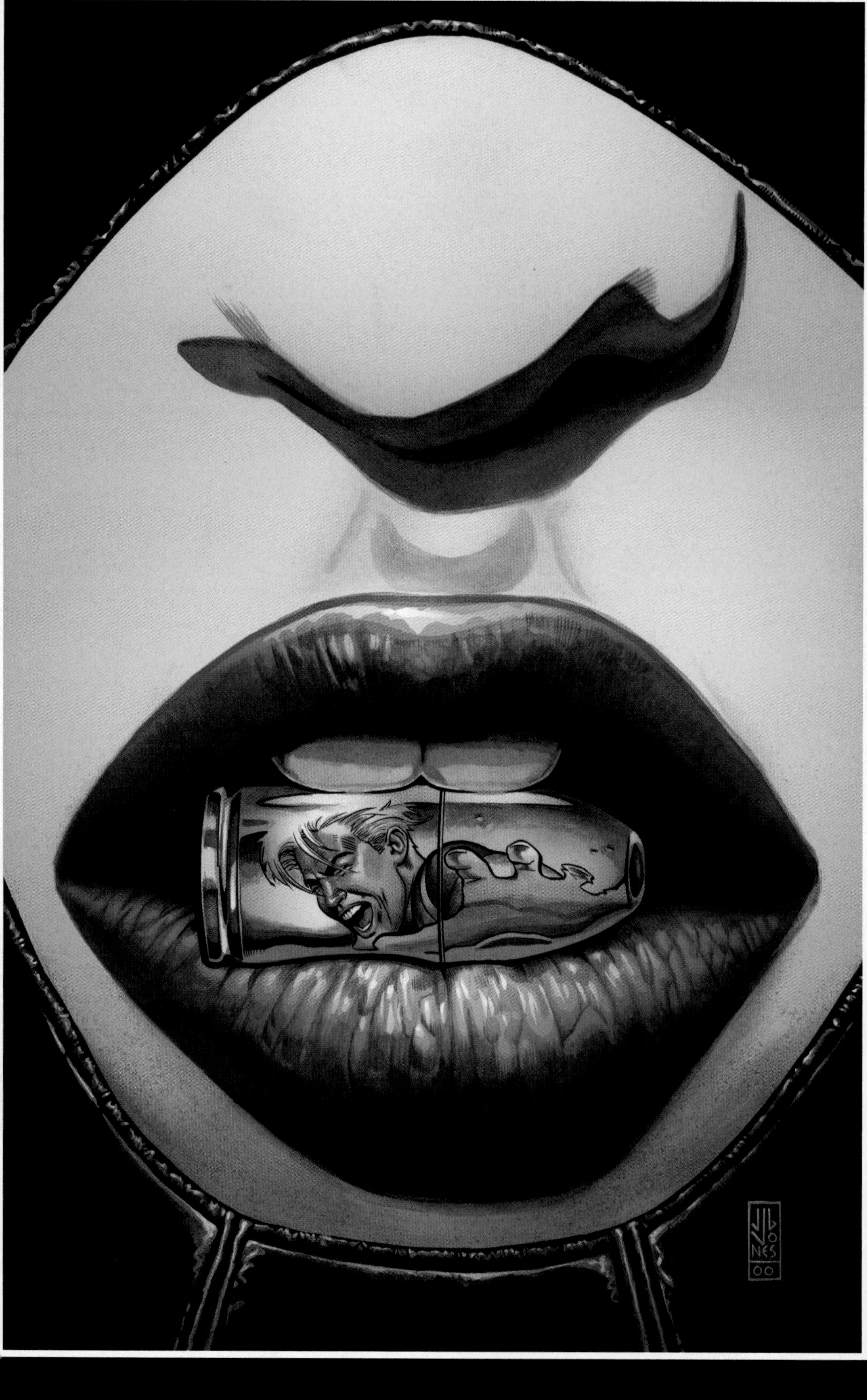

(4)

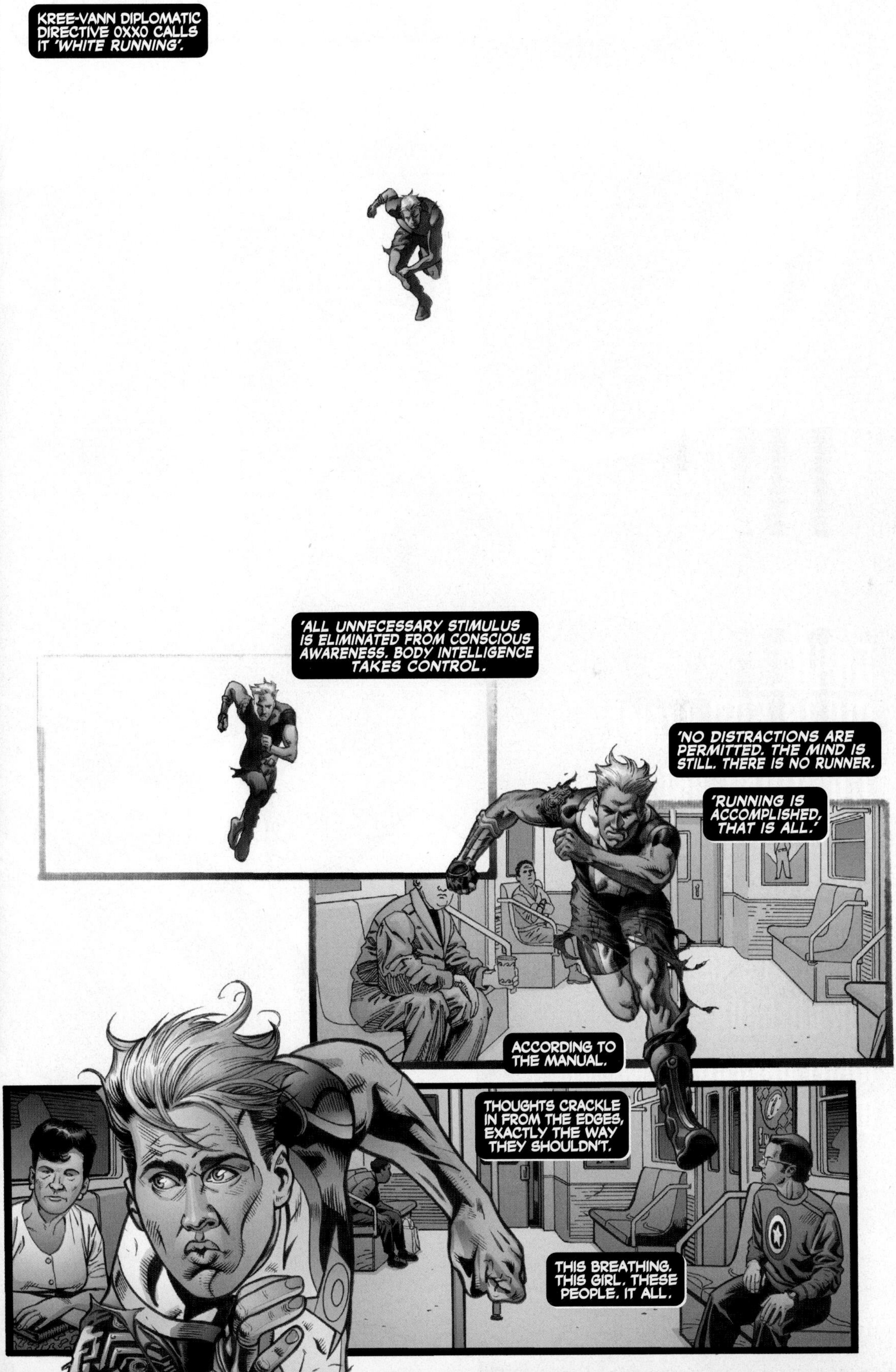
KREE-VANN DIPLOMATIC DIRECTIVE 0XX0 CALLS IT 'WHITE RUNNING'.
'ALL UNNECESSARY STIMULUS IS ELIMINATED FROM CONSCIOUS AWARENESS. BODY INTELLIGENCE TAKES CONTROL.
'NO DISTRACTIONS ARE PERMITTED. THE MIND IS STILL. THERE IS NO RUNNER.
'RUNNING IS ACCOMPLISHED, THAT IS ALL.'
ACCORDING TO THE MANUAL.
THOUGHTS CRACKLE IN FROM THE EDGES, EXACTLY THE WAY THEY SHOULDN'T.
THIS BREATHING. THIS GIRL. THESE PEOPLE. IT ALL.

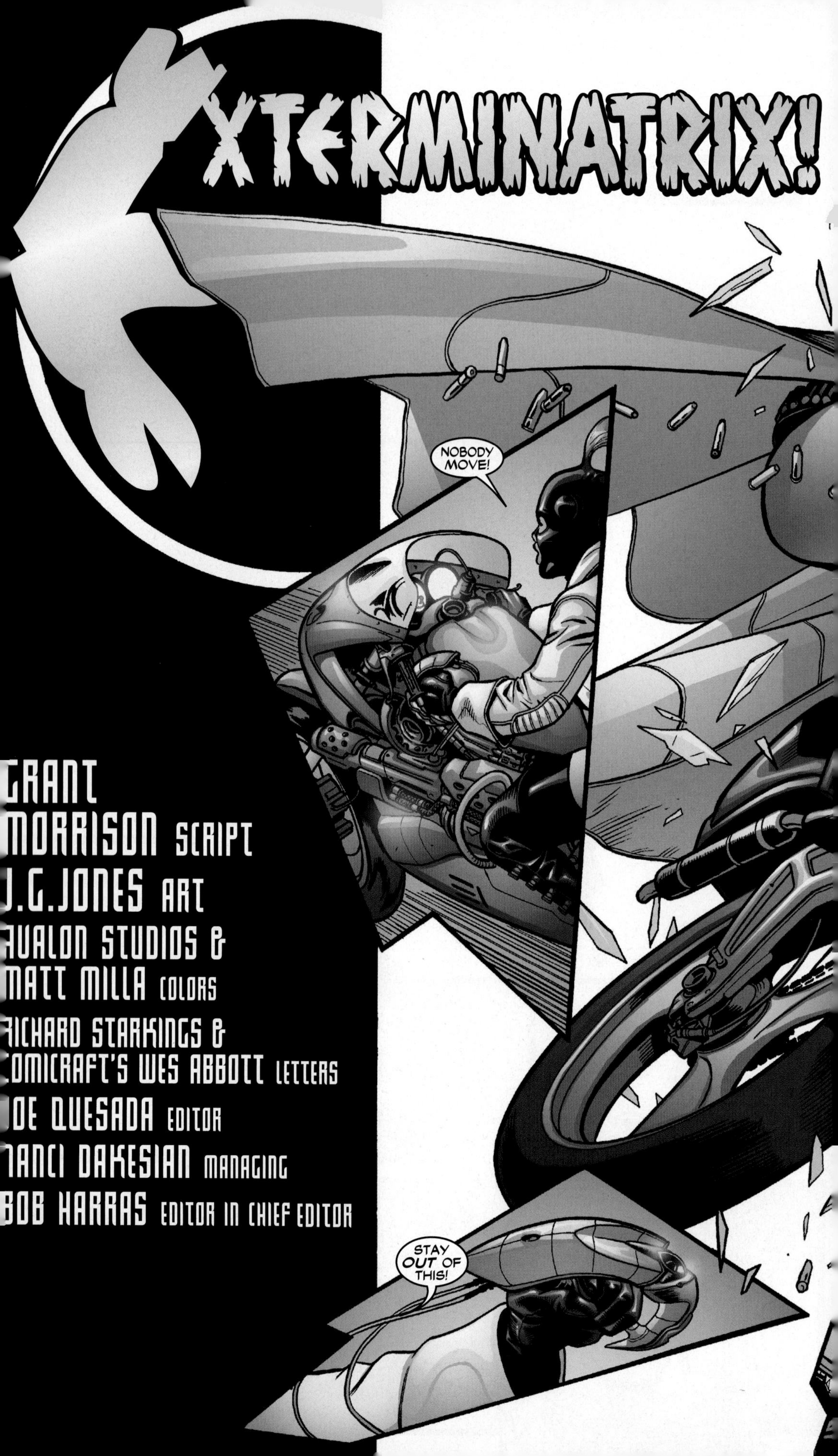
XTERMINATRIX!
NOBODY MOVE!
GRANT MORRISON SCRIPT
J.G. JONES ART
AVALON STUDIOS & MATT MILLA COLORS
RICHARD STARKINGS & COMICRAFT'S WES ABBOTT LETTERS
JOE QUESADA EDITOR
NANCI DAKESIAN MANAGING
BOB HARRAS EDITOR IN CHIEF EDITOR
STAY OUT OF THIS!

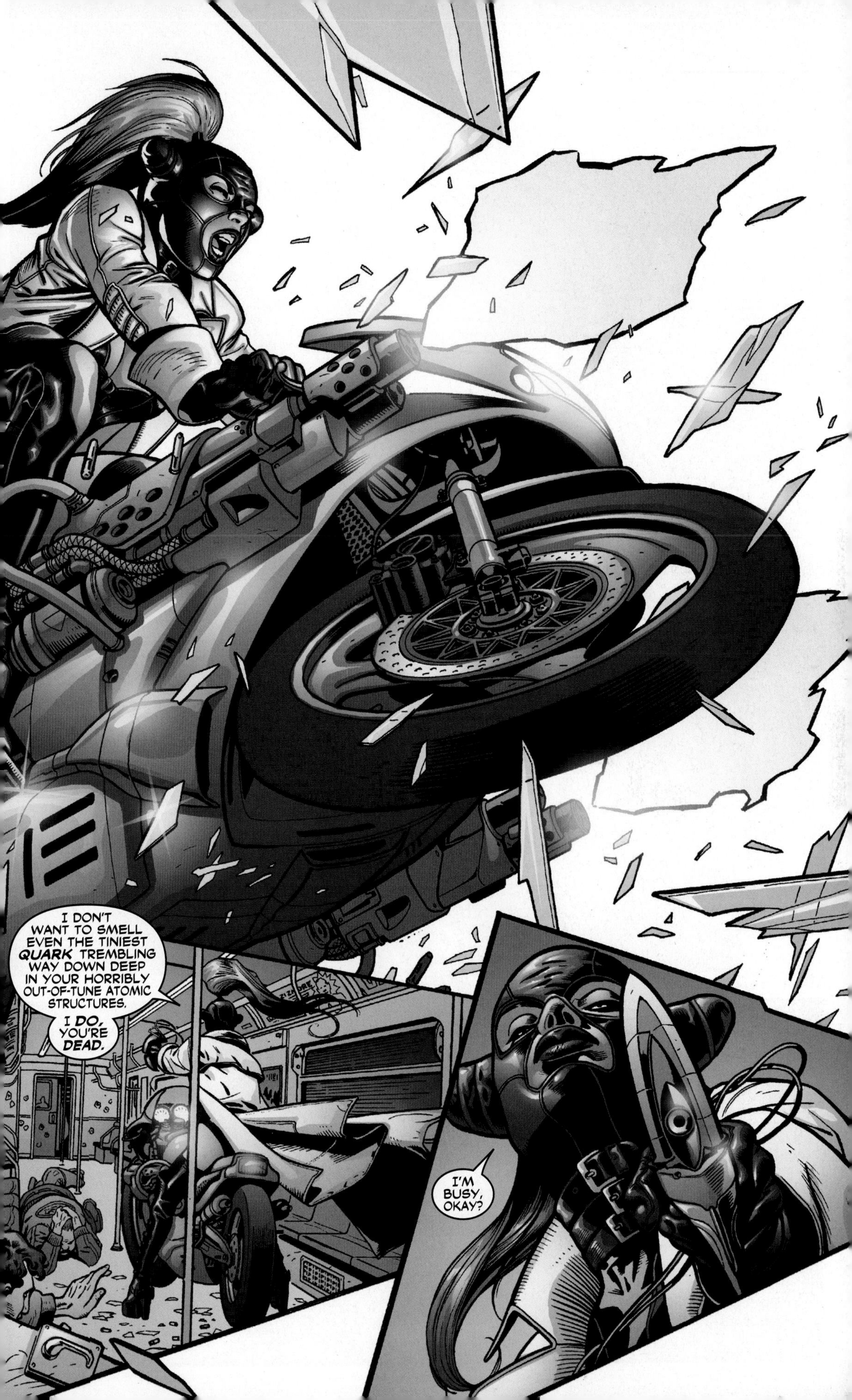
I DON'T WANT TO SMELL EVEN THE TINIEST QUARK TREMBLING WAY DOWN DEEP IN YOUR HORRIBLY OUT-OF-TUNE ATOMIC STRUCTURES.
I DO, YOU'RE DEAD.
I'M BUSY, OKAY?

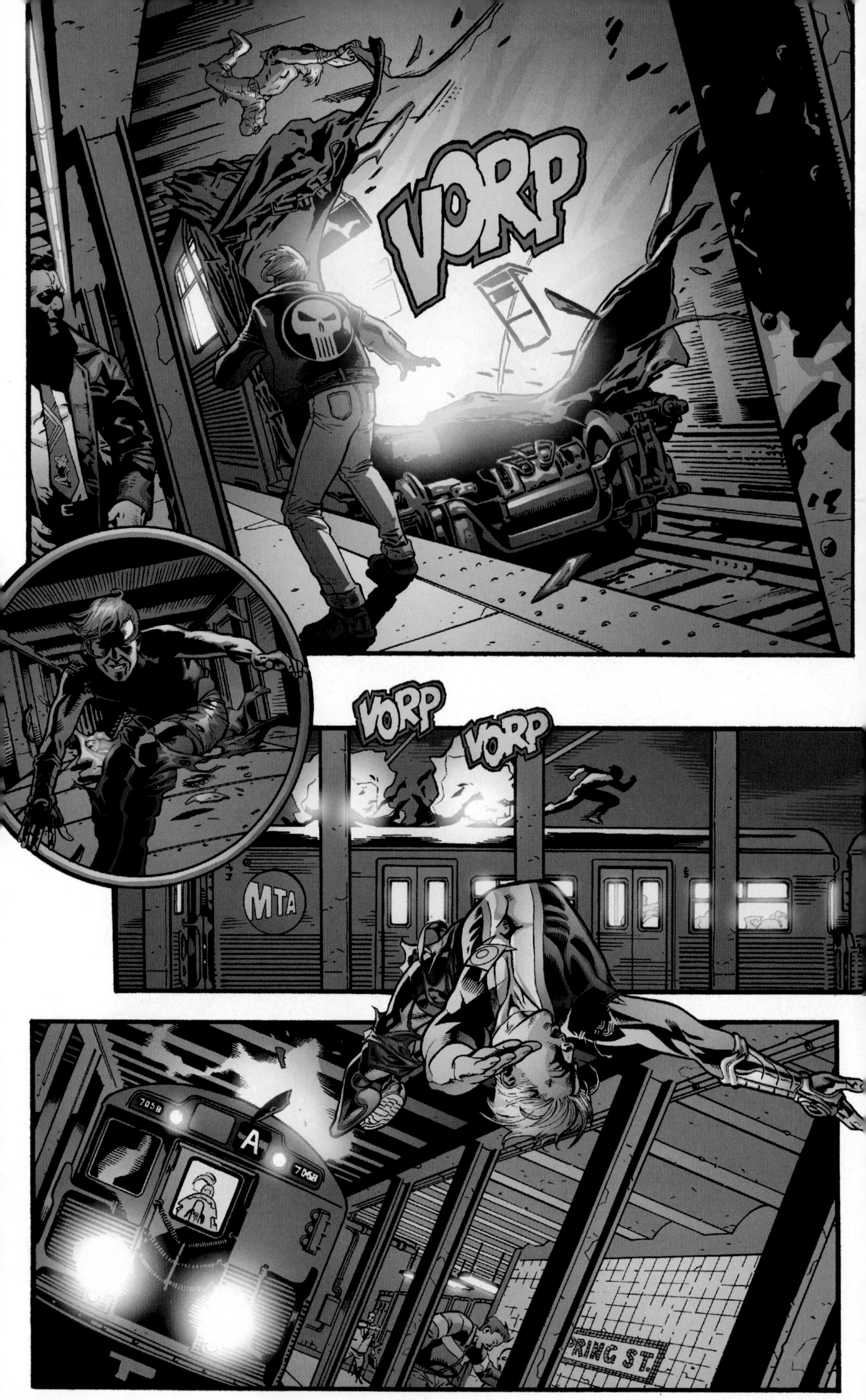
VORP
VORP
VORP
MTA
A
PRING ST.

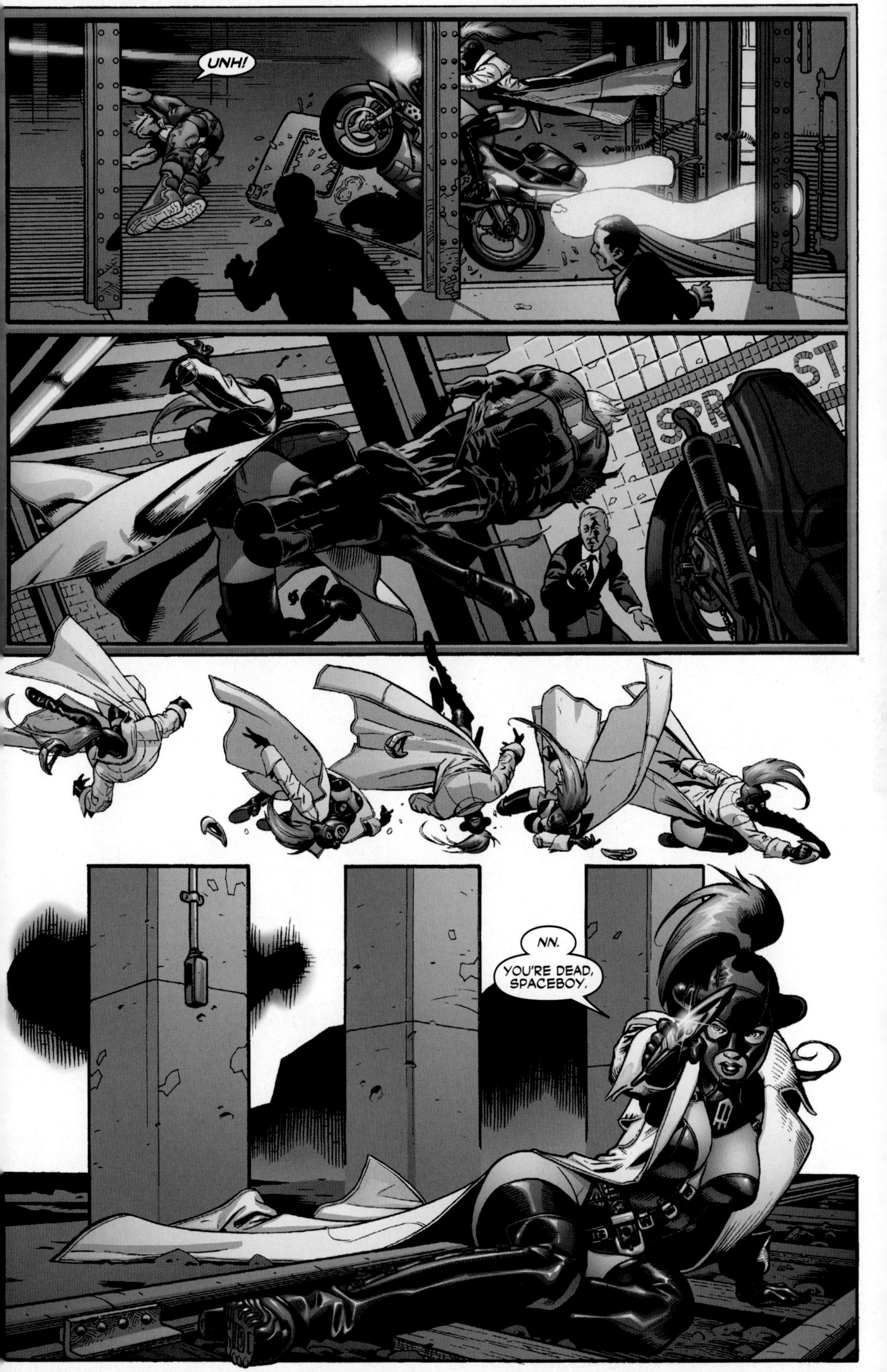
UNH!
NN.
YOU'RE DEAD, SPACEBOY.

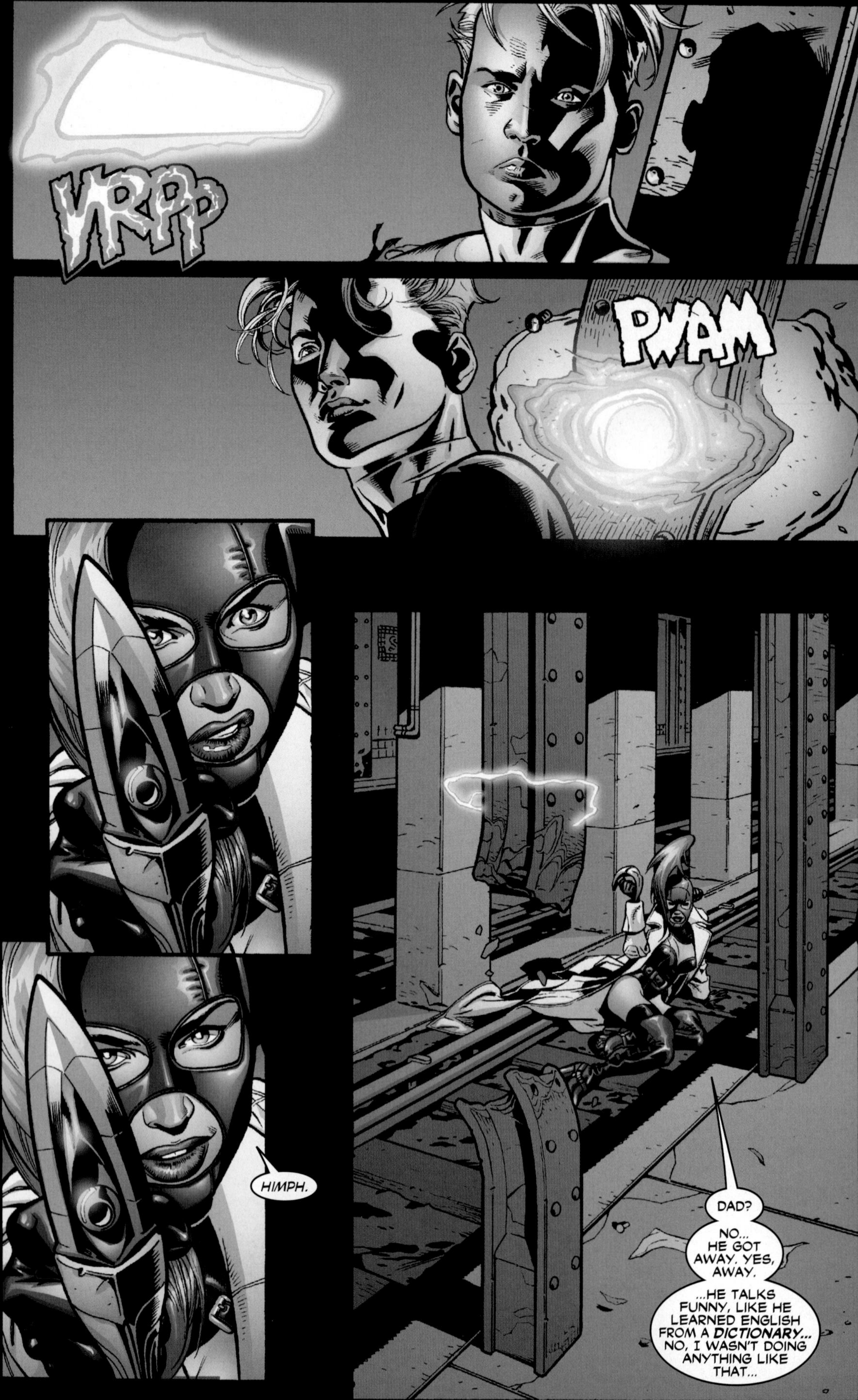
VRPP
PWAM
HIMPH.
DAD?
NO... HE GOT AWAY. YES, AWAY.
...HE TALKS FUNNY, LIKE HE LEARNED ENGLISH FROM A *DICTIONARY...* NO, I WASN'T DOING ANYTHING LIKE THAT...

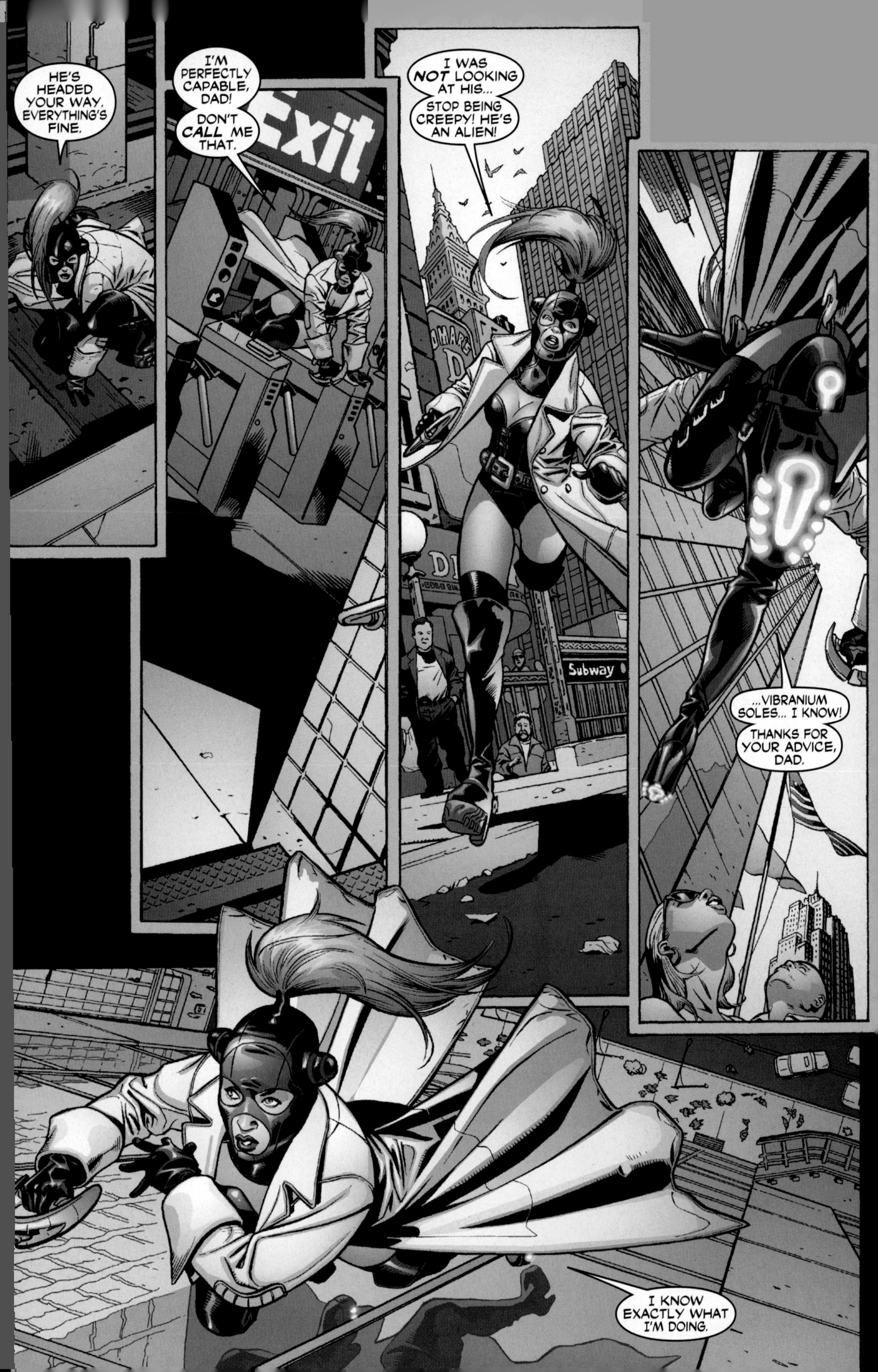
HE'S HEADED YOUR WAY. EVERYTHING'S FINE.
I'M PERFECTLY CAPABLE, DAD!
DON'T CALL ME THAT.
Exit
I WAS NOT LOOKING AT HIS...
STOP BEING CREEPY! HE'S AN ALIEN!
Subway
...VIBRANIUM SOLES... I KNOW!
THANKS FOR YOUR ADVICE, DAD.
I KNOW EXACTLY WHAT I'M DOING.

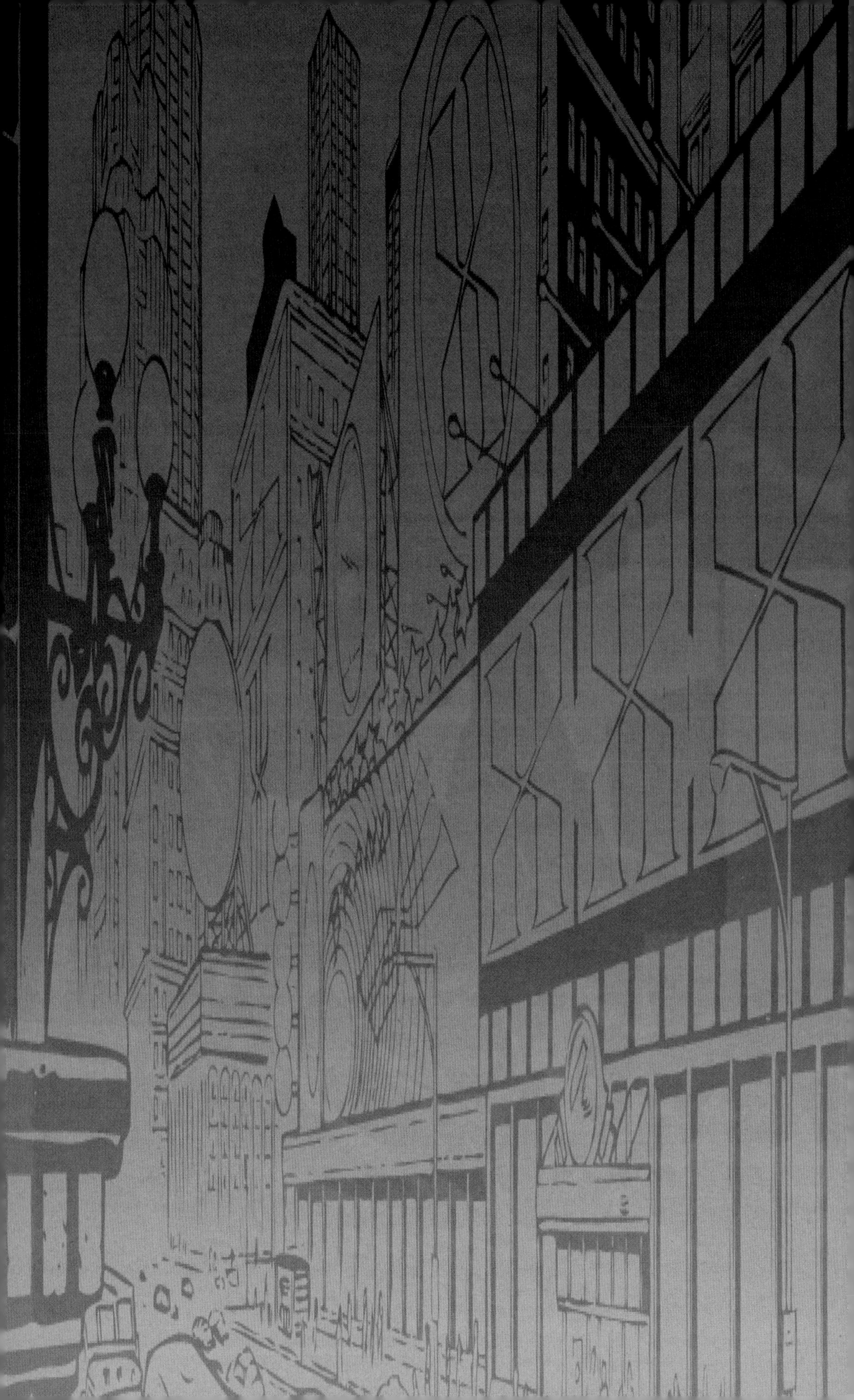

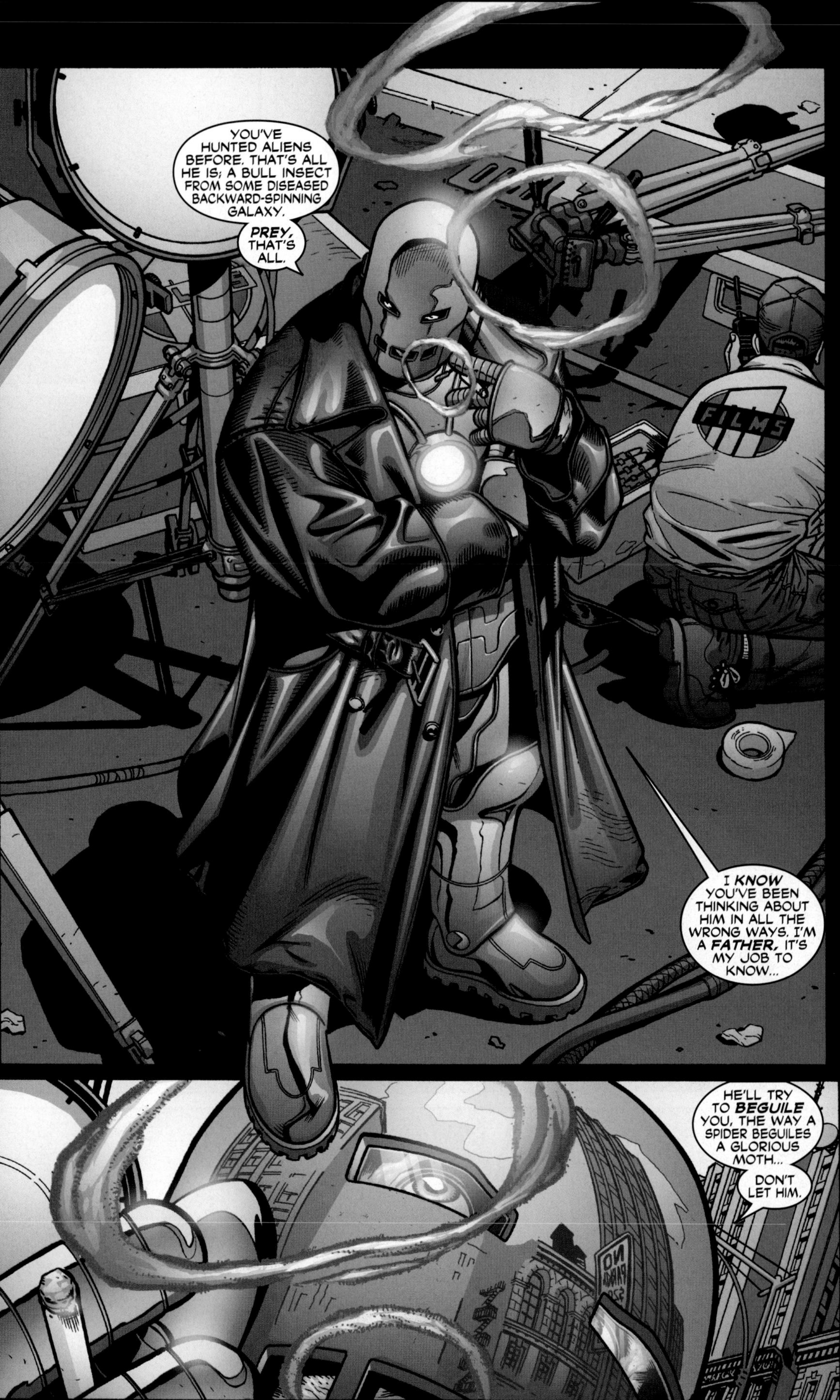
YOU'VE HUNTED ALIENS BEFORE. THAT'S ALL HE IS; A BULL INSECT FROM SOME DISEASED BACKWARD-SPINNING GALAXY.
PREY, THAT'S ALL.
FILMS
I KNOW YOU'VE BEEN THINKING ABOUT HIM IN ALL THE WRONG WAYS. I'M A FATHER, IT'S MY JOB TO KNOW...
HE'LL TRY TO BEGUILE YOU, THE WAY A SPIDER BEGUILES A GLORIOUS MOTH...
DON'T LET HIM.

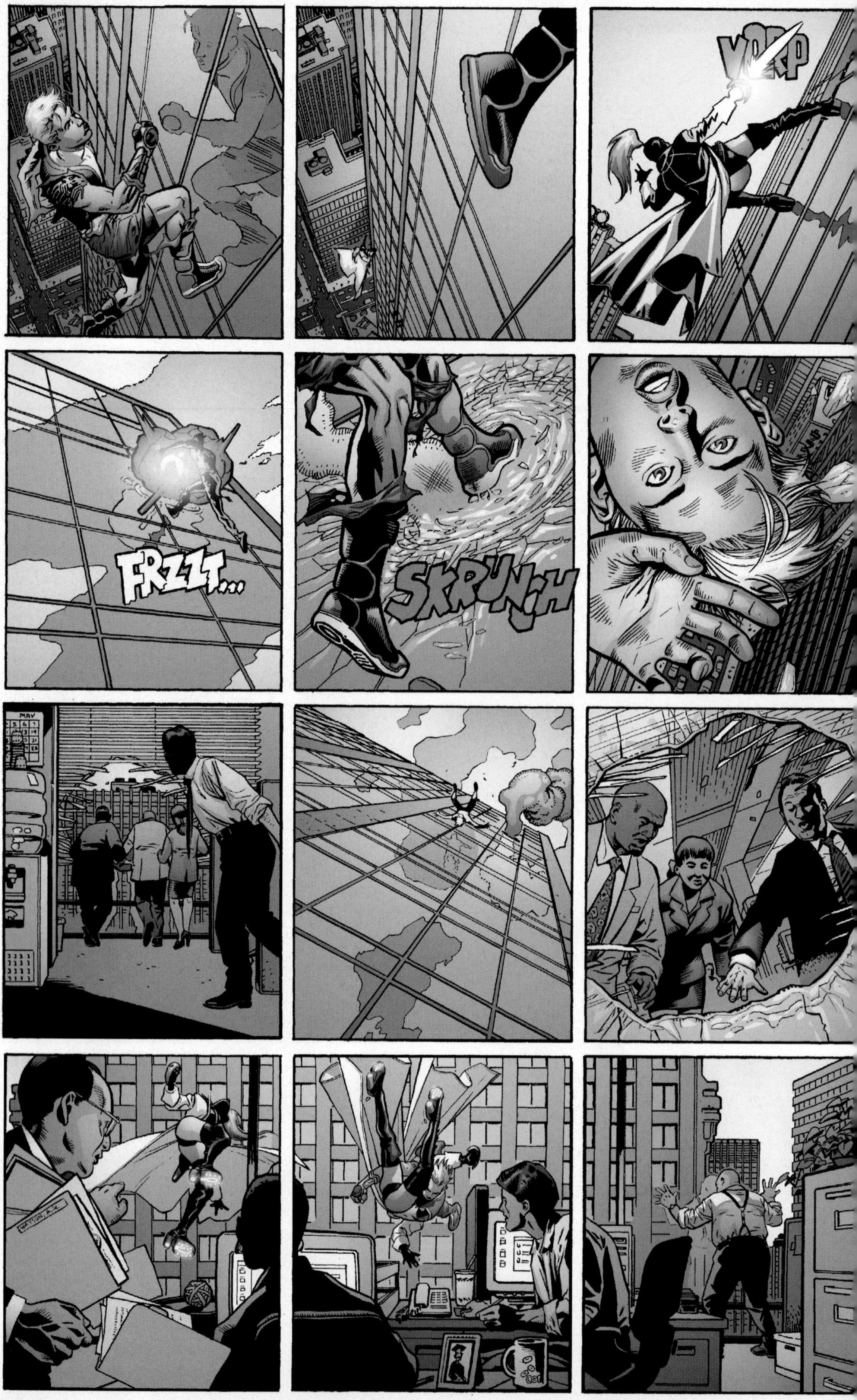

VORP
FRZZT...
SKRUNCH

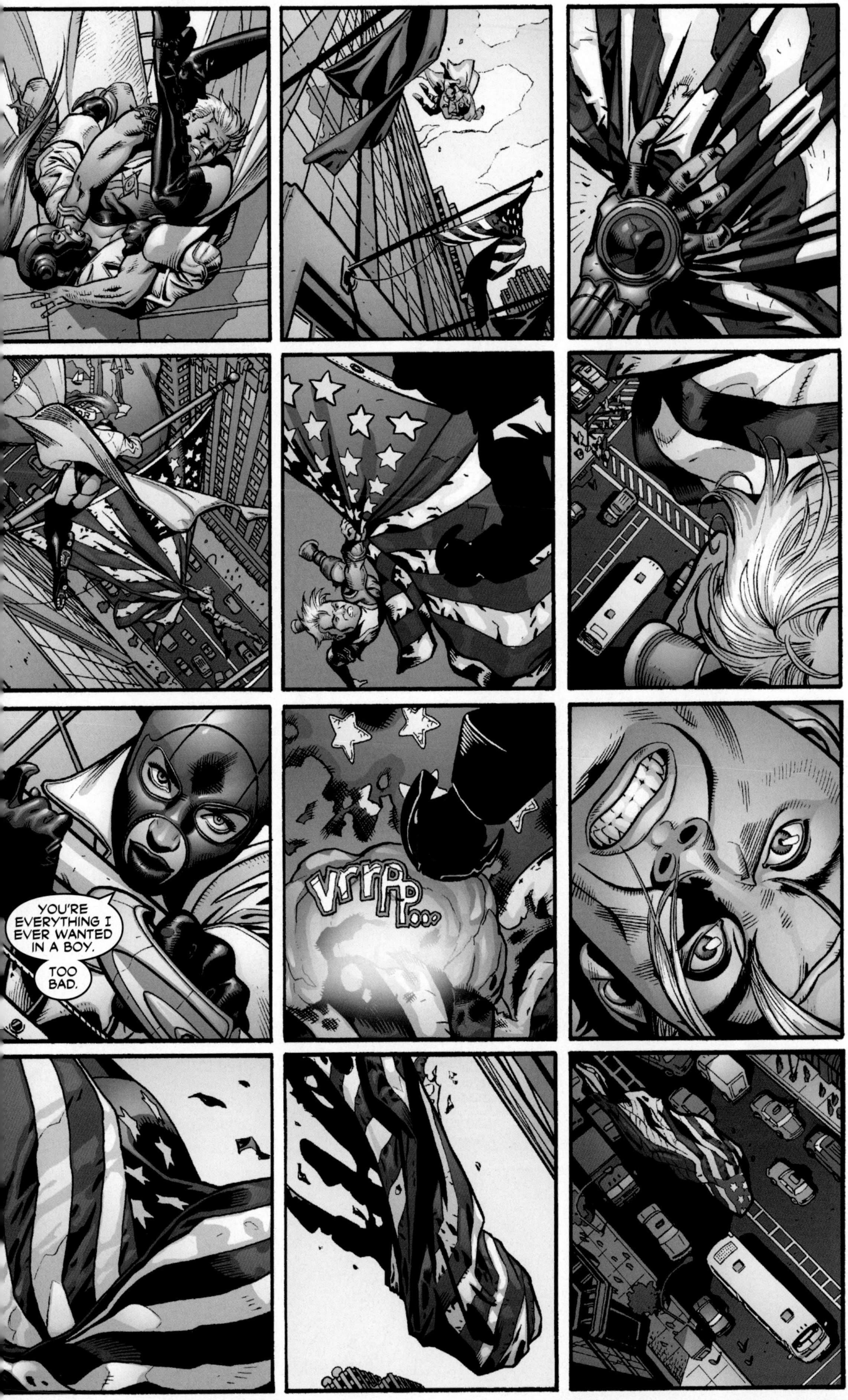
YOU'RE EVERYTHING I EVER WANTED IN A BOY.
TOO BAD.
VRRRP...

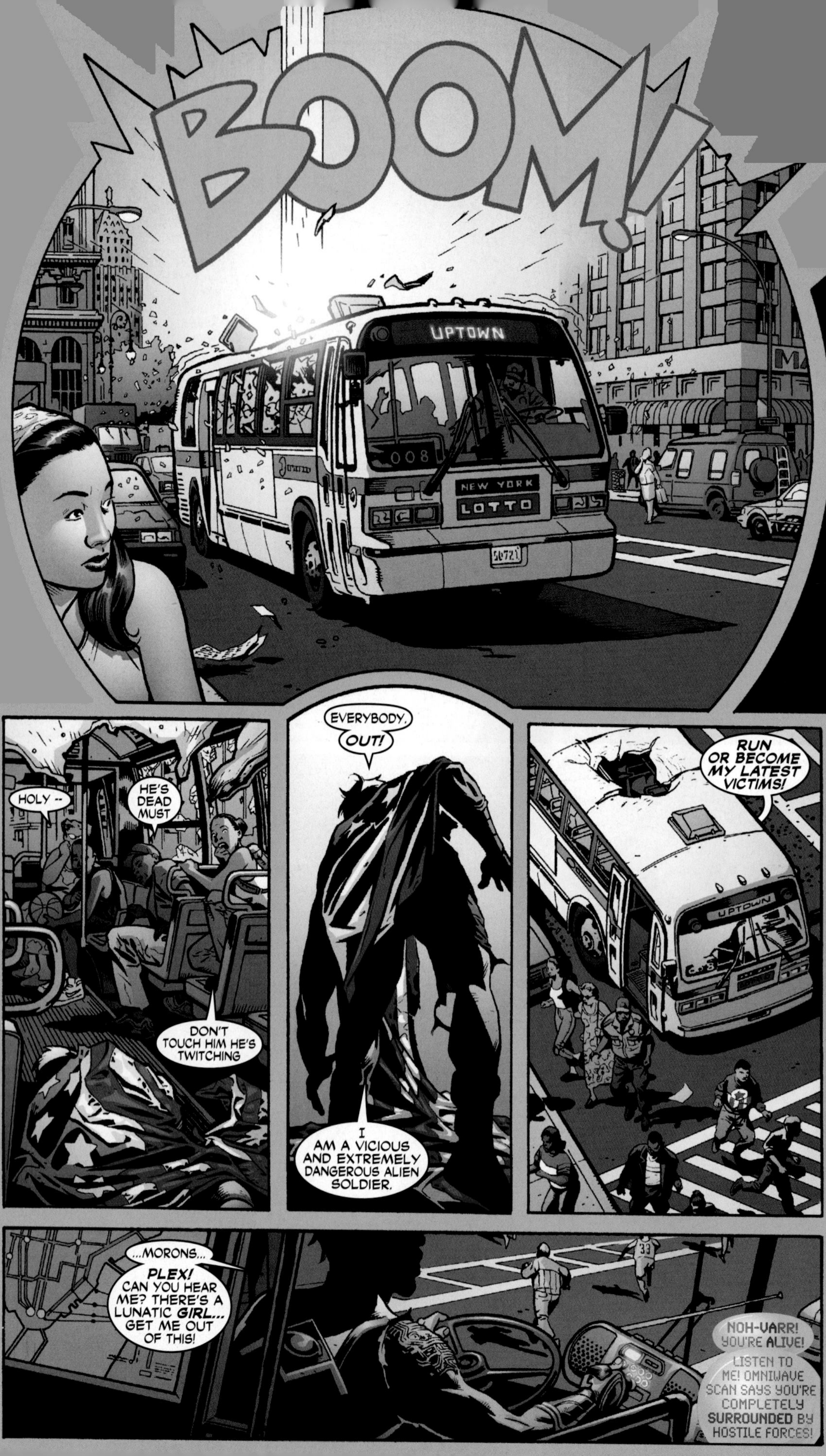
BOOM!
UPTOWN
NEW YORK LOTTO
HOLY --
HE'S DEAD MUST
DON'T TOUCH HIM HE'S TWITCHING
EVERYBODY. OUT!
I AM A VICIOUS AND EXTREMELY DANGEROUS ALIEN SOLDIER.
RUN OR BECOME MY LATEST VICTIMS!
UPTOWN
...MORONS...
PLEX! CAN YOU HEAR ME? THERE'S A LUNATIC GIRL... GET ME OUT OF THIS!
NOH-VARR! YOU'RE ALIVE!
LISTEN TO ME! OMNIWAVE SCAN SAYS YOU'RE COMPLETELY SURROUNDED BY HOSTILE FORCES!

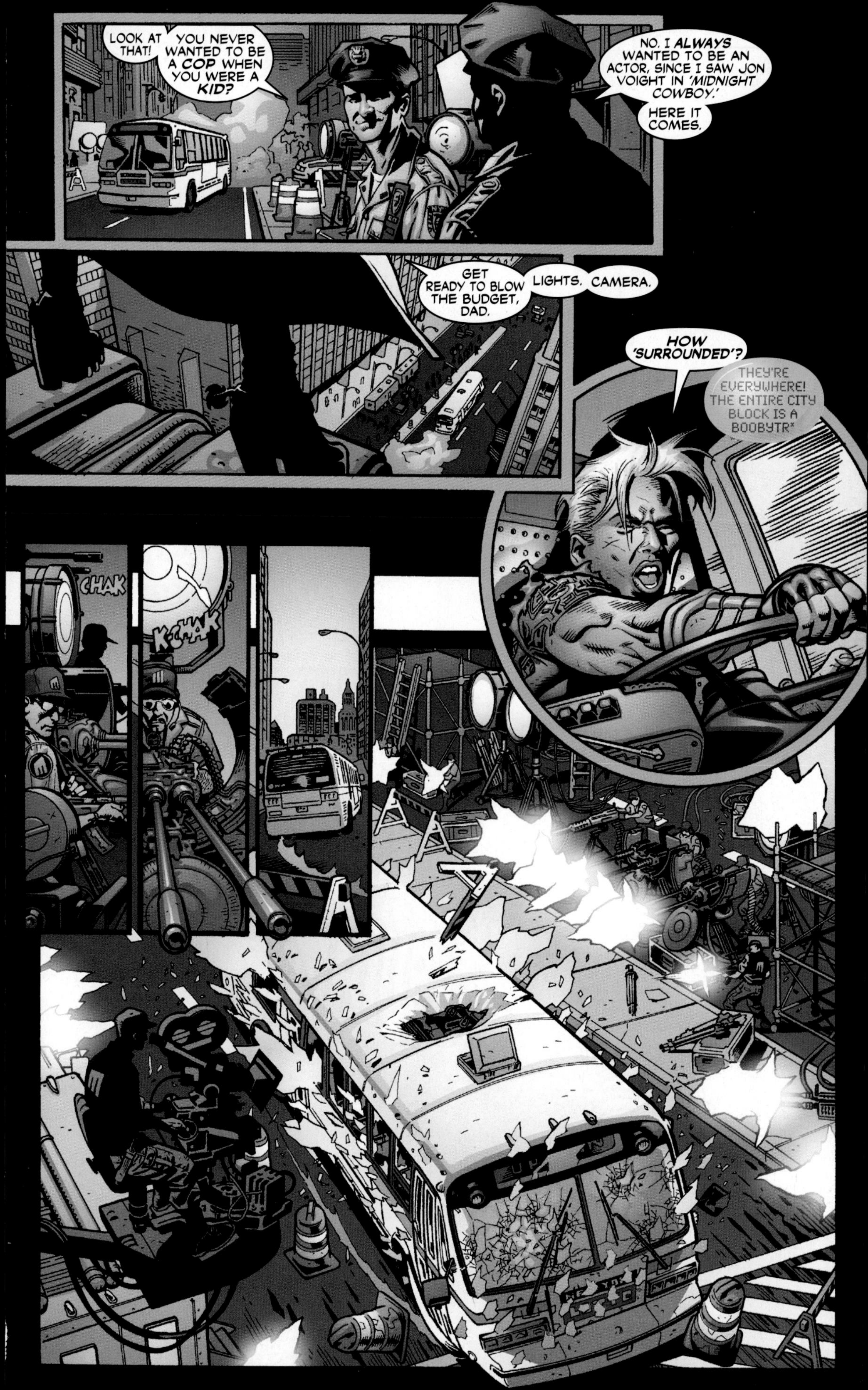
LOOK AT THAT!
YOU NEVER WANTED TO BE A COP WHEN YOU WERE A KID?
NO. I ALWAYS WANTED TO BE AN ACTOR, SINCE I SAW JON VOIGHT IN 'MIDNIGHT COWBOY.'
HERE IT COMES.
GET READY TO BLOW THE BUDGET, DAD.
LIGHTS.
CAMERA.
HOW 'SURROUNDED'?
THEY'RE EVERYWHERE! THE ENTIRE CITY BLOCK IS A BOOBYTR*
CHAK
K-CHAK

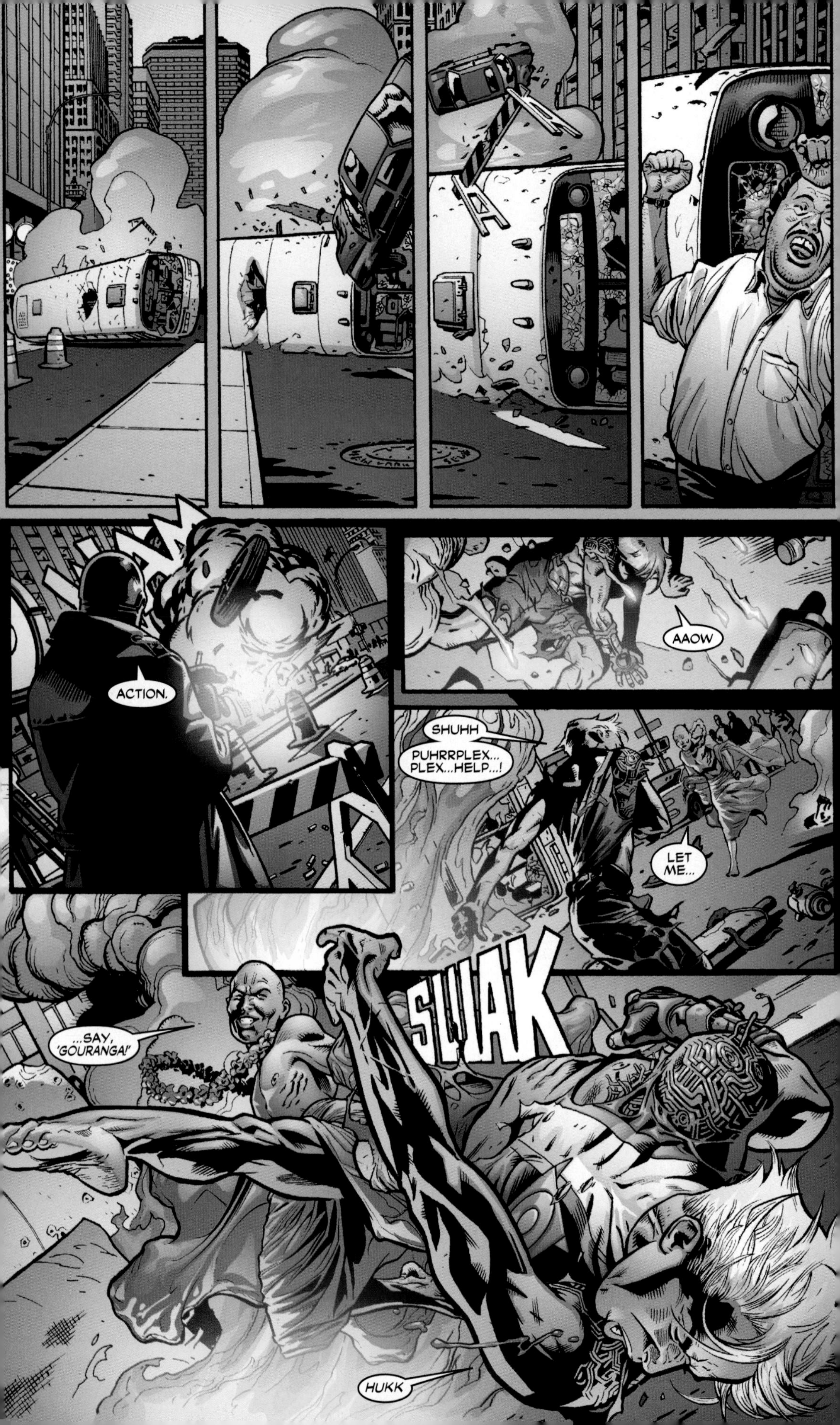
ACTION.
AAOW
SHUHH
PUHRRPLEX... PLEX...HELP...!
LET ME...
...SAY, 'GOURANGA!'
SWAK
HUKK

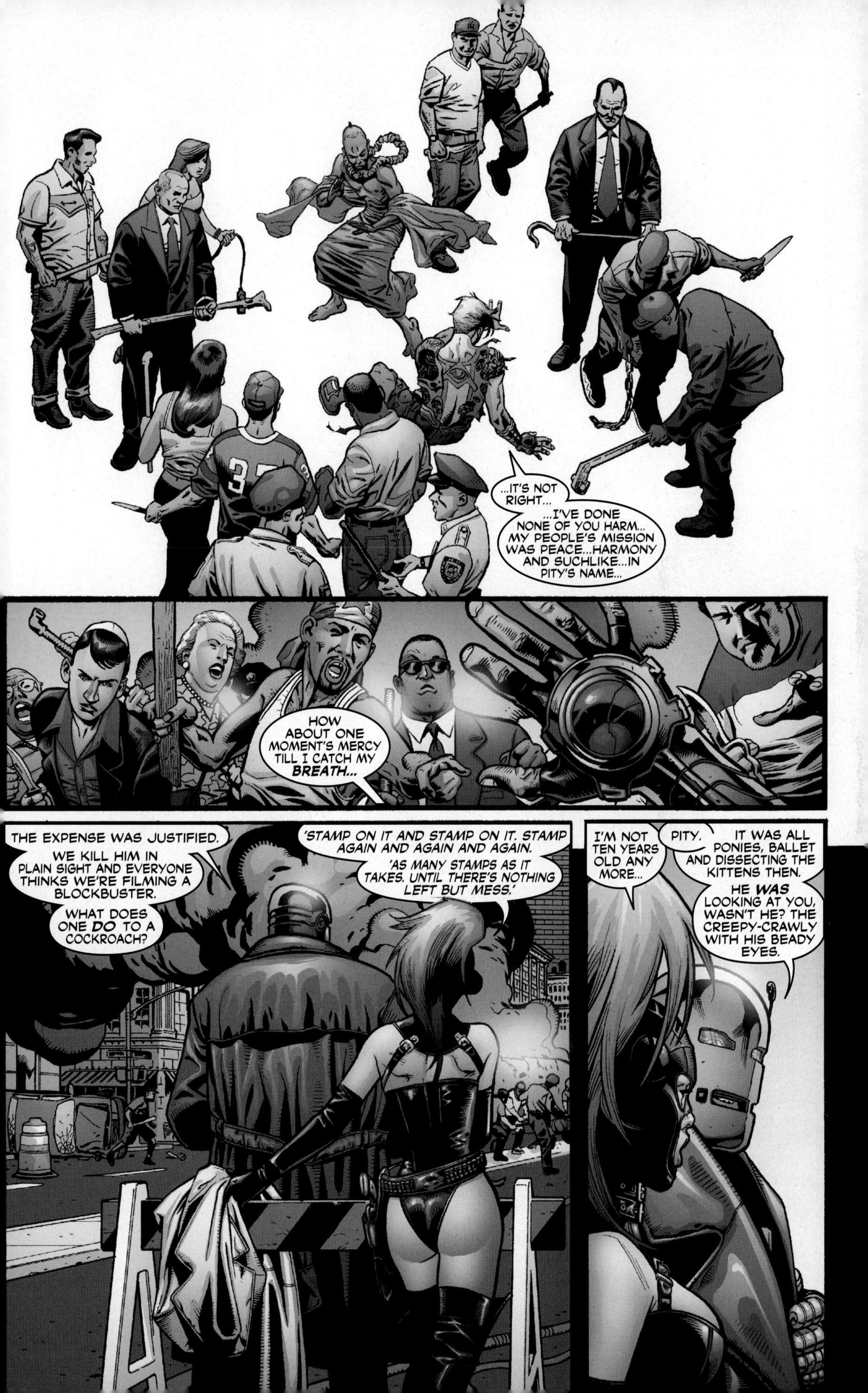
...IT'S NOT RIGHT...
...I'VE DONE NONE OF YOU HARM... MY PEOPLE'S MISSION WAS PEACE...HARMONY AND SUCHLIKE...IN PITY'S NAME...
HOW ABOUT ONE MOMENT'S MERCY TILL I CATCH MY BREATH...
THE EXPENSE WAS JUSTIFIED.
WE KILL HIM IN PLAIN SIGHT AND EVERYONE THINKS WE'RE FILMING A BLOCKBUSTER.
WHAT DOES ONE DO TO A COCKROACH?
'STAMP ON IT AND STAMP ON IT. STAMP AGAIN AND AGAIN AND AGAIN.
'AS MANY STAMPS AS IT TAKES. UNTIL THERE'S NOTHING LEFT BUT MESS.'
I'M NOT TEN YEARS OLD ANY MORE...
PITY.
IT WAS ALL PONIES, BALLET AND DISSECTING THE KITTENS THEN.
HE WAS LOOKING AT YOU, WASN'T HE? THE CREEPY-CRAWLY WITH HIS BEADY EYES.

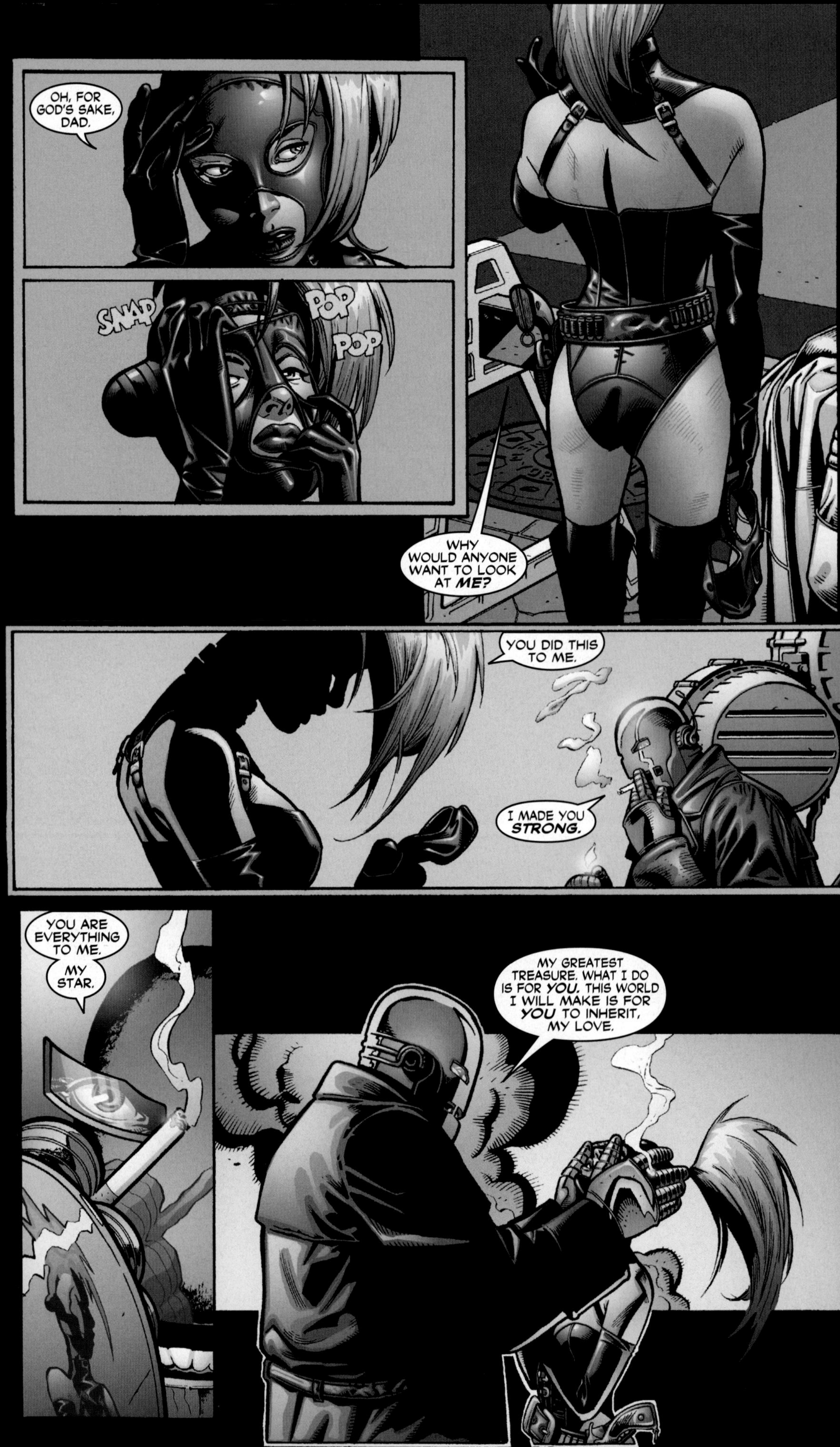
OH, FOR GOD'S SAKE, DAD.
SNAP
POP
POP
WHY WOULD ANYONE WANT TO LOOK AT *ME?*
YOU DID THIS TO ME.
I MADE YOU *STRONG.*
YOU ARE EVERYTHING TO ME.
MY STAR.
MY GREATEST TREASURE. WHAT I DO IS FOR *YOU.* THIS WORLD I WILL MAKE IS FOR *YOU* TO INHERIT, MY LOVE.

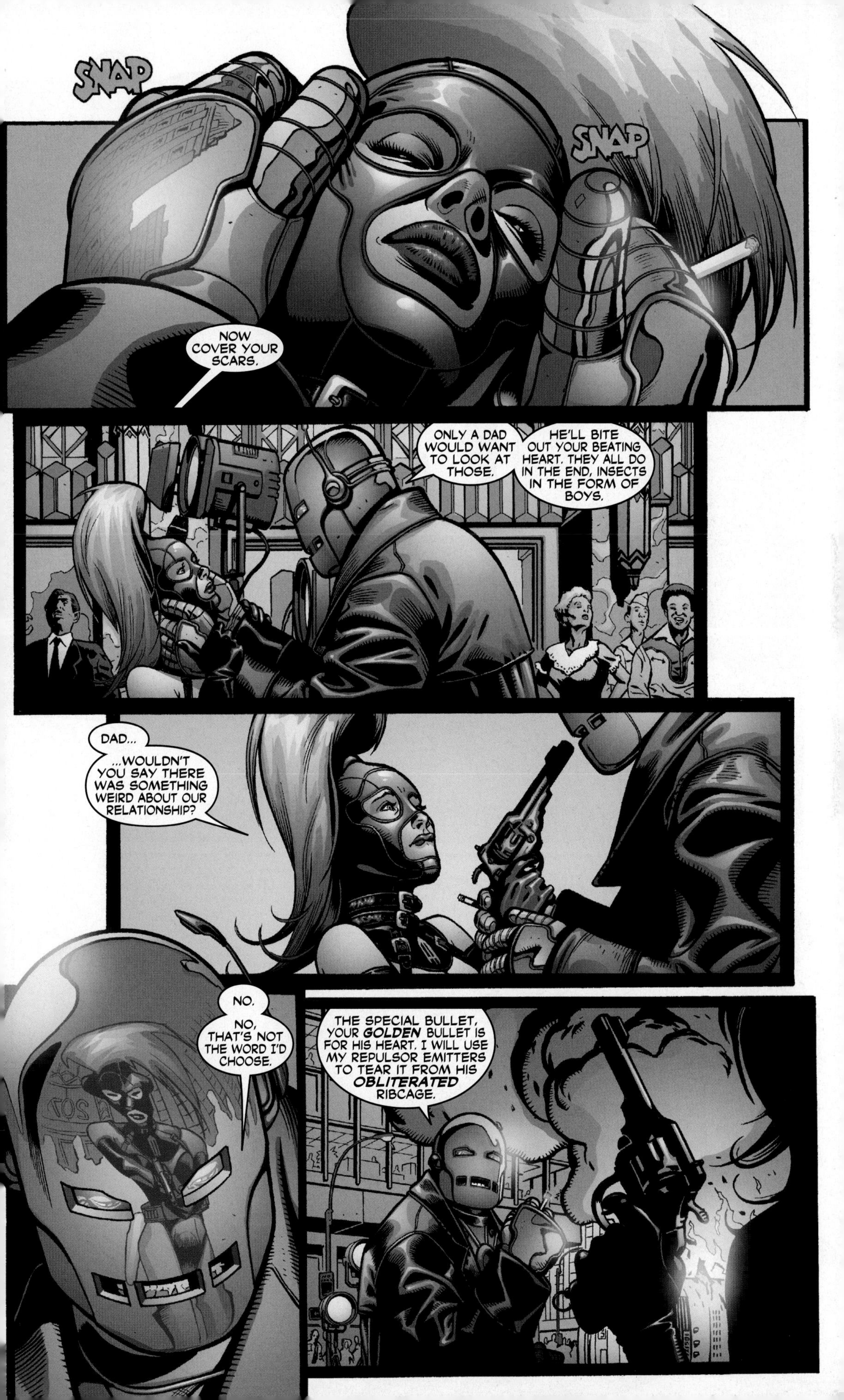
SNAP
SNAP
NOW COVER YOUR SCARS.
ONLY A DAD WOULD WANT TO LOOK AT THOSE.
HE'LL BITE OUT YOUR BEATING HEART. THEY ALL DO IN THE END, INSECTS IN THE FORM OF BOYS.
DAD...
...WOULDN'T YOU SAY THERE WAS SOMETHING WEIRD ABOUT OUR RELATIONSHIP?
NO.
NO, THAT'S NOT THE WORD I'D CHOOSE.
THE SPECIAL BULLET, YOUR GOLDEN BULLET IS FOR HIS HEART. I WILL USE MY REPULSOR EMITTERS TO TEAR IT FROM HIS OBLITERATED RIBCAGE.

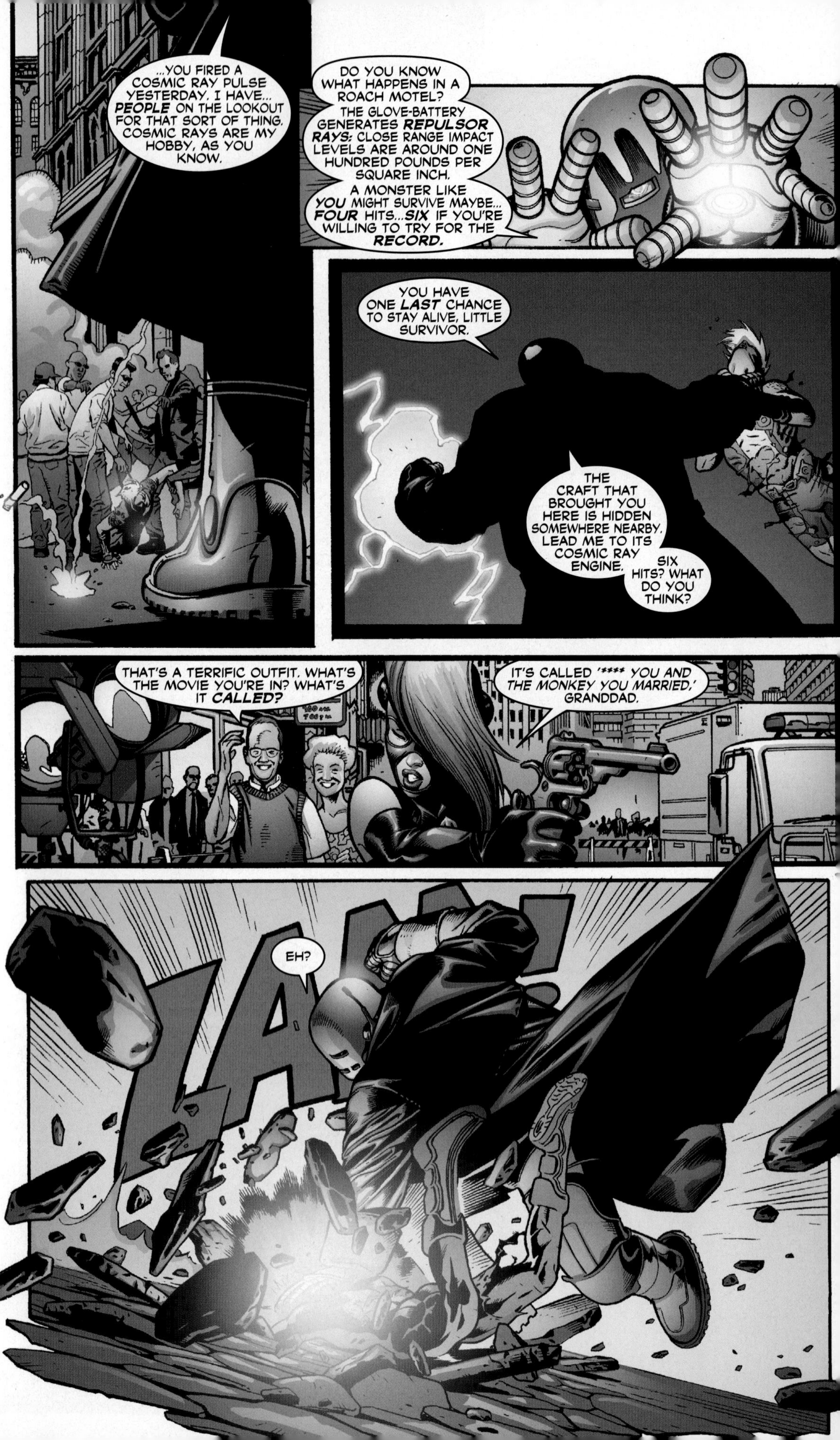

...YOU FIRED A COSMIC RAY PULSE YESTERDAY. I HAVE... PEOPLE ON THE LOOKOUT FOR THAT SORT OF THING. COSMIC RAYS ARE MY HOBBY, AS YOU KNOW.
DO YOU KNOW WHAT HAPPENS IN A ROACH MOTEL? THE GLOVE-BATTERY GENERATES REPULSOR RAYS: CLOSE RANGE IMPACT LEVELS ARE AROUND ONE HUNDRED POUNDS PER SQUARE INCH.
A MONSTER LIKE YOU MIGHT SURVIVE MAYBE... FOUR HITS...SIX IF YOU'RE WILLING TO TRY FOR THE RECORD.
YOU HAVE ONE LAST CHANCE TO STAY ALIVE, LITTLE SURVIVOR.
THE CRAFT THAT BROUGHT YOU HERE IS HIDDEN SOMEWHERE NEARBY. LEAD ME TO ITS COSMIC RAY ENGINE.
SIX HITS? WHAT DO YOU THINK?
THAT'S A TERRIFIC OUTFIT. WHAT'S THE MOVIE YOU'RE IN? WHAT'S IT CALLED?
IT'S CALLED '**** YOU AND THE MONKEY YOU MARRIED,' GRANDDAD.
EH?

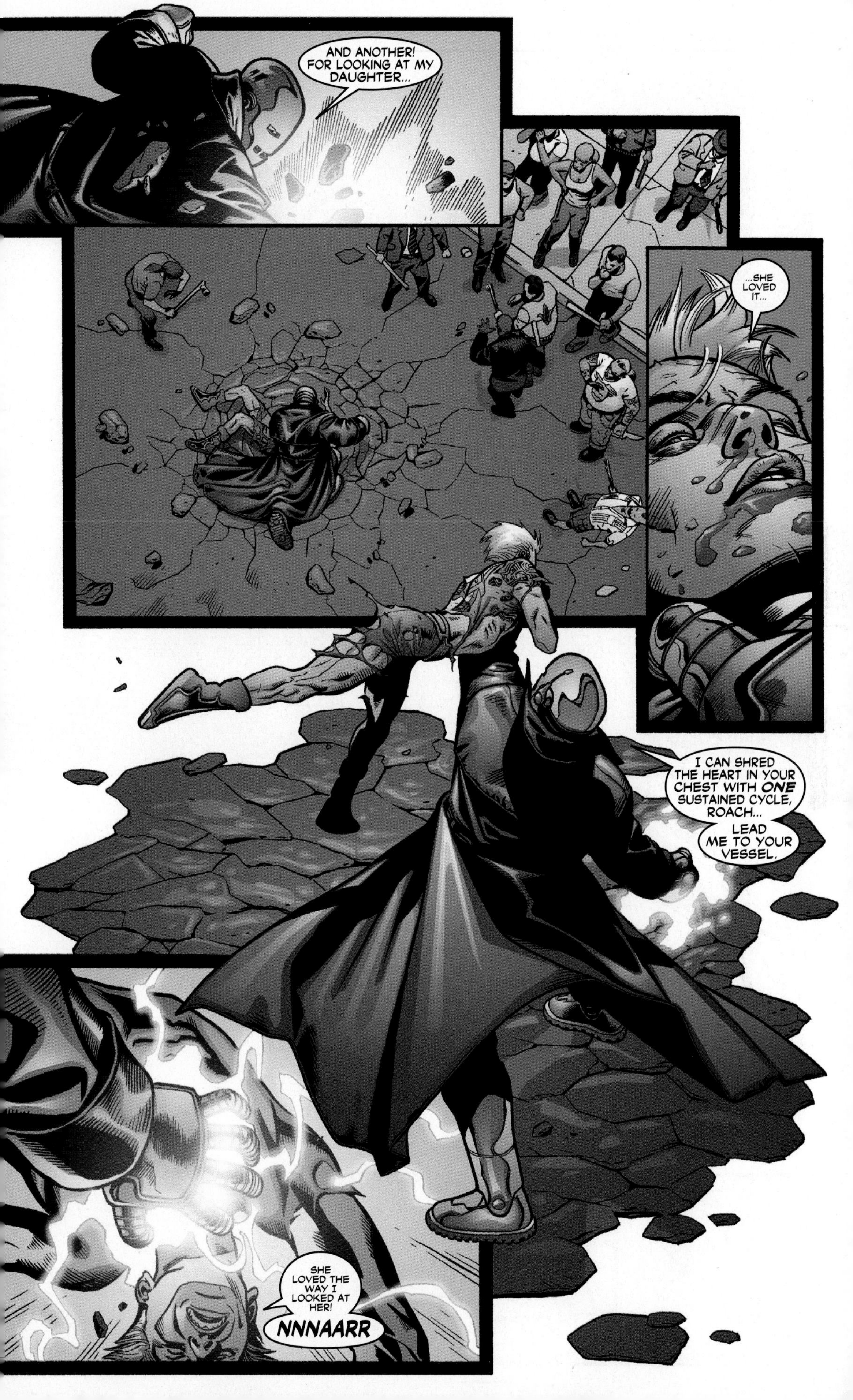
AND ANOTHER! FOR LOOKING AT MY DAUGHTER...
...SHE LOVED IT...
I CAN SHRED THE HEART IN YOUR CHEST WITH *ONE* SUSTAINED CYCLE, ROACH...
LEAD ME TO YOUR VESSEL.
SHE LOVED THE WAY I LOOKED AT HER!
NNNAARR

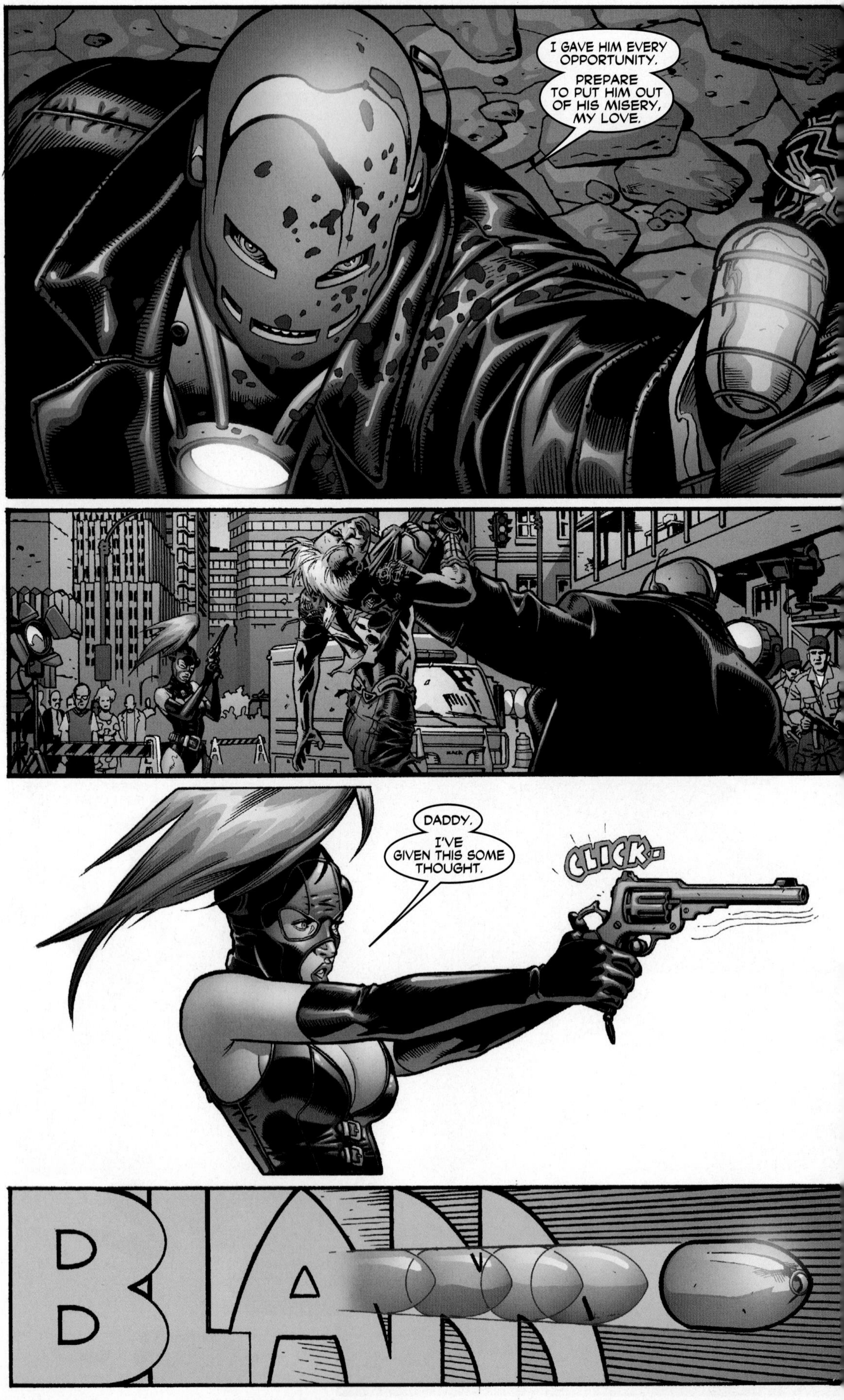
I GAVE HIM EVERY OPPORTUNITY.
PREPARE TO PUT HIM OUT OF HIS MISERY, MY LOVE.
DADDY.
I'VE GIVEN THIS SOME THOUGHT.
CLICK
BLAM

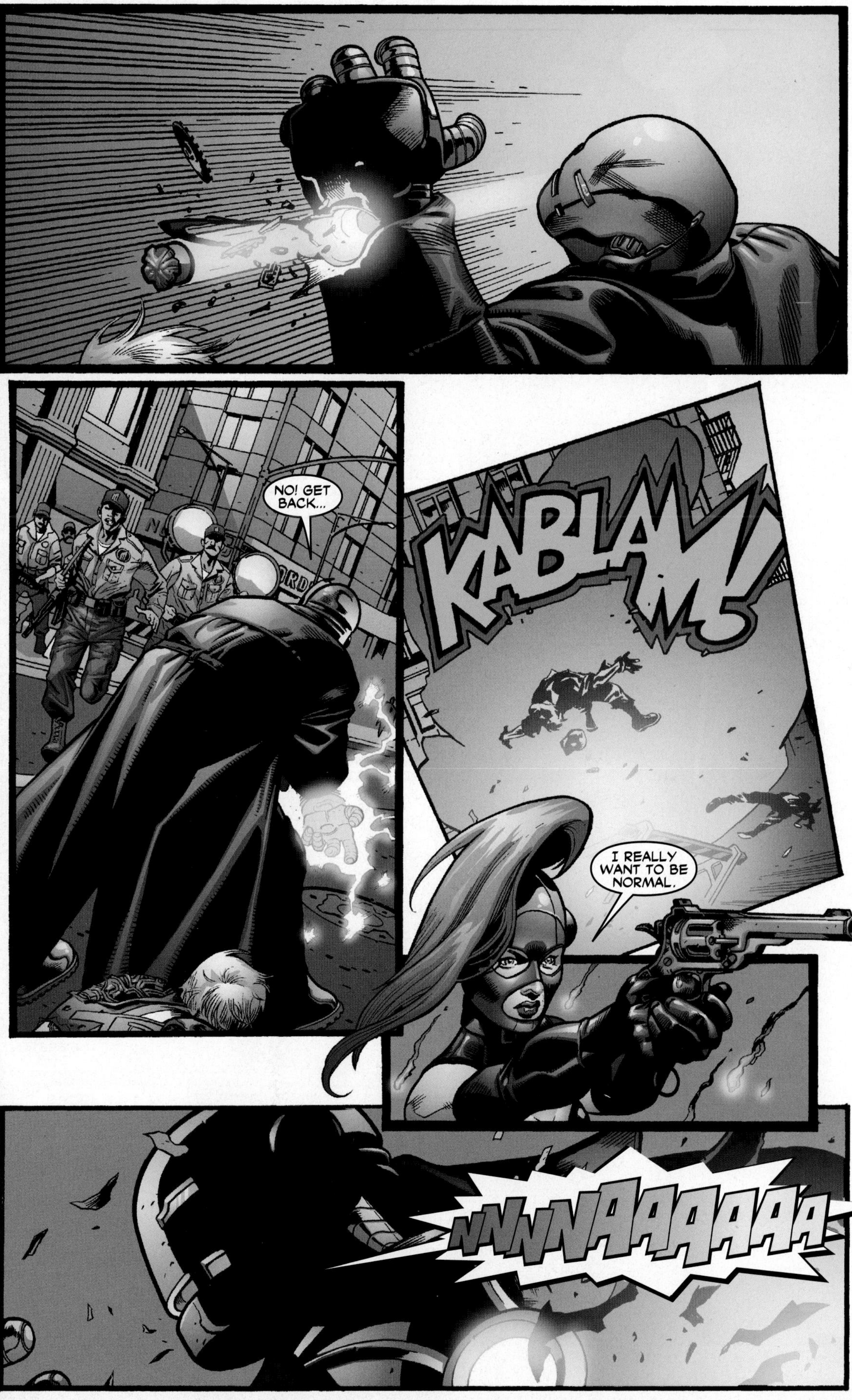
NO! GET BACK...
KABLAM!
I REALLY WANT TO BE NORMAL.
NNNNAAAAAAA

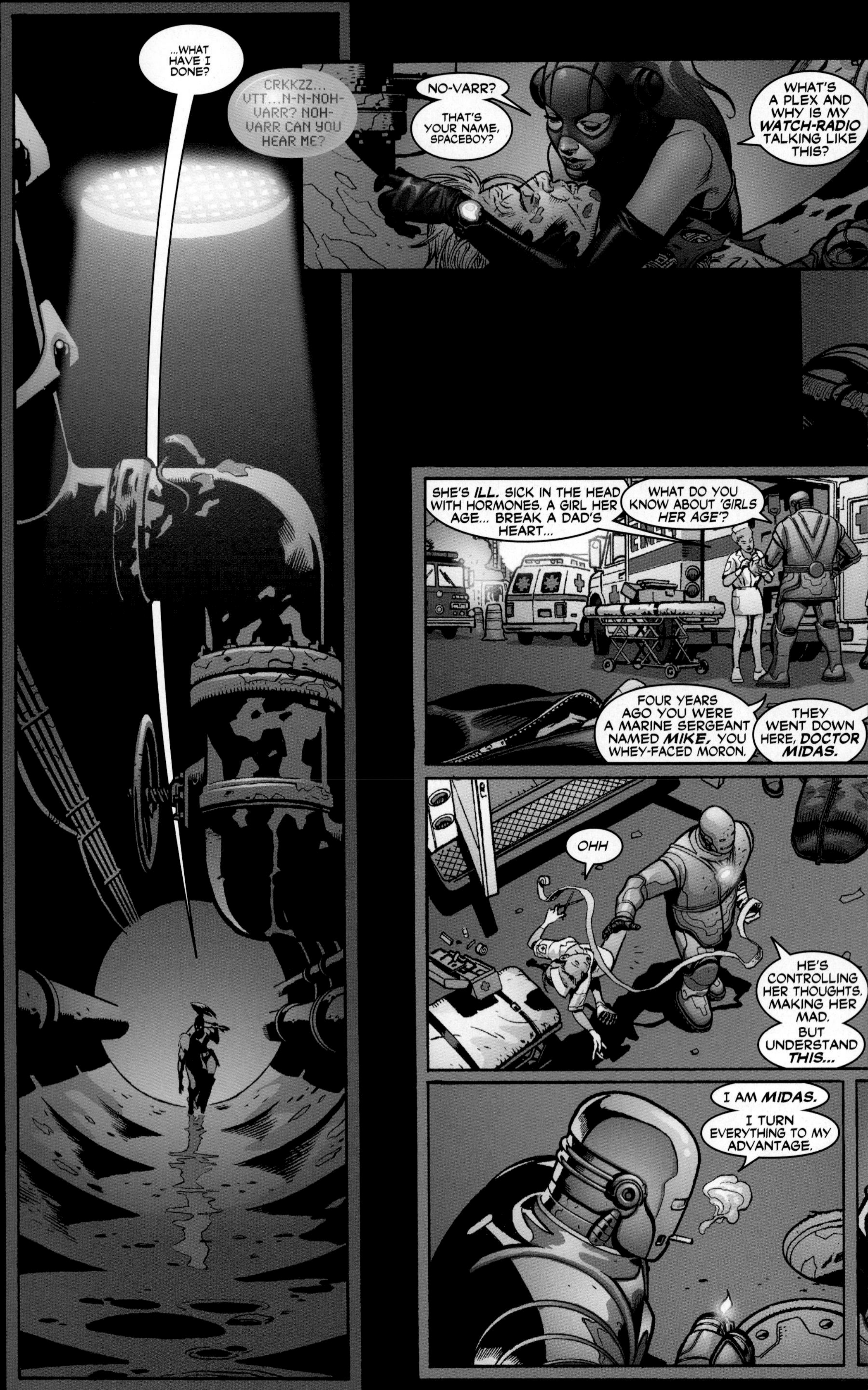
...WHAT HAVE I DONE?
CRKKZZ... VTT...N-N-NOH-VARR? NOH-VARR CAN YOU HEAR ME?
NO-VARR?
THAT'S YOUR NAME, SPACEBOY?
WHAT'S A PLEX AND WHY IS MY WATCH-RADIO TALKING LIKE THIS?
SHE'S ILL. SICK IN THE HEAD WITH HORMONES. A GIRL HER AGE... BREAK A DAD'S HEART...
WHAT DO YOU KNOW ABOUT 'GIRLS HER AGE'?
FOUR YEARS AGO YOU WERE A MARINE SERGEANT NAMED MIKE, YOU WHEY-FACED MORON.
THEY WENT DOWN HERE, DOCTOR MIDAS.
OHH
HE'S CONTROLLING HER THOUGHTS, MAKING HER MAD. BUT UNDERSTAND THIS...
I AM MIDAS.
I TURN EVERYTHING TO MY ADVANTAGE.

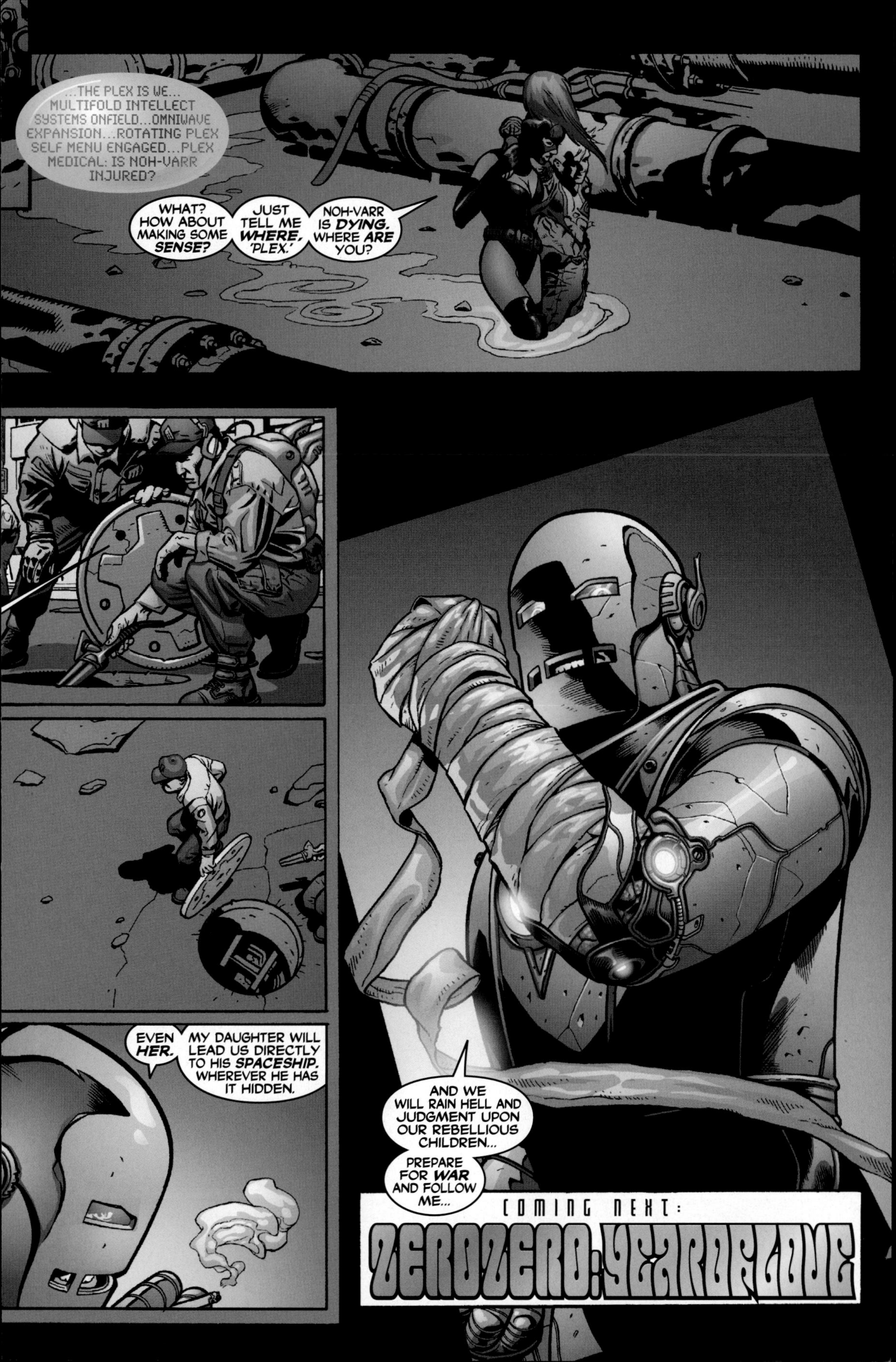
...THE PLEX IS WE... MULTIFOLD INTELLECT SYSTEMS ONFIELD...OMNIWAVE EXPANSION...ROTATING PLEX SELF MENU ENGAGED...PLEX MEDICAL: IS NOH-VARR INJURED?
WHAT? HOW ABOUT MAKING SOME SENSE?
JUST TELL ME WHERE, 'PLEX.'
NOH-VARR IS DYING. WHERE ARE YOU?
EVEN HER.
MY DAUGHTER WILL LEAD US DIRECTLY TO HIS SPACESHIP, WHEREVER HE HAS IT HIDDEN.
AND WE WILL RAIN HELL AND JUDGMENT UPON OUR REBELLIOUS CHILDREN...
PREPARE FOR WAR AND FOLLOW ME...
COMING NEXT:
ZEROZERO: YEAROFLOVE

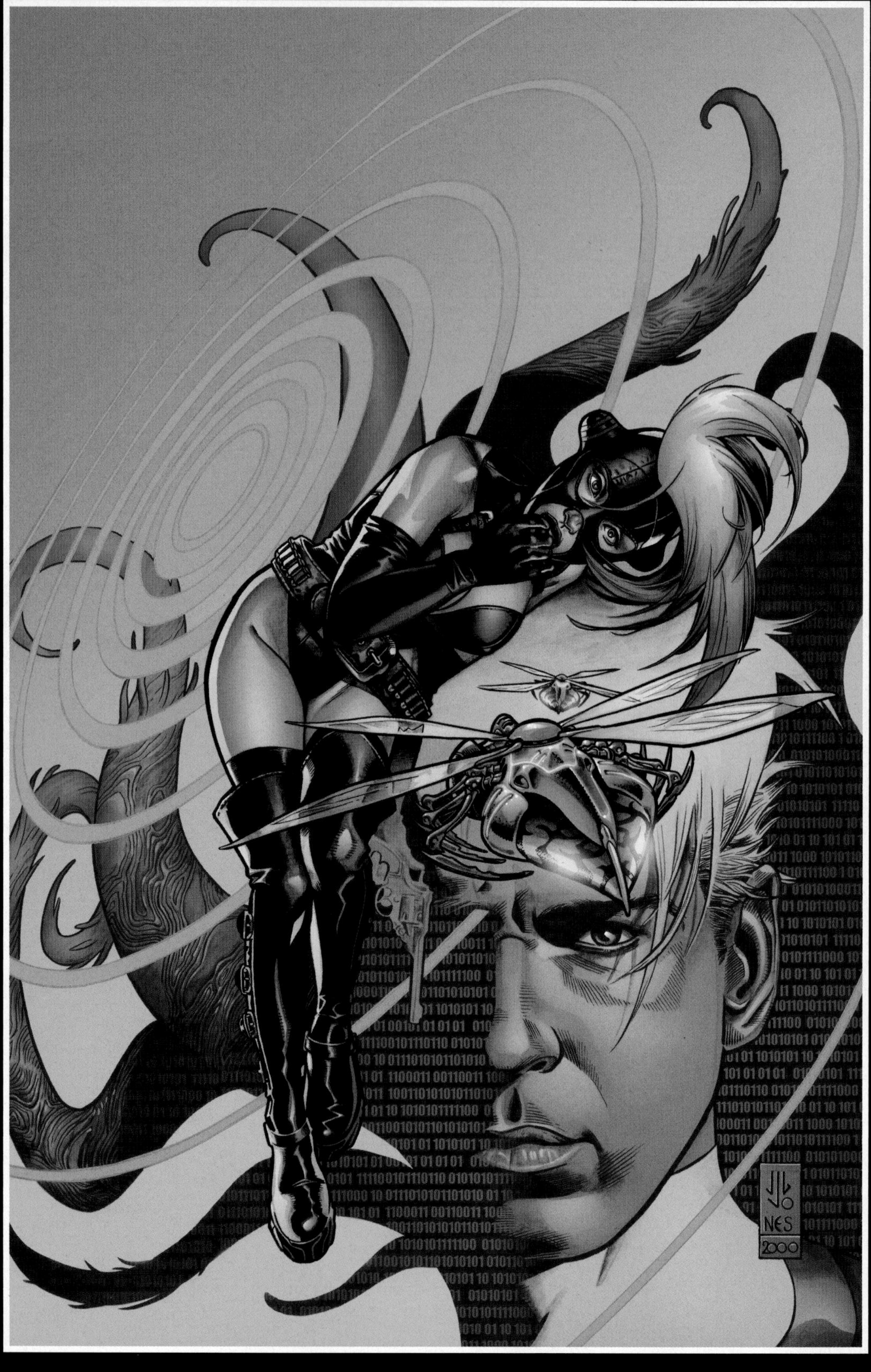

(5)

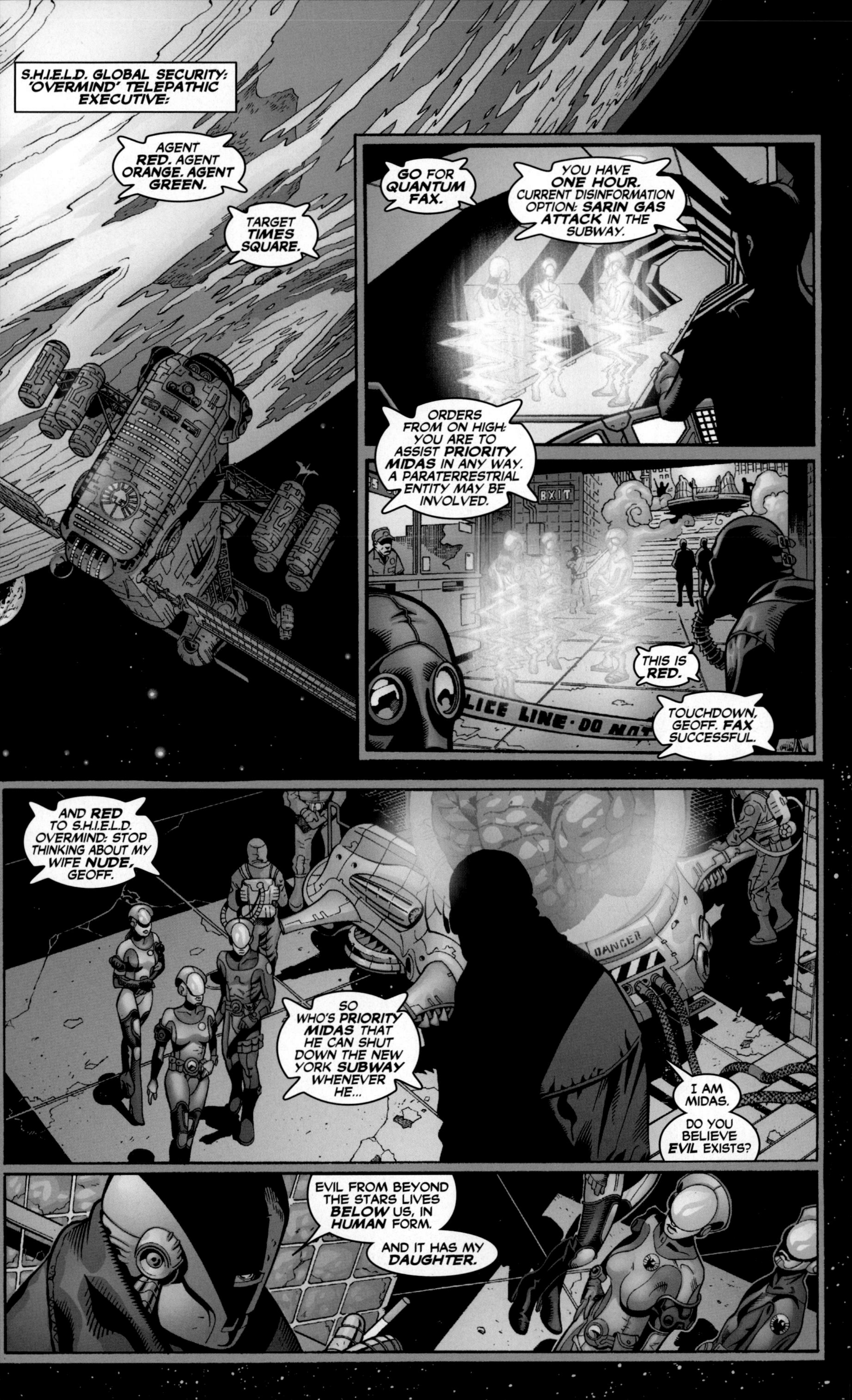
S.H.I.E.L.D. GLOBAL SECURITY: 'OVERMIND' TELEPATHIC EXECUTIVE:
AGENT RED. AGENT ORANGE. AGENT GREEN.
TARGET TIMES SQUARE.
GO FOR QUANTUM FAX.
YOU HAVE ONE HOUR. CURRENT DISINFORMATION OPTION: SARIN GAS ATTACK IN THE SUBWAY.
ORDERS FROM ON HIGH: YOU ARE TO ASSIST PRIORITY MIDAS IN ANY WAY. A PARATERRESTRIAL ENTITY MAY BE INVOLVED.
EXIT
THIS IS RED.
LICE LINE · DO NOT
TOUCHDOWN, GEOFF. FAX SUCCESSFUL.
AND RED TO S.H.I.E.L.D. OVERMIND: STOP THINKING ABOUT MY WIFE NUDE, GEOFF.
SO WHO'S PRIORITY MIDAS THAT HE CAN SHUT DOWN THE NEW YORK SUBWAY WHENEVER HE...
DANGER
I AM MIDAS.
DO YOU BELIEVE EVIL EXISTS?
EVIL FROM BEYOND THE STARS LIVES BELOW US, IN HUMAN FORM.
AND IT HAS MY DAUGHTER.

marvel boy

ZERO ZERO: YEAR OF LOVE

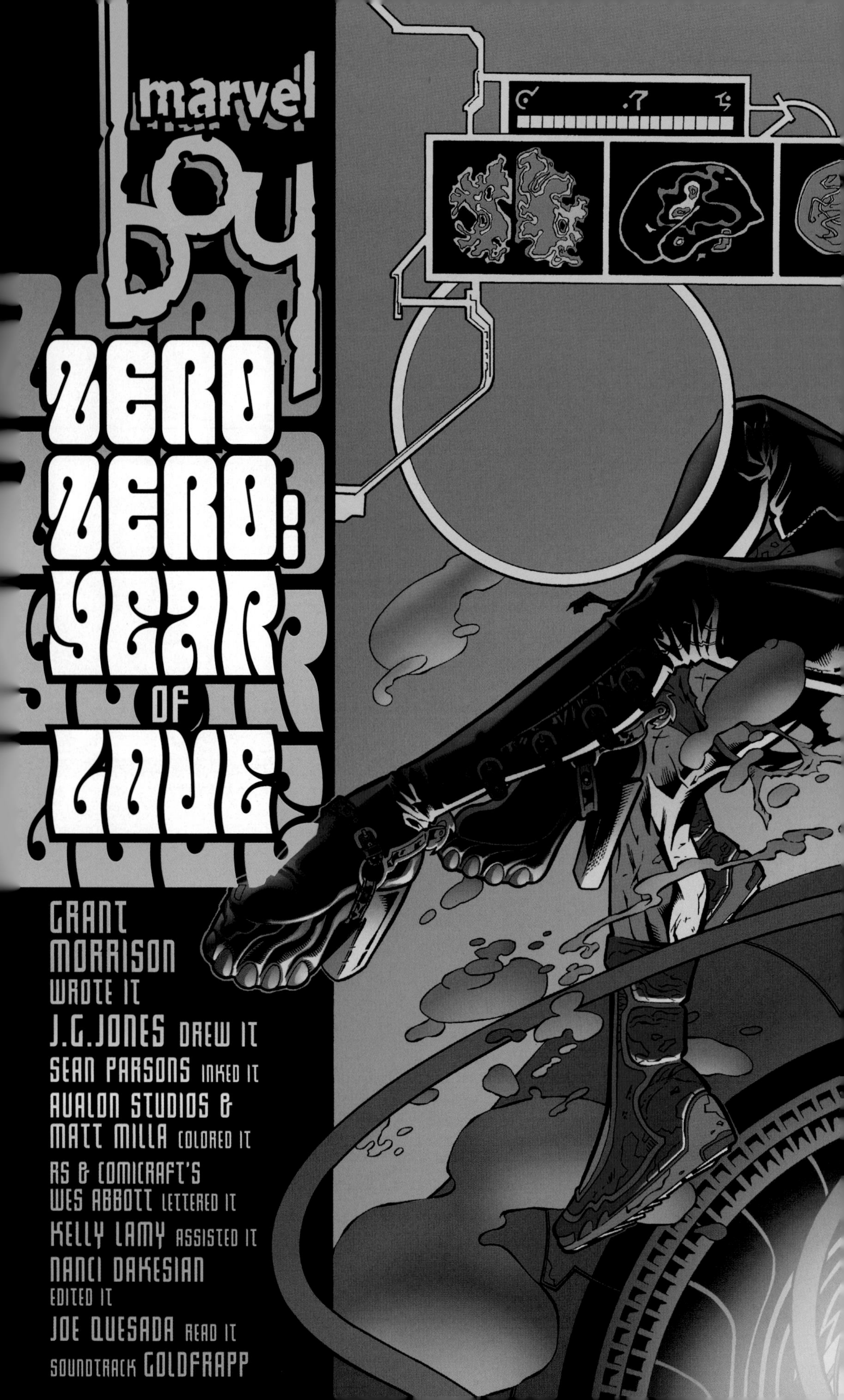

GRANT MORRISON WROTE IT
J.G.JONES DREW IT
SEAN PARSONS INKED IT
AVALON STUDIOS & MATT MILLA COLORED IT
RS & COMICRAFT'S WES ABBOTT LETTERED IT
KELLY LAMY ASSISTED IT
NANCI DAKESIAN EDITED IT
JOE QUESADA READ IT
SOUNDTRACK GOLDFRAPP

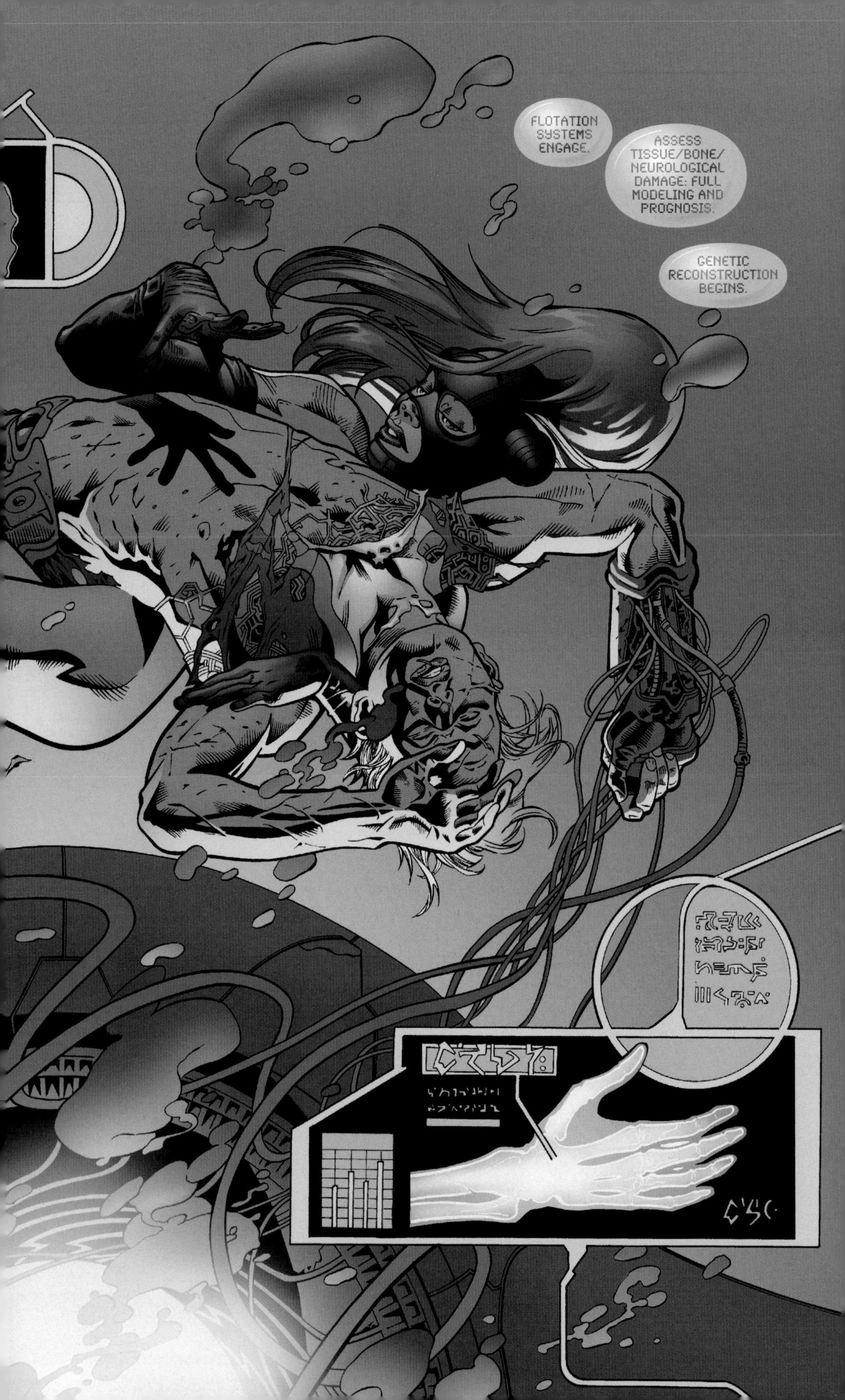
FLOTATION SYSTEMS ENGAGE.
ASSESS TISSUE/BONE/ NEUROLOGICAL DAMAGE: FULL MODELING AND PROGNOSIS.
GENETIC RECONSTRUCTION BEGINS.

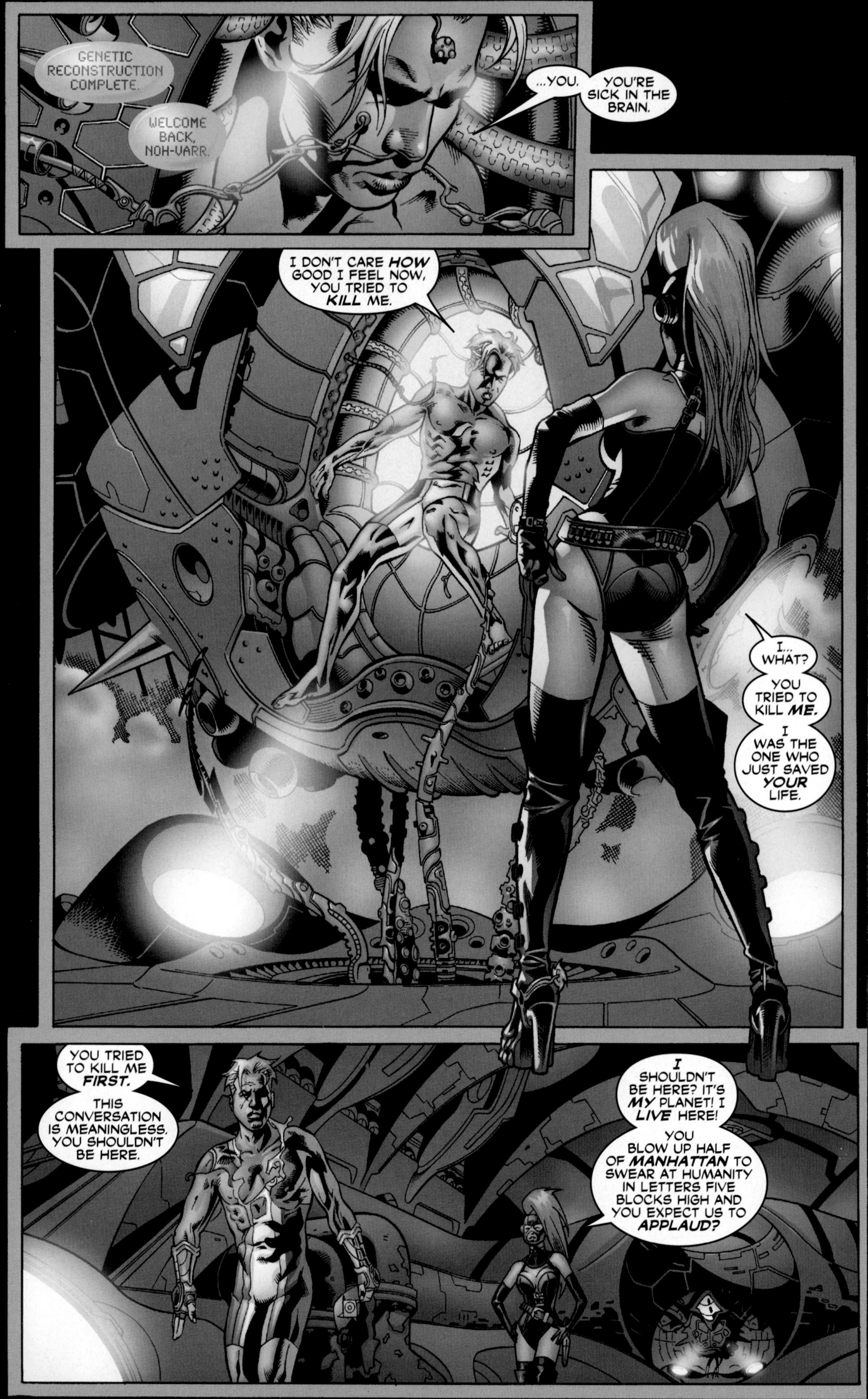
GENETIC RECONSTRUCTION COMPLETE.
WELCOME BACK, NOH-VARR.
...YOU.
YOU'RE SICK IN THE BRAIN.
I DON'T CARE HOW GOOD I FEEL NOW, YOU TRIED TO KILL ME.
I... WHAT?
YOU TRIED TO KILL ME.
I WAS THE ONE WHO JUST SAVED YOUR LIFE.
YOU TRIED TO KILL ME FIRST.
THIS CONVERSATION IS MEANINGLESS. YOU SHOULDN'T BE HERE.
I SHOULDN'T BE HERE? IT'S MY PLANET! I LIVE HERE!
YOU BLOW UP HALF OF MANHATTAN TO SWEAR AT HUMANITY IN LETTERS FIVE BLOCKS HIGH AND YOU EXPECT US TO APPLAUD?

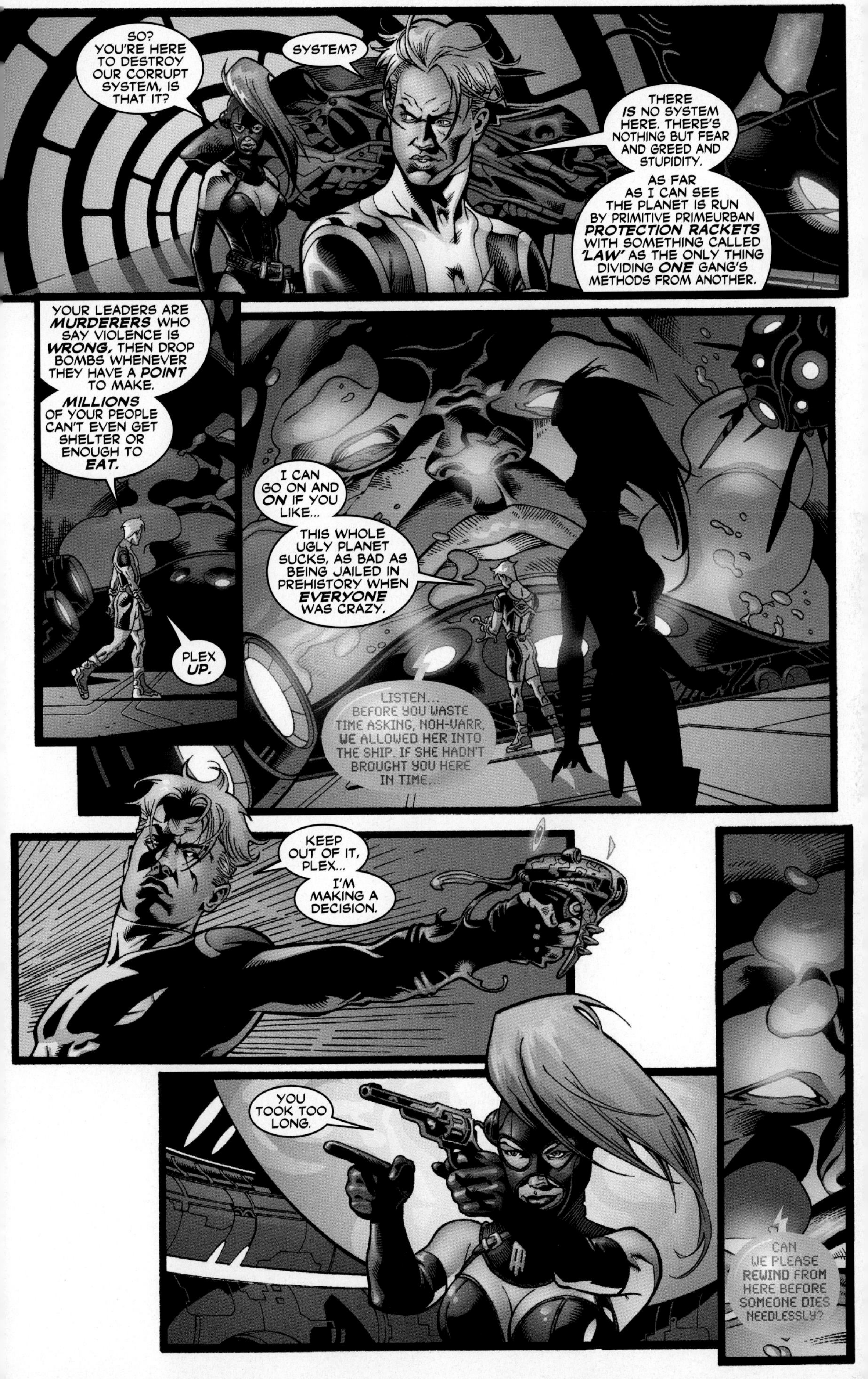
SO? YOU'RE HERE TO DESTROY OUR CORRUPT SYSTEM, IS THAT IT?
SYSTEM?
THERE IS NO SYSTEM HERE. THERE'S NOTHING BUT FEAR AND GREED AND STUPIDITY.
AS FAR AS I CAN SEE THE PLANET IS RUN BY PRIMITIVE PRIMEURBAN PROTECTION RACKETS WITH SOMETHING CALLED 'LAW' AS THE ONLY THING DIVIDING ONE GANG'S METHODS FROM ANOTHER.
YOUR LEADERS ARE MURDERERS WHO SAY VIOLENCE IS WRONG, THEN DROP BOMBS WHENEVER THEY HAVE A POINT TO MAKE.
MILLIONS OF YOUR PEOPLE CAN'T EVEN GET SHELTER OR ENOUGH TO EAT.
PLEX UP.
I CAN GO ON AND ON IF YOU LIKE...
THIS WHOLE UGLY PLANET SUCKS, AS BAD AS BEING JAILED IN PREHISTORY WHEN EVERYONE WAS CRAZY.
LISTEN... BEFORE YOU WASTE TIME ASKING, NOH-VARR, WE ALLOWED HER INTO THE SHIP. IF SHE HADN'T BROUGHT YOU HERE IN TIME...
KEEP OUT OF IT, PLEX...
I'M MAKING A DECISION.
YOU TOOK TOO LONG.
CAN WE PLEASE REWIND FROM HERE BEFORE SOMEONE DIES NEEDLESSLY?

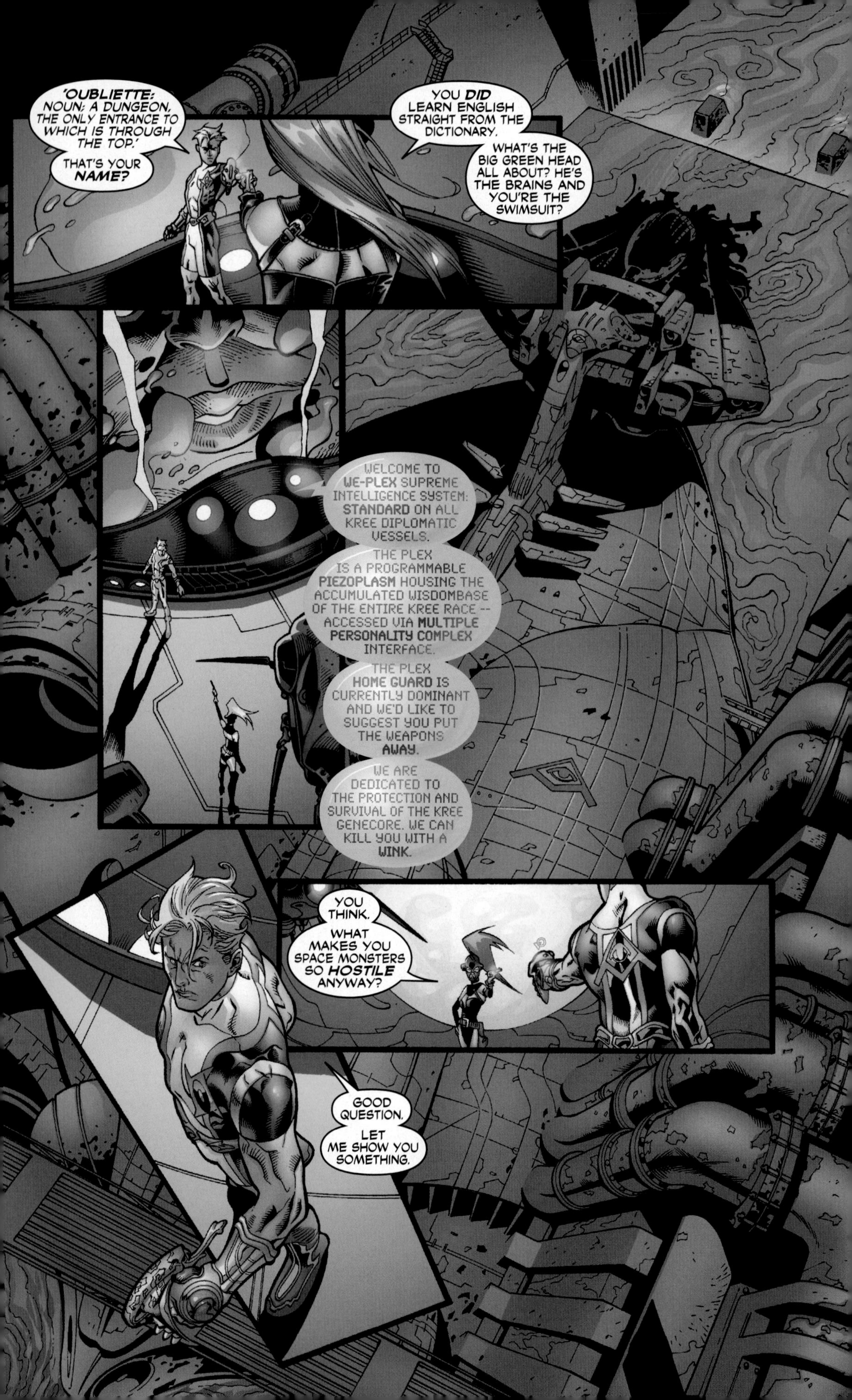
'OUBLIETTE: NOUN; A DUNGEON, THE ONLY ENTRANCE TO WHICH IS THROUGH THE TOP.'
THAT'S YOUR NAME?
YOU DID LEARN ENGLISH STRAIGHT FROM THE DICTIONARY.
WHAT'S THE BIG GREEN HEAD ALL ABOUT? HE'S THE BRAINS AND YOU'RE THE SWIMSUIT?
WELCOME TO WE-PLEX SUPREME INTELLIGENCE SYSTEM: STANDARD ON ALL KREE DIPLOMATIC VESSELS.
THE PLEX IS A PROGRAMMABLE PIEZOPLASM HOUSING THE ACCUMULATED WISDOMBASE OF THE ENTIRE KREE RACE -- ACCESSED VIA MULTIPLE PERSONALITY COMPLEX INTERFACE.
THE PLEX HOME GUARD IS CURRENTLY DOMINANT AND WE'D LIKE TO SUGGEST YOU PUT THE WEAPONS AWAY.
WE ARE DEDICATED TO THE PROTECTION AND SURVIVAL OF THE KREE GENECORE. WE CAN KILL YOU WITH A WINK.
YOU THINK.
WHAT MAKES YOU SPACE MONSTERS SO HOSTILE ANYWAY?
GOOD QUESTION.
LET ME SHOW YOU SOMETHING.

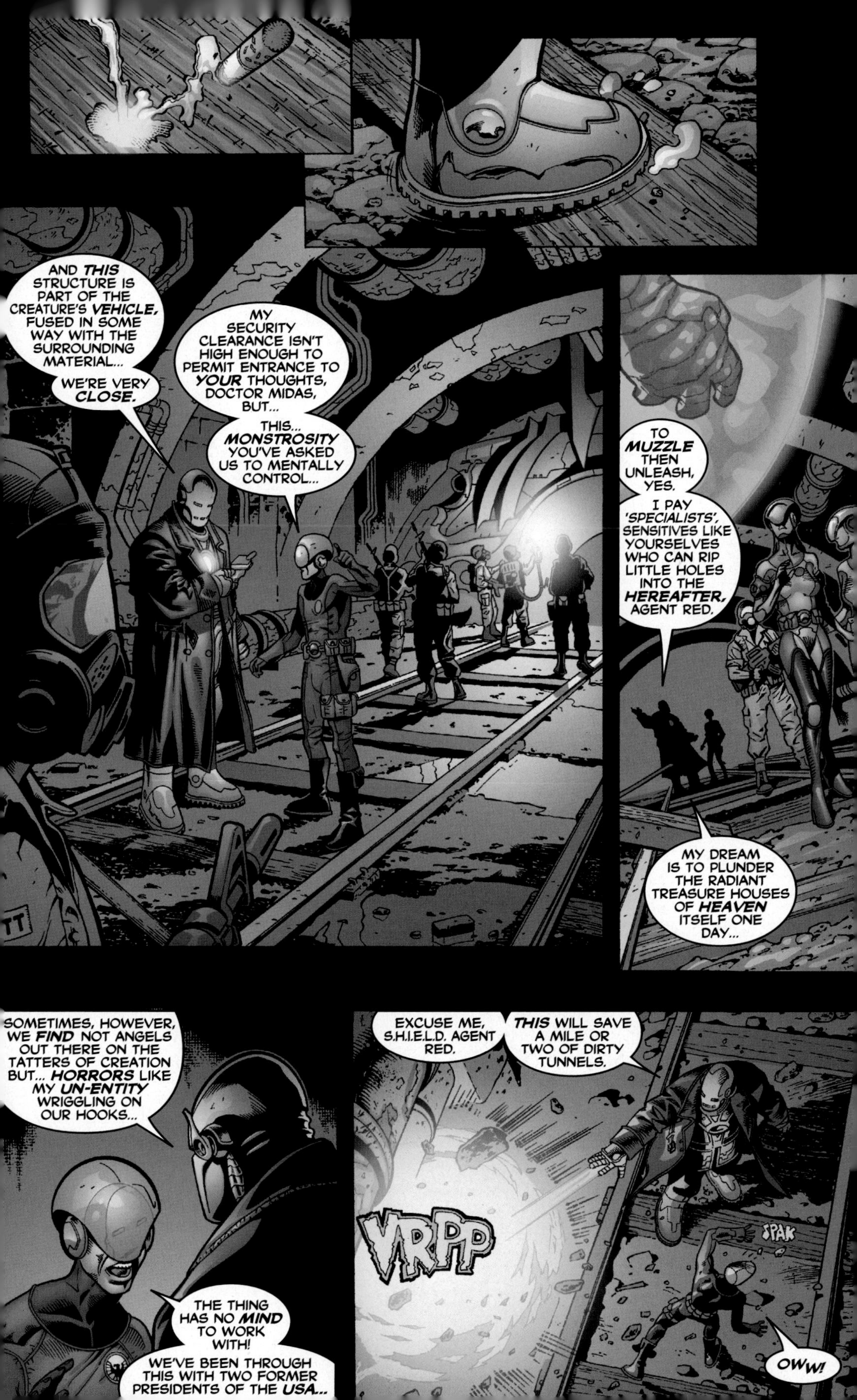
AND THIS STRUCTURE IS PART OF THE CREATURE'S VEHICLE, FUSED IN SOME WAY WITH THE SURROUNDING MATERIAL...
WE'RE VERY CLOSE.
MY SECURITY CLEARANCE ISN'T HIGH ENOUGH TO PERMIT ENTRANCE TO YOUR THOUGHTS, DOCTOR MIDAS, BUT...
THIS... MONSTROSITY YOU'VE ASKED US TO MENTALLY CONTROL...
TO MUZZLE THEN UNLEASH, YES.
I PAY 'SPECIALISTS', SENSITIVES LIKE YOURSELVES WHO CAN RIP LITTLE HOLES INTO THE HEREAFTER, AGENT RED.
MY DREAM IS TO PLUNDER THE RADIANT TREASURE HOUSES OF HEAVEN ITSELF ONE DAY...
SOMETIMES, HOWEVER, WE FIND NOT ANGELS OUT THERE ON THE TATTERS OF CREATION BUT... HORRORS LIKE MY UN-ENTITY WRIGGLING ON OUR HOOKS...
THE THING HAS NO MIND TO WORK WITH!
WE'VE BEEN THROUGH THIS WITH TWO FORMER PRESIDENTS OF THE USA...
EXCUSE ME, S.H.I.E.L.D. AGENT RED.
THIS WILL SAVE A MILE OR TWO OF DIRTY TUNNELS.
VRPP
SPAK
OWW!

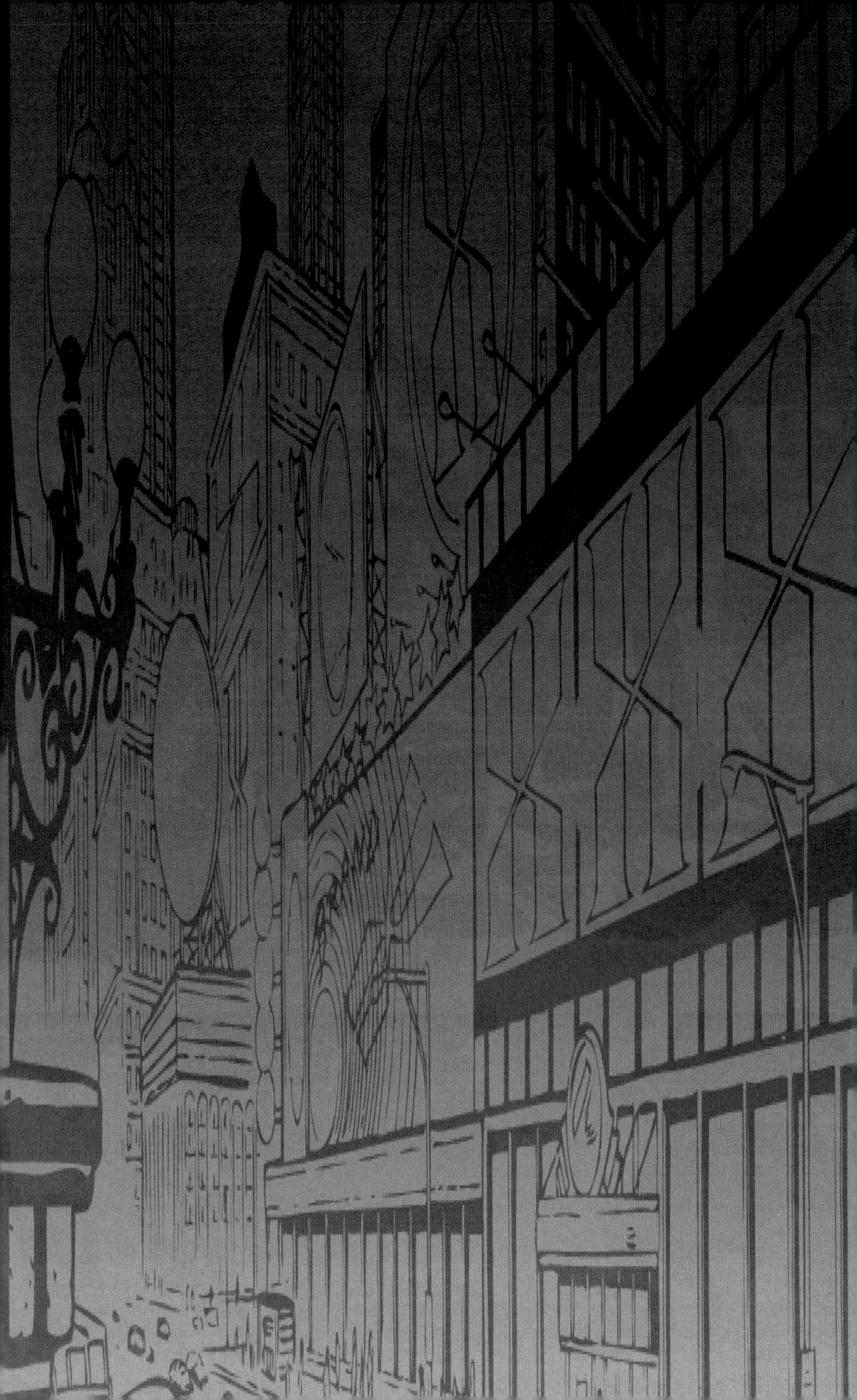

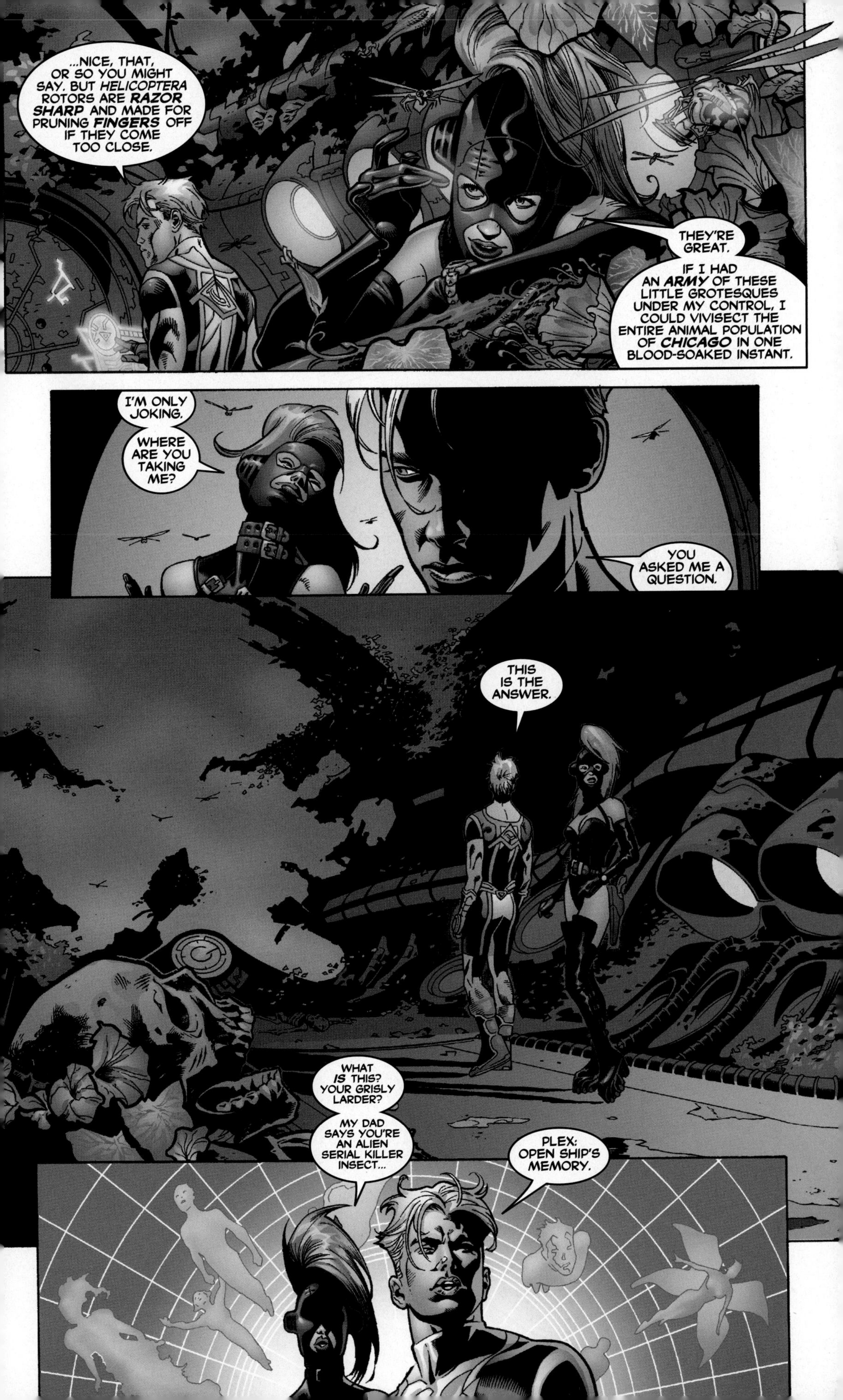

...NICE, THAT, OR SO YOU MIGHT SAY. BUT HELICOPTERA ROTORS ARE RAZOR SHARP AND MADE FOR PRUNING FINGERS OFF IF THEY COME TOO CLOSE.
THEY'RE GREAT.
IF I HAD AN ARMY OF THESE LITTLE GROTESQUES UNDER MY CONTROL, I COULD VIVISECT THE ENTIRE ANIMAL POPULATION OF CHICAGO IN ONE BLOOD-SOAKED INSTANT.
I'M ONLY JOKING.
WHERE ARE YOU TAKING ME?
YOU ASKED ME A QUESTION.
THIS IS THE ANSWER.
WHAT IS THIS? YOUR GRISLY LARDER?
MY DAD SAYS YOU'RE AN ALIEN SERIAL KILLER INSECT...
PLEX: OPEN SHIP'S MEMORY.

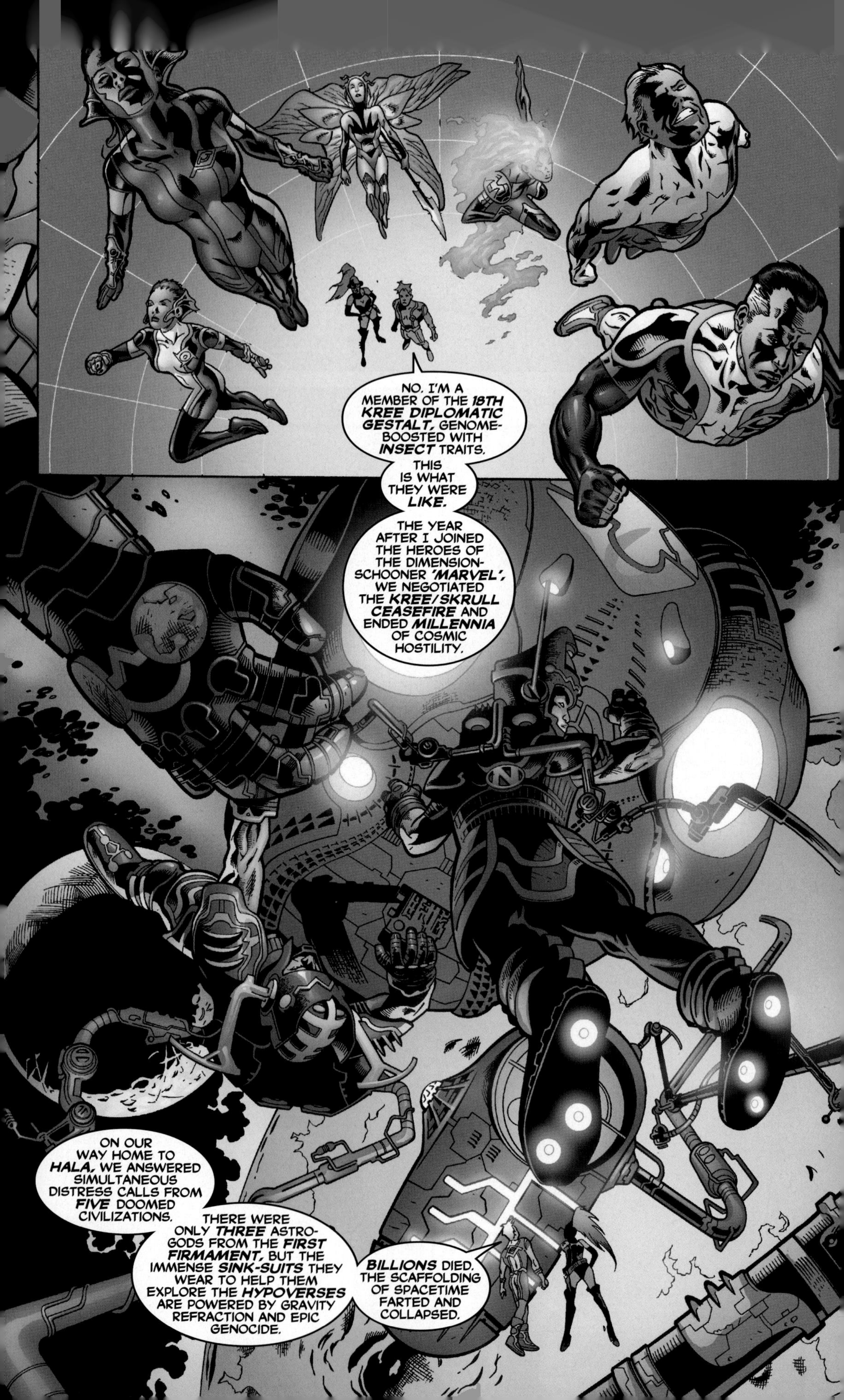
NO. I'M A MEMBER OF THE 18TH KREE DIPLOMATIC GESTALT, GENOME-BOOSTED WITH INSECT TRAITS.
THIS IS WHAT THEY WERE LIKE.
THE YEAR AFTER I JOINED THE HEROES OF THE DIMENSION-SCHOONER 'MARVEL', WE NEGOTIATED THE KREE/SKRULL CEASEFIRE AND ENDED MILLENNIA OF COSMIC HOSTILITY.
ON OUR WAY HOME TO HALA, WE ANSWERED SIMULTANEOUS DISTRESS CALLS FROM FIVE DOOMED CIVILIZATIONS.
THERE WERE ONLY THREE ASTRO-GODS FROM THE FIRST FIRMAMENT, BUT THE IMMENSE SINK-SUITS THEY WEAR TO HELP THEM EXPLORE THE HYPOVERSES ARE POWERED BY GRAVITY REFRACTION AND EPIC GENOCIDE.
BILLIONS DIED. THE SCAFFOLDING OF SPACETIME FARTED AND COLLAPSED.

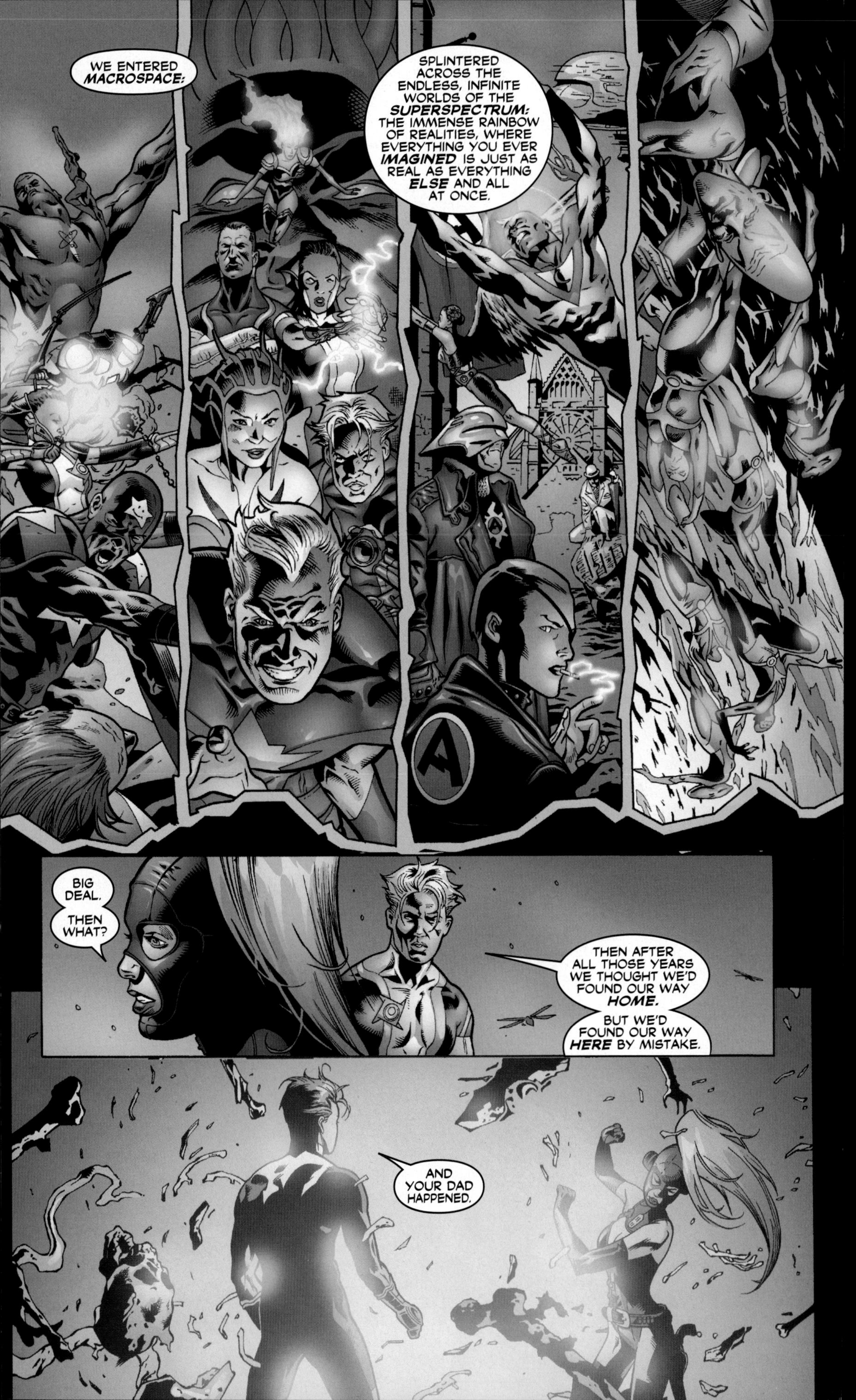
WE ENTERED *MACROSPACE:*
SPLINTERED ACROSS THE ENDLESS, INFINITE WORLDS OF THE *SUPERSPECTRUM:* THE IMMENSE RAINBOW OF REALITIES, WHERE EVERYTHING YOU EVER *IMAGINED* IS JUST AS REAL AS EVERYTHING *ELSE* AND ALL AT ONCE.
BIG DEAL.
THEN WHAT?
THEN AFTER ALL THOSE YEARS WE THOUGHT WE'D FOUND OUR WAY *HOME.*
BUT WE'D FOUND OUR WAY *HERE* BY MISTAKE.
AND YOUR DAD HAPPENED.

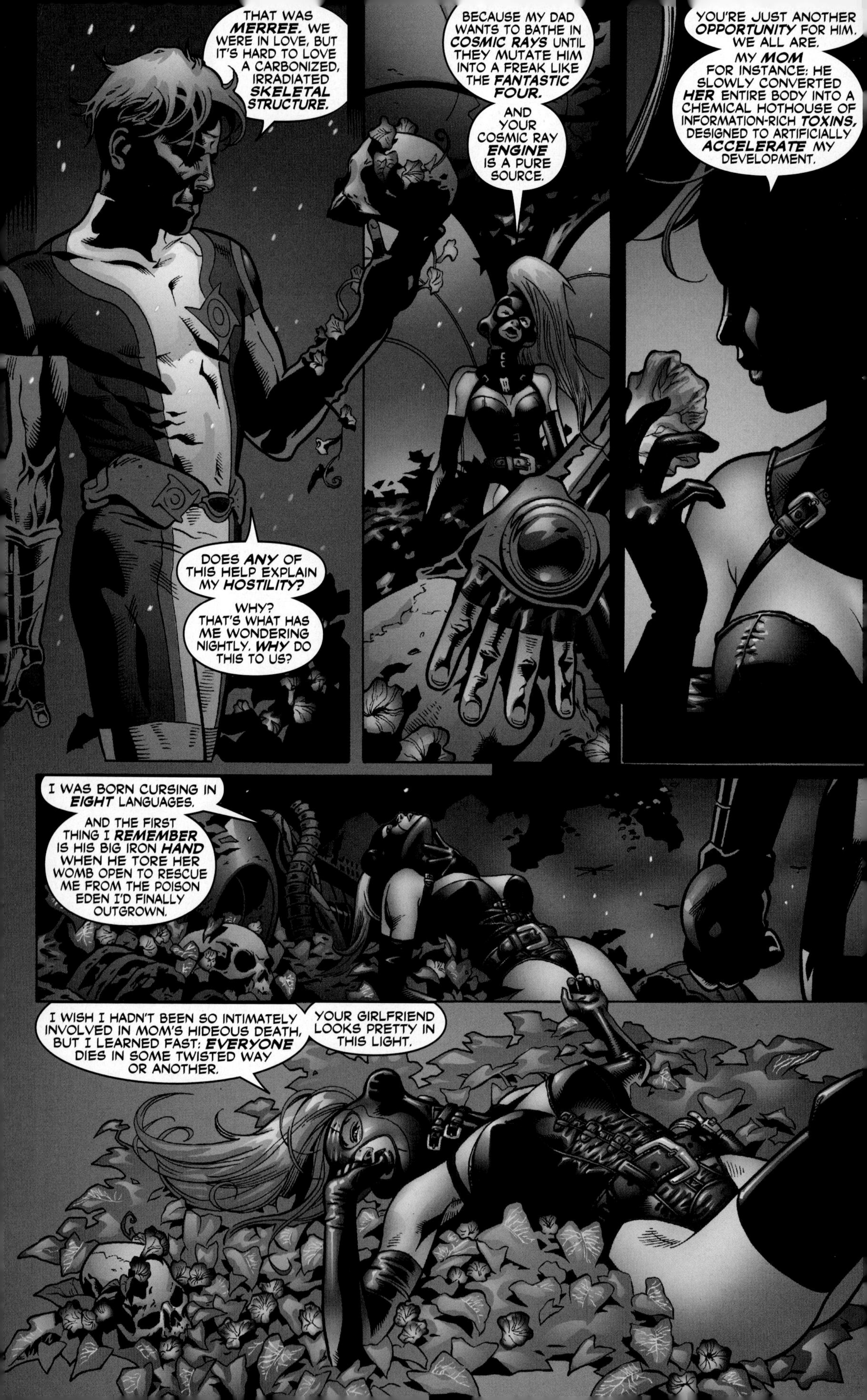
THAT WAS MERREE. WE WERE IN LOVE, BUT IT'S HARD TO LOVE A CARBONIZED, IRRADIATED SKELETAL STRUCTURE.
DOES ANY OF THIS HELP EXPLAIN MY HOSTILITY?
WHY? THAT'S WHAT HAS ME WONDERING NIGHTLY. WHY DO THIS TO US?
BECAUSE MY DAD WANTS TO BATHE IN COSMIC RAYS UNTIL THEY MUTATE HIM INTO A FREAK LIKE THE FANTASTIC FOUR.
AND YOUR COSMIC RAY ENGINE IS A PURE SOURCE.
YOU'RE JUST ANOTHER OPPORTUNITY FOR HIM. WE ALL ARE.
MY MOM FOR INSTANCE: HE SLOWLY CONVERTED HER ENTIRE BODY INTO A CHEMICAL HOTHOUSE OF INFORMATION-RICH TOXINS, DESIGNED TO ARTIFICIALLY ACCELERATE MY DEVELOPMENT.
I WAS BORN CURSING IN EIGHT LANGUAGES.
AND THE FIRST THING I REMEMBER IS HIS BIG IRON HAND WHEN HE TORE HER WOMB OPEN TO RESCUE ME FROM THE POISON EDEN I'D FINALLY OUTGROWN.
I WISH I HADN'T BEEN SO INTIMATELY INVOLVED IN MOM'S HIDEOUS DEATH, BUT I LEARNED FAST: EVERYONE DIES IN SOME TWISTED WAY OR ANOTHER.
YOUR GIRLFRIEND LOOKS PRETTY IN THIS LIGHT.

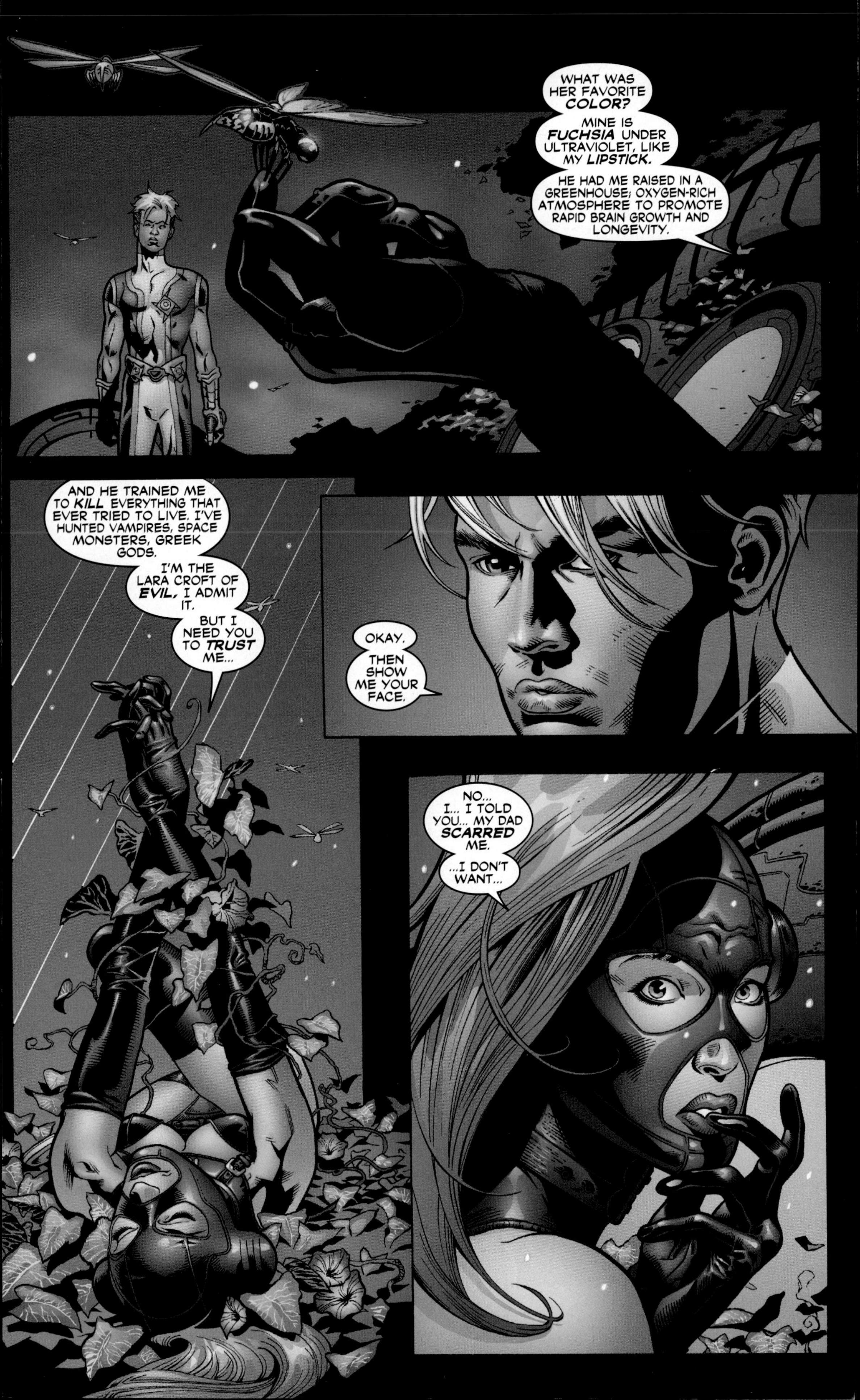
WHAT WAS HER FAVORITE COLOR?
MINE IS FUCHSIA UNDER ULTRAVIOLET, LIKE MY LIPSTICK.
HE HAD ME RAISED IN A GREENHOUSE; OXYGEN-RICH ATMOSPHERE TO PROMOTE RAPID BRAIN GROWTH AND LONGEVITY.
AND HE TRAINED ME TO KILL EVERYTHING THAT EVER TRIED TO LIVE. I'VE HUNTED VAMPIRES, SPACE MONSTERS, GREEK GODS.
I'M THE LARA CROFT OF EVIL, I ADMIT IT.
BUT I NEED YOU TO TRUST ME...
OKAY.
THEN SHOW ME YOUR FACE.
NO... I... I TOLD YOU... MY DAD SCARRED ME.
...I DON'T WANT...

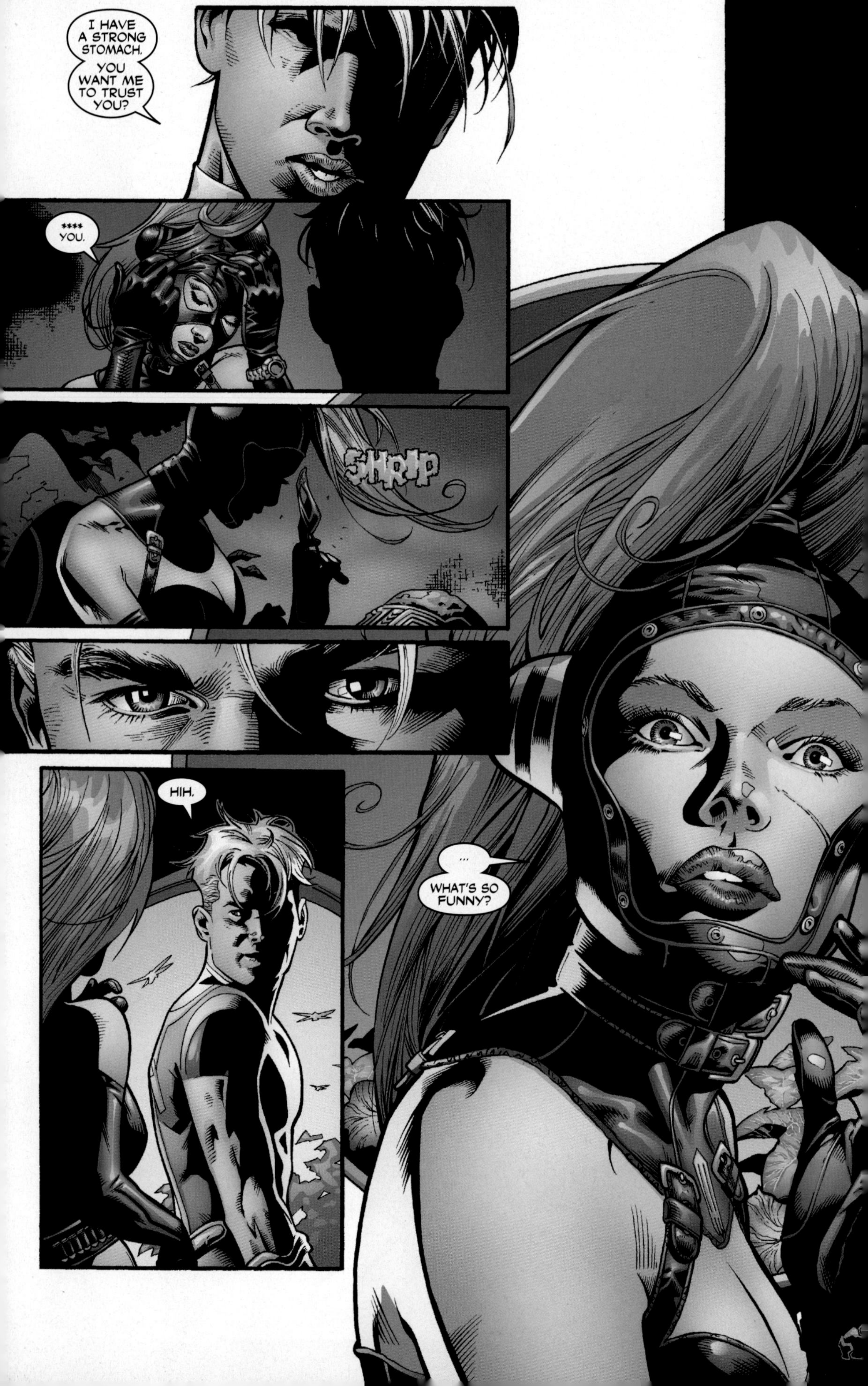
I HAVE A STRONG STOMACH.
YOU WANT ME TO TRUST YOU?
**** YOU.
SHRIP
HIH.
... WHAT'S SO FUNNY?

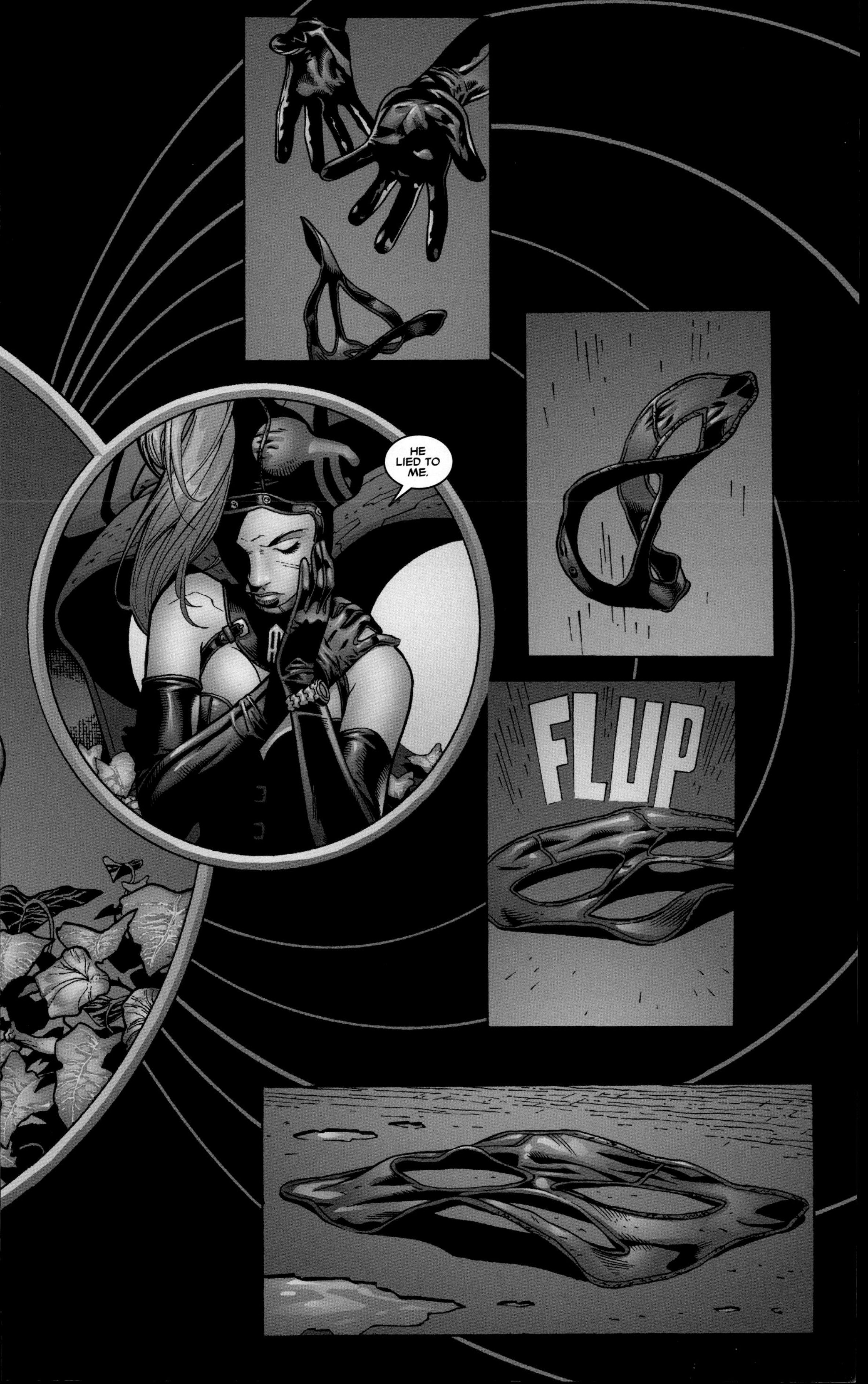
HE LIED TO ME.
FLUP

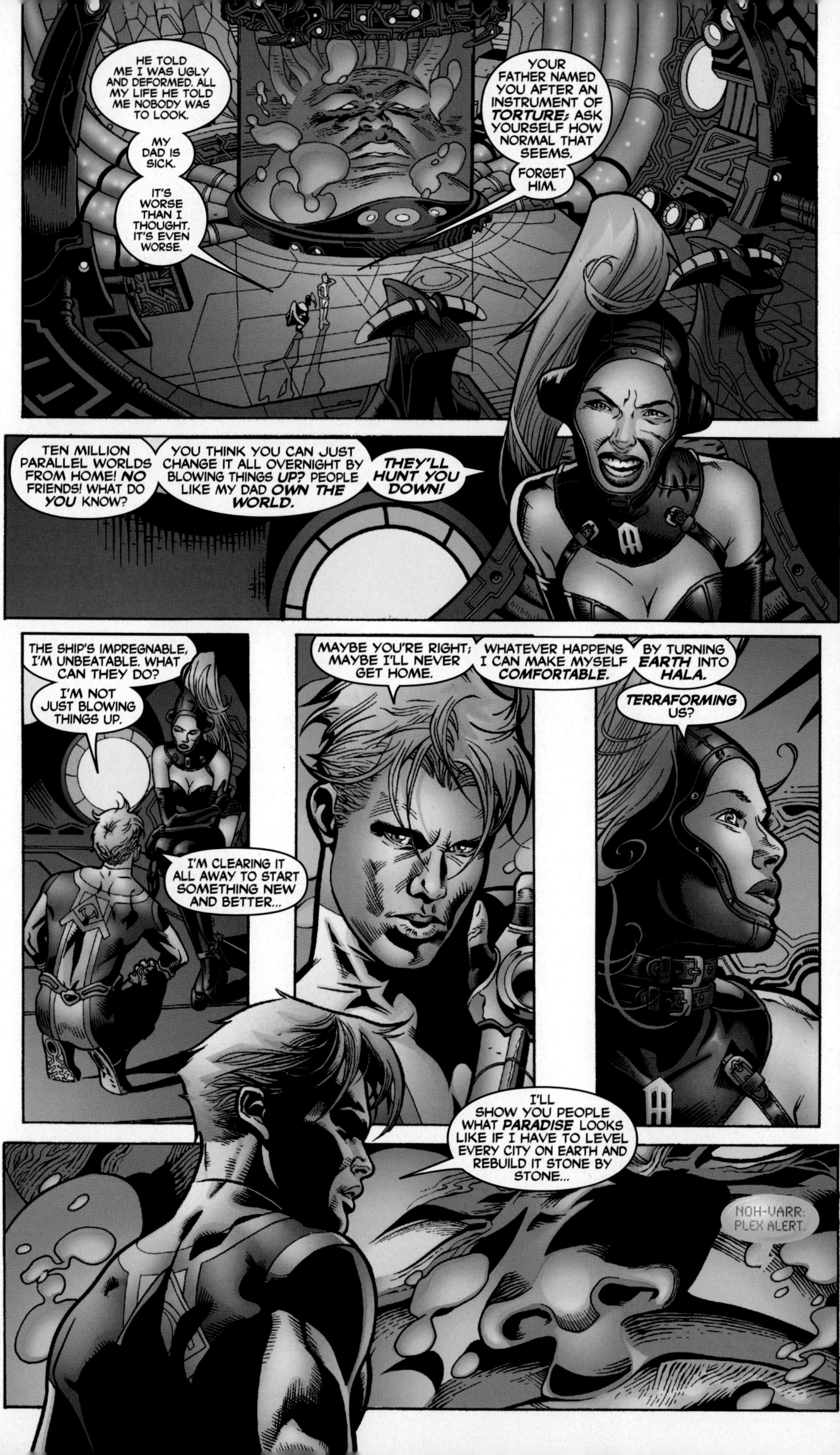
HE TOLD ME I WAS UGLY AND DEFORMED. ALL MY LIFE HE TOLD ME NOBODY WAS TO LOOK.
MY DAD IS SICK.
IT'S WORSE THAN I THOUGHT. IT'S EVEN WORSE.
YOUR FATHER NAMED YOU AFTER AN INSTRUMENT OF TORTURE; ASK YOURSELF HOW NORMAL THAT SEEMS.
FORGET HIM.
TEN MILLION PARALLEL WORLDS FROM HOME! NO FRIENDS! WHAT DO YOU KNOW?
YOU THINK YOU CAN JUST CHANGE IT ALL OVERNIGHT BY BLOWING THINGS UP? PEOPLE LIKE MY DAD OWN THE WORLD.
THEY'LL HUNT YOU DOWN!
THE SHIP'S IMPREGNABLE, I'M UNBEATABLE. WHAT CAN THEY DO?
I'M NOT JUST BLOWING THINGS UP.
I'M CLEARING IT ALL AWAY TO START SOMETHING NEW AND BETTER...
MAYBE YOU'RE RIGHT; MAYBE I'LL NEVER GET HOME.
WHATEVER HAPPENS I CAN MAKE MYSELF COMFORTABLE.
BY TURNING EARTH INTO HALA.
TERRAFORMING US?
I'LL SHOW YOU PEOPLE WHAT PARADISE LOOKS LIKE IF I HAVE TO LEVEL EVERY CITY ON EARTH AND REBUILD IT STONE BY STONE...
NOH-VARR: PLEX ALERT.

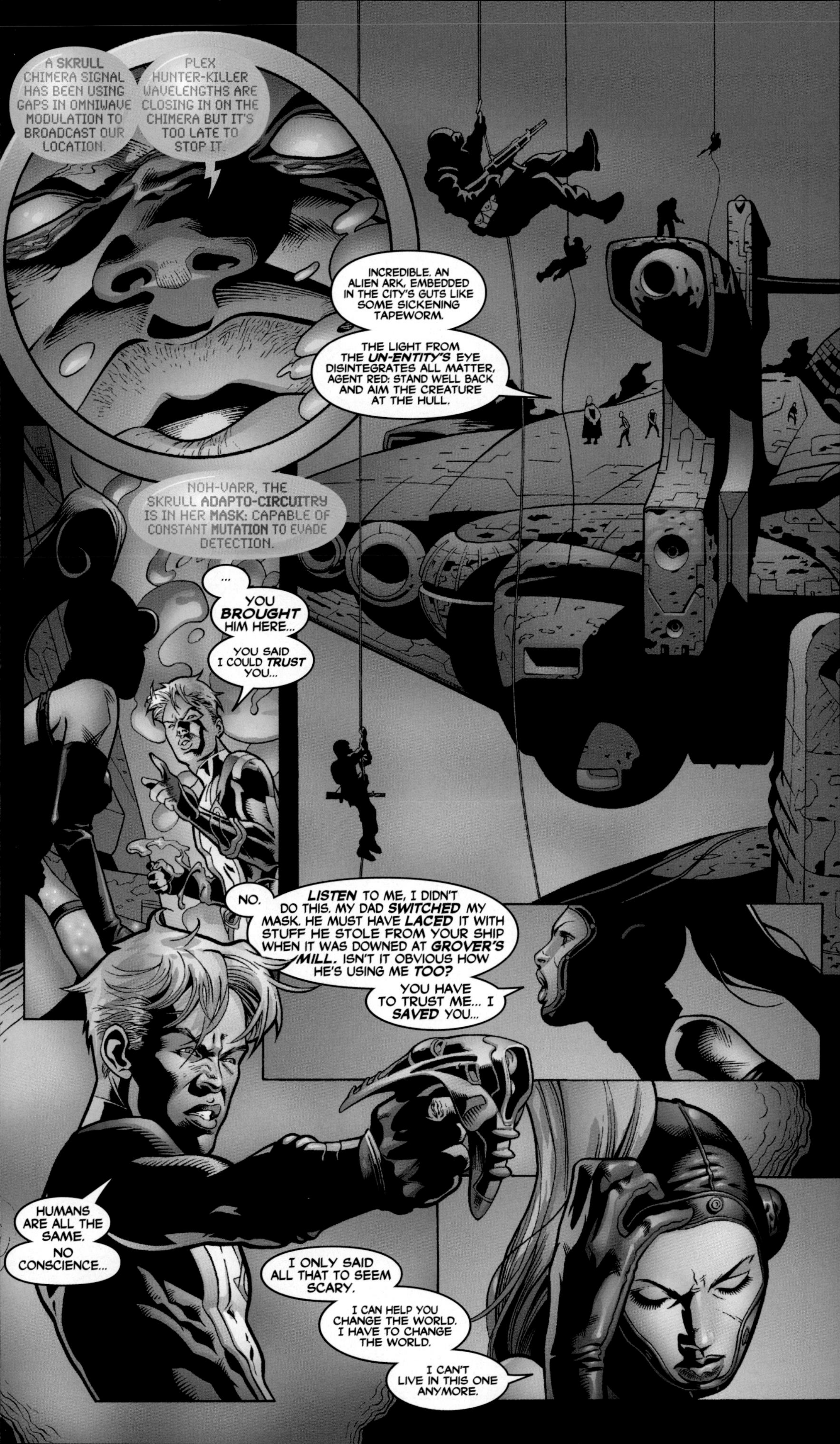

A SKRULL CHIMERA SIGNAL HAS BEEN USING GAPS IN OMNIWAVE MODULATION TO BROADCAST OUR LOCATION.
PLEX HUNTER-KILLER WAVELENGTHS ARE CLOSING IN ON THE CHIMERA BUT IT'S TOO LATE TO STOP IT.
INCREDIBLE. AN ALIEN ARK, EMBEDDED IN THE CITY'S GUTS LIKE SOME SICKENING TAPEWORM.
THE LIGHT FROM THE UN-ENTITY'S EYE DISINTEGRATES ALL MATTER, AGENT RED: STAND WELL BACK AND AIM THE CREATURE AT THE HULL.
NOH-VARR, THE SKRULL ADAPTO-CIRCUITRY IS IN HER MASK: CAPABLE OF CONSTANT MUTATION TO EVADE DETECTION.
...
YOU BROUGHT HIM HERE...
YOU SAID I COULD TRUST YOU...
NO.
LISTEN TO ME, I DIDN'T DO THIS. MY DAD SWITCHED MY MASK. HE MUST HAVE LACED IT WITH STUFF HE STOLE FROM YOUR SHIP WHEN IT WAS DOWNED AT GROVER'S MILL. ISN'T IT OBVIOUS HOW HE'S USING ME TOO?
YOU HAVE TO TRUST ME... I SAVED YOU...
HUMANS ARE ALL THE SAME.
NO CONSCIENCE...
I ONLY SAID ALL THAT TO SEEM SCARY.
I CAN HELP YOU CHANGE THE WORLD. I HAVE TO CHANGE THE WORLD.
I CAN'T LIVE IN THIS ONE ANYMORE.

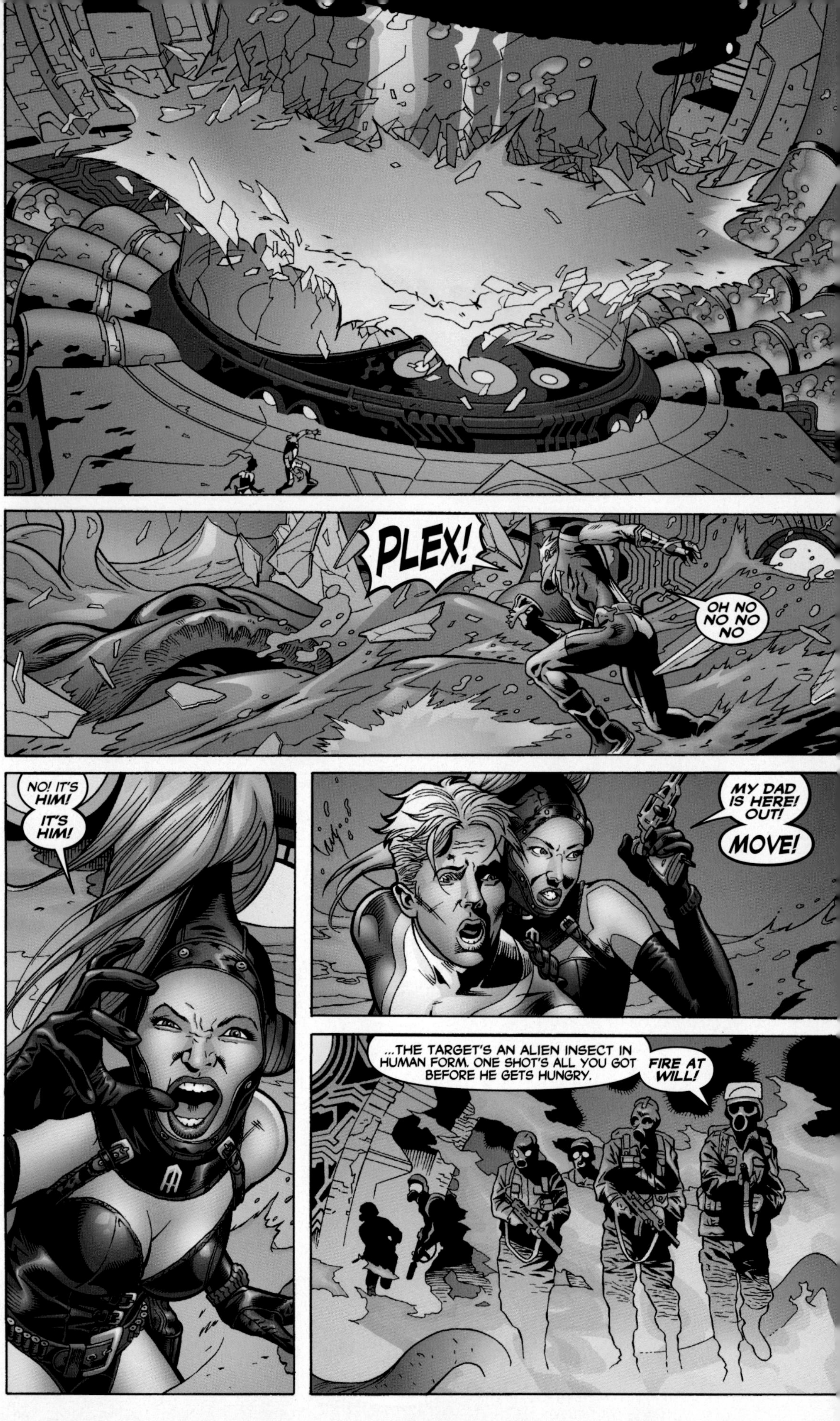
PLEX!
OH NO NO NO NO
NO! IT'S HIM!
IT'S HIM!
MY DAD IS HERE! OUT!
MOVE!
...THE TARGET'S AN ALIEN INSECT IN HUMAN FORM. ONE SHOT'S ALL YOU GOT BEFORE HE GETS HUNGRY.
FIRE AT WILL!

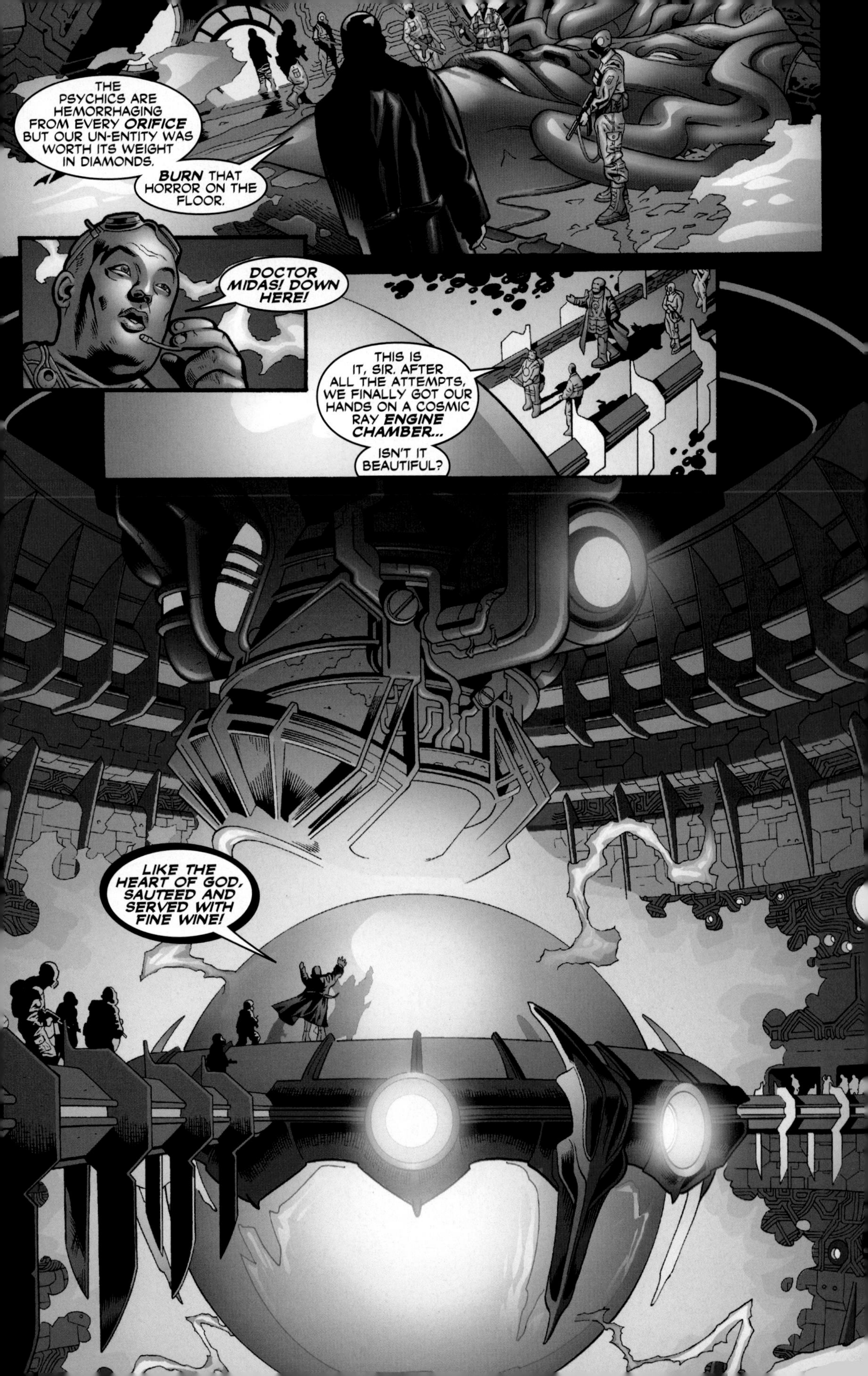
THE PSYCHICS ARE HEMORRHAGING FROM EVERY ORIFICE BUT OUR UN-ENTITY WAS WORTH ITS WEIGHT IN DIAMONDS.
BURN THAT HORROR ON THE FLOOR.
DOCTOR MIDAS! DOWN HERE!
THIS IS IT, SIR. AFTER ALL THE ATTEMPTS, WE FINALLY GOT OUR HANDS ON A COSMIC RAY ENGINE CHAMBER...
ISN'T IT BEAUTIFUL?
LIKE THE HEART OF GOD, SAUTEED AND SERVED WITH FINE WINE!

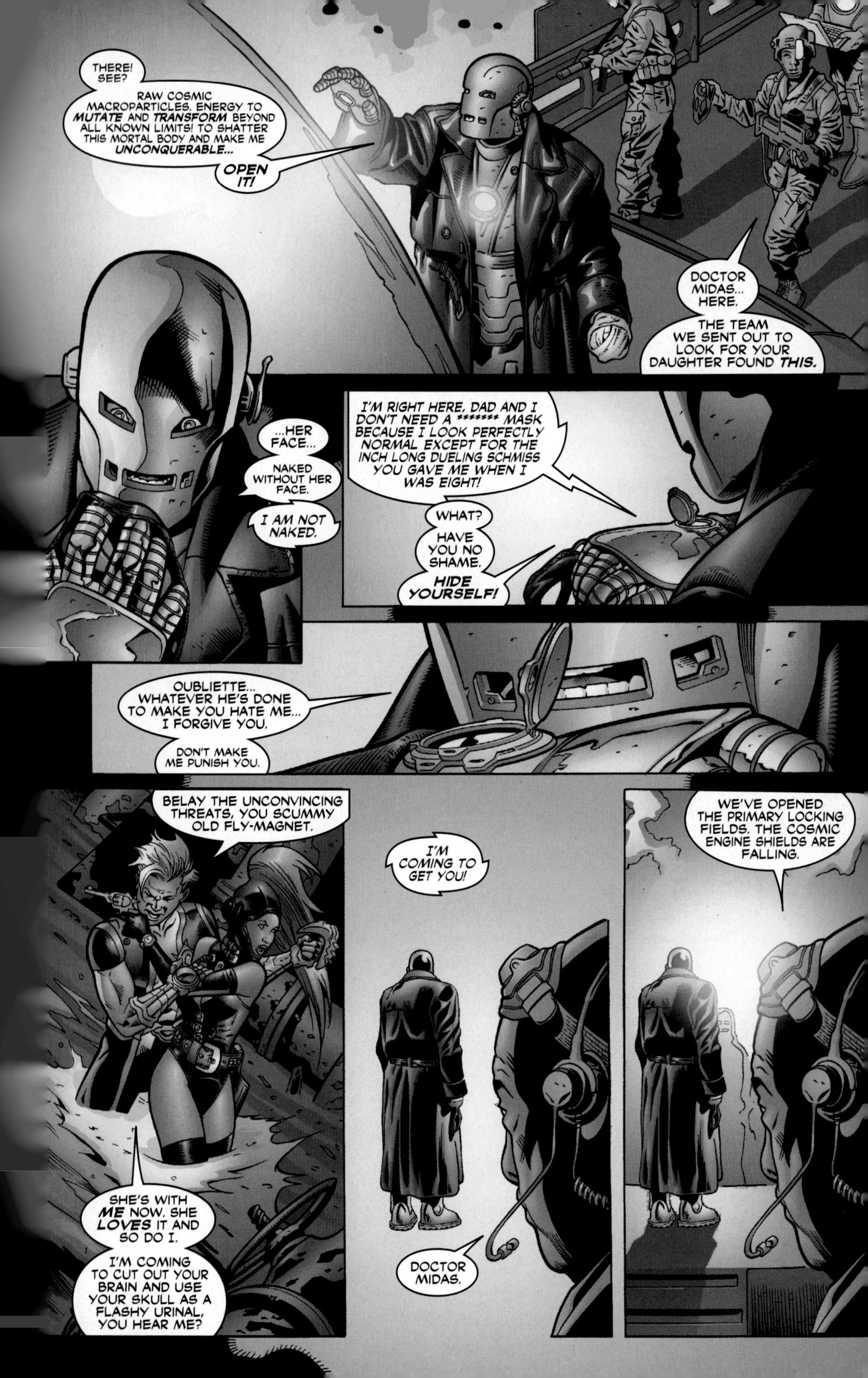
THERE! SEE?
RAW COSMIC MACROPARTICLES, ENERGY TO MUTATE AND TRANSFORM BEYOND ALL KNOWN LIMITS! TO SHATTER THIS MORTAL BODY AND MAKE ME UNCONQUERABLE...
OPEN IT!
DOCTOR MIDAS... HERE.
THE TEAM WE SENT OUT TO LOOK FOR YOUR DAUGHTER FOUND THIS.
...HER FACE...
NAKED WITHOUT HER FACE.
I AM NOT NAKED.
I'M RIGHT HERE, DAD AND I DON'T NEED A ******* MASK BECAUSE I LOOK PERFECTLY NORMAL EXCEPT FOR THE INCH LONG DUELING SCHMISS YOU GAVE ME WHEN I WAS EIGHT!
WHAT?
HAVE YOU NO SHAME.
HIDE YOURSELF!
OUBLIETTE... WHATEVER HE'S DONE TO MAKE YOU HATE ME... I FORGIVE YOU.
DON'T MAKE ME PUNISH YOU.
BELAY THE UNCONVINCING THREATS, YOU SCUMMY OLD FLY-MAGNET.
SHE'S WITH ME NOW. SHE LOVES IT AND SO DO I.
I'M COMING TO CUT OUT YOUR BRAIN AND USE YOUR SKULL AS A FLASHY URINAL, YOU HEAR ME?
I'M COMING TO GET YOU!
DOCTOR MIDAS.
WE'VE OPENED THE PRIMARY LOCKING FIELDS. THE COSMIC ENGINE SHIELDS ARE FALLING.

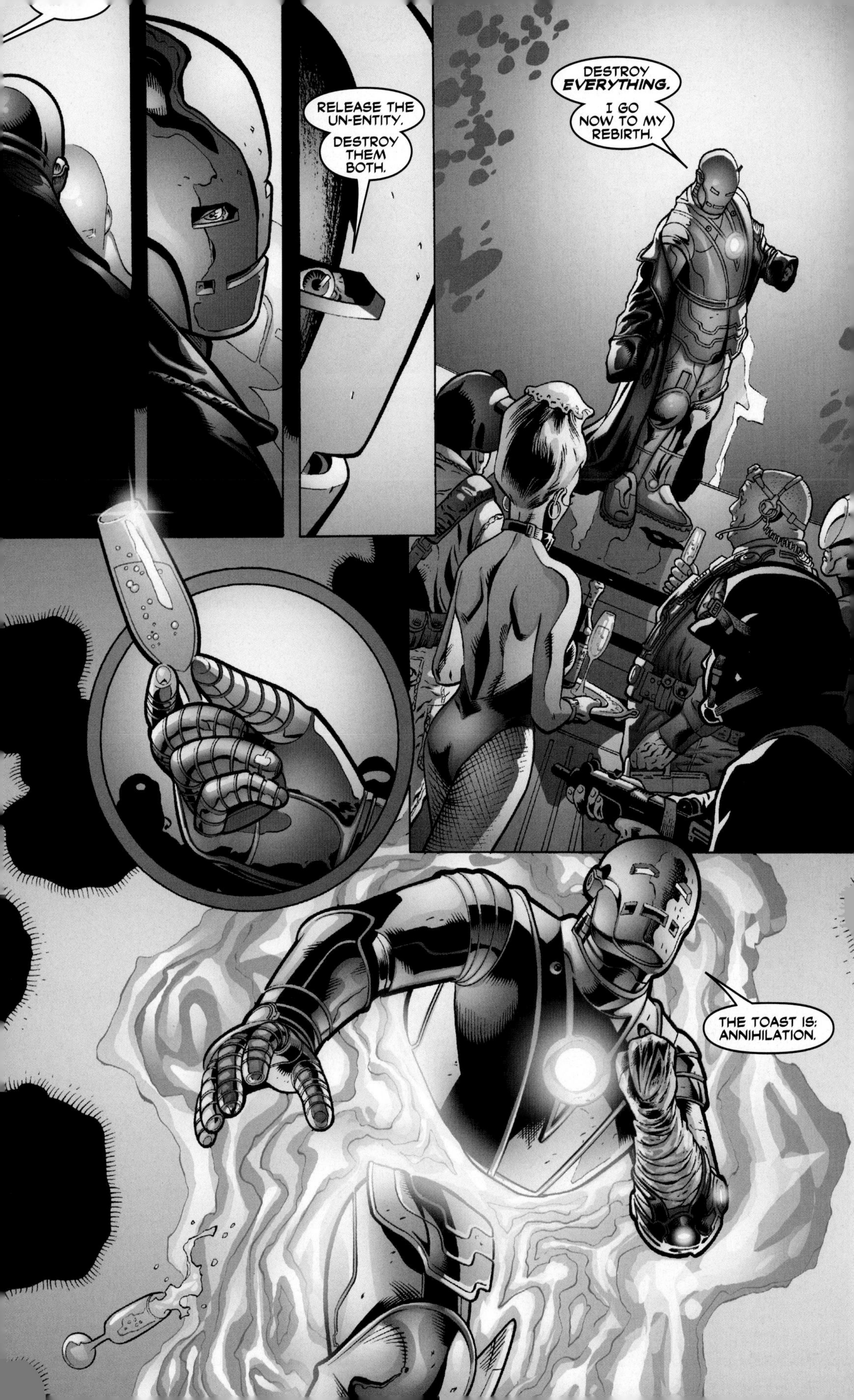
RELEASE THE UN-ENTITY.
DESTROY THEM BOTH.
DESTROY *EVERYTHING.*
I GO NOW TO MY REBIRTH.
THE TOAST IS: ANNIHILATION.

YOU SHOULDN'T HAVE SAID ALL THAT. HE'LL THINK WE'VE BEEN DOING SOMETHING *SEXUAL;* HE WON'T BELIEVE WE'VE *HONESTLY* BEEN TRYING TO *KILL* ONE ANOTHER.

WHAT'S THE BEST WAY OUT OF HERE...?

UP THE WAY, BUT I HAVE TO GO BACK FOR *PLEX.* IF...

...WHAT'S THAT NOISE?

THERE! CAN YOU HEAR?

...FOOTSTEPS... BUT THEY'D HAVE TO BE COMING THROUGH... SOLID ROCK.

NOH-VARR. SAY SOMETHING TO ME IN *KREE.* IN CASE WE DIE.

SOMETHING SEXY.

RRRM.

WHAT WAS *THAT?*

'THIS AREA IS NO LONGER INFECTED. YOU MAY PROCEED.'

HEH.

ME AND YOU, SPACEBOY.

I HOPE YOU'RE READY FOR THE MIDAS FAMILY.

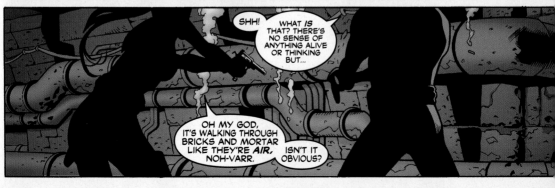

SHH! WHAT *IS* THAT? THERE'S NO SENSE OF ANYTHING ALIVE OR THINKING BUT...

OH MY GOD, IT'S WALKING THROUGH BRICKS AND MORTAR LIKE THEY'RE *AIR,* NOH-VARR.

ISN'T IT OBVIOUS?

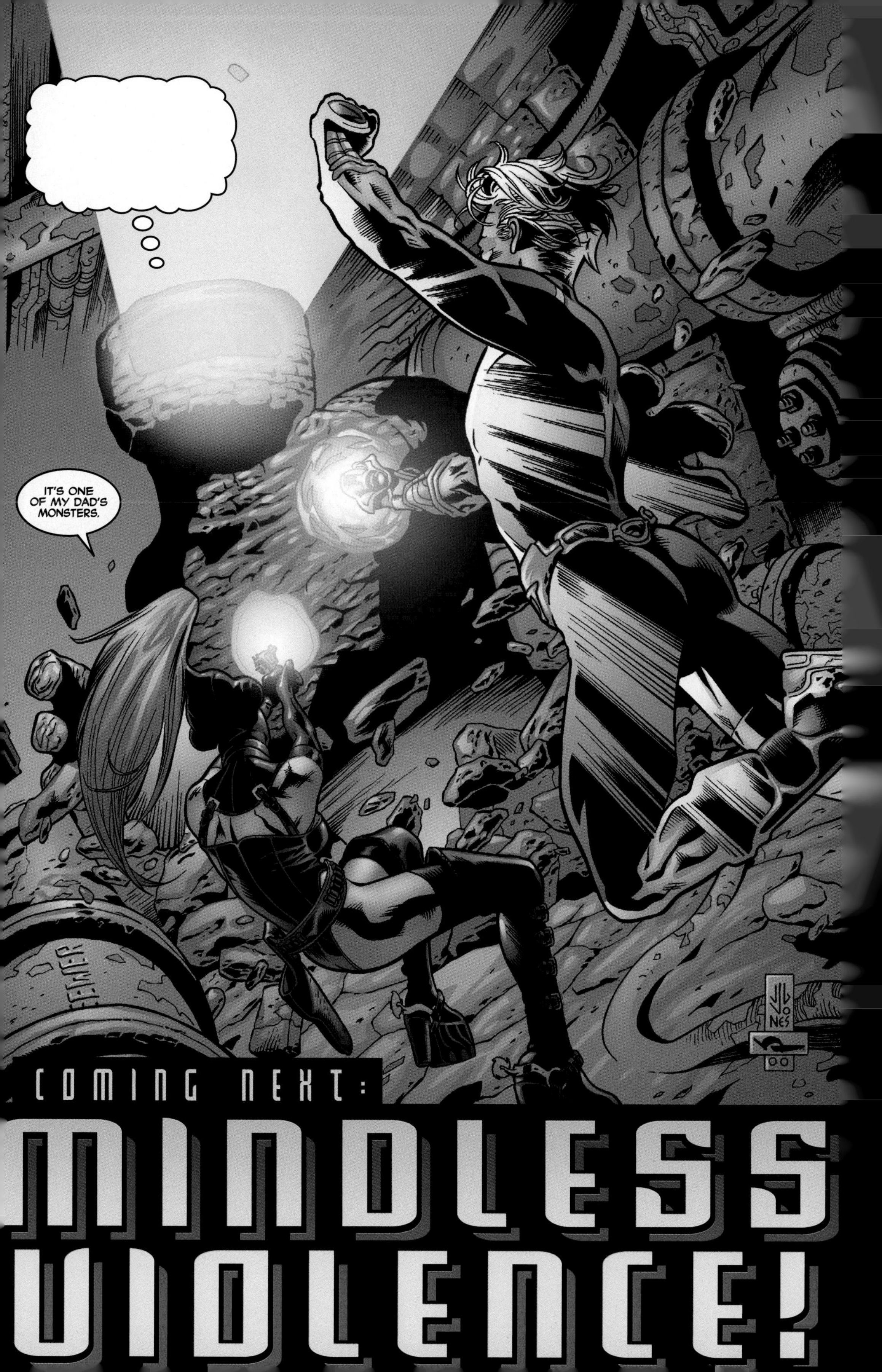
IT'S ONE OF MY DAD'S MONSTERS.
COMING NEXT:
MINDLESS VIOLENCE!

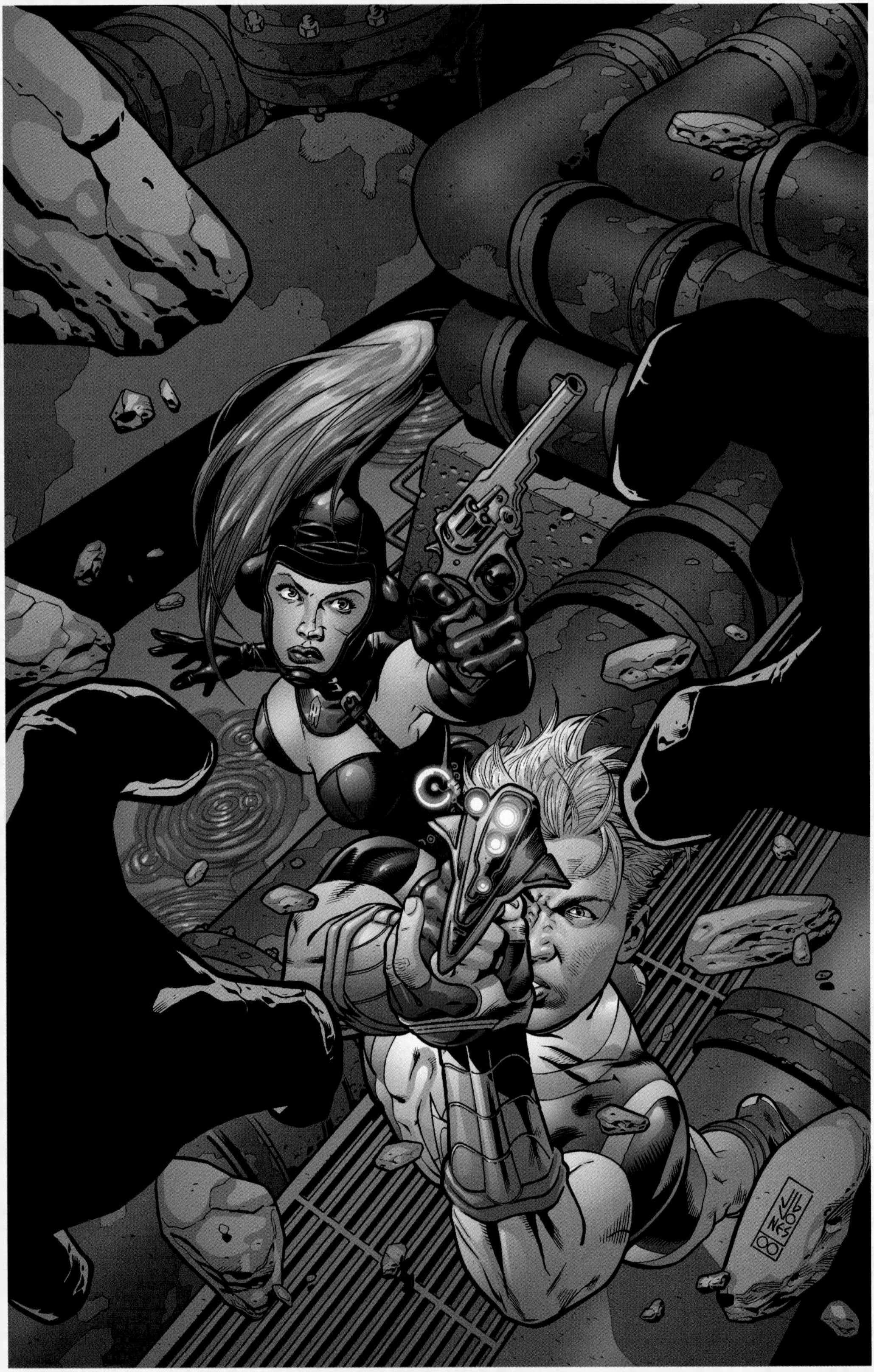

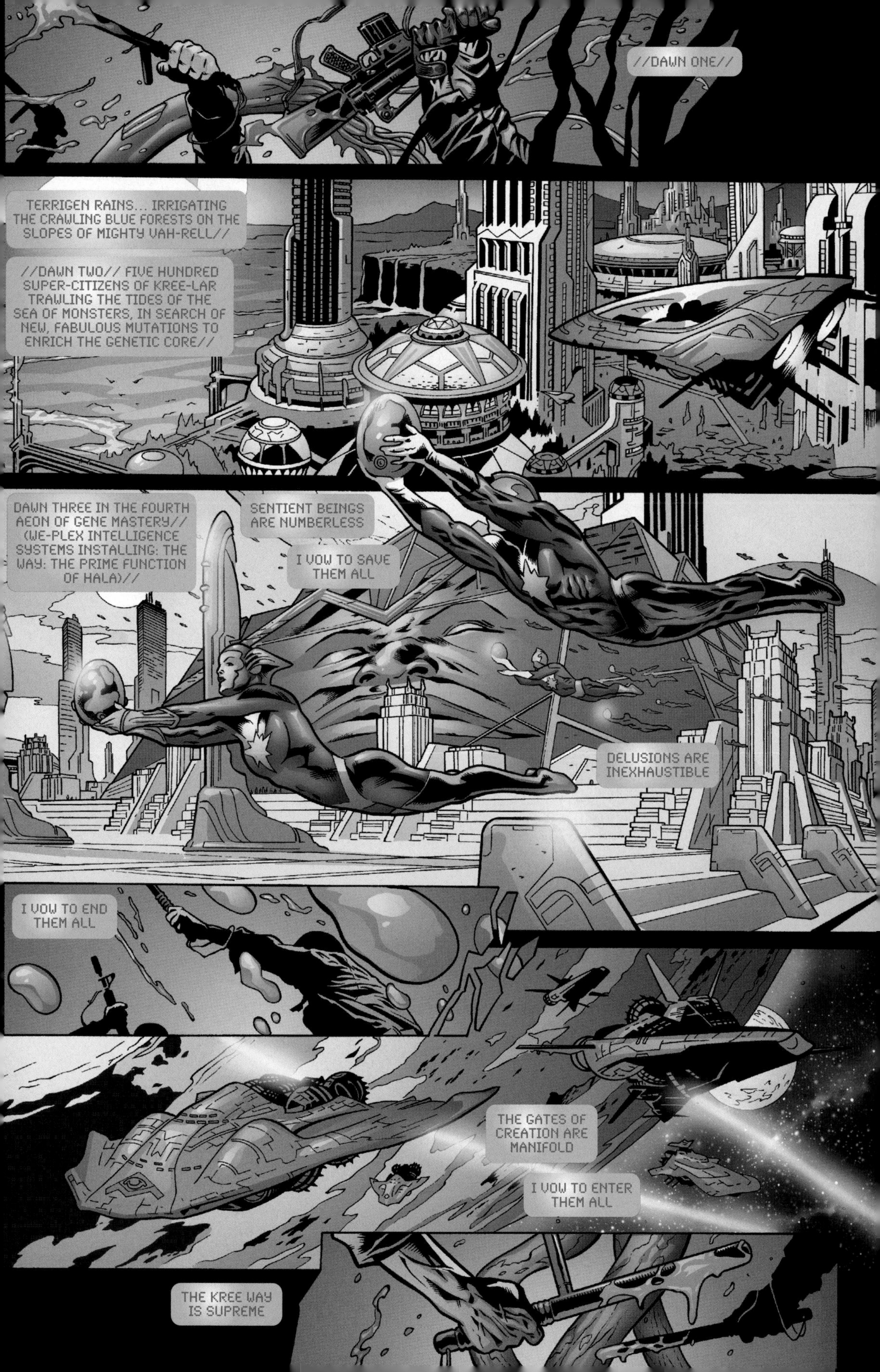
//DAWN ONE//
TERRIGEN RAINS... IRRIGATING THE CRAWLING BLUE FORESTS ON THE SLOPES OF MIGHTY VAH-RELL//
//DAWN TWO// FIVE HUNDRED SUPER-CITIZENS OF KREE-LAR TRAWLING THE TIDES OF THE SEA OF MONSTERS, IN SEARCH OF NEW, FABULOUS MUTATIONS TO ENRICH THE GENETIC CORE//
DAWN THREE IN THE FOURTH AEON OF GENE MASTERY// (WE-PLEX INTELLIGENCE SYSTEMS INSTALLING: THE WAY: THE PRIME FUNCTION OF HALA)//
SENTIENT BEINGS ARE NUMBERLESS
I VOW TO SAVE THEM ALL
DELUSIONS ARE INEXHAUSTIBLE
I VOW TO END THEM ALL
THE GATES OF CREATION ARE MANIFOLD
I VOW TO ENTER THEM ALL
THE KREE WAY IS SUPREME

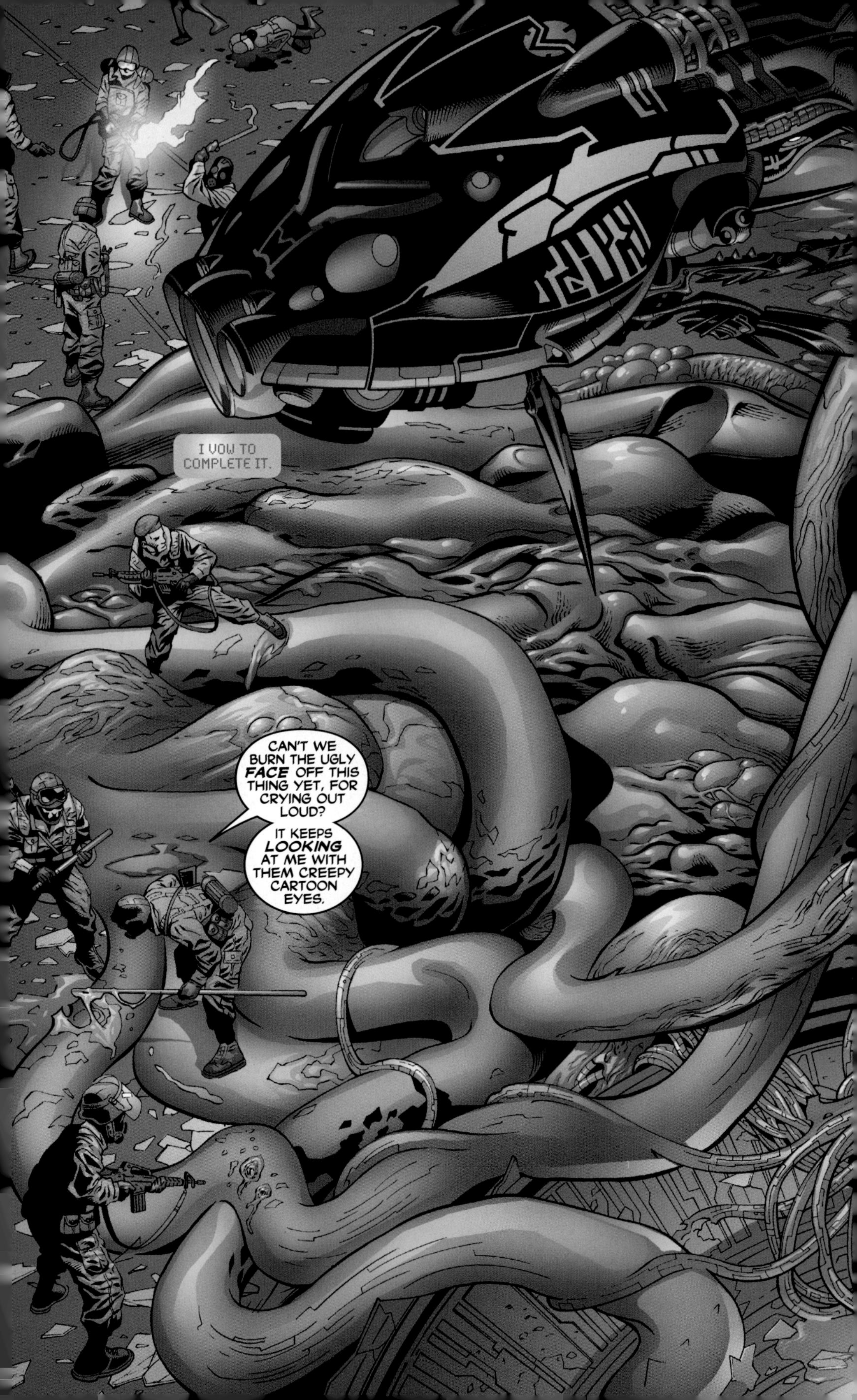
I VOW TO COMPLETE IT.
CAN'T WE BURN THE UGLY FACE OFF THIS THING YET, FOR CRYING OUT LOUD?
IT KEEPS LOOKING AT ME WITH THEM CREEPY CARTOON EYES.

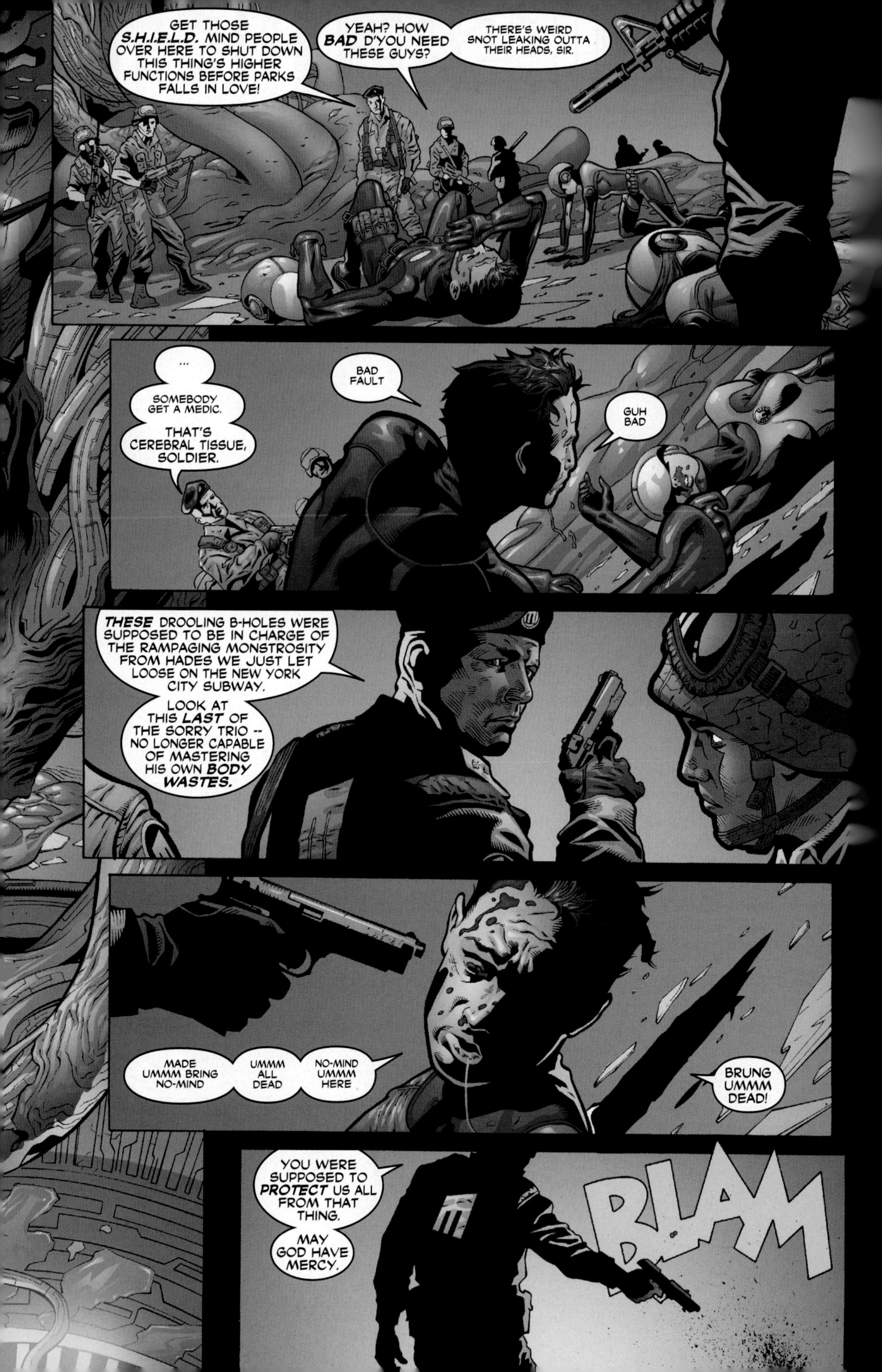
GET THOSE S.H.I.E.L.D. MIND PEOPLE OVER HERE TO SHUT DOWN THIS THING'S HIGHER FUNCTIONS BEFORE PARKS FALLS IN LOVE!
YEAH? HOW BAD D'YOU NEED THESE GUYS?
THERE'S WEIRD SNOT LEAKING OUTTA THEIR HEADS, SIR.
...
SOMEBODY GET A MEDIC.
THAT'S CEREBRAL TISSUE, SOLDIER.
BAD FAULT
GUH BAD
THESE DROOLING B-HOLES WERE SUPPOSED TO BE IN CHARGE OF THE RAMPAGING MONSTROSITY FROM HADES WE JUST LET LOOSE ON THE NEW YORK CITY SUBWAY.
LOOK AT THIS LAST OF THE SORRY TRIO -- NO LONGER CAPABLE OF MASTERING HIS OWN BODY WASTES.
MADE UMMM BRING NO-MIND
UMMM ALL DEAD
NO-MIND UMMM HERE
BRUNG UMMM DEAD!
YOU WERE SUPPOSED TO PROTECT US ALL FROM THAT THING.
MAY GOD HAVE MERCY.
BLAM

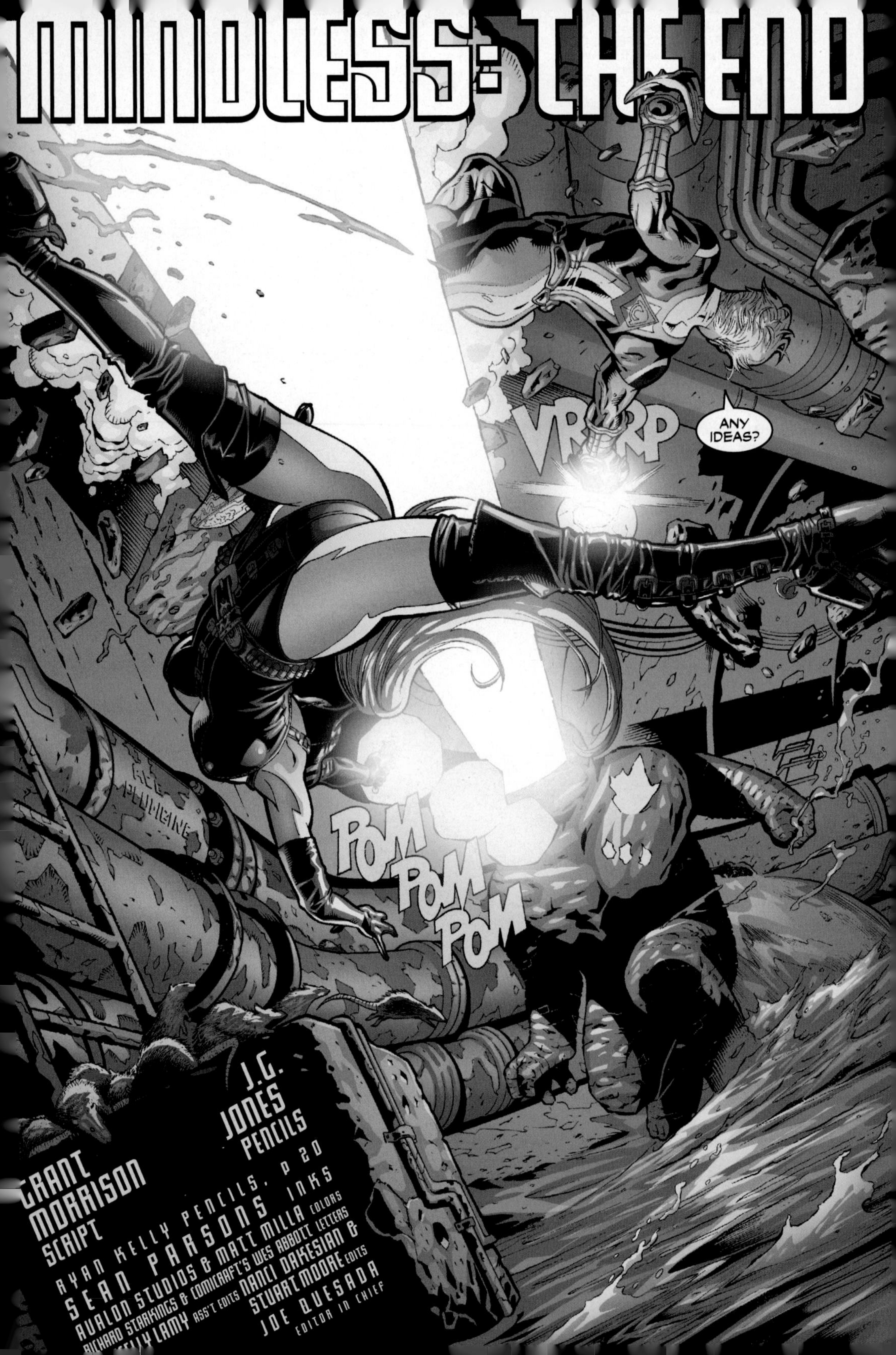
MINDLESS: THE END
VRRRP
ANY IDEAS?
POM POM POM POM
GRANT MORRISON SCRIPT
J.G. JONES PENCILS
RYAN KELLY PENCILS, P 20
SEAN PARSONS INKS
AVALON STUDIOS & MATT MILLA COLORS
RICHARD STARKINGS & COMICRAFT'S WES ABBOTT LETTERS
LAMY ASS'T EDITS
NANCI DAKESIAN &
STUART MOORE EDITS
JOE QUESADA EDITOR IN CHIEF

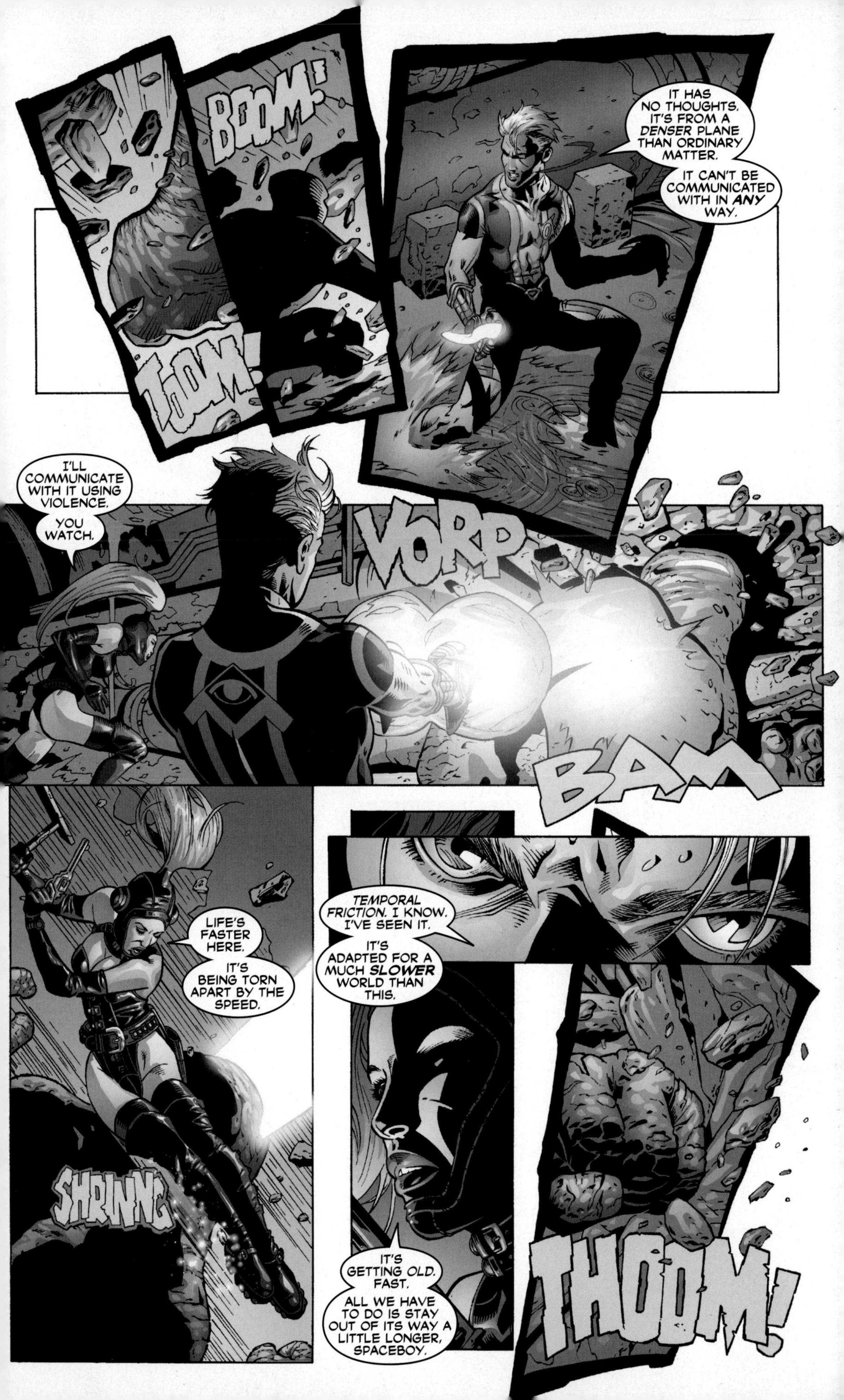
TOOM!
BOOM!
IT HAS NO THOUGHTS. IT'S FROM A DENSER PLANE THAN ORDINARY MATTER.
IT CAN'T BE COMMUNICATED WITH IN ANY WAY.
I'LL COMMUNICATE WITH IT USING VIOLENCE.
YOU WATCH.
VORP
BAM
LIFE'S FASTER HERE.
IT'S BEING TORN APART BY THE SPEED.
SHRINNG
TEMPORAL FRICTION. I KNOW. I'VE SEEN IT.
IT'S ADAPTED FOR A MUCH SLOWER WORLD THAN THIS.
IT'S GETTING OLD. FAST.
ALL WE HAVE TO DO IS STAY OUT OF ITS WAY A LITTLE LONGER, SPACEBOY.
THOOM!

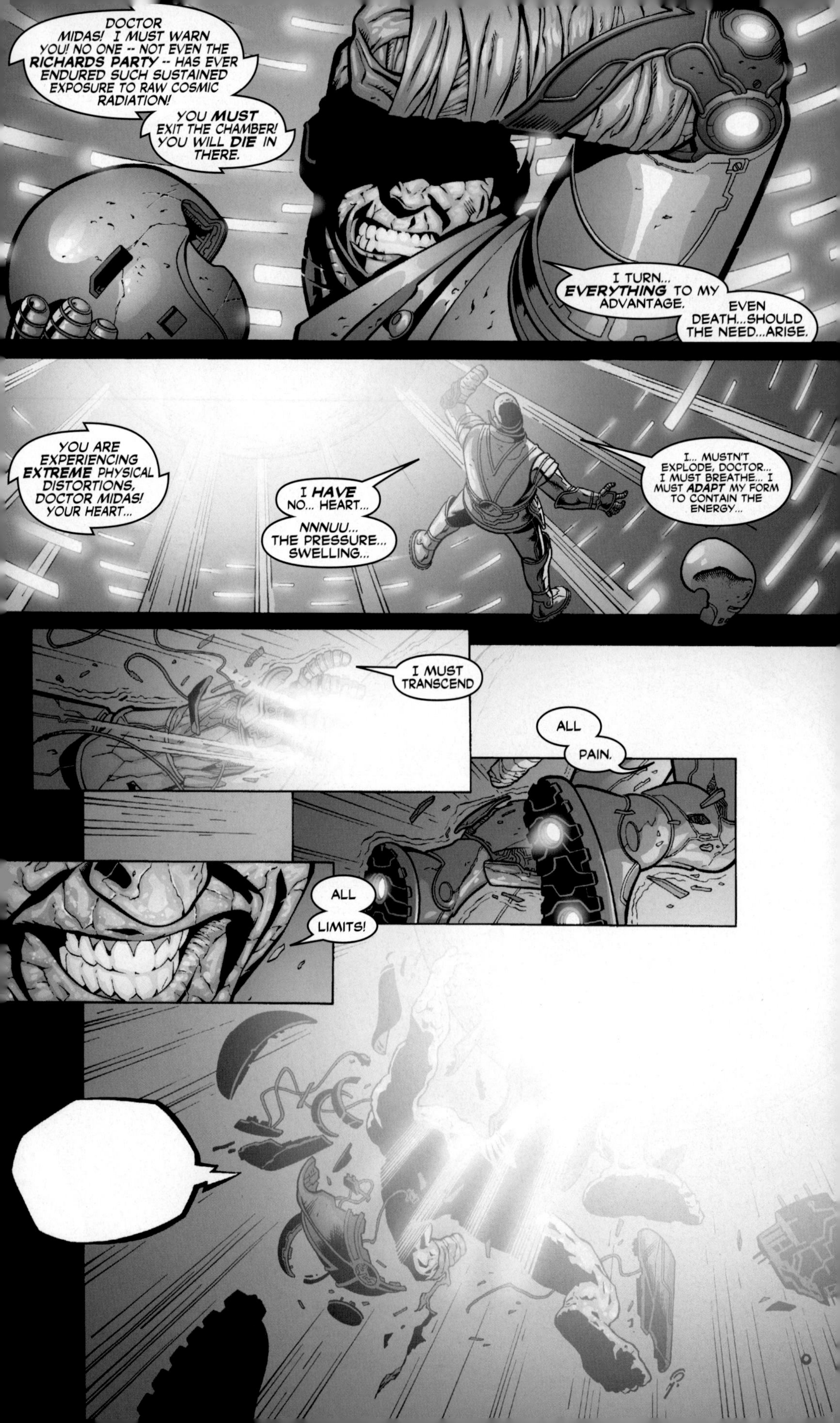
DOCTOR MIDAS! I MUST WARN YOU! NO ONE -- NOT EVEN THE RICHARDS PARTY -- HAS EVER ENDURED SUCH SUSTAINED EXPOSURE TO RAW COSMIC RADIATION!
YOU MUST EXIT THE CHAMBER! YOU WILL DIE IN THERE.
I TURN... EVERYTHING TO MY ADVANTAGE.
EVEN DEATH...SHOULD THE NEED...ARISE.
YOU ARE EXPERIENCING EXTREME PHYSICAL DISTORTIONS, DOCTOR MIDAS! YOUR HEART...
I HAVE NO... HEART...
NNNUU... THE PRESSURE... SWELLING...
I... MUSTN'T EXPLODE, DOCTOR... I MUST BREATHE... I MUST ADAPT MY FORM TO CONTAIN THE ENERGY...
I MUST TRANSCEND
ALL
PAIN.
ALL
LIMITS!

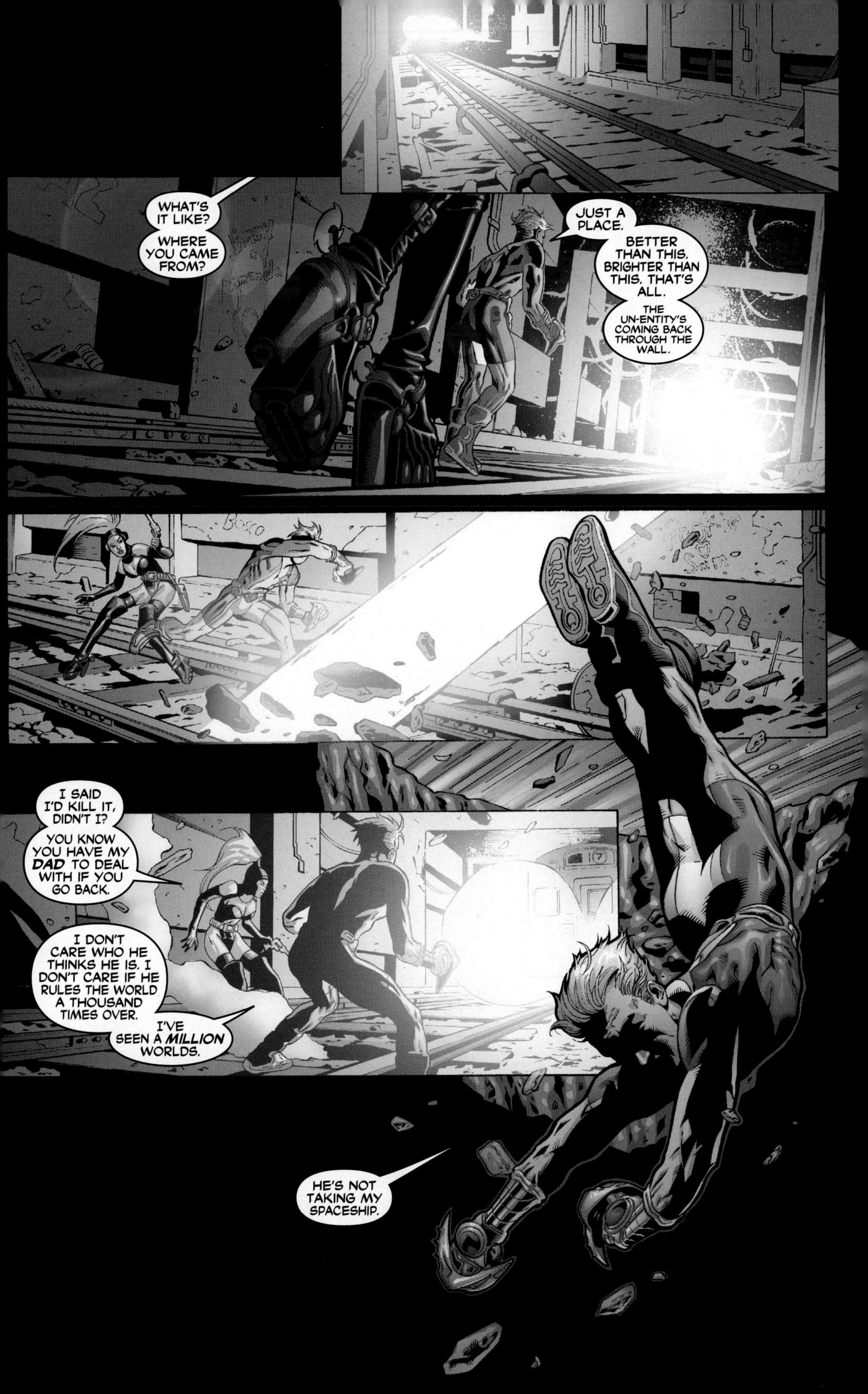

WHAT'S IT LIKE? WHERE YOU CAME FROM?
JUST A PLACE.
BETTER THAN THIS. BRIGHTER THAN THIS. THAT'S ALL.
THE UN-ENTITY'S COMING BACK THROUGH THE WALL.
I SAID I'D KILL IT, DIDN'T I?
YOU KNOW YOU HAVE MY DAD TO DEAL WITH IF YOU GO BACK.
I DON'T CARE WHO HE THINKS HE IS. I DON'T CARE IF HE RULES THE WORLD A THOUSAND TIMES OVER.
I'VE SEEN A MILLION WORLDS.
HE'S NOT TAKING MY SPACESHIP.

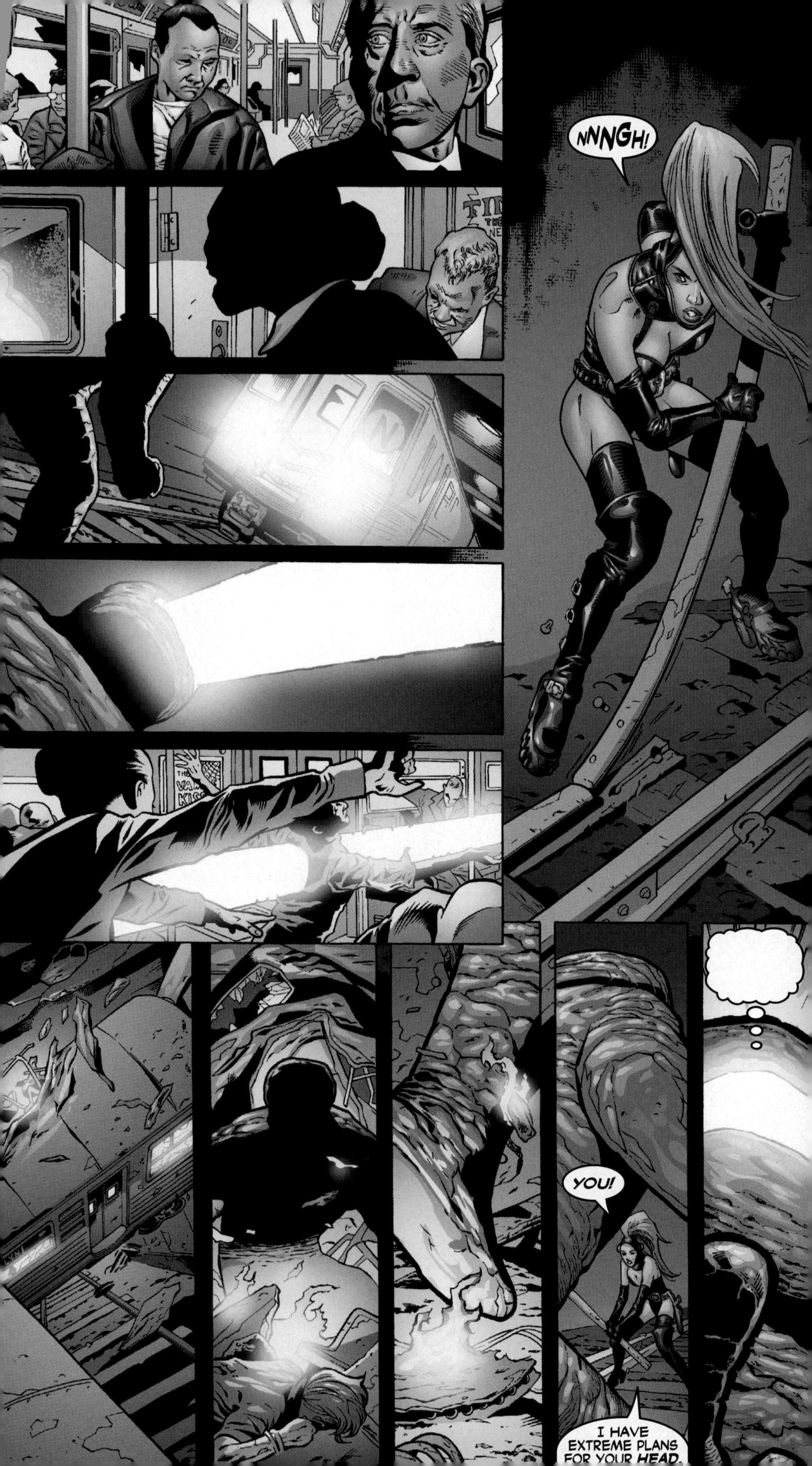

NNNGH!
YOU!
I HAVE EXTREME PLANS FOR YOUR HEAD.

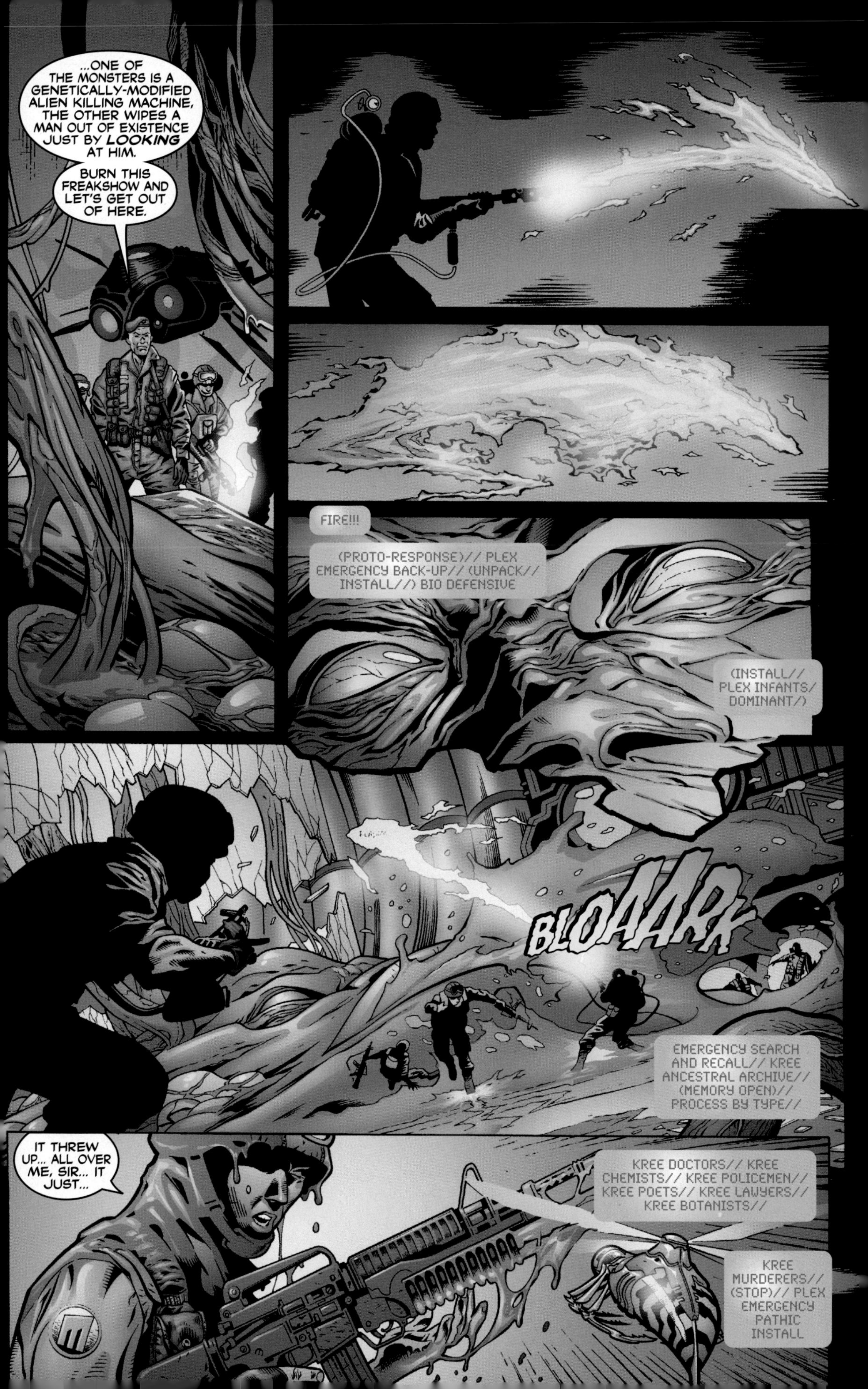
...ONE OF THE MONSTERS IS A GENETICALLY-MODIFIED ALIEN KILLING MACHINE, THE OTHER WIPES A MAN OUT OF EXISTENCE JUST BY LOOKING AT HIM.
BURN THIS FREAKSHOW AND LET'S GET OUT OF HERE.
FIRE!!!
(PROTO-RESPONSE)// PLEX EMERGENCY BACK-UP// (UNPACK// INSTALL//) BIO DEFENSIVE
(INSTALL// PLEX INFANTS/ DOMINANT/)
BLOAARK
EMERGENCY SEARCH AND RECALL// KREE ANCESTRAL ARCHIVE// (MEMORY OPEN)// PROCESS BY TYPE//
IT THREW UP... ALL OVER ME, SIR... IT JUST...
KREE DOCTORS// KREE CHEMISTS// KREE POLICEMEN// KREE POETS// KREE LAWYERS// KREE BOTANISTS//
KREE MURDERERS// (STOP)// PLEX EMERGENCY PATHIC INSTALL

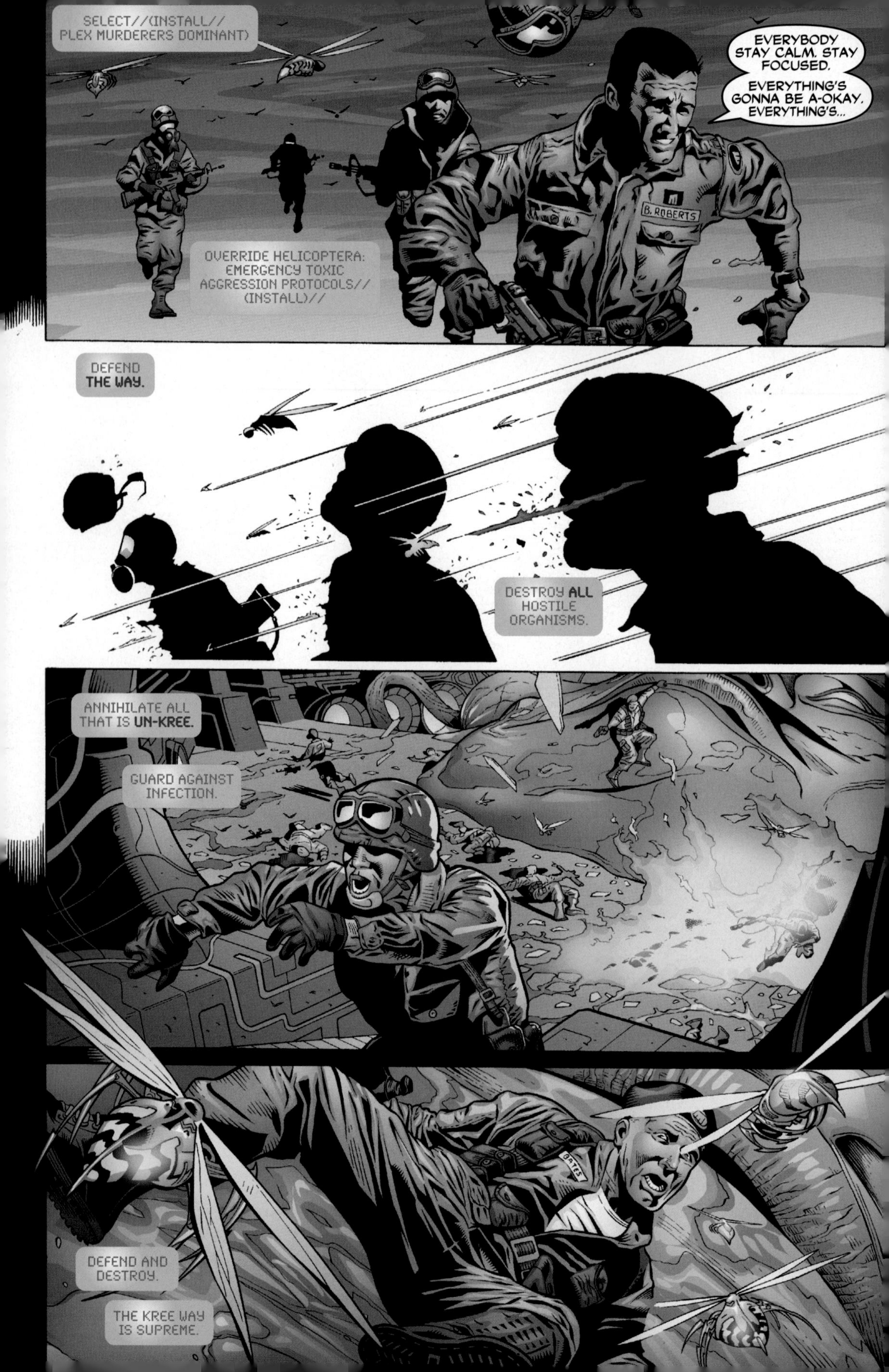
SELECT//(INSTALL// PLEX MURDERERS DOMINANT)
EVERYBODY STAY CALM. STAY FOCUSED.
EVERYTHING'S GONNA BE A-OKAY. EVERYTHING'S...
B. ROBERTS
OVERRIDE HELICOPTERA: EMERGENCY TOXIC AGGRESSION PROTOCOLS// (INSTALL)//
DEFEND **THE WAY.**
DESTROY **ALL** HOSTILE ORGANISMS.
ANNIHILATE ALL THAT IS **UN-KREE.**
GUARD AGAINST INFECTION.
GATES
DEFEND AND DESTROY.
THE KREE WAY IS SUPREME.

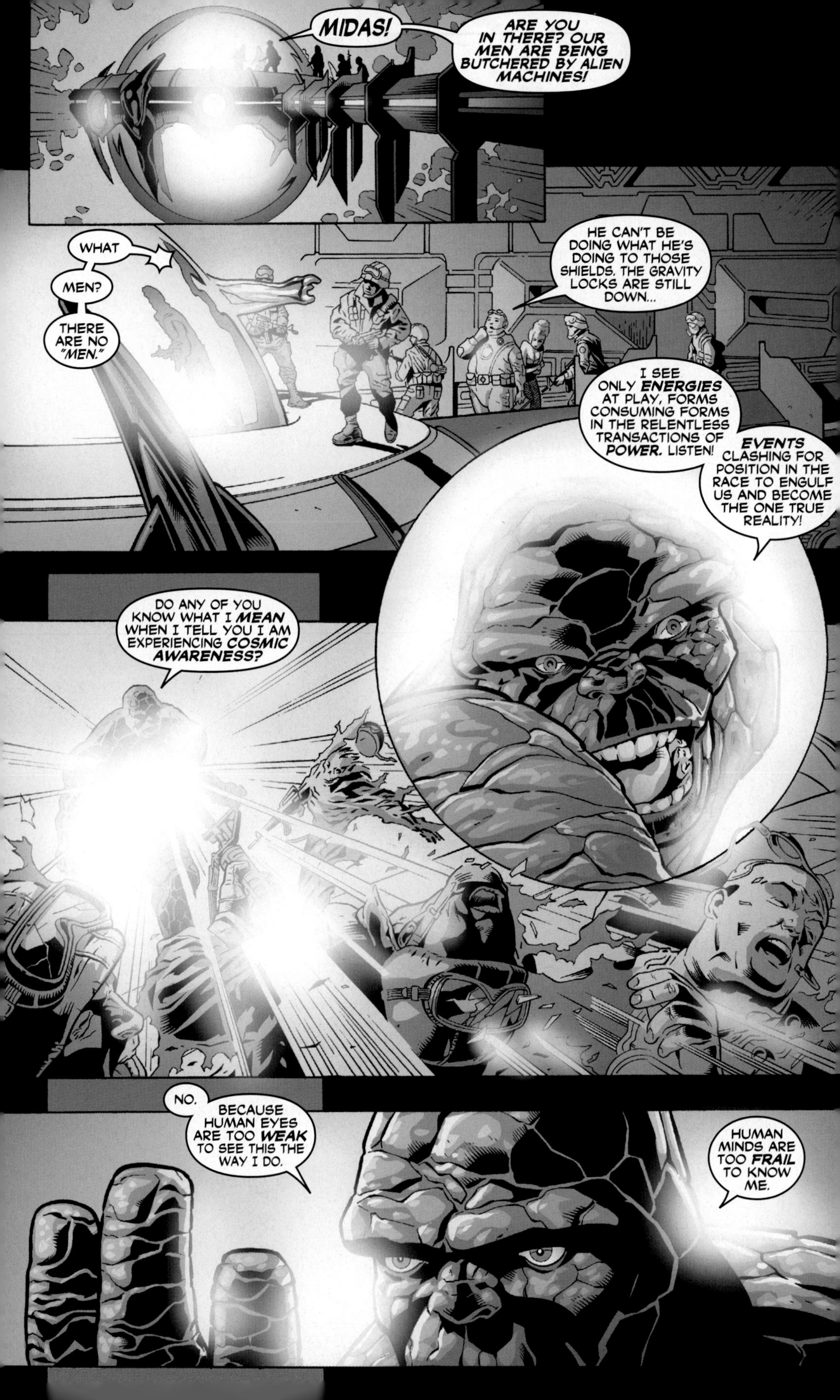
MIDAS!
ARE YOU IN THERE? OUR MEN ARE BEING BUTCHERED BY ALIEN MACHINES!
HE CAN'T BE DOING WHAT HE'S DOING TO THOSE SHIELDS. THE GRAVITY LOCKS ARE STILL DOWN...
WHAT
MEN?
THERE ARE NO "MEN."
I SEE ONLY ENERGIES AT PLAY, FORMS CONSUMING FORMS IN THE RELENTLESS TRANSACTIONS OF POWER. LISTEN!
EVENTS CLASHING FOR POSITION IN THE RACE TO ENGULF US AND BECOME THE ONE TRUE REALITY!
DO ANY OF YOU KNOW WHAT I MEAN WHEN I TELL YOU I AM EXPERIENCING COSMIC AWARENESS?
NO.
BECAUSE HUMAN EYES ARE TOO WEAK TO SEE THIS THE WAY I DO.
HUMAN MINDS ARE TOO FRAIL TO KNOW ME.

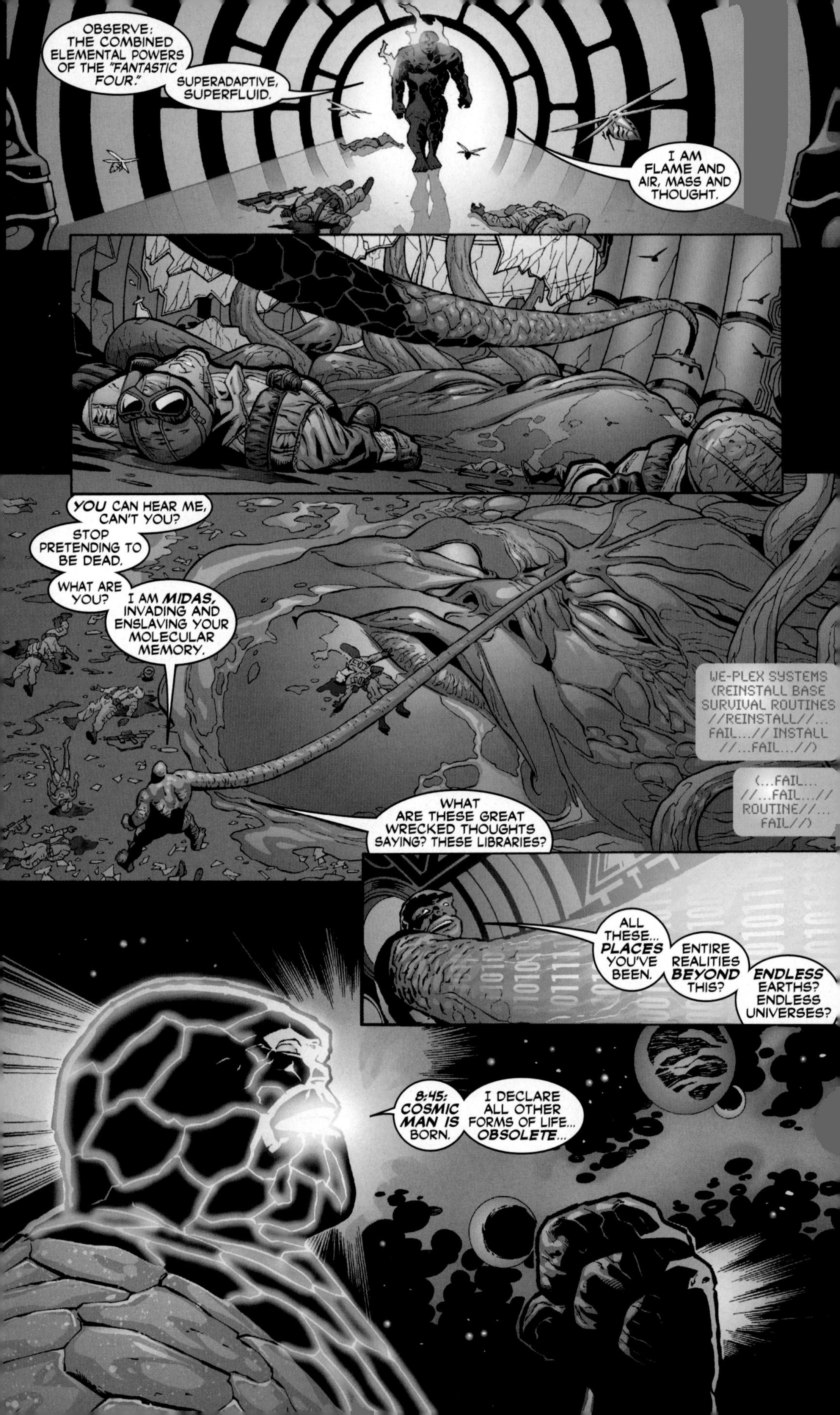
OBSERVE: THE COMBINED ELEMENTAL POWERS OF THE "FANTASTIC FOUR."
SUPERADAPTIVE, SUPERFLUID.
I AM FLAME AND AIR, MASS AND THOUGHT.
YOU CAN HEAR ME, CAN'T YOU?
STOP PRETENDING TO BE DEAD.
WHAT ARE YOU?
I AM MIDAS, INVADING AND ENSLAVING YOUR MOLECULAR MEMORY.
WE-PLEX SYSTEMS (REINSTALL BASE SURVIVAL ROUTINES //REINSTALL//... FAIL...// INSTALL //...FAIL...//)
(...FAIL... //...FAIL...// ROUTINE//... FAIL//)
WHAT ARE THESE GREAT WRECKED THOUGHTS SAYING? THESE LIBRARIES?
ALL THESE... PLACES YOU'VE BEEN.
ENTIRE REALITIES BEYOND THIS?
ENDLESS EARTHS? ENDLESS UNIVERSES?
8:45: COSMIC MAN IS BORN.
I DECLARE ALL OTHER FORMS OF LIFE... OBSOLETE...

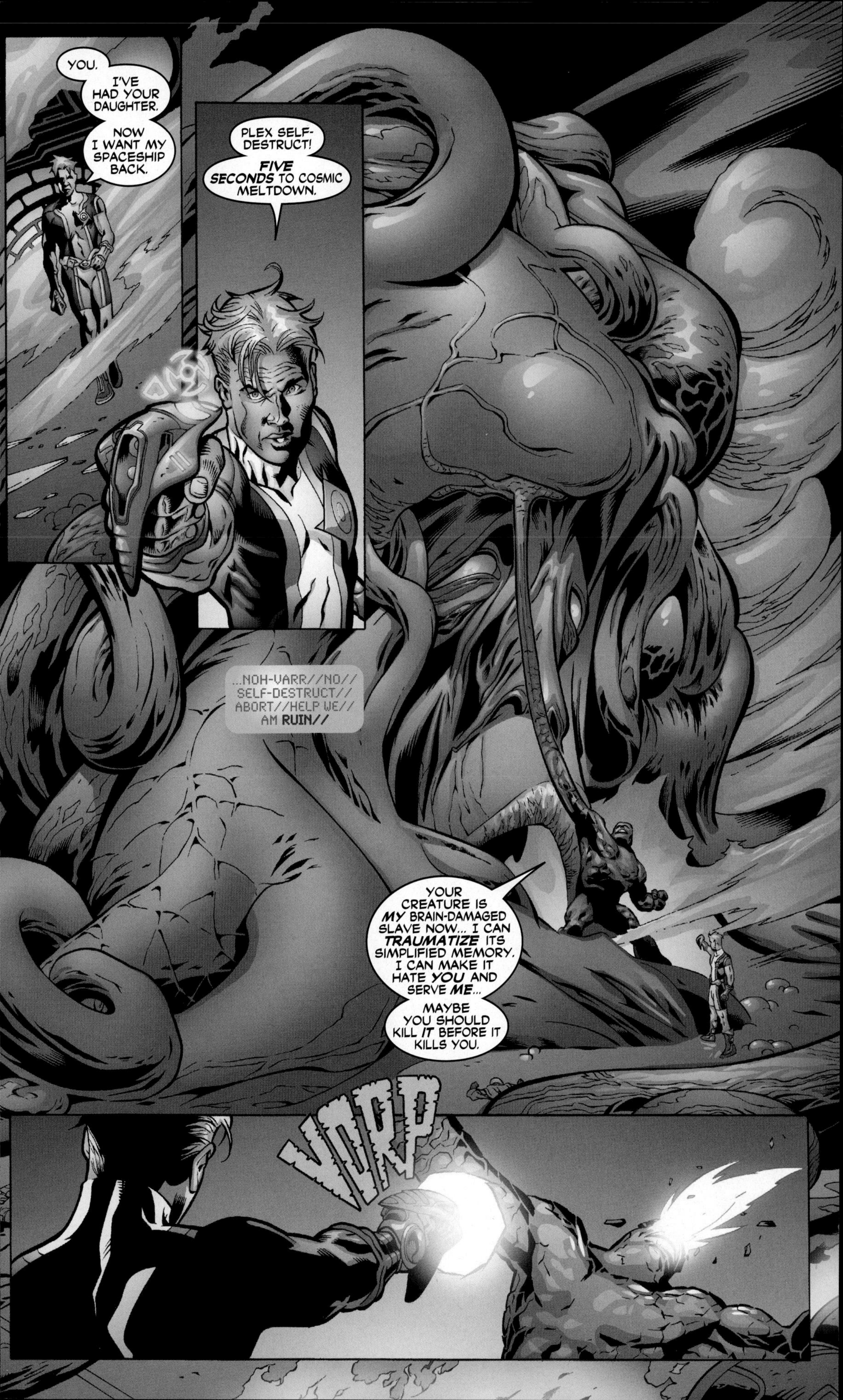
YOU.
I'VE HAD YOUR DAUGHTER.
NOW I WANT MY SPACESHIP BACK.
PLEX SELF-DESTRUCT!
FIVE SECONDS TO COSMIC MELTDOWN.
...NOH-VARR//NO// SELF-DESTRUCT// ABORT//HELP WE// AM RUIN//
YOUR CREATURE IS MY BRAIN-DAMAGED SLAVE NOW... I CAN TRAUMATIZE ITS SIMPLIFIED MEMORY. I CAN MAKE IT HATE YOU AND SERVE ME...
MAYBE YOU SHOULD KILL IT BEFORE IT KILLS YOU.
VORP

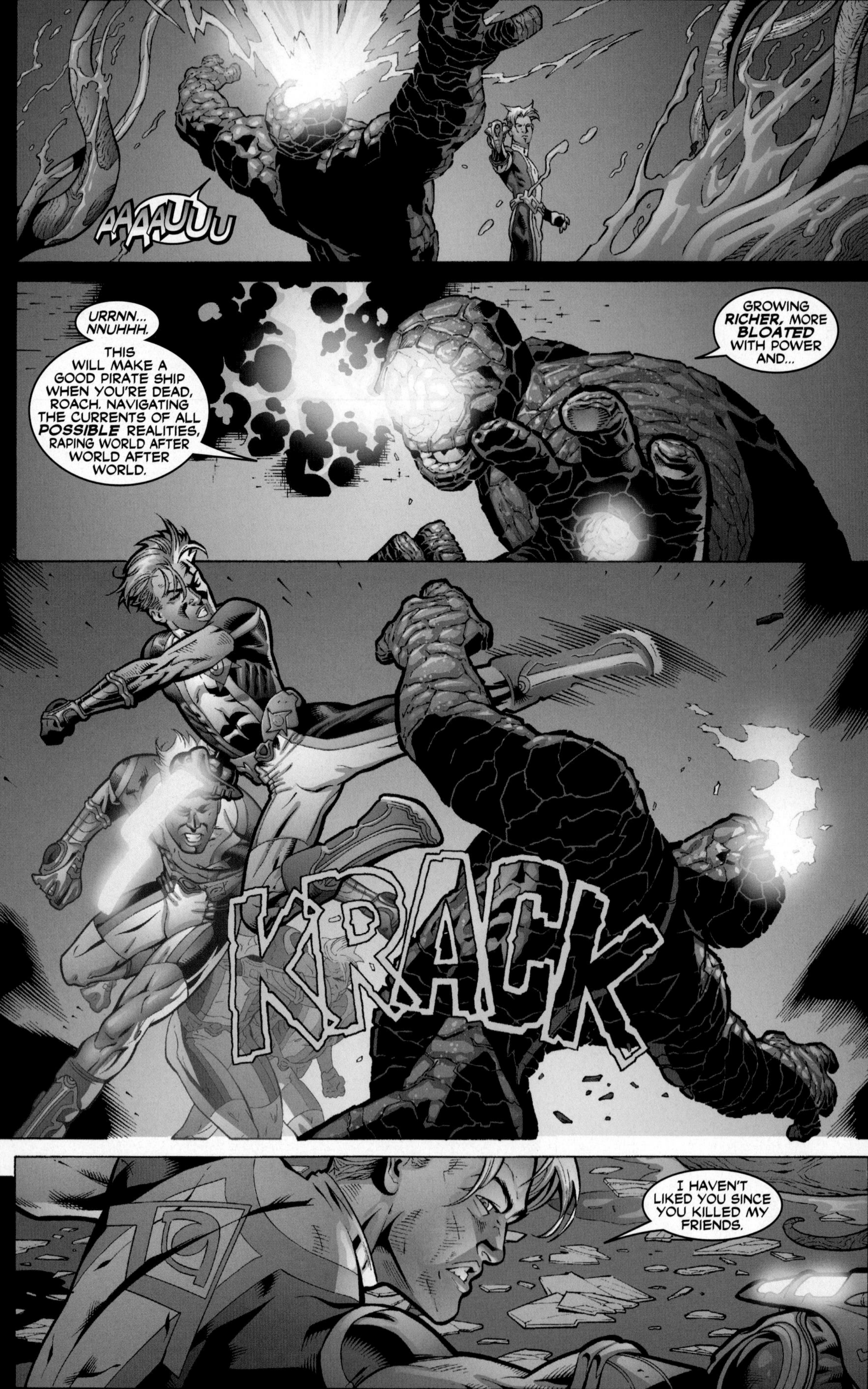
AAAAUUU
URRNN... NNUHHH.
THIS WILL MAKE A GOOD PIRATE SHIP WHEN YOU'RE DEAD, ROACH. NAVIGATING THE CURRENTS OF ALL POSSIBLE REALITIES, RAPING WORLD AFTER WORLD AFTER WORLD.
GROWING RICHER, MORE BLOATED WITH POWER AND...
KRACK
I HAVEN'T LIKED YOU SINCE YOU KILLED MY FRIENDS.

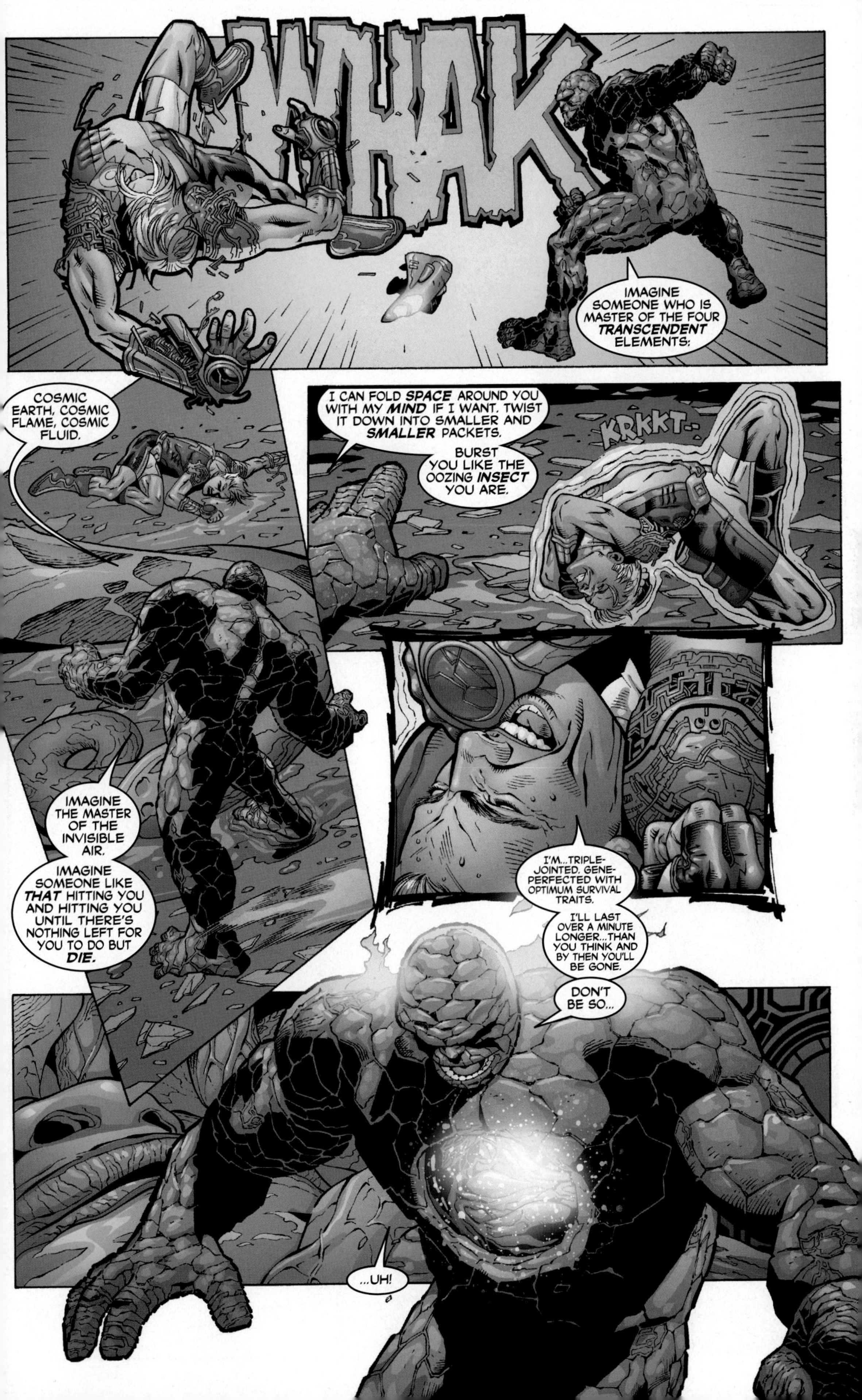
WHAK
IMAGINE SOMEONE WHO IS MASTER OF THE FOUR TRANSCENDENT ELEMENTS:
COSMIC EARTH, COSMIC FLAME, COSMIC FLUID.
I CAN FOLD SPACE AROUND YOU WITH MY MIND IF I WANT. TWIST IT DOWN INTO SMALLER AND SMALLER PACKETS.
BURST YOU LIKE THE OOZING INSECT YOU ARE.
KRKKT-
IMAGINE THE MASTER OF THE INVISIBLE AIR.
IMAGINE SOMEONE LIKE THAT HITTING YOU AND HITTING YOU UNTIL THERE'S NOTHING LEFT FOR YOU TO DO BUT DIE.
I'M...TRIPLE-JOINTED. GENE-PERFECTED WITH OPTIMUM SURVIVAL TRAITS.
I'LL LAST OVER A MINUTE LONGER...THAN YOU THINK AND BY THEN YOU'LL BE GONE.
DON'T BE SO...
...UH!

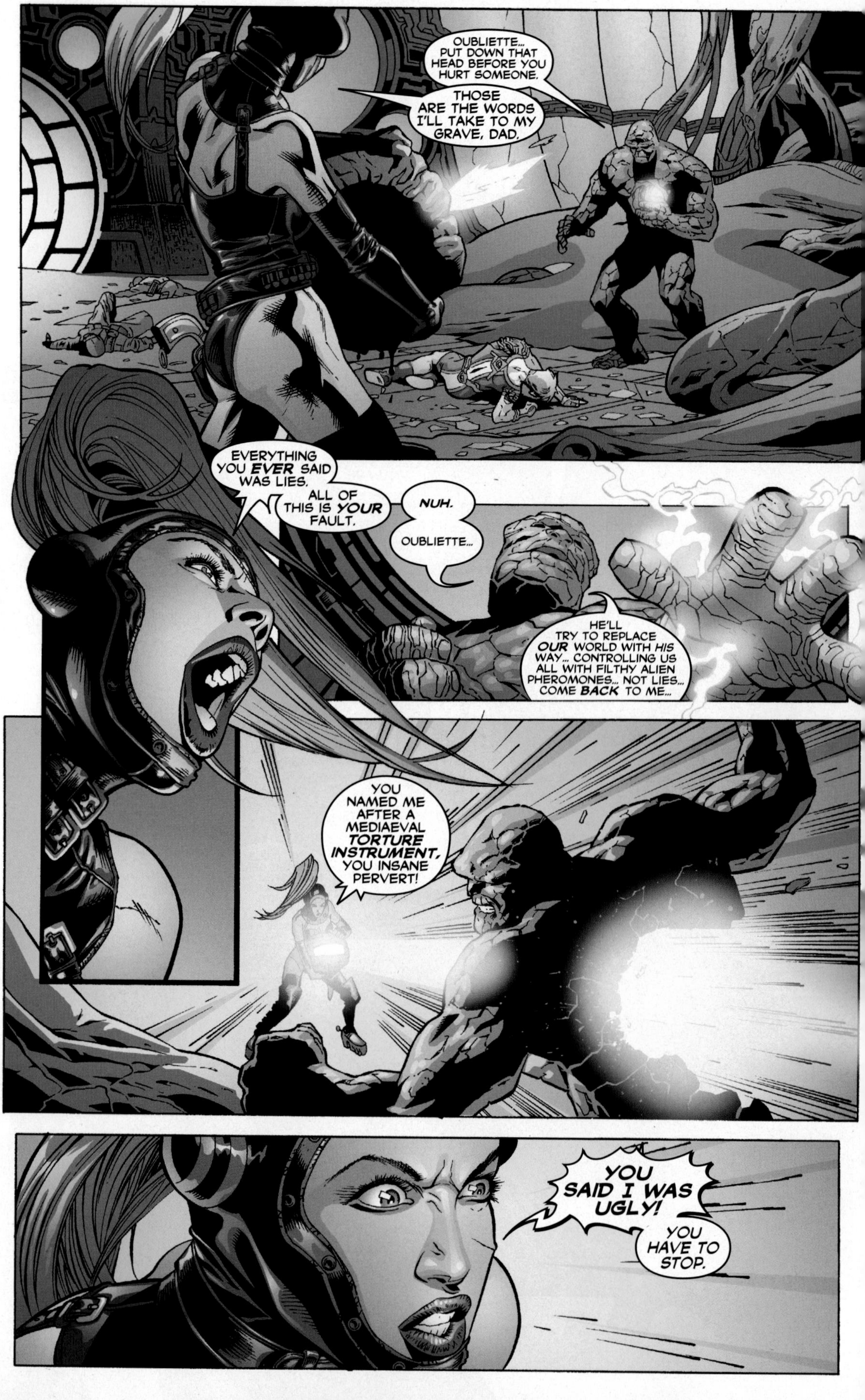
OUBLIETTE... PUT DOWN THAT HEAD BEFORE YOU HURT SOMEONE.
THOSE ARE THE WORDS I'LL TAKE TO MY GRAVE, DAD.
EVERYTHING YOU **EVER** SAID WAS LIES.
ALL OF THIS IS **YOUR** FAULT.
NUH.
OUBLIETTE...
HE'LL TRY TO REPLACE **OUR** WORLD WITH *HIS* WAY... CONTROLLING US ALL WITH FILTHY ALIEN PHEROMONES... NOT LIES... COME **BACK** TO ME...
YOU NAMED ME AFTER A MEDIAEVAL **TORTURE INSTRUMENT,** YOU INSANE PERVERT!
YOU SAID I WAS UGLY!
YOU HAVE TO STOP.

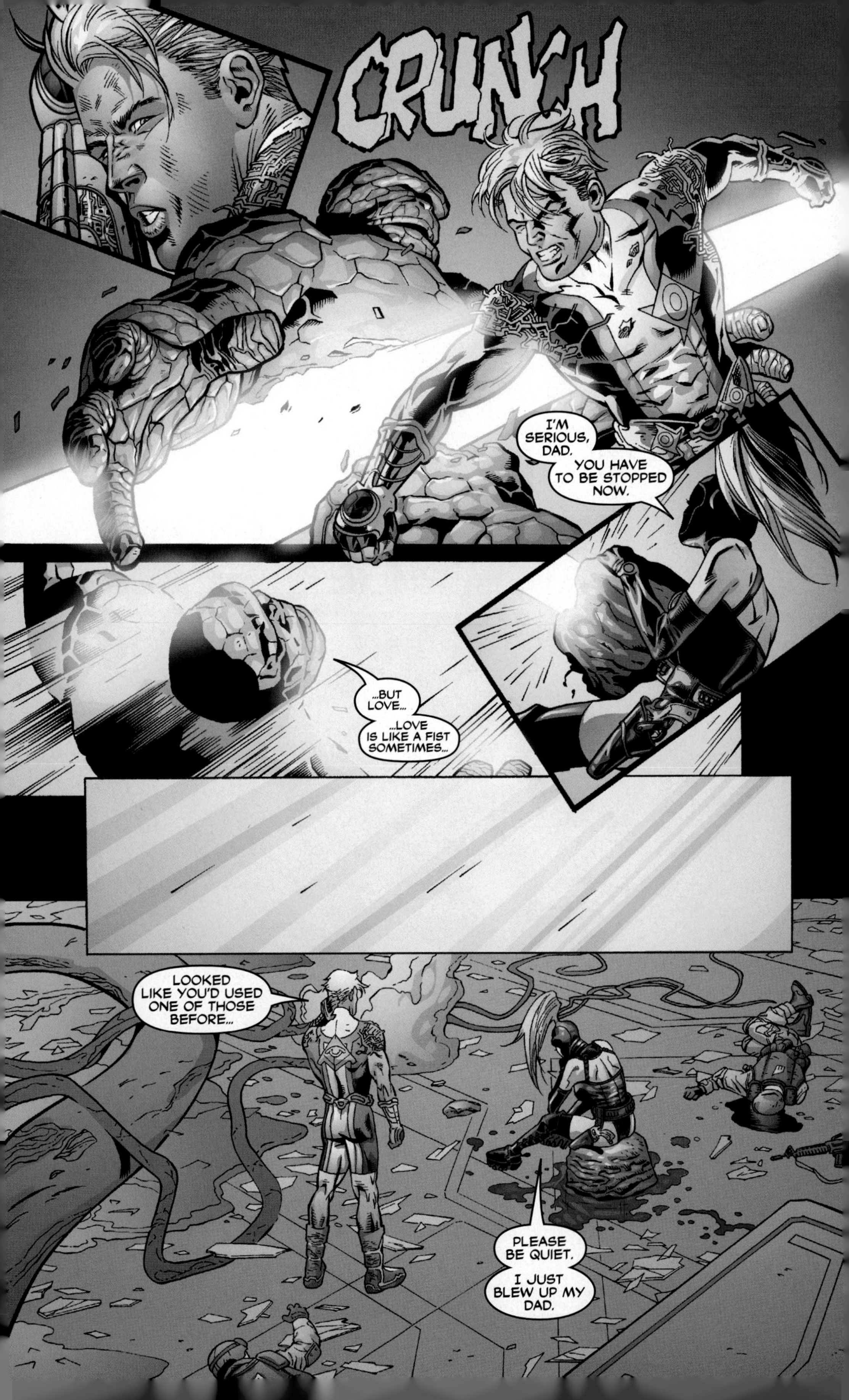
CRUNCH
I'M SERIOUS, DAD.
YOU HAVE TO BE STOPPED NOW.
...BUT LOVE...
...LOVE IS LIKE A FIST SOMETIMES...
LOOKED LIKE YOU'D USED ONE OF THOSE BEFORE...
PLEASE BE QUIET.
I JUST BLEW UP MY DAD.

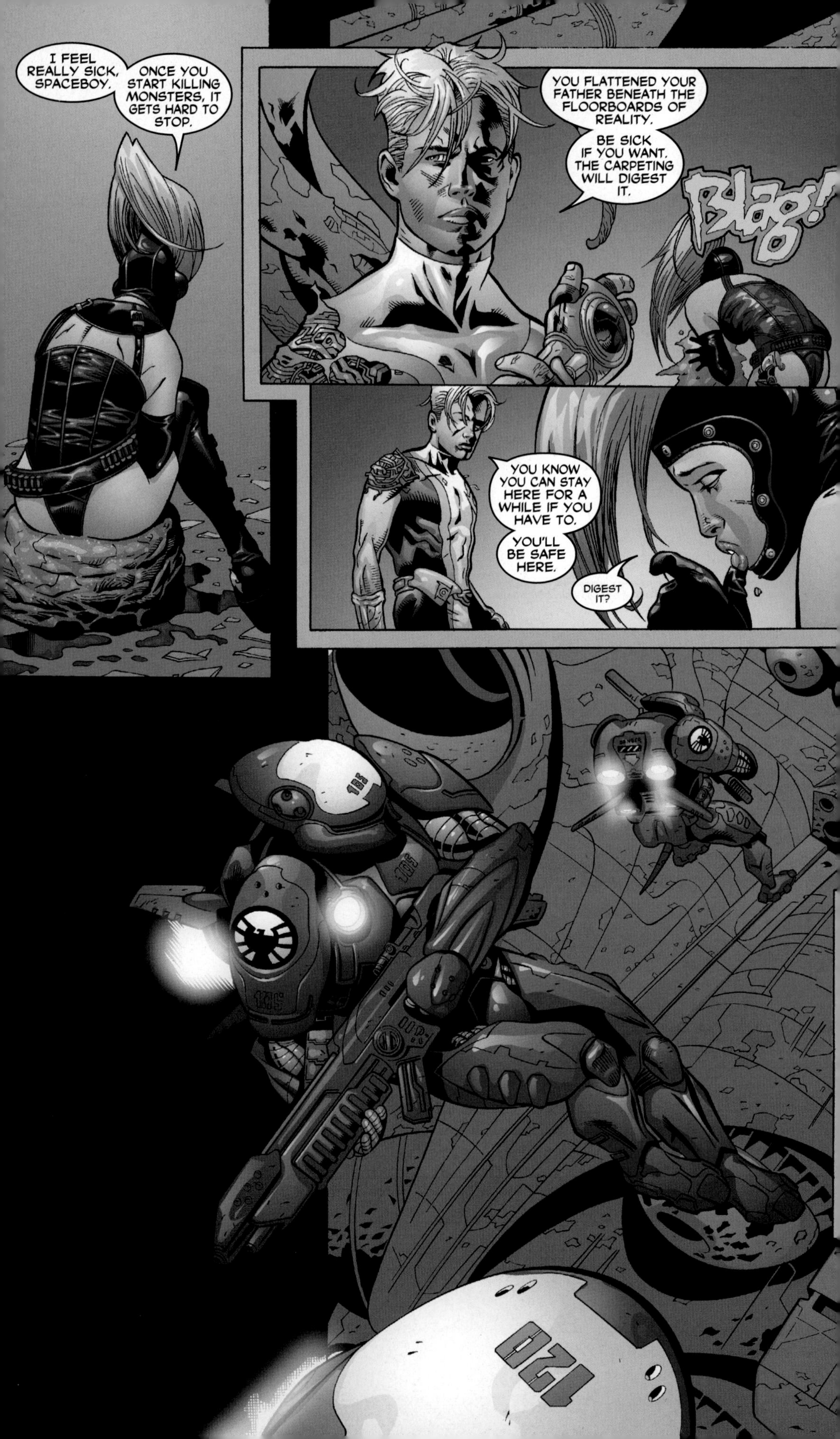
I FEEL REALLY SICK, SPACEBOY.
ONCE YOU START KILLING MONSTERS, IT GETS HARD TO STOP.
YOU FLATTENED YOUR FATHER BENEATH THE FLOORBOARDS OF REALITY.
BE SICK IF YOU WANT. THE CARPETING WILL DIGEST IT.
BLAG!
YOU KNOW YOU CAN STAY HERE FOR A WHILE IF YOU HAVE TO.
YOU'LL BE SAFE HERE.
DIGEST IT?
120

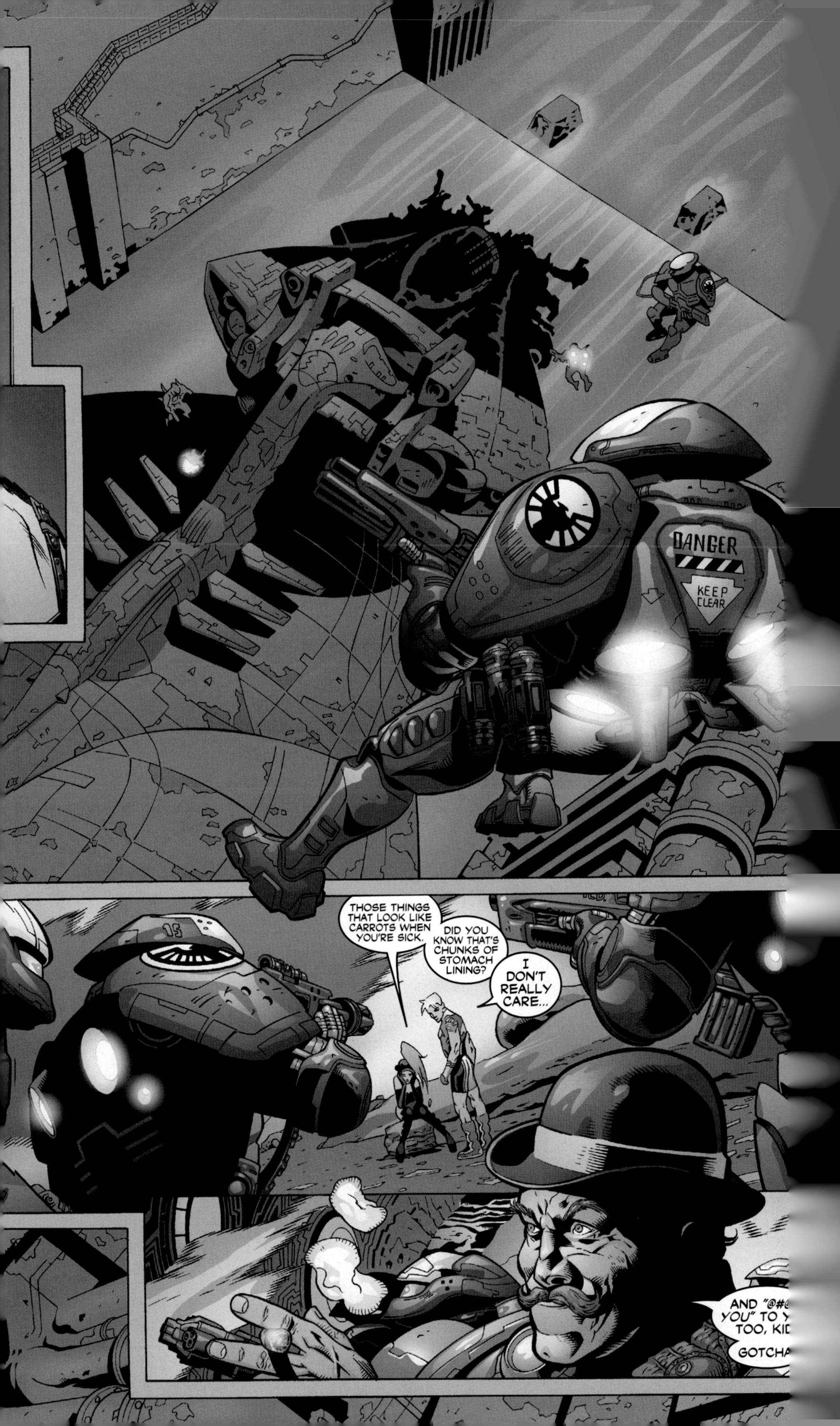
DANGER
KEEP CLEAR
THOSE THINGS THAT LOOK LIKE CARROTS WHEN YOU'RE SICK.
DID YOU KNOW THAT'S CHUNKS OF STOMACH LINING?
I DON'T REALLY CARE...
AND "@#
YOU" TO
TOO, KI
GOTCH

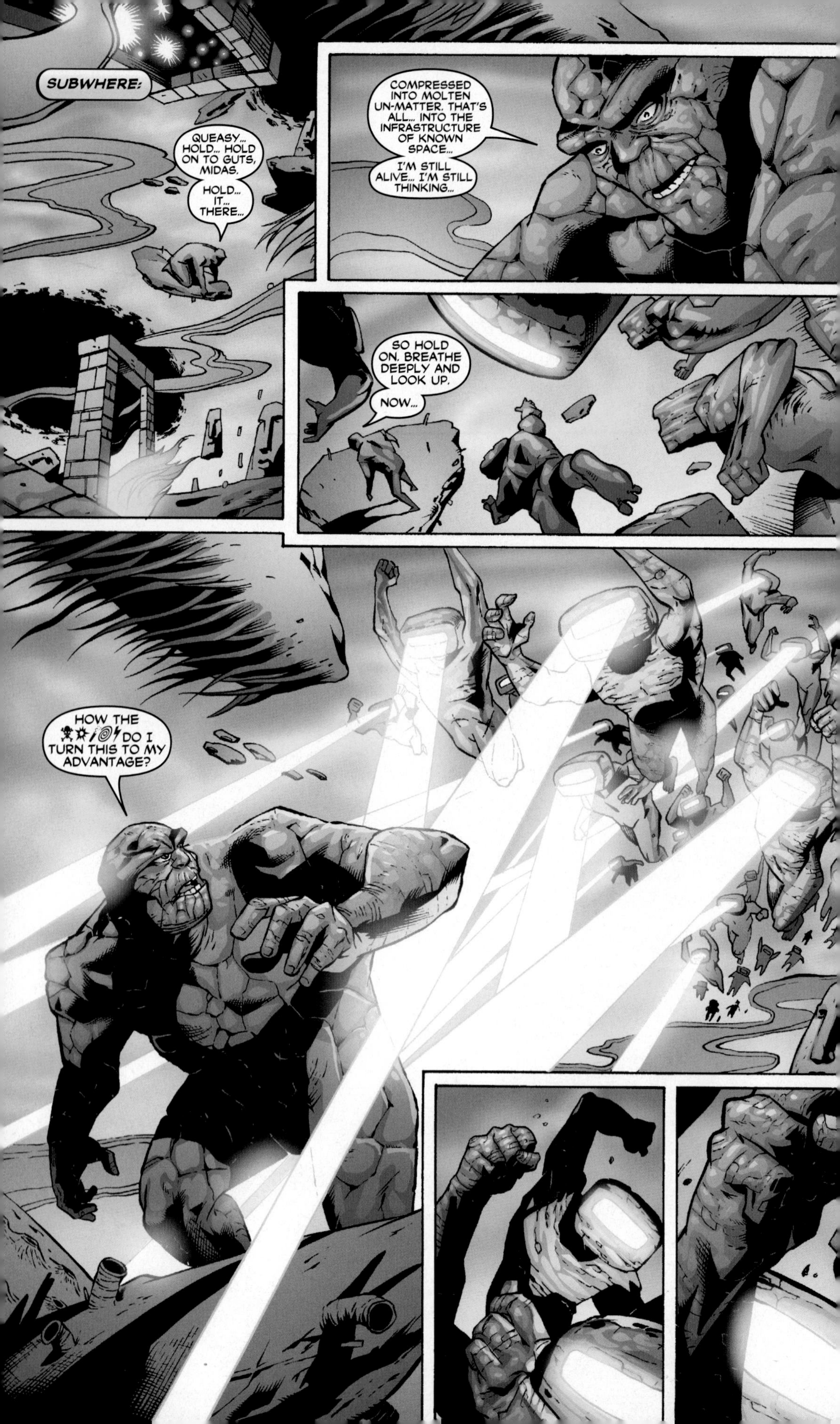
SUBWHERE:
QUEASY... HOLD... HOLD ON TO GUTS, MIDAS.
HOLD... IT... THERE...
COMPRESSED INTO MOLTEN UN-MATTER. THAT'S ALL... INTO THE INFRASTRUCTURE OF KNOWN SPACE...
I'M STILL ALIVE... I'M STILL THINKING...
SO HOLD ON. BREATHE DEEPLY AND LOOK UP.
NOW...
HOW THE DO I TURN THIS TO MY ADVANTAGE?

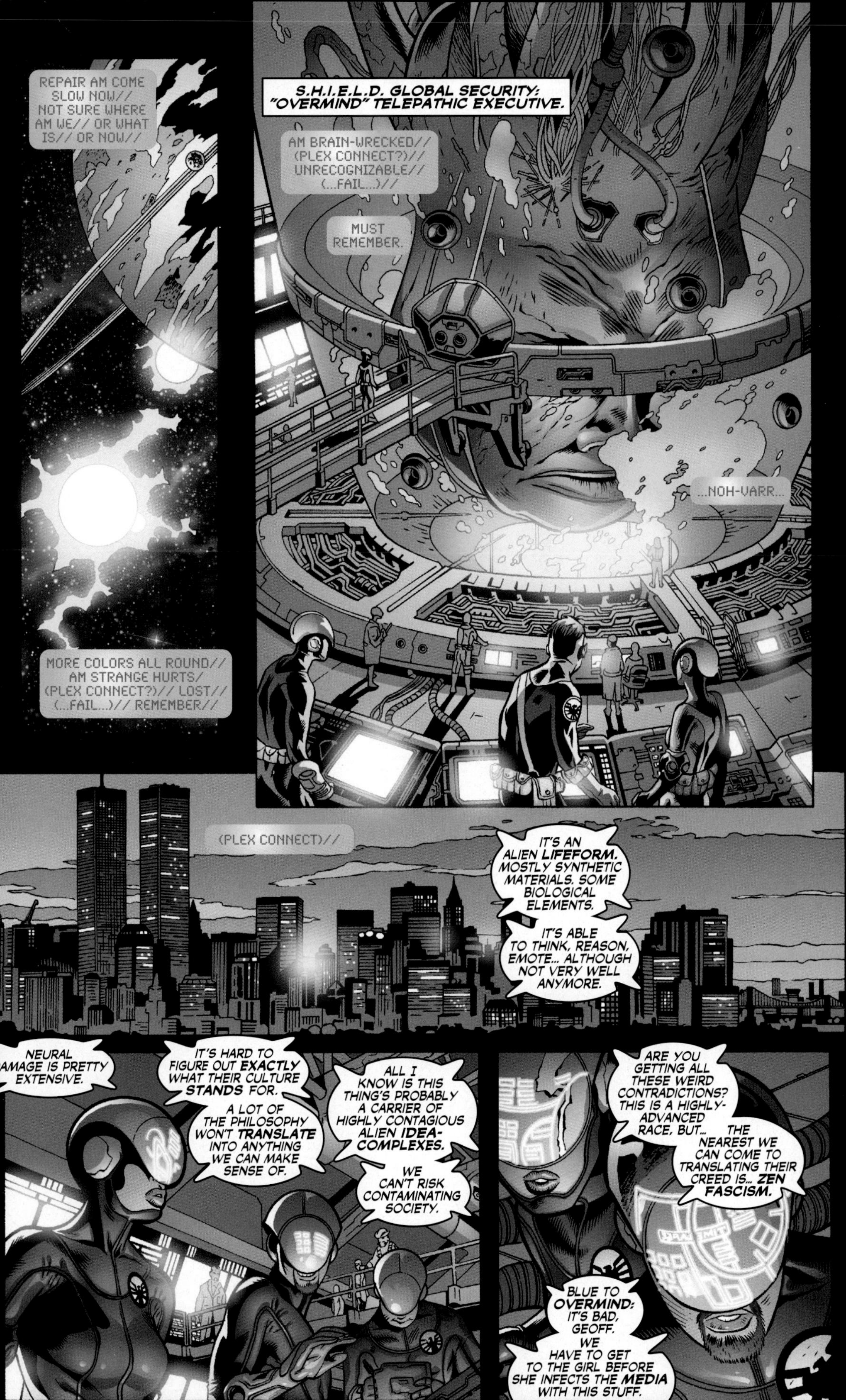
REPAIR AM COME SLOW NOW// NOT SURE WHERE AM WE// OR WHAT IS// OR NOW//
MORE COLORS ALL ROUND// AM STRANGE HURTS/ (PLEX CONNECT?)// LOST// (...FAIL...)// REMEMBER//
S.H.I.E.L.D. GLOBAL SECURITY: "OVERMIND" TELEPATHIC EXECUTIVE.
AM BRAIN-WRECKED// (PLEX CONNECT?)// UNRECOGNIZABLE// (...FAIL...)//
MUST REMEMBER.
...NOH-VARR...
(PLEX CONNECT)//
IT'S AN ALIEN LIFEFORM. MOSTLY SYNTHETIC MATERIALS. SOME BIOLOGICAL ELEMENTS.
IT'S ABLE TO THINK, REASON, EMOTE... ALTHOUGH NOT VERY WELL ANYMORE.
NEURAL AMAGE IS PRETTY EXTENSIVE.
IT'S HARD TO FIGURE OUT EXACTLY WHAT THEIR CULTURE STANDS FOR.
A LOT OF THE PHILOSOPHY WON'T TRANSLATE INTO ANYTHING WE CAN MAKE SENSE OF.
ALL I KNOW IS THIS THING'S PROBABLY A CARRIER OF HIGHLY CONTAGIOUS ALIEN IDEA-COMPLEXES.
WE CAN'T RISK CONTAMINATING SOCIETY.
ARE YOU GETTING ALL THESE WEIRD CONTRADICTIONS? THIS IS A HIGHLY-ADVANCED RACE, BUT...
THE NEAREST WE CAN COME TO TRANSLATING THEIR CREED IS... ZEN FASCISM.
BLUE TO OVERMIND: IT'S BAD, GEOFF.
WE HAVE TO GET TO THE GIRL BEFORE SHE INFECTS THE MEDIA WITH THIS STUFF.

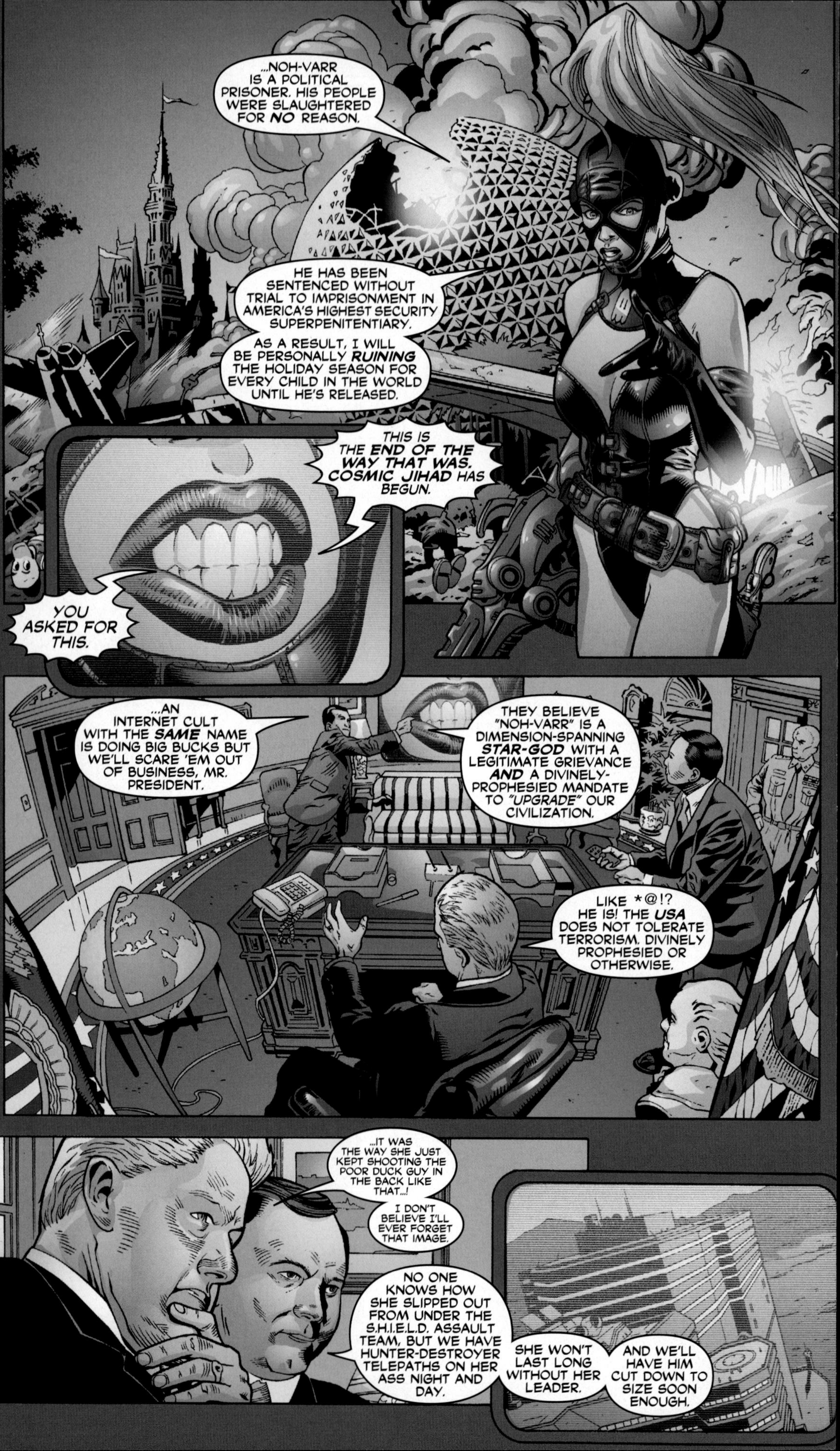
...NOH-VARR IS A POLITICAL PRISONER. HIS PEOPLE WERE SLAUGHTERED FOR NO REASON.
HE HAS BEEN SENTENCED WITHOUT TRIAL TO IMPRISONMENT IN AMERICA'S HIGHEST SECURITY SUPERPENITENTIARY.
AS A RESULT, I WILL BE PERSONALLY RUINING THE HOLIDAY SEASON FOR EVERY CHILD IN THE WORLD UNTIL HE'S RELEASED.
THIS IS THE END OF THE WAY THAT WAS. COSMIC JIHAD HAS BEGUN.
YOU ASKED FOR THIS.
...AN INTERNET CULT WITH THE SAME NAME IS DOING BIG BUCKS BUT WE'LL SCARE 'EM OUT OF BUSINESS, MR. PRESIDENT.
THEY BELIEVE "NOH-VARR" IS A DIMENSION-SPANNING STAR-GOD WITH A LEGITIMATE GRIEVANCE AND A DIVINELY-PROPHESIED MANDATE TO "UPGRADE" OUR CIVILIZATION.
LIKE *@!? HE IS! THE USA DOES NOT TOLERATE TERRORISM. DIVINELY PROPHESIED OR OTHERWISE.
...IT WAS THE WAY SHE JUST KEPT SHOOTING THE POOR DUCK GUY IN THE BACK LIKE THAT...!
I DON'T BELIEVE I'LL EVER FORGET THAT IMAGE.
NO ONE KNOWS HOW SHE SLIPPED OUT FROM UNDER THE S.H.I.E.L.D. ASSAULT TEAM, BUT WE HAVE HUNTER-DESTROYER TELEPATHS ON HER ASS NIGHT AND DAY.
SHE WON'T LAST LONG WITHOUT HER LEADER.
AND WE'LL HAVE HIM CUT DOWN TO SIZE SOON ENOUGH.

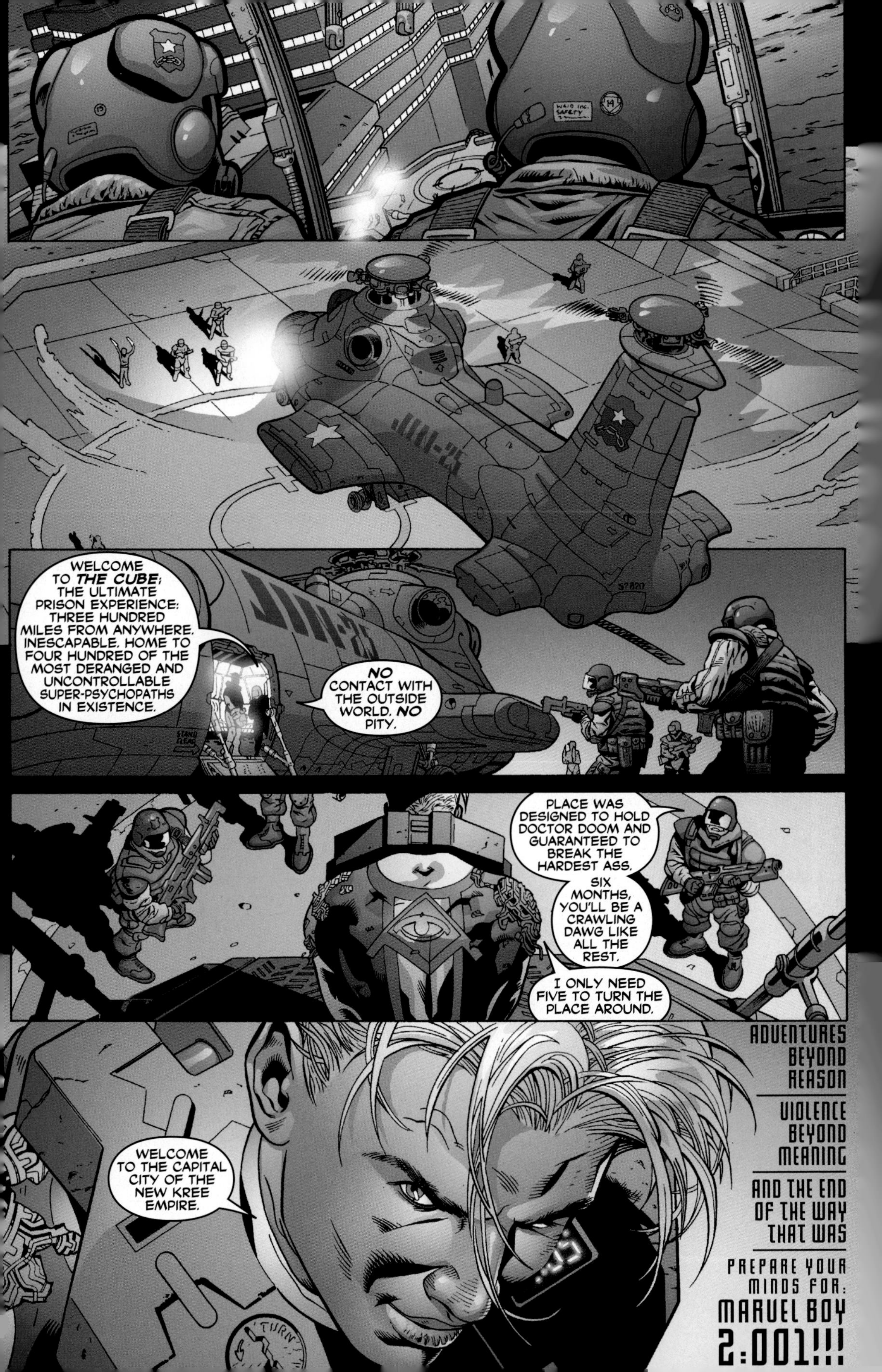

WELCOME TO THE CUBE; THE ULTIMATE PRISON EXPERIENCE: THREE HUNDRED MILES FROM ANYWHERE. INESCAPABLE. HOME TO FOUR HUNDRED OF THE MOST DERANGED AND UNCONTROLLABLE SUPER-PSYCHOPATHS IN EXISTENCE.
NO CONTACT WITH THE OUTSIDE WORLD. NO PITY.
PLACE WAS DESIGNED TO HOLD DOCTOR DOOM AND GUARANTEED TO BREAK THE HARDEST ASS.
SIX MONTHS, YOU'LL BE A CRAWLING DAWG LIKE ALL THE REST.
I ONLY NEED FIVE TO TURN THE PLACE AROUND.
WELCOME TO THE CAPITAL CITY OF THE NEW KREE EMPIRE.
ADVENTURES BEYOND REASON
VIOLENCE BEYOND MEANING
AND THE END OF THE WAY THAT WAS
PREPARE YOUR MINDS FOR:
MARVEL BOY 2:001!!!

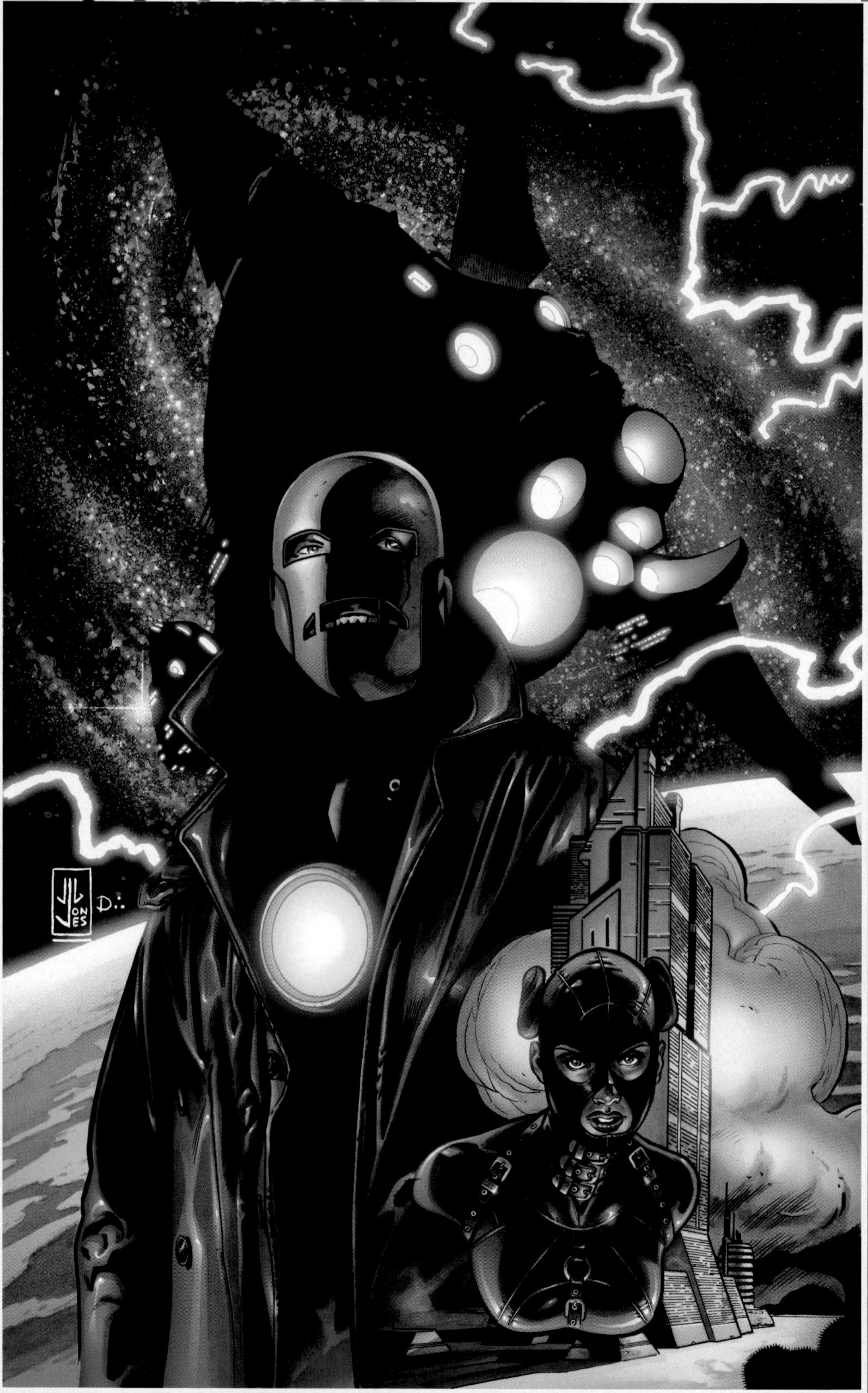

(1 Variant)

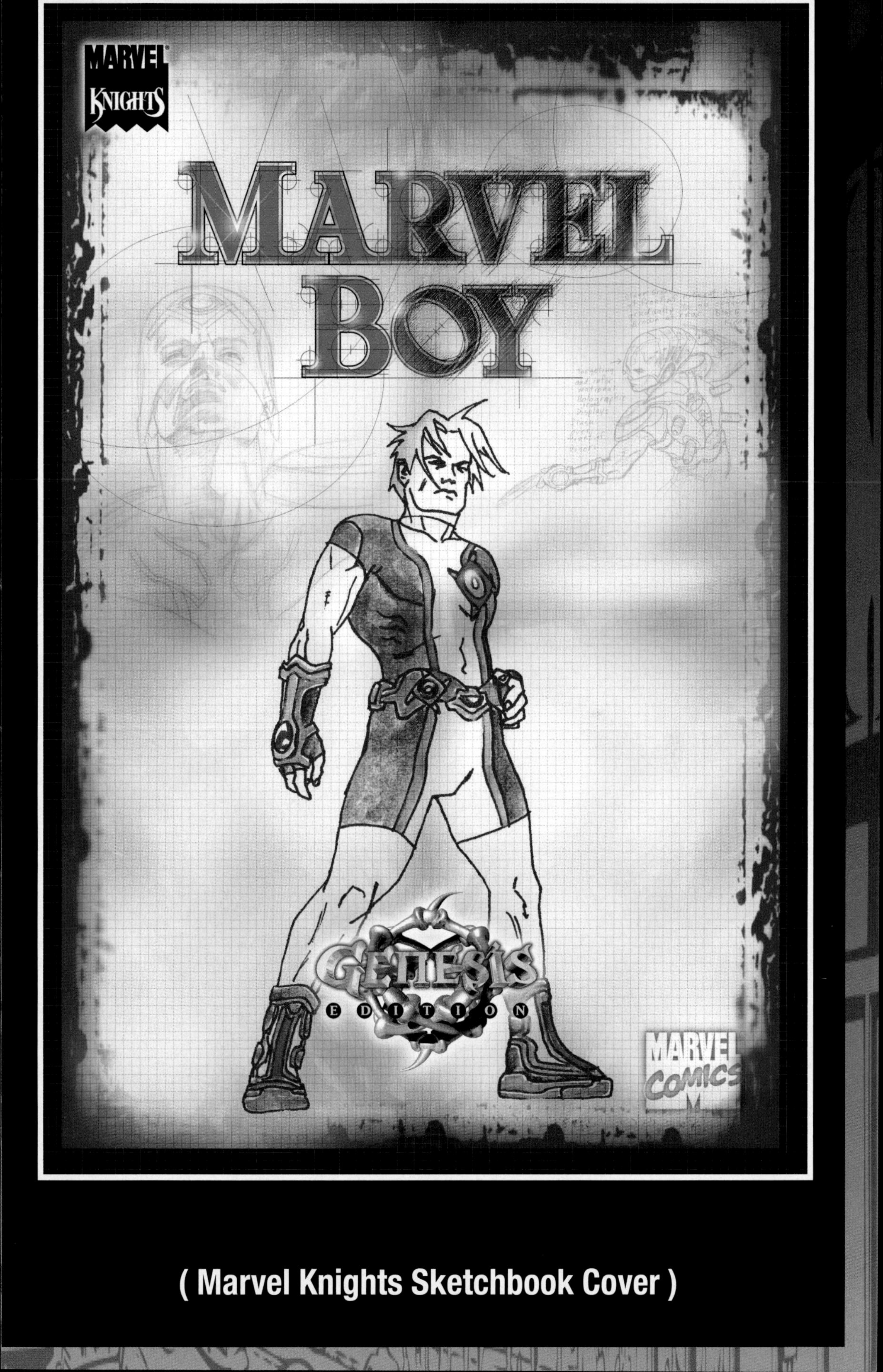
MARVEL KNIGHTS
MARVEL BOY
GENESIS EDITION
MARVEL COMICS

(Marvel Knights Sketchbook Cover)

Writer
Mike Raicht

Artist
J.G. Jones

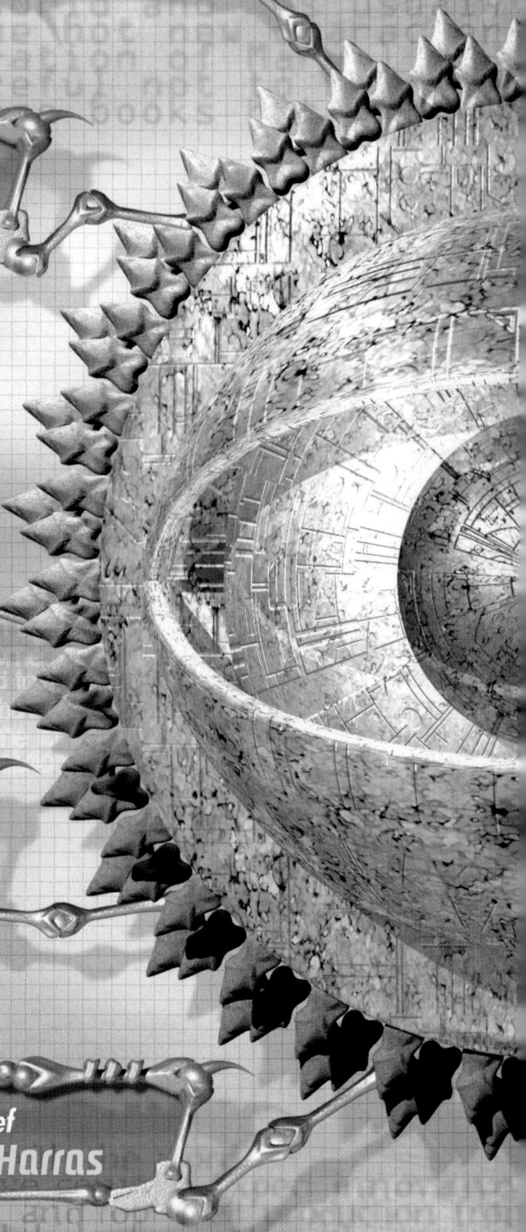

Designer
Jeffrey Huang

Editor
Polly Watson

Editor in Chief
Bob Harras

Introduction

MARVEL KNIGHTS: The name is synonymous with the word "quality." We've come to expect innovative storytelling, cutting-edge art and top-shelf production from any book bearing the Knightly banner. Now, the tradition continues with a vengeance as we come to the next step in the MARVEL KNIGHTS evolution: MARVEL BOY!

Written by Grant Morrison and featuring the mind-blowing art of J.G. Jones, fresh off his stint on the sharp and sexy BLACK WIDOW limited series, MARVEL BOY takes a twisted look at the Marvel Universe you didn't know existed, and reveals it to be chock-full of action, adventure and intrigue! Awe-inspiring stories as only Grant Morrison can deliver them, with art that will knock you on your butt!

When you pick up a MARVEL KNIGHTS book you expect to see art that is out of this world and, as usual, the KNIGHTS deliver! Take a look at the hot new character who just may be the next generation of Marvel super hero! But be careful not to burn your eyeballs — you'll need 'em when these books hit the stands next month!

GENESIS EDITION

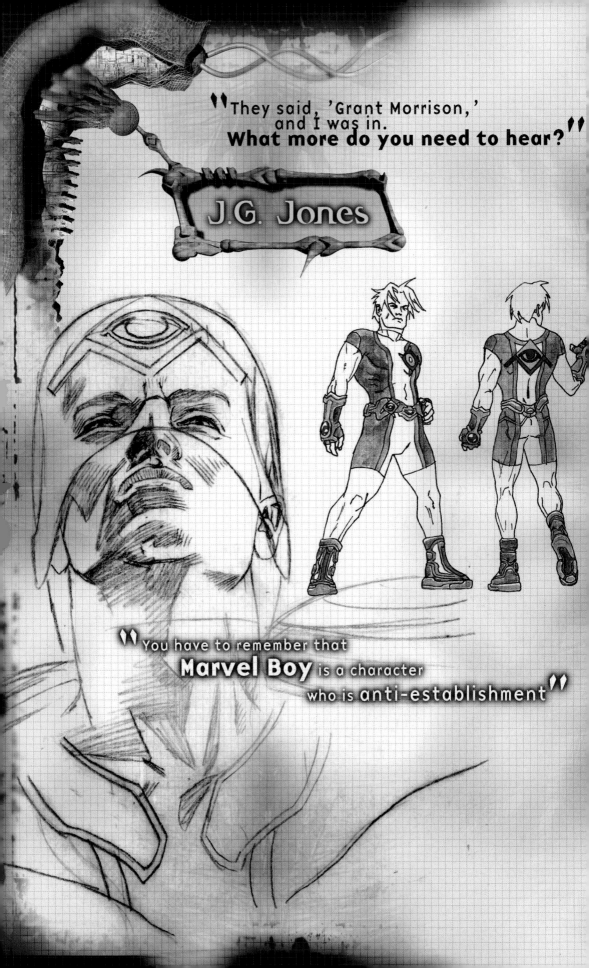

"They said, 'Grant Morrison,' and I was in. **What more do you need to hear?**"

J.G. Jones

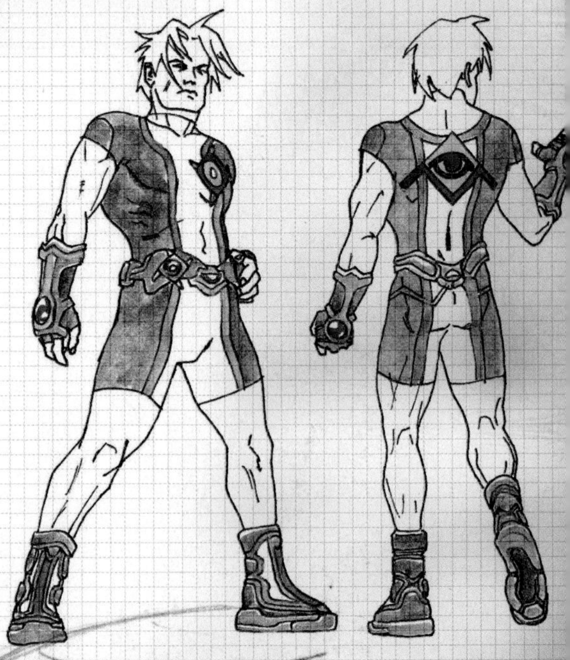

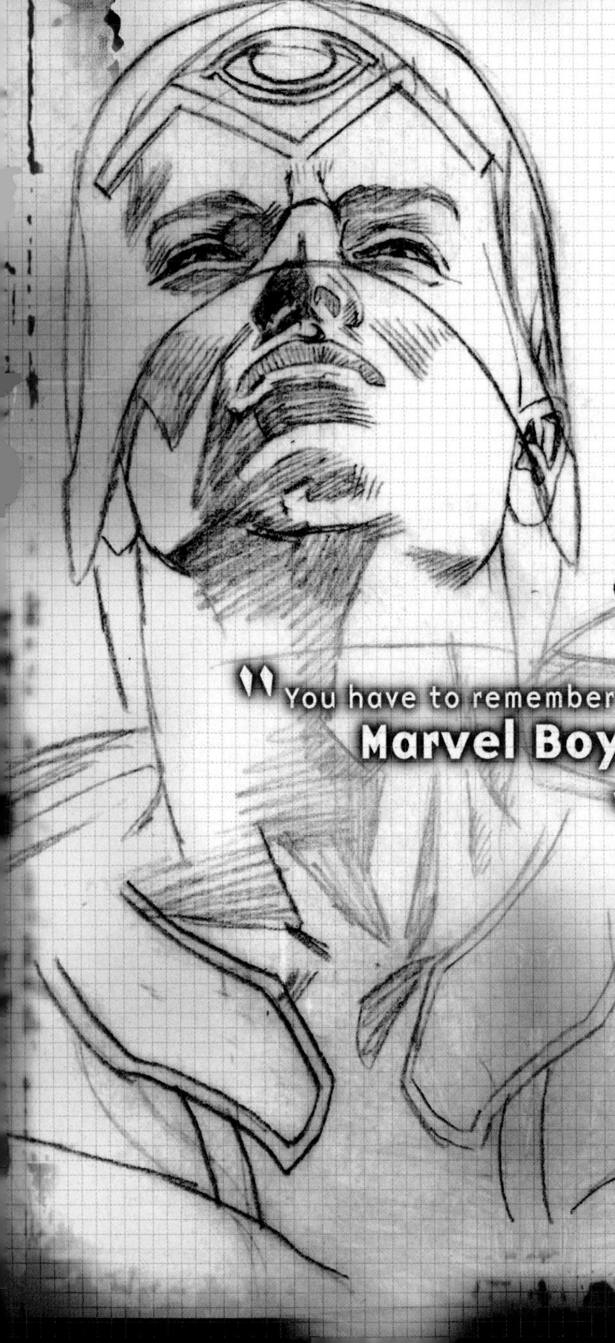

"You have to remember that **Marvel Boy** is a character who is anti-establishment"

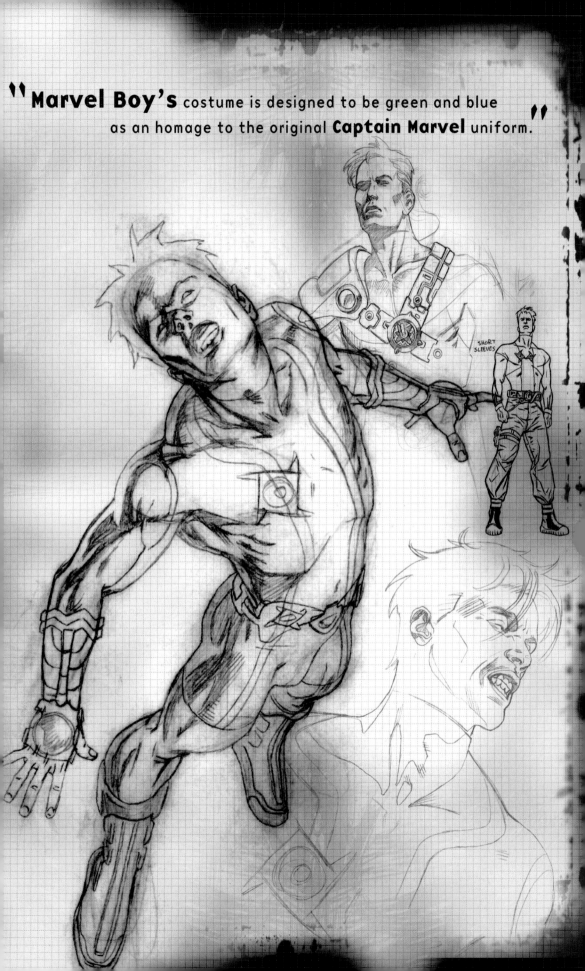

"Marvel Boy's costume is designed to be green and blue as an homage to the original **Captain Marvel** uniform.**"**

SHORT SLEEVES

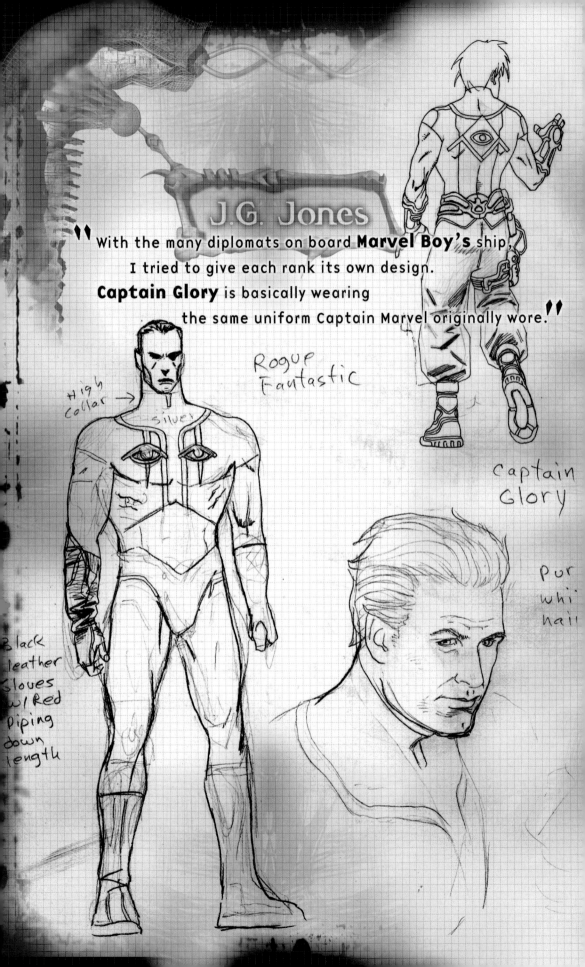

J.G. Jones

"With the many diplomats on board **Marvel Boy's** ship, I tried to give each rank its own design. **Captain Glory** is basically wearing the same uniform Captain Marvel originally wore."

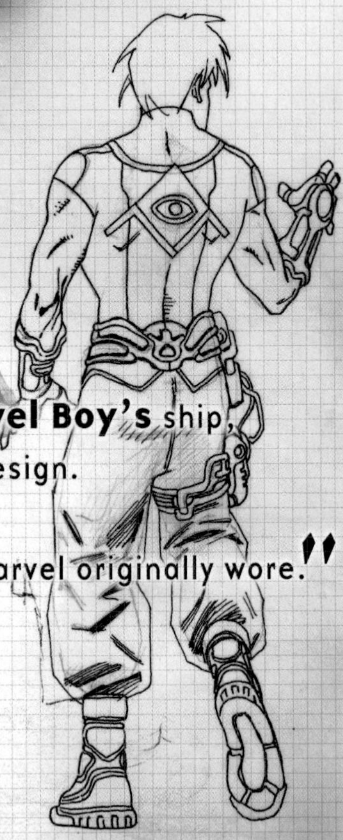

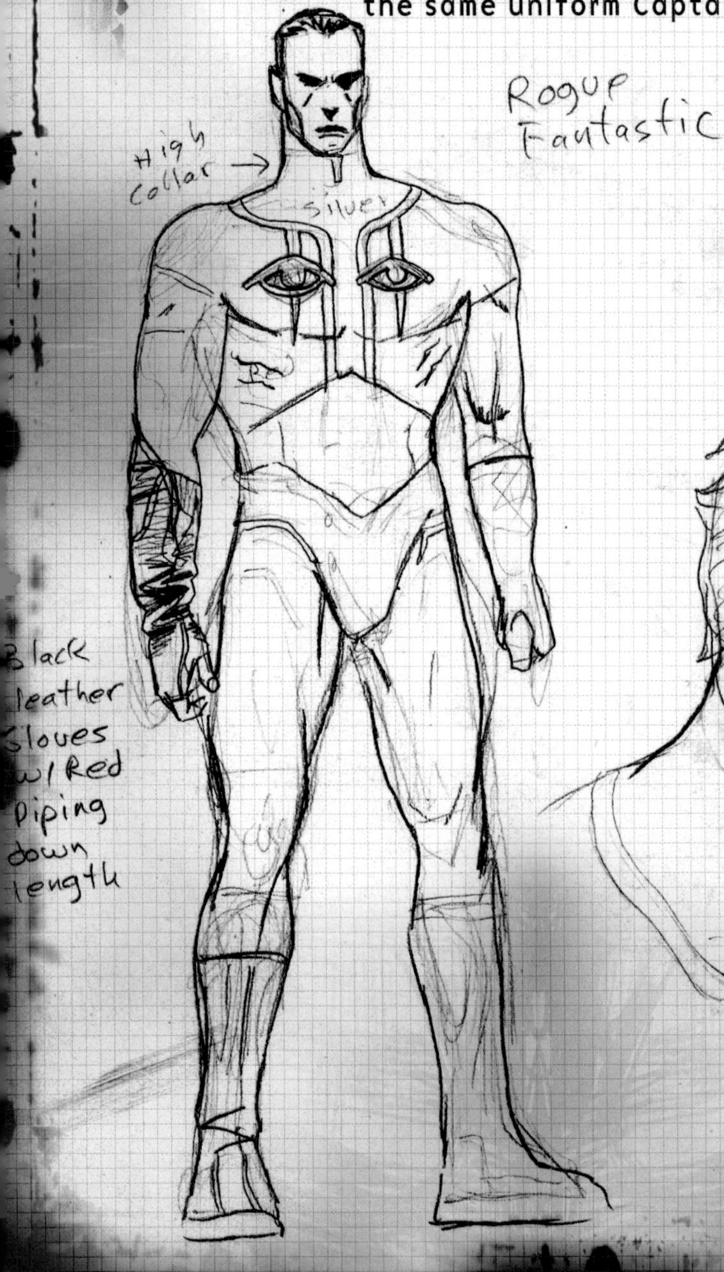
Rogue Fantastic
High collar
Silver
Black leather Gloves w/ Red piping down length

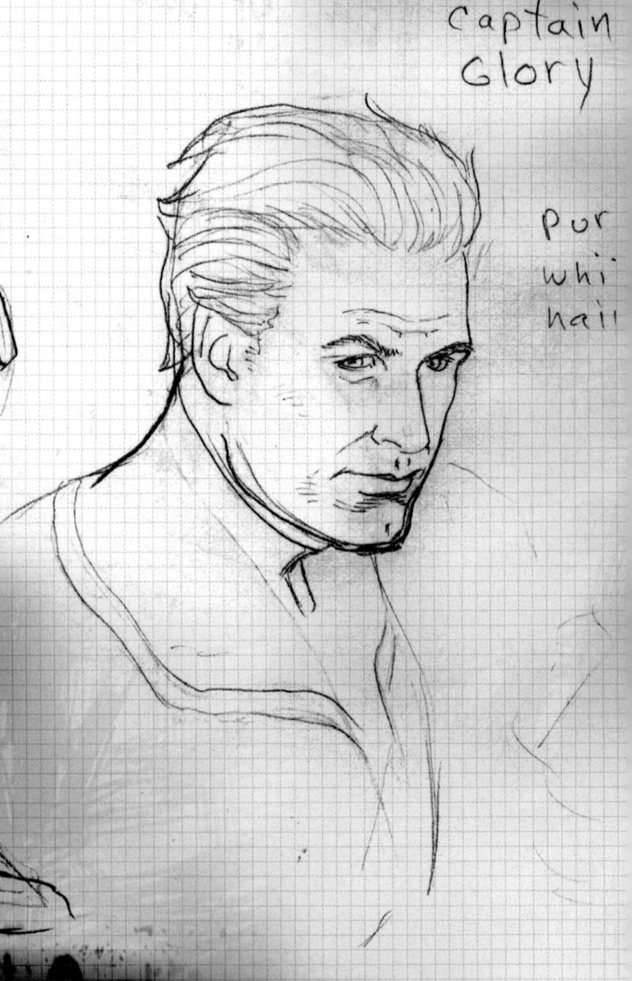
Captain Glory

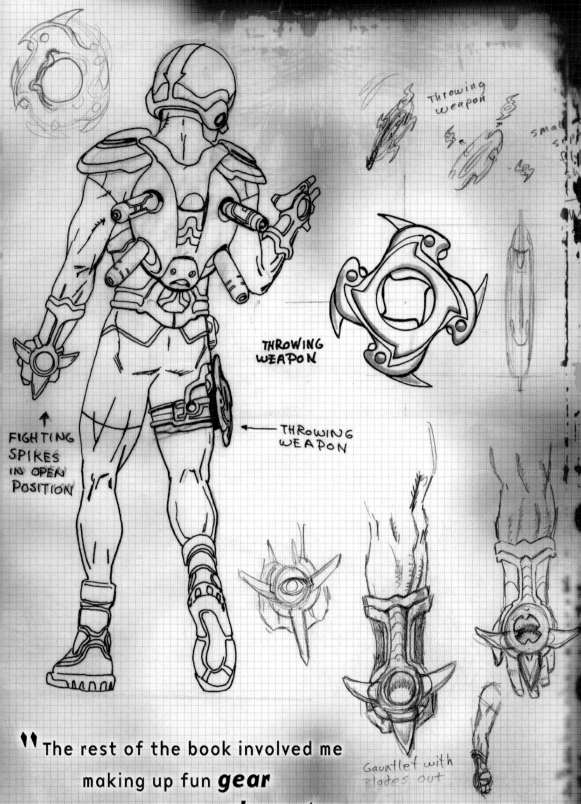

throwing weapon

small
sep

THROWING
WEAPON

THROWING
WEAPON

FIGHTING
SPIKES
IN OPEN
POSITION

Gauntlet with
blades out

"The rest of the book involved me
making up fun *gear*
for the *character* which was a blast!
Each issue **Marvel Boy** changes gear
so I had a lot of fun dreaming stuff up."

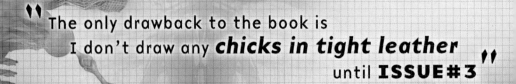

"The only drawback to the book is I don't draw any ***chicks in tight leather*** until **ISSUE#3**"

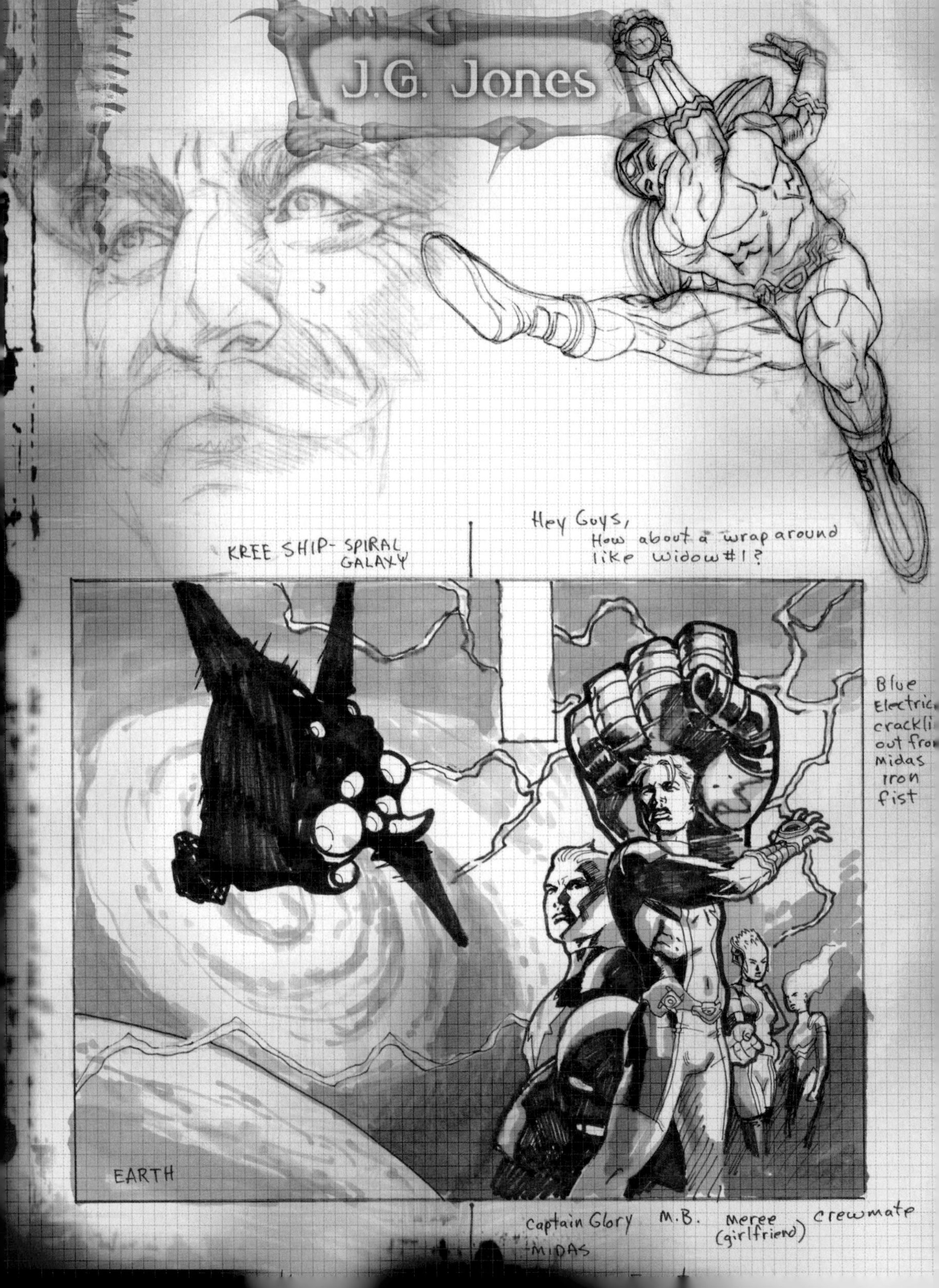

J.G. Jones
KREE SHIP- SPIRAL GALAXY
Hey Guys,
How about a wrap around like Widow #1?
Blue
Midas
iron
fist
EARTH
Captain Glory
MIDAS
M.B.
Meree (girlfriend)
crewmate

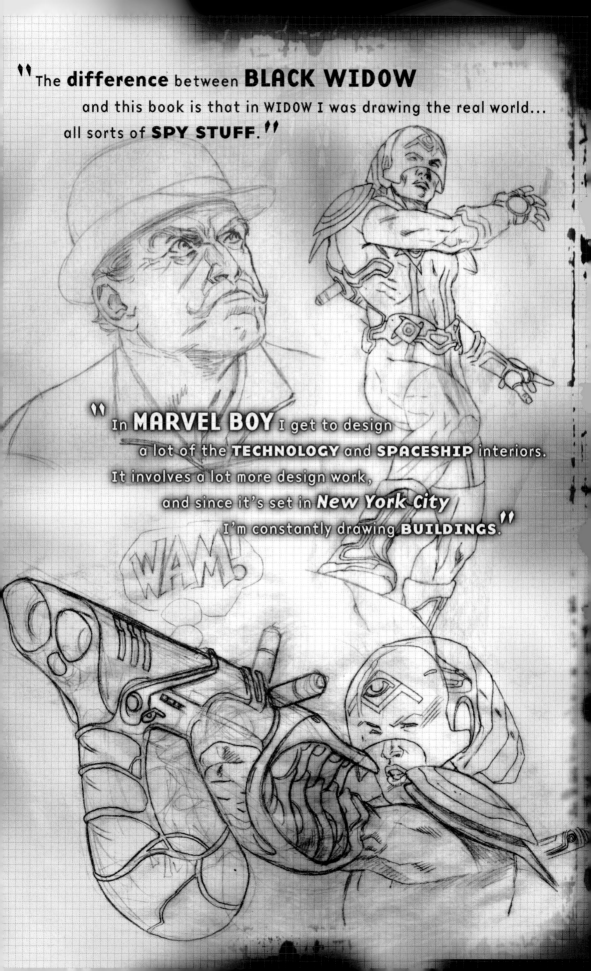

"The **difference** between **BLACK WIDOW** and this book is that in WIDOW I was drawing the real world... all sorts of **SPY STUFF**."

"In **MARVEL BOY** I get to design a lot of the **TECHNOLOGY** and **SPACESHIP** interiors. It involves a lot more design work, and since it's set in *New York City* I'm constantly drawing **BUILDINGS**."

WAM!

"I'm having a ball on this book. It's **ACTION-ORIENTED** all the way with Grant's political bent thrown in. Playing on the edges of the **Marvel Universe** in this book has been great."

J.G. Jones

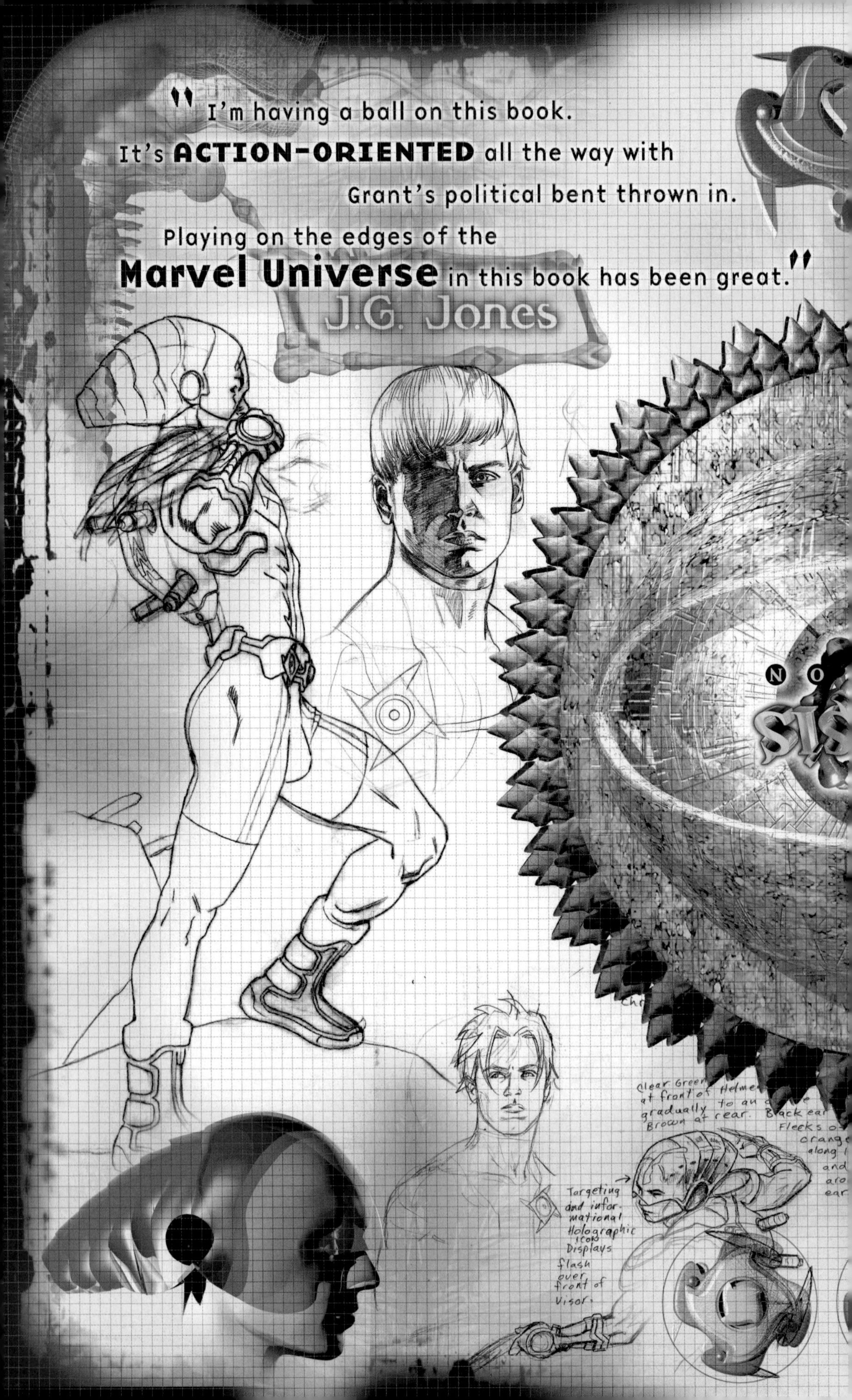

Targeting and informational Holographic icon Displays flash over front of Visor.
at front of
gradually to an
Brown at rear. Black ear

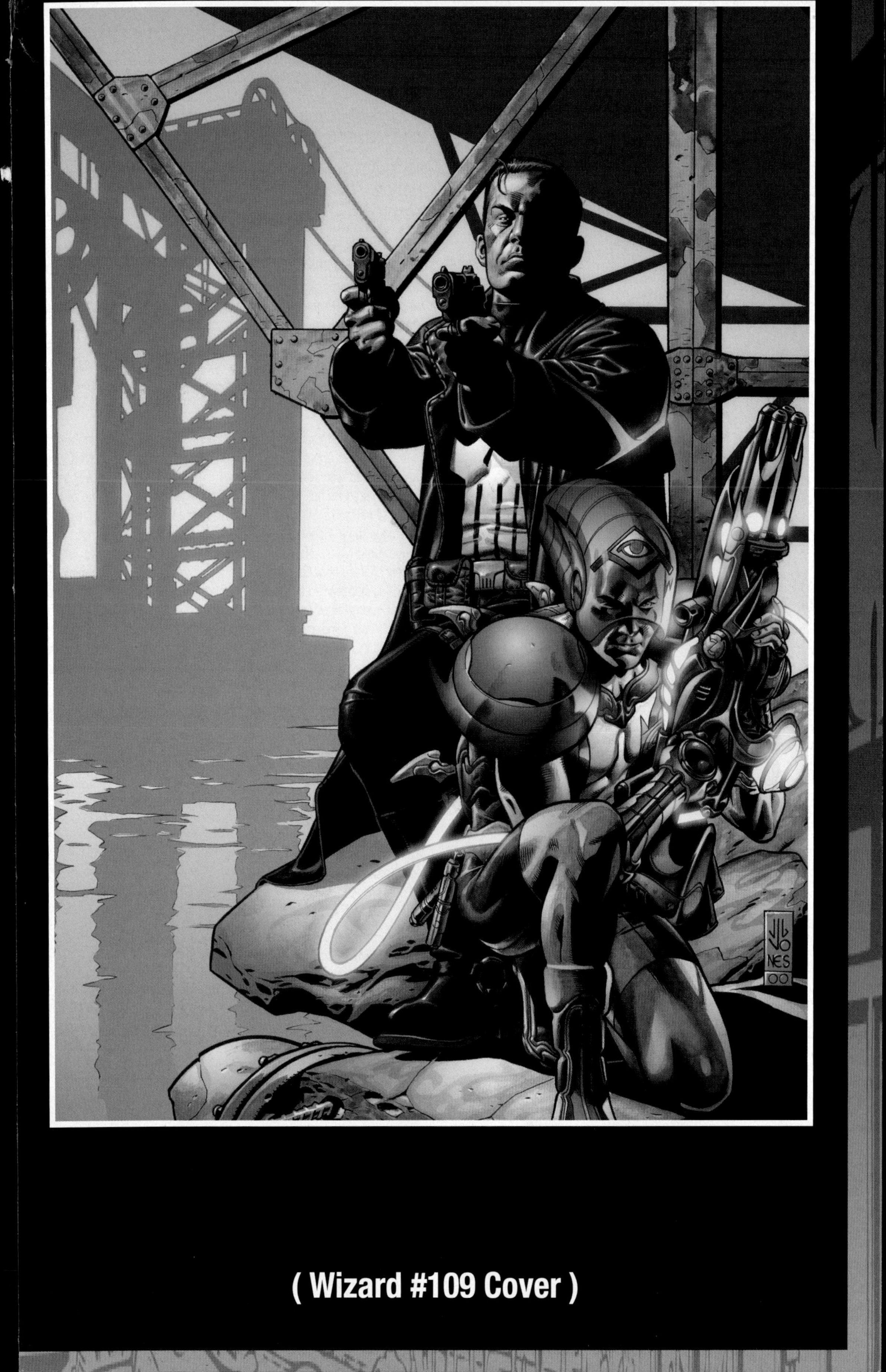

(Wizard #109 Cover)

MARVEL BOY

REAL NAME: Noh-Varr
ALIASES: Ensign Marvel
OCCUPATION: Extradimensional peacekeeper, Kree missionary
CITIZENSHIP: Kree Empire (otherdimensional version)
PLACE OF BIRTH: Unrevealed (alternate reality)
KNOWN RELATIVES: None
GROUP AFFILIATION: Formerly 18th Kree Diplomatic Gestalt
EDUCATION: Unrevealed
FIRST APPEARANCE: Marvel Boy #1 (2000)

HISTORY: Genetically engineered with cockroach DNA, the extradimensional Kree Noh-Varr joined the 18th Kree Diplomatic Gestalt, a team of intergalactic peacekeepers who became lost in transdimensional space when they encountered 3 astro-gods siphoning energy to explore Hypospace (the Omniverse). During the encounter, space-time collapsed, and the group was forced to escape through Macrospace. They careened through the Microverse and explored a multitude of realities while trapped there, until the alien-obsessed Midas caught their S.O.S., trapped them on Earth-616, and destroyed their ship. The sole survivor, Noh-Varr escaped Midas and destroyed his building before retreating to the New York subway system, which he made his temporary home. The enraged Noh-Varr, who had lost his lover Merree in the crash, took his aggression out on New York City, battling S.H.I.E.L.D. and their new experimental superteam, the Bannermen, a team of genetically enhanced superhumans pumped with gamma radiation and laced with Adamantium, whom he easily defeated. After destroying the living, planet-conquering corporation Hexus by sending their trade secrets to other companies and making them obsolete, Noh-Varr met Midas' head assassin and daughter, Exterminatrix.

Battling the Exterminatrix and Midas throughout New York City, Noh-Varr lost. Midas was about to kill him when Exterminatrix rescued Noh-Varr and escaped with him. Noh-Varr and Exterminatrix bonded over their mutual hatred for her father before Midas' agents, including one of the Dark Dimension's Mindless Ones, discovered them, forcing them to flee once more. Encountering the Cosmic Man, a renamed and newly empowered Midas, Noh-Varr immediately shot him in the head, which barely affected him. As Cosmic Man toyed with Noh-Varr, Exterminatrix used the decapitated Mindless One's head to shunt her father into the Dark Dimension, where he was attacked and seemingly killed by a large horde of the Mindless Ones. While Exterminatrix mourned her father, S.H.I.E.L.D. captured Noh-Varr and dragged him away to the Cube, a giant prison for super-villains, which Noh-Varr promised would be the capital of the new Kree empire within five months.

| HEIGHT: 5'10" | EYES: Black |
| WEIGHT: 165 lbs. | HAIR: White |

ABILITIES/ACCESSORIES: Noh-Varr is incredibly strong and fast, and much more durable than an average human being or Kree. His reaction time is high enough to dodge bullets with ease. Possibly due to his super-speed, Noh-Varr can walk up walls, defying gravity. His saliva is full of nanotechnology and triggers hallucinations in anybody it comes into contact with. He can grow or solidify his hair at will. When he finds himself in great danger, Noh-Varr can perform a "White Run" where his instincts fully take over, allowing him to run with no distractions at top speeds capable of outrunning a speeding motorcycle.

Due to his ancestry and space travels, Noh-Varr has many advanced weapons, most of which he has some idea of how to use, including the Marvel, his spaceship. His notable accessories include the Plex Intelligence, his ship's living databank, his gauntlet (which he can transform into a gun at will), his super-dense costume (lined with alien metals), and the Pocket Battlefield, which chooses between nine different battlefield situations, depending on whatever is needed at the time, and shifts whoever enters it into a pocket dimension with its own specialized physics.

POWER GRID	1	2	3	4	5	6	7
INTELLIGENCE							
STRENGTH							
SPEED							
DURABILITY							
ENERGY PROJECTION							
FIGHTING SKILLS							

Text by Bill Lentz   *Art by J.G. Jones*